WESTMAR COLLEGE

KIERKEGAARD
ON CHRIST AND CHRISTIAN
COHERENCE

SÖREN KIERKEGAARD

KIERKEGAARD ON CHRIST AND CHRISTIAN COHERENCE

PAUL SPONHEIM

1817

HARPER & ROW, PUBLISHERS

NEW YORK AND EVANSTON

To Nell

FIRST EDITION

LIBRARY OF CONGRESS CATALOG CARD NUMBER: 68-17590

CONTENTS

PART FOUR

THE LEGACY OF KIERKEGAARD AS A SYSTEMATIC THINKER

EDITOR'S PREFACE

AT the end of the nineteenth century very few historians or theologians would have suggested that a series of studies dealing with its leading theological figures should include a monograph on Sören Kierkegaard. Now that the twentieth century is two-thirds over, it is clear that this critic of academic theology, whose mordant wit and intellectual modesty would have thought the title utterly presumptuous, has turned out to be more of a "maker of modern theology" than almost any of his contemporaries.

There are many reasons for this change. Poets and thinkers who write in the minor languages of Europe may remain obscure for generations: Ibsen and Undset were well served by their translators, but even today who knows very much about Petöfi or Orszagh-Hviezdoslav? The pioneering work of his German interpreters and American translators began introducing Kierkegaard to the broader philosophical and theological public a century or more after his birth, and the *Papirer* have still not been translated in full. But it was more than his being Danish that denied him his due recognition until our own time. So long as theologians believed it to be their vocation to speculate in the grand manner and to create universal systems, the embarrassing questions of the *Concluding Unscientific Postscript* seemed to be *lèse majesté* toward the fathers and doctors. Only after the chastening work of its critics had cut down many of its pretensions could Christian thought accept the force of Kierkegaard's ideas as a liberation rather than a menace.

Now the theologians seem to have moved to the opposite extreme. As Kierkegaard argued that the Reformation's fear of works-righteousness had been learned only too well by the Danish church of his time, so Kierkegaard's attacks upon "the System" have become part of the conventional wisdom of this generation. Karl Holl pointed out fifty years ago that the notion of "the irrational" in religion was ambiguous and could cover up all manner of shoddy thinking. And today Sören Kierkegaard, with his passion for the precise thought and the fitting word, is being used to justify a trivialization of the assignment of theology into the composition of discrete essays on sundry topics. The case for Christian faith is presented as though believing were as arbitrary as preferring rye bread to white, and the quest of Christian thinkers from Origen to Tillich for the meaning in the whole of things is dismissed as hostile to authentic discipleship. Kierkegaard's scorn of mere pedantry is remembered, his respect for genuine scholarship is overlooked. His critique of system-building has been canonized, but the deeper unity of his own thought is lost amid the rhetoric.

It is this deeper unity which Paul Sponheim is attempting to recover in the present volume. He is not insensitive to Kierkegaard's abrasive comments on anyone who would attempt to construct an edifice of systematic theology on his foundation. Nor does he slight the philosophical and theological implications of Kierkegaard's highly personal style of authorship, especially his employment of pseudonymity. All of these points are scored, and their totals are properly recorded. But Sponheim argues that it is an injustice to Kierkegaard to leave it at that. He also resists the suggestion that it is necessary to smuggle Hegelian categories back into Kierkegaard to make sense of him. Instead, he chooses the simple device —which, in the event, proves to be anything but simple—of taking Kierkegaard at his word when he claims to make Jesus Christ the God-man the center of his life and thought. That claim took various forms in the authorship, especially the form of acknowledging how imperfectly it was being realized. In the speculations of H. L. Martensen Kierkegaard saw the dangers of a new Gnosticism in which the relation between the two natures in Christ was being universalized into a cosmic principle. But this recognition did not keep him from finding in the Christ a key to meaning both in human existence and in the world. Only the person and work of Jesus Christ could be concrete enough, inclusive enough, dialectical enough to provide the key. "Christian coherence" is the phrase used here to designate Kierkegaard's vision of this meaning.

Not every devotee of Kierkegaard will be pleased with this argument. The anti-systematists will be shocked by the integrated structure into which some of their favorite epigrams about the Hegelian system are fitted. Among the most enthusiastic Kierkegaardians in our day are certain literary critics who see in him, and accurately, profound resources for the interpretation of their texts. They, too, will be offended; for if Sponheim is right in his conclusions, no major component of Kierkegaard's thought, not even his theories of criticism, can finally be separated from the radical Christocentrism of what may properly be called his system. Historians like myself, who prefer contextual to immanent analysis and who therefore interpret a thinker in relation both to his epoch and to his career, will find some of Sponheim's constructs rather artificial and will wonder whether Kierkegaardian concreteness does not demand more attention to biography and history. But all of these readers will be obliged to come to terms with the implications of this closely reasoned monograph. Less erudite than either Baur or Harnack, less speculative than either Schleiermacher or Ritschl, Sören Kierkegaard may nevertheless prove to be, *pace* his own distinction, both a genuis and an apostle.

JAROSLAV PELIKAN

Yale University

AUTHOR'S PREFACE

THE names of three men would dominate any accurate autobiographical account of my work on Kierkegaard. Dr Reidar Thomte, Professor of Philosophy at Concordia College, Moorhead, Minnesota, introduced me to Kierkegaard in 1952 and has freely shared his library and his learning with me since that time. Dr Neils Thulstrup, Secretary of the Sören Kierkegaard Society, gave generously of his vast knowledge of the primary and secondary literature as adviser to a period of Fullbright study of 1953-4, and did so again—this time wholly without formal occasion—during a shorter research visit to Copenhagen in 1964. Dr Jaroslav Pelikan, now of Yale University, guided the process by which these earlier studies deepened to bear fruit in a doctoral dissertation at the University of Chicago. As the editor of this series he has provoked and superintended a fresh study of Kierkegaard yielding a manuscript notably different from the dissertation. None of these men may recognize their influence in this work, of course, but then none of them have sought disciples either!

Other men have made quite specific contributions in the later stages of my study. While the book was being written three colleagues at Concordia College read all or part of the manuscript. In addition to Professor Thomte, they were Dr Albert Anderson (currently Visiting Professor of Philosophy at St Olaf College, Northfield, Minnesota) and Dr Lloyd Svendsbye (now Editor-in-Chief of Augsburg Publishing House, Minneapolis). I have tried to profit from their comments as the book developed, but I am sure they will still find much occasion for the exercise of their critical faculties. Furthermore, I want to say a special word of thanks to Professor Gregor Malantschuk who received me most graciously into his home to respond to several questions concerning matters of Kierkegaard interpretation.

I also wish to express my gratitude to corporate bodies 'who' have assisted me by making funds available. In addition to the Fullbright grant already mentioned, sustained periods of Kierkegaard research have been made possible for me in the main by fellowships from the Rockefeller and David F. Swenson-Sören Kierkegaard Memorial Foundations, and by a faculty leave from Concordia College.

I cannot here even adequately acknowledge and surely not pay my debt to a great number of colleagues—teachers, students, and others—who have strongly contributed to my own development and so made their mark on my reading of Kierkegaard. But I hope they will know that they have made Kierkegaard's formula about self and race meaningful for me in the specific making of this book as well as otherwise. In expressing my gratitude for these relationships I have tried to speak broadly of the kind of essential indebtedness which I have sought to recognize in its most outstanding instance by dedicating this book to my wife.

I regret that due to the somewhat extended process of editing and publication, it has not been possible to cite some of the recent translations of Kierkegaard (such as the work of Ronald Gregor Smith and Howard Hong in the *Papirer*, and Lee M. Capel's *The Concept of Irony*) or to let the book have the benefit of contact with recent major secondary works (such as Niels Thulstrup's *Kierkegaards Forhold til Hegel*). It has been possible to identify some of this work at the beginning (the acknowledgements) and end (bibliography) of this volume. Other contributions very probably have even now—and by the actual time of publication surely will have—gone without mention. That is at once unfortunate and inevitable. But since I take it that we do together regard the study of Kierkegaard as a process to be continued rather than as a point to be passed, it is acceptable that this plainly penultimate effort should make its way out of the process and back into it once again.

ACKNOWLEDGEMENTS

GRATEFUL acknowledgement is made to the following for permission to use certain materials. For the nature of the use of the Kierkegaard translations, see the Bibliographical Note, pages xv–xvii.

Augsburg Publishing House, Minneapolis, for the use of material from *Edifying Discourses*, by Sören Kierkegaard, translated by David M. Swenson and Lillian M. Swenson, 4 vols, 1943–6. This work is now available in a revised and re-edited two-volume work, copyright, Augsburg, 1962.

Curtis Brown Ltd, London, and Henry Regnery Company, Chicago, for the use of material from *The Mind of Kierkegaard* by James Collins, copyright 1953.

George Allen & Unwin Ltd, London, for the use of material from *The Phenomenology of Mind*, by G. W. F. Hegel, translated by J. B. Baillie, second edition, 1910.

Harper and Row, Publishers, New York, for the use of material from *A Kierkegaard Critique*, ed. Howard A. Johnson and Niels Thulstrup, copyright, 1962, by Howard A. Johnson and Niels Thulstrup; for the use of material from *The Point of View for my Work as an Author* by Sören Kierkegaard, translated by Walter Lowrie, newly edited with a preface by Benjamin Nelson, copyright, Harper, 1962.

Howard A. Johnson for the use of material from *Christian Discourses*, by Sören Kierkegaard, translated by Walter Lowrie, London: Oxford University Press, 1939.

Princeton University Press, Princeton, for the use of material from *The Concept of Dread* by Sören Kierkegaard, translated by Walter Lowrie, Princeton University Press, 1944; for the use of material from *Concluding Unscientific Postscript*, by Sören Kierkegaard, translated by David F. Swenson and Walter Lowrie, Princeton, 1941; for the use of material from *Either-Or* by Sören Kierkegaard, translated by David F. Swenson, Lillian M. Swenson, and Walter Lowrie, 2 vols, Princeton, 1944; for the use of material from *For Self-Examination* and *Judge For Yourselves* by Sören Kierkegaard, translated by Walter Lowrie, Princeton, 1941; for the use of material from *Philosophical*

Fragments by Sören Kierkegaard, translated by David F. Swenson, Princeton, 1936; second edition, 1962, with new introduction and commentary by Niels Thulstrup and revised translation by Howard V. Hong; for the use of material from *Training in Christianity* by Sören Kierkegaard, translated by Walter Lowrie, Princeton, 1944.

The University of Chicago Press, Chicago, for the use of material from *The Journal of Religion*, 'Kierkegaard and Apologetics', by Malcolm L. Diamond, Vol. LXIV, number 2 (April, 1964), 122–32; for the use of material from *Systematic Theology* by Paul Tillich, 3 vols, copyright, The University of Chicago Press, 1951, 1957, 1963.

BIBLIOGRAPHICAL NOTE AND TABLE OF ABBREVIATIONS

WE HAVE used *Sören Kierkegaards Samlede Vaerker*, edited by A. B. Drachmann, J. L. Heiberg, and H. O. Lange. 15 vols. Copenhagen: Gyldendals, 1901–36; *Sören Kierkegaards Papirer*, edited by P. A. Heiberg and Victor Kuhr. 11 vols. Copenhagen: Gyldendals, 1909–48; *Sören Kierkegaards Efterladte Papirer*, edited by H. P. Barfod. 9 vols. Copenhagen: C. A. Reitzel, 1869–81; and *Breve og Aktstykker vedrörende Sören Kierkegaard*, edited by N. Thulstrup. 2 vols. Copenhagen: Munksgaard, 1953–4.

All translations from the primary and secondary literature are ours, except where other translators are noted. Where an English translation is available for a passage from Kierkegaard, we have cited the reference first in the Danish and then, in parentheses, in the English. We have had much good from the work of the Swensons, Lowrie, Dru and their company. (Lowrie's service includes not only the many volumes from the *Samlede Vaerker*, but also the numerous renderings of *Papirer* passages he included in his large *Kierkegaard*.) Yet nearly all of the translations have been revised in this volume— in varying degrees. The general tendency apparent in the revisions is toward a more literal translation. One may renew the quarrel with this tendency, but it may well be that what is lost is more the mind-benumbing familiarity of key passages rather than the essential beauty of Kierkegaard's prose. In any case the serious student should be the better for the new translations. He can the more carefully fit his mind to Kierkegaard's meaning in those cases where the variance in translation is not great. And major differences will surely put him on his guard, and may drive him to learn Danish! The system of abbreviations used in the citations is as follows:

AC   *Attack upon 'Christendom'*. Translated by Walter Lowrie. Princeton: Princeton University, 1946.
AR   *On Authority and Revelation: The Book on Adler*. Translated by Walter Lowrie. Princeton: Princeton University, 1955.
'AW'   *My Activity as a Writer* published with *The Point of View for My Work as an Author* (*PV*).

CD   *The Concept of Dread*. Translated by Walter Lowrie. Princeton: Princeton University, 1946.

CDi   *Christian Discourses* and *The Lilies of the Field and the Birds of the Air* and *Three Discourses at the Communion on Fridays*. Translated by Walter Lowrie. London: Oxford, 1939.

CUP   *Concluding Unscientific Postscript to the Philosophical Fragments*. Translated by David F. Swenson and Walter Lowrie. Princeton: Princeton University, 1944.

DIARY *The Diary of Sören Kierkegaard*. Translated by G. M. Anderson. Edited by P. P. Rohde. London: Peter Owen, 1961.

DO   *Johannes Climacus* or *De Omnibus Dubitandum Est* and a *Sermon*. Translated by T. H. Croxall. Stanford: Stanford University, 1958.

Dru   *The Journals of Sören Kierkegaard*. Edited and translated by Alexander Dru. London: Oxford, 1951.

ED   *Edifying Discourses*. Translated by David F. Swenson and Lillian M. Swenson. 4 vols. Minneapolis: Augsburg, 1943–6.

'EE' 'The Expectation of an Eternal Happiness', *Edifying Discourses*, (*ED*), III.

'EF' 'The Expectation of Faith', *Edifying Discourses* (*ED*), I.

E-O   *Either/Or*. Translated by David F. Swenson, Lillian M. Swenson, and Walter Lowrie. 2 vols. Princeton: Princeton University, 1944.

FT   *Fear and Trembling*. Translated by Walter Lowrie. Princeton: Princeton University, 1941.

GS   *The Gospel of Suffering*. Translated by David F. Swenson and Lillian M. Swenson. Minneapolis; Augsburg, 1948.

'HM' 'Has a Man the Right to Let Himself Be Put to Death for the Truth?', published with *The Present Age* (*PA*).

'HP' 'The High Priest', published with *Christian Discourses* (*CDi*).

JY   *Judge for Yourselves!* Translated by Walter Lowrie. London: Oxford, 1941.

'LC' 'Love Shall Cover a Multitude of Sins', *Edifying Discourses* (*ED*), I.

'LF' 'The Lilies of the Field and the Birds of the Air', published with *CDi*.

'MN' 'Man's Need of God Constitutes His Highest Perfection', *Edifying Discourses* (*ED*), IV.

PA   *The Present Age.* Translated by Walter Lowrie and A. Dru. London: Oxford, 1940.

Pap.   *Sören Kierkegaards Papirer.*

PF   *Philosophical Fragments or a Fragment of Philosophy.* Translated by David F. Swenson. Princeton: Princeton University, 1936.

PH   *Purity of Heart Is to Will One Thing.* Translated by Douglas Steere. New York: Harper, 1938.

PV   *The Point of View for my Work as an Author* and *My Activity as an Author.* Translated by Walter Lowrie. New York: Harper, 1962.

REP   *Repetition.* Translated by Walter Lowrie. Princeton: Princeton University, 1946.

SD   *The Sickness Unto Death.* Translated by Walter Lowrie. Princeton: Princeton University, 1951.

SE   *For Self-Examination.* Translated by Walter Lowrie. London: Oxford, 1941.

S.V.   *Sören Kierkegaards Samlede Vaerker.*

SW   *Stages on Life's Way.* Translated by Walter Lowrie. Princeton: Princeton University, 1940.

TC   *Training in Christianity.* Translated by Walter Lowrie. London: Oxford, 1941.

TCS   *Thoughts on Crucial Situations in Human Life.* Translated by David F. Swenson. Minneapolis: Augsburg, 1941.

'UG'   'The Unchangeableness of God', published with *SE*.

WL   *Works of Love.* Translated by David F. Swenson and Douglas Steere. Princeton: Princeton University, 1946.

'WLF' 'What We Learn from the Lilies of the Field and the Birds of the Air', published with *GS*.

'WS'   'The Woman that Was a Sinner', published with *CDi*.

PART ONE

I

THE SENSE OF A SYSTEMATIC STUDY OF KIERKEGAARD

1. *The Penultimate Scope of the Systematic*

AN AUTHOR'S intentions in stressing the systematic character of his study of Kierkegaard are not self evident. Or it may be that the sense of the term 'systematic' seems clear and wholly unobjectionable, except, perhaps, for the fact that it is a sense quite without significance. Would not every author claim as much—or as little? These many writers of words surely believe their sentences so to refer to the writings of Kierkegaard as to describe clearly those entities real or imagined to which his sentences referred. In facing, then, the vast Kierkegaard literature are we not dealing in every case with a systematic study—that is, with books professing such respect on the author's part and assuming such respect on Kierkegaard's part for rudimentary logical values as is requisite for the impartation of meaning?

One may, of course, confess some doubt as to the success of some of these 'systematic' ventures. Indeed such doubt—or more likely, disbelief—seems inevitable to any one confronting the massive chorus of contradictory voices making up the Kierkegaard literature. Yet every one of those voices would also concede that other men's studies may be so related to the 'real' Kierkegaard as to forfeit all claim to the term 'systematic'.

This essay does intend something more by its persistent reference to the 'systematic'. It quests after the pulse of order within or underneath the minimal referential order which transforms strings of words into meaningful sentences. Are there affirmations which impart a structure to Kierkegaard's thought and so distinguish it from a mass of isolated units of meaning? May one speak of rhythm in Kierkegaard's reflection? This interest in the systematic in a second sense may be bold, but it is not blindly so. While finding such systematic tendencies in Kierkegaard's thought, it does not deny that these tendencies are often nearly completely hidden under details in an authorship marked by an almost excessive rhetorical brilliance and a strongly situationalist sighting of the enemy under attack. Yet the study claims that these tendencies are visible to the disciplined reader who will not require of Kierkegaard the revelling in the obvious which can be consumed in half-hour doses as casual entertainments.

While we claim that this study does deal with discernible systematic tendencies in Kierkegaard's authorship, we acknowledge that several limitations form the boundaries of our study of these tendencies. (1) The study is not exhaustively systematic, for it does not follow the structuring tendencies through the entirety of Kierkegaard's thought. It does claim, however, to identify these tendencies very near the centre of Kierkegaard's thought and to follow them through a few major areas of manifestation. (2) The study is not rigidly systematic, for it acknowledges that a structuring tendency in thought may—and in Kierkegaard's case often does—involve the formulation of a field of genuine alternatives. Since the process of selection from that field cannot be reduced to a single principle, one is consistently brought up short of predictability. One begins to sense that the consistency of the systematic tendencies seems better suggested by the employment of an organic model than a geometric one. The systematic description of the alternative selected does not, then, claim to settle the question of casuality. Indeed the presence of such evident selection within a field of systematic alternatives can well remind the systematician that at *every* point he is dealing with the thought of a thinker. Anyone who would confuse the discernment of relationships in thought with a causal explanation of that thought will, after all, have Kierkegaard to face. (3) The study is not rigidly systematic, for it recognizes Kierkegaard's affirmation of such realities as mystery and risk—and beyond that, positive paradox and offence. It will not be argued that these references represent the inflation of the Danish poet's hyperbole or that they stand at the fringe of his thought. What does become evident, however, is that these very affirmations of mystery and discontinuity occur in an interconnected way. These references are seen to reveal the systematic impulse itself—partly in the sense that when they are juxtaposed to another tendency in Kierkegaard's thought, they represent a formally structuring principle despite their material negation of system.[1] The other aspect of the systematic to be seen in these references leads us on to a final qualification. (4) The study is not syste-

---

[1] Henning Schröer expresses a related concern when he turns to Kierkegaard for the answer to his question whether (and if so, how) the thought form of

matic in a simplistic sense for it does not claim that Kierkegaard's thought can be described adequately by the use of any single systematizing principle. We rather acknowledge the presence of at least two—and in a way, three—systematic rhythms within Kierkegaard's thought. Indeed we give considerable attention to the complex interaction of these rhythms. We shall see that much of Kierkegaard's discourse about paradox reflects this interaction in a pattern of formulations which is very consistent for all its complexity.

This delimitation of the sense of systematic provokes a number of questions. One may wish to explore the relationships of this penultimate sense for system with the minimal concern for the consistency required of all meaningful discourse, on the one hand, and with the quest for the ultimate relatedness of all meaningful utterance, on the other hand. These questions are discussed obliquely in the course of the essay, but a full probing exceeds the reach of this study. It is harder to silence the question concerning the desirability of such a study. One may venture the opinion that man, for all his capacity for caprice, basically quests after a relatedness which well exceeds the limits of the minimal meaning of 'systematic'. The theologian seems not to find—nor really to seek—exemption from that quest.[2]

Paradoxalität is a theological thought form. Schröer helpfully distinguishes the thought form from its products—in this case, paradoxes. *Die Denkform der Paradoxalität als Theologisches Problem* (Göttingen: Vandenhoeck & Ruprecht, 1960), especially pp. 11–28, 76, 131.

[2] On the relation of system and theology see Kenneth Hamilton, *The System and the Gospel* (New York: Macmillan; London: SCM Press, 1963); especially Chapter one: Hamilton criticizes Paul Tillich for his 'refusal to be content with anything less than a whole. All problems must be solved by absorbing them within one grand over-arching scheme' (ibid., p. 14). Hamilton sees Tillich's error to lie in the fact that he lets his understanding of the system-building nature of philosophical (metaphysical) thought influence his understanding of the nature of theological thought. Hamilton himself prefers to view theology as 'the orderly arrangement of material which does not need to be given coherence through being interpreted in terms of a system, since it is self-authenticating and needs only to be displayed in such a manner that it can be readily grasped' (ibid., p. 16). As champion of this most stringent limitation of the systematic impulse, Hamilton offers Sören Kierkegaard! We shall seek to make clear that Hamilton, while rightly rooting this methodological problem in the substance of Kierkegaard's thought, has reached his solution by a very selective reading of that substance. It seems to us that a more balanced view of the Kierkegaardian corpus does not permit one so simple a solution to the question of the role of the systematic principle in Kierkegaard. Tillich's own theology offers a formulation which may be useful in understanding the point we are trying to make. It seems a contradiction in terms to speak of a 'systematic impulse' or 'bent'. Yet we can find no other term which better recognizes the ordering function without eliminating the living reality of the thinker. One may take this to be part of what Tillich has in mind in his discussion of the ontological polarity of dynamics and form. *Systematic Theology*, Vol. I (Chicago: University of Chicago,

The value of indulging this bent in confronting this particular figure is a matter which concerns us later in this introductory chapter and again at the end of our study. We need first to answer some pointed objections against the very possibility of such a study. We can best attempt to make that response after giving these remarks about rhythms of reflection something more than purely formal identity.[3]

1951 [London: Nisbet, 1953]), pp. 178–82 [197–201]. Tillich writes: 'On the human level form is the rational structure of subjective reason actualized in a life-process. . . . We recommend the use of the term "intentionality", which means being related to meaningful structures, living in universals, grasping and shaping reality. . . . Man's dynamics, his creative vitality, is not undirected, chaotic, self-contained activity. It is directed, formed; it transcends itself toward meaningful contents. There is no vitality as such and no intentionality as such. They are inter-dependent' (ibid., pp. 180–1 [199–200]).

[3] We have not tried to establish metaphysical citizenship for the argument of this section, for this understanding of the quest for order does not seem limited to a single metaphysical orientation. For a discussion of non-idealistic ways of systematic thinking, see Paul Weiss, ' "Existenz" and Hegel', *Philosophy and Phenomenological Research*, 1947–8, pp. 206–16. It should be emphasized that the term 'rhythm' in this study is used to refer not to some sovereign structure of reality to which mortal beings must conform, but to the style of reflection of a most emphatically alive individual. Linguists isolate for analysis terministic cycles which come to constitute distinct dynasties in the living use of language. (See Kenneth Burke, *A Grammar of Motives* [New York: Prentice-Hall, 1945] and *The Rhetoric of Religion: Studies in Logology* [Boston: Beacon Press, 1961].) In somewhat less ambitious fashion but with specific reference to religious discourse, Ninian Smart writes: '. . . a complex doctrinal scheme has a certain artistic composition, so to speak, which makes the disparate elements hang together. This point is relevant to the way moral propositions are incorporated into the fabric of spiritual discourse. That is, moral discourse, in the context of religion, functions like one of the strands of specifically religious discourse. . . .' The likeness permits differences to be noted. So Smart allows that 'the similarities justifying identifications in religion are looser than those criteria which would justify a mundane claim that A and B are identical'. Nonetheless, the difference is not sufficient to set religious discourse in a land apart, for Smart is seeking to justify the integration of moral and religious discourse by drawing attention to the agreement between certain moral concepts and certain specifically religious ones. (See Ninian Smart, 'God, Bliss and Morality', *Christian Ethics and Contemporary Philosophy*, edited by Ian T. Ramsey [London: SCM Press; New York: The Macmillan Company, 1966], pp. 15–30.) In like manner this study of Kierkegaard resists both the tendency to refer the religious discourse involved to a region where irrationality is challenged only by the order of succession or to restrict the dynamic of that discourse by positing a pattern sovereign over the speaker. The structures of the study are employed to draw near what is actually going on in Kierkegaard's speech, rather than to suppress his amazing life under some static schema. As such, this effort is an empirical hypothesis to be tested by the texts treated in the pages that lie ahead and not a nonsensical invitation to some never-never land beyond the lines Kierkegaard wrote. After identifying the rhythms of Kierkegaard's reflec*ting* (to avoid the substantive fiction), it may be observed (see below, pages 27–28) that the tyranny of metaphysical generalization is missing not only from the formal step of introducing the rhythms, but from Kierkegaard's material employment of them as well.

2. The Divine-Human Polarity, the Rhythms of Reflection, and the Christological Centre

This study will seek to show that Kierkegaard's religious thought moves between two poles formed by his affirmations regarding God and man. This proposal may seem commonplace and wholly non-controversial.[4] It would be easy enough to produce lexicographical evidence attesting the prominence of these themes in the authorship.[5] That would, however, be a very small step, indeed, towards the demonstration of our claim. In so assessing such evidence we do not have in mind merely the point that one would have to inquire of the degree (if any) of systematic unity within the verbal unity. Our thesis requires us to show more than that, for our contention is that the character of the polarity is such that a relationship of inter-dependence characterizes Kierkegaard's discourse regarding God and man. We will seek to show that the interdependence in Kierke-gaard's discourse has its roots in the substantive interrelatedness of his thought as it moves between these poles. Thus the opening 'psy-chological' half of the *Sickness unto Death*—with cause celebrated as one of Kierkegaard's most brilliant pieces of anthropological analysis—moves the reader towards the second half's statement of the theo-logical context and solution for despair. Or, observing the flow of Kierkegaard's thought in the other direction, one can note that even passages in which divine sovereignty is the major theme acknowledge this polar interdependence: 'Even the ultimate certitude, revelation itself, becomes *eo ipso* dialectic so soon as I endeavour to appropriate it. . . .'[6] Or the polar interdependence of Kierkegaard's thought can focus more directly, if less obviously, in the quest for a synthesis of the eternal and the temporal.[7]

This polar interdependence is widely ignored or denied. This holds

---

[4] The identification of the poles is not itself a particularly original suggestion. See, for example, James Collins. *The Mind of Kierkegaard* (Chicago: Henry Regnery, 1953), p. 179: 'God and the human individual are the organizing principles which give unity and hierarchy to his various findings'.

[5] A. Ibsen's *Register til Sören Kierkegaards Samlede Vaerker* (with J. Himmelstrup, Copenhagen: Gyldendals, 1936) provides precisely such an unsorted collection of references.

[6] *S.V.* VII, p. 24 note (*CUP*, p. 35, note).

[7] Thus Walter Schulz in 'Existenz und System bei S. Kierkegaard', *Wesen und Wirklichkeit des Menschen* (Göttingen: Vandenhoeck & Ruprecht, 1957), can find 'the question concerning the possibility of this synthesis is the fundamental problem of all the stages'. Cf. Johannes Slök, *Die Anthropologie Kierkegaards* (Copen-hagen: Rosenkilde und Bagger, 1954). We shall see that the unity so designated encompasses sharp diversity within itself.

true of works presenting themselves as descriptive studies of Kierke-gaard. Thus George Price can praise Kierkegaard's description of man as having first rate significance, even though his theology might be questionable, his philosophy even worse.[8] One seems to find further illustration of this tendency when one ponders the appeal of certain existentialist philosophers to Kierkegaard.[9] That appeal will concern us in the concluding section of this work when it will be possible to note the extent to which the severance involved represents an acceleration of a tendency already present in Kierke-gaard's thought. On the other hand we are not seeking to argue that Kierkegaard's statements regarding man are somehow arrived at by a process of rigid dictation from his views regarding God. We *do* mean to speak of the *inter*dependence of the poles. Surely Kierkegaard's keen eye did not fail to record and ponder many observations regarding the humanity about and within him. But as his thought took shape it constantly ordered itself with reference to both poles.[10]

The ambiguity which makes it difficult to identify the poles which give structure to Kierkegaard's thought is related to the fact that more than one rhythm can be detected within that structure. Indeed one must not only say that as a result of the duality of the major

[8] George Price, *The Narrow Pass* (London: Hutchinson, 1963), p. 11. Price continues: 'If man was to be the key to reality, then he must provide the key to his own. And this meant trying to understand him afresh in the light of the material his own self provided. To this end Kierkegaard initiated a new approach to the study of man, one of introspection and self analysis. He admitted no metaphysical questions about the nature of the soul nor about an "ultimate reality", but sought a concept of man entirely in terms of a certain psychology of himself' (ibid., p. 12). Oddly, Price can find Kierkegaard to be saying that man's 'reality as a person rested wholly upon the reality of God', and that 'outside of a radical encounter with God man simply did not exist' (ibid., pp. 217–8). Yet Price does not let this acknowledgement affect his analysis of Kierkegaard's methodology, or his assessment's separation of Kierkegaard's analysis of man from his 'theology'.

[9] K. E. Lögstrup, *Kierkegaards und Heideggers Existenzanalyse und ihr Verhältnis zur Verkündigung* (Berlin: Erich Blaschker, 1950) strongly affirms the formal legitimacy of such an appeal. Thus Lögstrup argues that in his discourse concerning the infinite and the finite, the eternal and the temporal, Kierkegaard is not dealing with Christianity: 'His understanding of existence is, to be sure, religious; but in a human immanent way. . . . Putting it briefly, Kierkegaard is doing philosophy and not theology' (ibid., p. 35).

[10] Perhaps one may find a suggestion of the breadth of Kierkegaard's sources and the constancy and precision of the polar structure of his reflection in Niels Thulstrup's identification of the 'two stable factors' in Kierkegaard's work as the claims of the New Testament witness and the individual person in his concrete situation. 'The Complex of Problems Called "Kierkegaard"', *A Kierkegaard Critique*, ed. H. Johnson and N. Thulstrup (New York: Harper, 1962), p. 294. See also Thulstrup's 'Kierkegaard og den filosofiske Idealisme', *Kierkegaardiana*, ed. N. Thulstrup, 1962, pp. 88–105.

currents of thought the poles take on different appearances from time to time, but also that there is a fluidity in their very determination relative to each other. That fluidity is held in check by yet a third systematizing force in Kierkegaard's thought—but that is getting ahead of ourselves. We speak at this point of two basic movements of thought. On the one hand, there is discernible a centrifugal current by which the opposition between the poles is ensured and enhanced. That opposition may be defined in widely differing ways, but in every case the emphasis is on disengagement—on withdrawal to stress the separateness of God and man. We may call this movement *diastasis*. On the other hand, the diastatic current is balanced by a centripetal one which perceives and emphasizes the relatedness, the co-involvement of God and man. We shall speak of this movement as *synthesis*. The choice of this word must not be understood to suggest that the distinct identity of the poles is obliterated or even compromised. The two rhythms seem to check each other.[11] Surely it is not the case that they function alternately—as if, say, by pre-arrangement. While one movement may be seen to be the dominant one in a particular body of discourse, the movements constantly infiltrate what appears to be alien terrain, so that one really never finds a passage of significant length reflecting only one rhythm. Yet we believe that we can show that the movements of *diastasis* and *synthesis* can be distinguished without violence to Kierkegaard's writings, even though they are never fully isolated from each other.

The material demonstration of the value of this line of interpretation falls, of course, to the analysis undertaken in Part Three of this

---

[11] That checking activity can be illustrated in this way. In the rhythm of diastasis a centrifugal movement is to be noted by which the opposition between the poles is *ensured and enhanced*. This diastatic movement's relatedness to the synthesizing movement is expressed in the tendency to *ensure* opposition; the movement's systematic initiative is expressed in the tendency to *enhance* or potentiate opposition. In turn, the synthesizing rhythm responds to that initiative by affirming that God and man, however distinct ('opposed') are *related*. And that rhythm moves beyond the balancing act of location to speak of the actual activity of *co-involvement*. It seems best to state the rhythms here in as broad terms as possible, though they surely never lack concreteness in the literature itself. The striking diversity of these concrete determinations (running the course of ethical, religious, and metaphysical categories) requires the common denominator characterization to acquire the pallor of neutrality. Unfortunately the systematic advantages to be had by the formal introduction of the rhythms here may be offset if the aforementioned pallor arouses the suspicion that we have here to do with death, not life. Life is not chaos and Kierkegaard's work is never capricious. It is precisely because these rhythms are internal to Kierkegaard's thought and hence highly useful for the elucidation of that thought that we deem the risk involved in their highly generalized statement here to be worth taking.

work. The formal demonstration of the possibility of the interpretation will concern us a few pages hence. Our interpretation will be
related to others in the course of the substantive analysis and in a
general way within this introductory chapter.[12] Yet even this brief
statement of our approach to Kierkegaard calls for some clarification
of its relationship to two other studies. Most obviously Werner
Elert's *Der Kampf um das Christentum* employed the interpretative
categories of diastasis and synthesis and in the course of discussing a
wide range of theological types devoted a few pages to the analysis of
Kierkegaard's thought.[13] While the formal reference of the terms in
our study is the same as Elert's, the differences separating the studies
are more significant. Most important, perhaps, is the fact that Elert
used the categorical schema to discuss change in the relationship of
Christianity to the general development of human thought. Our study
on the other hand, points first of all to the appropriateness of these
categories for the elucidation of Kierkegaard's own substantive
theological position and only secondarily to the role of these categories in the task of correlating that position with views held outside
the household of faith. We deem this order to be instructive and welcome the fact that the far narrower scope of this book permits the twin-
faceted employment of the categories. The two studies also differ quite
sharply in their material analysis and evaluation of Kierkegaard.[14]

A more subtle and significant relatedness to our study characterizes

[12] Restraint must be exercised at this point or the argument of this essay would
evaporate in a hopelessly allusive appendix to the massive Kierkegaard literature.
Jens Himmelstrup's *Sören Kierkegaard, International Bibliografi* (Copenhagen: Nyt
Nordisk, 1962) runs only to 1956 and yet totals nearly 7,000 entries. To be sure,
the collection is inflated by the inclusion of a large number of tit-bits which can
hardly claim much significance; yet a number of important studies have apparently
eluded the editor's eye. Readers of this note will know that the highly diverse
torrent of Kierkegaardiana did not run dry at year's end, 1955. But for all the
massiveness of the literature, a significant orientation and confrontation seems
possible by restricting oneself in the main to the major studies and by emphasizing
tendencies, if not schools, of interpretation.

[13] Werner Elert, *Der Kampf um das Christentum* (Munich: C. H. Beck'sche, 1921),
especially pp. 430–4.

[14] Elert saw Kierkegaard's position as almost purely diastatic in character,
which happened also to be the direction in which Elert thought theology ought to
move if it were to be sensitive to the 'demands of the future'. Parts Three and Four
will make clear our divergence from these views. It is worth adding here, however,
that the very scope Elert seeks for the application of his categories calls forth
suspicion about their formal structure. While our analysis stays close to the living
particularity of one man, the effort to cover centuries of human thought makes it
difficult to see how Elert can avoid rather grandiose metaphysical-historical commitments. While he likes the organic image of breathing, he does permit himself
such phrases as 'the inner necessity of the counter-movements' (ibid., p. 4).

Henning Schröer's *Die Denkform der Paradoxalität als Theologisches Problem*.[15] Using a highly complex set of categories, Schröer seems to cover much of the ground touched in our work and often reaches conclusions which also elicit our assent. He sees Kierkegaard's dialectic as the paradigmatic attempt to place the thought form of the paradoxical in the service of theology. While Schröer resists the suggestion that Kierkegaard's dialectic is purely antithetical in character, he nonetheless seems most impressed with what we have called the diastatic movement. Our analysis does not reach Schröer's conclusion that the fundamental paradox animating the dialectic is the ontological one. We shall concede that ontological affirmations are involved in the rhythms under discussion, but we seek to point to an independent religious dialectic which at times enlists ontological designations, and does so—we suspect—to its own detriment.[16]

Before leaving this comparison of lines of interpretation we may note by way of anticipation that Elert and (perhaps to a lesser extent) Schröer alert us to the fact that our study will probably find its larger task—surely its lonelier one—in pointing persuasively to the presence of the movement of synthesis in Kierkegaard's thought. While Kierkegaard scholars have frequently attacked Torsten Bohlin's great Kierkegaard studies, they seem to join Bishop Bohlin in holding that Kierkegaard 'is always stronger in destroying false connections and in sundering apparent unities and all invalid harmonizing than in knitting the sundered together in a new unity; analysis is the passion of his thought; he always (*ater*) mistrusts striving after synthesis as an expression on the whole for the levelling effort of a (*forsätlig*) quantitative dialectic'.[17]

In the heavy stress which we have laid on the divine-human polarity we have not yet reached the centre of this study, for that

[15] Schröer, op. cit.

[16] On the ontological paradox, see ibid., pp. 78–80, 87, 200. It seems to us that Schröer, for all the precision and detail of his interpretive schema, has failed to distinguish adequately between an ontological opposition between being and becoming and a methodological opposition between concreteness and abstraction. Kierkegaard's espousal of the latter distinction does not necessarily carry with it the full weight of the ontological distinction. Schröer's concluding pages warn warmly against the reduction of the paradoxical to the status of a technique or gimmick and plead for an exploration of the specifically theological sense of the paradoxical. In these ways Schröer moves towards the rhythm of synthesis. Given the loose common usage of the term paradox, however, Schröer's interest in the synthesis strand, lacking thorough statement set free from the term paradox, probably has trouble making itself heard for many readers.

[17] Torsten Bohlin, *Sören Kierkegaards etiska aaskaadning* (Stockholm: Svenska Kyrkans Diakonistyrelses, 1918), p. 110.

lies in Kierkegaard's christology. Kierkegaardian statements identifying God and man as matters of concern shaping a whole authorship can easily enough be paralleled in the area of christology. Thus near the end of his life in pointing to the concept of contemporaneity, in which the Christ is both the ground and the goal of man's hope, Kierkegaard could say: 'And this is the decisive thing! This thought is for me my life's thought! I may also with truth say that I have had the honour to suffer in order to bring this truth to light. Therefore I die gladly, infinitely grateful to Governance that it was granted to me in such a way to become attentive to and make others attentive to this thought. Not that I have discovered it. God forbid that I should be guilty of such presumption. No, the discovery is old. It is the New Testament's. But yet it was granted to me, suffering, to bring this thought again to remembrance.'[18] In his dissertation for the doctorate in theology, Per Lönning has shown persuasively that the centrality of this theme does not depend on the formal frequency of its presence in the authorship.[19] Lönning's work can also serve to banish any impression that in citing the importance of christology for Kierkegaard's thought we are proposing a third systematic force which would be wholly isolated from the other two. For Lönning rightly finds that in discussing the situation of contemporaneity he is working with material concerning God and man.[20] Nor does this

[18] *S.V.* XIV, p. 300 (*AC*, p. 242). In a note Kierkegaard comments that the article in which this passage occurs dates from 1853, although it was not published until September 1855.

[19] Per Lönning, '*Samtidighedens Situation*' (Oslo: Land og Kirke, 1954). One of Lönning's critics at the disputation, P. Svendsen, did him one better by making a good case for finding the concept of contemporaneity expressed already in Kierkegaard's dissertation, *On the concept of Irony with particular reference to Socrates* (printed 16 September 1841). Svendsen particularly emphasizes the distinction which Kierkegaard draws between the two accounts of Socrates. See *S.V.* XIII, pp. 109–10, 112, 126; and Paulus Svendsen, 'Opposisjonsennlegg ved cand. teol. Per Lönning's disputas for den teologiske doktorgrad, 5 maj, 1955', *Norsk Teologisk Tidskrift*, 1956, pp. 1–23. Lönning seems to us clearly to have the better part of the argument in his criticism of Hayo Gerdes's contention (*Das Christus Bild Sören Kierkegaards* [Düsseldorf: Eugen Dietrichs, 1960]) that the decisive christological statements of Kierkegaard do not begin until 1848. See Lönning's 'Sören Kierkegaards Kristusbillede', *Kierkegaardiana*, ed. N. Thulstrup, 1962, pp. 75–88.

[20] We find Lönning's work impressive at a great many points and the reader will perhaps perceive a significant community of intention in the two studies. We believe the scope of our study to be broader—not only in the greater attention we give to the matrix and legacy of Kierkegaard's thought, but also in the internal analysis of Part Three. The adoption of a more comprehensive interpretative schema makes significant difference in the analysis. That difference may be seen by comparing the ways in which the two studies handle the problem of the relationship between the final tortuous period of Kierkegaard's authorship and the earlier portion of his work.

third force appear to be related to the other two as they are to each other. Kierkegaard's affirmations concerning the Christ seem rather to represent a field of intersection in the movement of thought between two poles. In the words of the decisively Christian Anti-Climacus: 'It is true for the first time in Christ that God is man's goal and measure.'[21] The evident textual elevation of the Christ does not itself, of course, warrant our identification of christology as an irreducibly basic systematizing force for Kierkegaard. Kierkegaard's discourse about the Christ might be precisely an intersection, and only that! Perhaps Kierkegaard's Christ is the logical derivative of a process of reflection born in his view of God and man and their relationship.[22] We believe that this suggestion is in part correct. The third part of this work will show that what Kierkegaard believes about God and man materially influences the content of the Christ for whom so many formal acolades are retained. At least that often seems to be the case, if the order of statement reflects the order of thought. Yet the truth of this suggestion is only partial. Our analysis will also point to passages where christological formulations are to be found whose relationship to Kierkegaard's discourse regarding God and man simply eludes and exceeds the logical relation of conclusion to premsises. One need not capitulate to a biographical-psychological interpretation of Kierkegaard, if one adds that these passages and

[21] *S.V.* XI, p. 224 (*SD*, p. 186). It is the frequency of this sort of passage which invites M. Diamond's statement: 'God apart from Christ did not very much interest Kierkegaard who was one of the most Christocentric thinkers in the history of Christendom': 'Kierkegaard and Apologetics', *The Journal of Religion*, 30 April 1964, p. 124. For a fuller statement see *Pap* X 2 A 643 (*Dru* 1089): 'The measure of man is: before how great a number of an age he dares appear and have his life judged by them. One could on this point go through a whole gamut of relativities (from those who only exist for a very few, for example their wives, to those who exist for greater and greater circles, though they always remain circles) to the highest of all, the God-Man who establishes the quality Man and therefore must and wishes to be judged by absolutely every man, eternally and divinely certain that he, only he, expresses the quality: to be a man, whereas all other men do not express the quality, but only the quality charged with relative contingencies. . . . Furthermore, one could go through every conceivable human relativity in order to establish to what extent it was commensurable with the God-Man, in the sense that he could have been the God-Man therein.'

[22] Schröer expresses a related concern. He finds it to be the case that 'the decisive problem of Kierkegaard's christology remains the relationship of anthropology and christology' (op. cit., p. 87). That the 'existentual reality be already regarded as Christian reality' is for Schröer one of the two dangers threatening the Kierkegaardian dialectic (ibid., p. 96). He further suggests that Kierkegaard's concept of God is shaped on anthropological rather than christological grounds, and traces that back to Kierkegaard's failure to make a precise determination of the relationship between ontology and theology. See note 16 above on the divergence of our analysis from Schröer's.

others seem to burn with the heart's own fire in a way which may remind the reader of the eloquent testimony Kierkegaard bore to the impact his father's dark-hued sketches of the Christ figure had for him as a child.[23] We find here the order of systematic intcrrelatedness of Kierkegaard's fundamental concerns to be of that sort suggested by the affirmations which form the living tissue of those concerns. The dominant line of our substantive interpretation may be forced upon us by our quarrel with the one-sided fascination of Kierkegaard's present public with the diastatic tendency in his thought. Thus we shall surely find ourselves opposing the view which would seek to exhaust Kierkegaard's discourse on the divine-human polarity with an exclusivist reference to a slender and at times apparently invisible point in the first century. Similarly we are not able to conclude that Kierkegaard's systematic concerns with God and man have only derivative significance. But we also wish to turn the coin. Kierkegaard's christology is not to be reduced to either anthropology or theology or to some curious blend of the two, any more than Christ's historical reality is dispensable for the believer. Indeed it seems to be the case that the christological concern not only possesses independent systematic significance for Kierkegaard within the movement between the poles of God and man, but also as such a fundamental irreducible systematic force so functions as to check the very movements of diastasis and synthesis between those poles.

3. *The Thinker's Freedom and his Necessity*

We cannot well delay longer the consideration of certain basic objections to the approach which we have proposed. An obvious source of criticism lies in that view which would limit meaningful studies to those of the biographical-psychological genre. Surely there is quite literally no important sense to the kind of systematic study we are proposing, if Kierkegaard's works are simply the reflection of a circuitous path of personality development or the mechanical response to the data fed him by his environment. The psychologizing approach

---

[23] So *Pap.* IX A 68 (*Dru* 773): I owe everything, from the beginning, to my father. When melancholy as he was, he saw me melancholy, his prayer to me was: Be sure that you can rightly love Jesus Christ.' Cf. the poignant passage from *Training in Christianity*, in which Kierkegaard asks the reader to ponder the effect an encounter with a picture of the crucified one will have on a child. Kierkegaard pointedly adds that when that child reached maturity 'he would not have forgotten the impression of childhood, but he understood it differently'. *S.V.* XII, pp. 162–6 (*TC*, pp. 174–8).

seems to have seized upon Kierkegaard as a particularly apt subject.[24] No diagnostic agreement regarding Kierkegaard's maladies appears to have been reached by the practitioners of this art.[25] While this absence of agreement may not reflect adversely on the results of these studies, one does wonder whether Kierkegaard was really *that* ill. In any case this field of Kierkegaard study does present a fascinating index to the shifting winds of fortune in the world of psychology and its over-eager disciples whose single-minded 'applications' often appear to this layman to cast a bad light over even the established reputation of the discipline.

Our quarrel pushes behind the results of such studies to their method and its presuppositions. It is not clear to us how one dismisses the possibility that Kierkegaard's melancholy might be related to his reaction to some things he saw in the real world about him and that that reaction might be on the order of a free response. Of course that possibility as a meaningful alternative is foreclosed by the invocation of a determinism which posits a causality of total equivalence. That Kierkegaard himself rejected this position can, of course, be explained in a similarly mechanistic way.[26] It follows, too, that any

[24] A useful summary of the Scandinavian pursuit of this line is provided by Aage Kabell, *Kierkegaardstudiet i Norden* (Copenhagen: H. Hagerup, 1948). For a briefer English summary of this approach see Aage Henriksen, *Methods and Results of Kierkegaard Studies in Scandinavia* (Copenhagen: Munksgaard, 1951), pp. 66–128. P. A. Heiberg's *Sören Kierkegaards religiöse Udvikling. Psykologisk Mikroskopi* (Copenhagen: Gyldendal, 1925) may be singled out as one of the most influential examples of this approach. Heiberg saw Kierkegaard as one struggling to be healed from a sickness composed of elements of melancholy and self-accusation. Kabell notes that Heiberg's study was enhanced by a thorough knowledge of the sources and was done with considerable restraint. It is doubtful whether those characterizations can be applied to many works in the deluge of psychological studies which followed Heiberg's.

[25] See, for example, John Björkhem, *Sören Kierkegaard i psykologisk belysning* (Uppsala: Nyblom, 1942) and H. Helweg, *Sören Kierkegaard. En psykiatrisk-psykologisk Studie* (Copenhagen: Hagerup, 1933).

[26] We refer, of course, to Kierkegaard's basic understanding of the human self and its relationship to the race. It will be our task to analyse that understanding in Part Three. It is that understanding which lies behind such specific passages as *The Concept of Dread*'s delimitation of the function of psychology by reference to the elusive but irreducible reality of human freedom: 'What psychology shall have to do with must be something at rest, which abides in an agitated state of quiet, not a restless thing, which constantly either produces itself or is repressed. But that which is abiding, that out of which sin constantly becomes—not with necessity, for a becoming with necessity is a condition, as, for example, the whole history of the plant is a condition, but with freedom—this abiding, the predisposing presupposition, sin's real possibility, this is an object for the interest of psychology. That which can occupy psychology and with which psychology can occupy itself is how sin can come into existence, not that it does come into existence. In its psychological

attempt to plead for a distinction between the questions of causality and validity is inadmissible in that the reductionist reading of Kierkegaard's 'thought' really eliminates any objective reference to that thought. Disproof of this point of view seems impossible, since it rejects the referential system basic for all proof. One may, however, wonder how the representatives of this view escape their own presuppositions—or if they do not seek to do so, why they take their 'view' so seriously and propagate it so zealously. Furthermore, while no conclusive disproof of this viewpoint may be at hand, one may be permitted to find it puzzling that Kierkegaard's works often seem rather to contradict than to reflect his own way of life.[27]

While rejecting the dogmatic extremes of the biographical-psychological school, we acknowledge that an understanding of the context provided by the world in which Kierkegaard lived is necessary if one is to understand the meaning of the sentences composing his works. We make an effort to state that context in Part Two of this

---

interest it can bring the matter so far that it is as if sin were there, but the next step, that it is there, is qualitatively different from this. Now how this presupposition for the painstaking psychological contemplation and observation shows itself to be more and more comprehensive—that is psychology's interest; yes, psychology will, as it were, abandon itself to the illusion that herewith sin exists. But this last illusion is the impotence of psychology which shows that it has put in its time.

That human nature must be such that it makes sin possible is, psychologically speaking, quite true; but to want to let this possibility of sin become its reality outrages ethics and sounds like blasphemy to dogmatics; for freedom is never possible, so soon as it is, it is real.' *S.V.* IV, p. 294 (*CD*, pp. 19–20).

[27] Kabell (op. cit., pp. 243ff.) traces the process by which Kierkegaard scholarship has destroyed a legendary idealized Kierkegaard constructed in large part on a model drawn from his works. Notable early ingredients in that process included P. A. Heiberg's *En Episode i Sören Kierkegaards Ungdomsliv* (Copenhagen: Gyldendal, 1912) and V. Ammundsen's *Sören Kierkegaards Ungdom, hans Slaegt og religiöse Udvikling* (Copenhagen: G. E. C. Gad, 1912). The image of the moral hero had some difficulty maintaining itself in the face of the revelation of Kierkegaard's apparent inclination to waste his prodigious talents in a round of activities which would have to be conventionally classified with the sins of the flesh. F. Brandt has suggested (*Sören Kierkegaard og Pengene* [Copenhagen: Levin & Munksgaard, 1935]) that Kierkegaard was not above (his worshippers promptly translated 'below') accepting interest and that his charitable contributions were rather too modest to fit the image of the great humanitarian dispensing his father's fortune. Even the history of research into Kierkegaard's physical appearance has witnessed a steady withdrawal from an idealized portrait. See Rikard Magnussen, *Sören Kierkegaard, set udefra* (Copenhagen: Munksgaard, 1942) and F. Brandt, *Syv Kierkegaard Studier* (Copenhagen: Munksgaard, 1962). On the lack of correspondence between Kierkegaard's life and his writings, see Torsten Bohlin's last book, *Kierkegaards Tro* (Uppsala; Svenska Kyrkans Diakonistyrelses, 1944), pp. 141–2. The cumulative weight of this material is such that the effort to find some biographical-psychological datum to account for the contradiction seems exceptionally bold.

book. An understanding of his life is undeniably useful at times by laying bare the occasion for a particular turn in his thought. Such data may even appear to involve events which so pressed in upon the self that one feels one is saying too little in speaking of 'occasions', if yet too much in speaking of 'causes'. Anyone who regards the freedom and originality of the author as the complete explanation of his works seems to us sorely to need the wisdom of Anti-Climacus' counsel regarding the relationship of necessity and possibility in the self.[28] In Part Two we shall make a modest effort to suggest how some of the more prominent features of Kierkegaard's life—features largely familiar to English readers from the standard biographies by Lowrie[29] —may be related to the development of the systematizing rhythms with which this study is in the main concerned. It *is* those rhythms which are our main concern, for we feel their elucidation is a task which is still far from complete and one which does not require of the reader massive exposure to biographical data. Thus we welcome and join the shift in recent Kierkegaard scholarship to the study of Kierkegaard's thought.[30]

4. *The Systematic Impulse and the Critique of the 'System'*

Many Kierkegaard students who would share our rejection of the extreme biographical-psychological approach would prefer still other company to ours when we offer as an alternative the kind of system-

---

[28] *S.V.* XI, pp. 148–54 (*SD*, pp. 53–65). We have already urged recognition of the distinction between systematic analysis and causal explanation; see above, p. 4. Johannes Hohlenberg seems wholly to ignore the element of necessity. He worships personality, which 'is not a combination of characteristics, but the power which chooses and groups them; as a poet groups the words wherewith he shapes his poem. They are the material through which personality expresses itself.

And it is equally impossible to infer a man's character from his milieu. This also is a revelation of the essence of personality and a part of his fate. Personality guides the outer circumstances, and makes them acquire a significance which corresponds to its aims. It searches them out, or goes out of the way for them, and makes out of them exactly what it needs for its purposes.' *Sören Kierkegaard*, trans. T. H. Croxall (New York: Pantheon, 1954), p. 4. In support of this view Hohlenberg appeals to the fact that 'we can imagine human personality as such a cosmic idea which has equipped the individual person (through which it expresses itself) with just those characteristics which it needs in order to reveal itself' (ibid., pp. 1–2).

[29] Walter Lowrie, *Kierkegaard* (London: Oxford, 1938) and *A Short Life of Kierkegaard* (Princeton: Princeton, 1942).

[30] Both Kabell and Henriksen note this shift. M. Theunissen, however, observes a parallel tendency to study Kierkegaard's life relatively independently of his works, 'Das Kierkegaardbild in der neuern Forschung und Deutung'. *Deutsche Vierteljahrsschrift für Literaturwissenschaft und Geistesgeschichte*, 1958, p. 598.

atic study which we have proposed. They would insist that Kierkegaard's writings can be said to be systematic only in the minimal
sense of referential consistency requisite for meaningful communication. Any fuller sense of the systematic surely falls before Kierkegaard's attack on Hegel. For, while 'Hegel had many critics in his
lifetime, . . . they were mostly those who attacked his system
because they believed that they could construct a better one themselves. But his Danish critic attacked him for being the most consistent system-builder among system-builders. In the name of the
Christian faith Kierkegaard rejected not this or that element in
Hegelianism but the whole, referring to it in mockery as "the
System". So it happens that the issue of system *versus* the Christian
faith has been debated more than a hundred years ago.'[31]

Such a view is understandable, perhaps, given the warmth of some
Kierkegaardian passages—but it is sorely mistaken concerning both
the nature and extent of Kierkegaard's disagreement with Hegel.
Actually Kierkegaard criticizes the 'System' because it is *un*systematic
in important respects. Rather than seeing the systematic impulse in
Kierkegaard's thought as an unhappy remnant of the 'System' he
meant to attack, we see it as fundamental in the assault itself.[32]

Kierkegaard's systematic critique of the 'System' draws the line of
battle by insisting that the principle of contradiction applies in life
and thought.[33] Near the end of the intoxicating outpourings of the

---

[31] Hamilton, op. cit., p. 37 [italics his]. Cf. ibid., pp. 89–95. Cf. also Marjorie
Grene, *Dreadful Freedom, A Critique of Existentialism* (Chicago: University of Chicago,
1948), p. 22 and note 14.

[32] Helmut Fahrenbach in his critical bibliographical essay *Die gegenwärtige
Kierkegaard Auslegung in der deutschsprachigen Literatur von 1948 bis 1962* (Tübingen:
J. C. B. Mohr, 1962), pp. 34–35 notes that until very recently what little interest
was shown in the presence of system in Kierkegaard was largely negative. Fahren-
bach makes important suggestions on the nature of the systematic element in
Kierkegaard (ibid., pp. 35–42). Gregor Malantschuk, 'Kierkegaard and Nietzsche',
A Kierkegaard Critique, article trans. by Margaret Grieve, ed. Johnson and N.
Thulstrup, p. 119: 'In Kierkegaard's case it was in particular the philosophy of
Hegel which stimulated an examination of his own position. The mixture of
Christianity and philosophy in Hegel's works incited Kierkegaard to think clearly
and consistently upon the relation between these two and at the same time to stress
the paradox of Christianity in contrast to all human knowledge. He discovered that
Hegel in his philosophical method abused logical thought, and this was for him
a reminder of the wariness with which logical conclusions should be drawn.
Perhaps we owe it largely to Hegel's inconsistencies that Kierkegaard has such a
well-grounded and strictly logical method of thought.'

[33] *Pap.* V A 68–69. In his commentary on the *Fragments* Neils Thulstrup sketches
the Danish background for this passage: 'As is known, Hegel in *Wissenschaft der
Logik* (W.a.A., IV, 57ff.; J. A., IV, 535ff.; *Science of Logic*, II, 58ff.) asserts that the
principle of contradiction has been repudiated. In Denmark this position was

diapsalmata the author of *Either-Or* affirms: 'Tautology is and remains still the supreme principle, the highest law of thought.'[34] A reference in Kierkegaard's journals suggests the significance this sentence bears for the work in which it stands:

My particular concern with the whole of *Either-Or* is that it should be quite clear that the metaphysical significance at the bottom of the whole work leads everything back to the dilemma. The same thing is also at the bottom of the little philosophical essay: Tautology as the highest principle of thought; that is to say (oh, but how many will understand it) if the principle of contradiction is true (and that is expressed in 'either-or'), it is the scientific expression for tautology, and that is the only unity in which it can be resolved, the only way in which the system is possible. It would not be aesthetically correct to write a treatise on the principle of contradiction in this work and so it is expressed personally—but the same thing, seen from a speculative point of view (if one does not wish to 'go further'), is the apotheosis of tautology.[35]

Kierkegaard's interest is not merely to chastise the Hegelians by delimiting logic by means of the much noted distinction between logical 'movement' and existential movement.[36] It is also—and this is our immediate concern—to show that disrespect for the principle of contradiction involves a blurring of the identities which in their distinctness make possible both passion in life and precision in thought. Thus the passage from *Either-Or*, on the one hand, in marking the

---

transferred from logic to theology by J. A. Bornemann (1813–90) and Martensen, in that they maintained that both rationalism and supernaturalism had been abrogated as "absolute points of view". J. P. Mynster, however, protested first of all, although F. C. Sibbern had already attacked J. L. Heiberg's Hegelian treatment of this logical principle. . . . It is clear that Kierkegaard, not only here but consistently, affirms the validity of the principle of contradiction, both in formal logic and in philosophy and theology, even though, as emphasized by J. Himmelstrup, he usually has the principle of exclusion in mind.' *Philosophical Fragments*, commentary trans. H. Hong (Princeton: Princeton, 1962), p. 259. At this point we do not assess the validity of the charges which Kierkegaard makes by appeal to this principle. We shall examine that question in Part Two. Here our concern is to show that Kierkegaard so understood his work—including his critique of Hegel— as to permit and encourage the kind of systematic study we are proposing.
[34] *S.V.*, I, p. 22 (*E-O*, I, p. 30).
[35] *Pap.* III B 177 (*Dru* 405).
[36] On this point, see J. Heywood Thomas, *Subjectivity and Paradox* (Oxford: Basil Blackwell, 1957), pp. 12–14: It might help us to grasp Kierkegaard's point better if we compared it with Hume's insight that no individual proposition about a contingent matter of fact can be established *a priori*. This means that if we wish to make a novel assertion then we assert something which is not true *a priori*, and conversely anything which is true *a priori* is not an empirical assertion and is therefore a tautology. . . . Kierkegaard's argument makes essentially the same criticism of *a priori* systematic thinking. His point is that the System does away with the dilemma that is the peculiar characteristic of contingency, especially the contingent human situation. The system tells us nothing about man (ibid., p. 14 [italics his]).

limit for logic, ridicules the kind of tautology which 'is especially useful in cathedrals and pulpits where one is supposed to say something profound'.[37] On the other hand, suggesting the positive side of the relationship of this principle to Kierkegaard's concern, the passage says regarding this law of thought: 'Nor is it so poor but that it may well fill out a whole life.'[38] The passion of choice is reduced to aimless futility, if no possibilities can attain or retain identity for the self.[39] And clearly thought loses all precision if this principle is denied. In fact in Part Two we shall seek to show that for Kierkegaard the System represents a mass of confusion because it fails to distinguish sharply between precisely those identities which constitute the polarity structuring his thought. Neither God nor man escapes violation in such a procedure. The problems are interrelated, for if Hegel had actually honoured the real distinctness of God and man he would have recognized that such a dualistic reality could not be defined and described in a monistic system in which movement can only be apparent. That system repudiates the genuine plurality which is needed as the means and measure for movement.[40]

The distinct inner act of the self generates movement and that act eludes the structures of necessity. The product of the act 'enters the order of things . . . which digests, so to speak, the free actions

[37] *S.V.*, loc. cit.

[38] ibid.

[39] In actual effects the Hegelian romance with mediation parallels the position of the aesthete. Victor Kuhr, *Modsigelsens Grundsaetning* (Copenhagen: Gyldendal, 1915) has argued 'that fundamentally the aesthete keeps to the principle of contradiction; but owing to his purely intellectual relation to existence he can construct opposed possibilities out of every phenomenon of reality, or conversely declare that the realization of opposed possibilities gives the same result (marry or do not marry, you will regret both); this use of the principle of contradiction may be called tautological, since to the aesthete the opposites in reality coincide because they are equally valid to him in relation to existence; either-or under the aspect of tautology becomes neither-nor', cited and trans. in Henriksen, op. cit., pp. 137–8. The aesthete by refusing to posit his self in genuine choice renders his acceptance of the principle of contradiction merely intellectual. The Hegelian philosopher, on the other hand, by repudiating the principle of contradiction, denies himself the very context needed for the act of positing: 'what philosophy has retained [is] recognition of the fact that there is an absolute mediation. This is naturally of the most extreme importance; for if one gives up mediation, one gives up speculation as well. On the other side it is a serious thing to admit it; for if one admits mediation, then there is no absolute choice, and if there is not such, then there is no absolute either-or.' *S.V.* II, p. 157 (*E-O*, II, pp. 146–7).

[40] Kuhr notes the connection: 'The principle of contradiction . . . thus has in Kierkegaard from the outset a practical, ethical interest, the interest of personality', cited in Kabell, op. cit., p. 221. For a fuller statement of the connection, see Niels Thulstrup, 'Kierkegaards Verhältnis zu Hegel', *Theologische Zeitschrift*, 1957, pp. 200–26.

and coordinates them in its eternal laws'.[41] Hence a relative mediation is possible—but no more, for 'with what one calls the inward work philosophy has nothing at all to do, but the inward work is the true life of freedom'[42] *Either-Or* sets out to measure Hegel's denial of this distinction. So the preface reads: 'It has perhaps from time to time occurred to you, dear reader, to doubt a little the correctness of the celebrated philosophical thesis that the outward is the inward and the inward the outward.'[43] The distinction made in these passages has its roots in Kierkegaard's affirmation of the fundamental duality of reality—a duality receiving its most insistent expression for Kierkegaard in the divine-human polarity.[44]

Perhaps the success of our argument undermines its goal. Appealing to the principle of contradiction, Kierkegaard lampoons the Hegelians for presuming to treat the mystery of existential movement in a monistic system. Our interest in the systematic can thus claim Kierkegaard as an ally on formal grounds. But does not the material content of his concern with existence defy systematic determination? Indeed would not such a systematic effort reap Kierkegaard's scorn for the professors?[45] This question is suggested by many of Paul Holmer's articles on Kierkegaard. Professor Holmer stresses that in order to understand Kierkegaard one must recognize that he was dealing with 'possibles'. Holmer then draws a distinction: 'Cognitive

[41] *S.V.*, II, p. 158 (*E-O*, II, p. 147).

[42] ibid.

[43] *S.V.* I, p. v (*E-O*, I, p. 3) So Climacus found that the 'misdirection of speculation . . . must not be something accidental, but must lie far deeper in the whole tendency of the time—it must indeed lie in the fact that one had with such great knowledge altogether forgotten what it is to *exist* and what *inwardness* means. *S.V.*, VII, p. 203 (*CUP*, p. 216). In this paragraph we have had to anticipate in very brief compass our fuller discussion in Part Three.

[44] Wilhelm Anz seems to have lost sight of this polarity when he contends that 'the spirit as the synthesis of the finite and the infinite knows only the self-posited reality and the self-fashioned truth and here the point is now reached in which the fundamental commonality of the dialectic of existence with the idealistic thought of Hegel finally penetrates, . . . [for] the dialectic of existence and speculative philosophy are inflections of the same modern philosophical self-consciousness and therein lies a latent commonality which is just as important as their more notorious contrast', *Kierkegaard und der deutsche Idealismus* (Tübingen: J. C. B. Mohr, 1956), p. 70. For a penetrating critique of this contention see N. Thulstrup, 'Kierkegaard og den filosofiske Idealisme', *Kierkegaardiana* ed. N. Thulstrup, 1962, pp. 88–105.

[45] The passages abound and are both pointed and painful. Among the best known is the piercing description of the man who 'became professor of . . . that Christ was crucified'. That passage ends by contending that 'just in the degree that the professor is accounted the highest thing, in that same degree is one the most disoriented in Christianity; by the way the "professor" is judged, one can perceive the state of Christendom and the judgement about Christianity'. *Pap.* X 3 A 122; cf. X 2 A 633 (*Dru* 1087); VI B 133f., pp. 225f.; X 1 A 609; XI 1 A 374.

possibles get their reference in virtue of an act of the thinker, which act does not change the cognitive agent but affects only the transition from unintelligible to intelligible. Ethical possibles get their reference in virtue of an interest and passion of the person. As possibles they too are neutral and without reference. They acquire "reference" only when they are chosen and willed as the model for one's future.'[46] 'All possibles *qua* possibles are objective, i.e., they can be described.'[47] While ethical possibles have as their correlatives human passions, 'it is Kierkegaard's radicalness to have . . . argued that the qualities of passion are cognizable and are statable as ethical and religious possibles'.[48] Now this way of stating the matter might seem to give the systematician room in which to work. But Holmer contends that a 'major error in philosophy is to treat such possibles as if they were true of objects, as if they were descriptive of actuality, hence could be synthesized into cognitive unities and propositions. Kierkegaard's books put these ethical possibles into linguistic form without making them tools of cognition'.[49] How shall one best approach Kierkegaard then? Surely not by massive biographical research, for 'his own historical immediacy was his accidental point of departure for his encounter with the qualitative dialectic of ethico-religious possibilities, and he believed that every man's contemporaneity permitted, but did not require or predispose, the same immediacy'.[50] Apparently systematic analysis is not a particularly significant ingredient in the relation of contemporaneity, for 'to grasp these possibles (and not the theory) as requirements is Kierkegaard's wish for his readers. This does not ask for philosophical talent as much as it does an ability to read and respond with fitting passion'.[51]

Herman Diem's prize-winning *Die Existenzdialektik von Sören Kierkegaard*[52] may be said to leave the systematician in about the same state of frustration. In this work Diem expounds a theme which he has already enunciated in *Philosophie und Christentum bei Sören Kierkegaard*: 'Kierkegaard has no Christian doctrine which could be reproduced as a system, but only a dialectical method of Christian

[46] Paul L. Holmer, 'On Understanding Kierkegaard', *A Kierkegaard Critique*, ed. H. Johnson and N. Thulstrup, 1962, p. 46.

[47] ibid., p. 48.

[48] ibid.

[49] ibid., pp. 46–47.

[50] ibid., p. 49.

[51] ibid., p. 52. Cf. ibid. pp. 50–51: 'These possibles are not hypotheses at all— they must be intuited directly as possibles and as ethico-religious possibles, not as are the cognitive possibles previously noted.'

[52] Zürich, Evangelischer, 1950.

communication which places near the one who receives it the possibility to exist as a Christian.'[53]

When asked to acknowledge so slender a role for the systematician one may echo Kierkegaard's lament: 'Yet understanding and reflection are also gifts from God. What shall one do with them and what make of them, if one must not use them?'[54] Perhaps our quarrel with Professor Holmer lies not so much in the question of the admissibility of systematic analysis as in the assessment of its worth and —doubtless—in the substance of its execution. Holmer, as we have seen, does not deny that the religious possibles can be 'objects of cognition'. Kierkegaard surely affirms that of the Christian possible: 'The Christian possible exists before any Christian exists, it must exist in order that one can become a Christian, it contains the determination by means of which it may be tested whether one has become a Christian. It retains its objective existence apart from all believers, while it is at the same time present in the inwardness of the believer. In short, here there is no identity between the subjective and the objective. Though Christianity comes into the heart of ever so many believers, every believer is conscious that it has not arisen in his heart.'[55] Diem would seem hard put to hold to his contention that Christian existence involves no Christian doctrine which could be the subject for systematic analysis.[56] At this point it seems to us

---

[53] Hermann Diem, *Philosophie und Christentum bei Sören Kierkegaard* (Munich: Kaiser, 1929) p. vii; cf. ibid., pp. 111, 348f., 364.

[54] *Pap.* IX A 222. On Kierkegaard's understanding of himself as a poet and thinker, see *Pap.* X 1 A 281 and IX A 161. See also the sketch by Climacus of the young man with so great a love for consistency, *Pap.* IV B 1, pp. 103–82 (*DO*, pp. 103–73). Kierkegaard contrasts himself as a dialectical thinker with one who would appeal to revelation, *S.V.*, XIII, p. 568 (*P.V.*, p. 83). Furthermore, even when Climacus is stressing that the wise man has no essential advantage in relation to Christianity, he can permit the simple wise man to say to the simple man: 'But you must never make light of this study, just as I never regret it, since on the contrary it pleases me the most, when I smile over it, and just then, excited again, take hold of the strenuous labour of thought.' *S.V.*, VII, pp. 191–2 (*CUP*, p. 204).

[55] *Pap.* VII 2 B 235, pp. 199–205 (*AR*, p. 168); cf. *Pap.* X 2 A 119; X 3 A 756; and X 5 A 121. Similarly, Kierkegaard may disclaim that he subjectively represents the Christian possible, but he asserts: 'I know what Christianity is.' *S.V.* XIII, p. 505 ('AW', *PV*, p. 153). See also *S.V.*, VII, pp. 320–1 (*CUP*, pp. 330–1) on raising the question of what Christianity is with an eye to the existential.

[56] Many critics have argued that Diem's own Kierkegaard books require greater unity of Kierkegaard than the personal unity Diem permits. See Fahrenbach, op. cit., pp. 30–31 and Lönning, op. cit., pp. 12–15. We detect in Diem's problem a strained effort both to stress Kierkegaard's use of the Socratic dialectic and to liberate God from the reproach of a delimiting description. The effort could only be successful if one could not only excise Kierkegaard's references to an objective content to the Christian possible, but also show that the employment of the Socratic method carried with it no substantive implications.

that unless Diem is willing to grant fuller place to the systematician, he will have to retract his statement that the goal of Kierkegaard's method did lie in that Christian existence. The noteworthy dispatch with which Dr Holmer joins Diem in dismissing the systematician is partly due to the fact that, while he affirms that Kierkegaard understood the Christian possible as objective, he apparently denies that the reader's appropriation of that possible represented the underlying purpose of the authorship: 'Kierkegaard's literature presents genuinely alternative possibles. No amount of evidence can reduce them to one. . . . Kierkegaard believed that the glory of being human was to realize in one's own personality the most pervading of passions and enthusiasms. Among these, those of Christian quality were the truth for him.'[57] Later in this section—and in the essential argument of the book itself—we take issue with this reading of Kierkegaard's intent. Here, though, we must confess that it seems to us that Holmer's analysis makes rather too little of the rational element in the presentation and appropriation of the Christian possible.[58] We are impressed both with Kierkegaard's references to the role of reason and with the role reason plays in his own works.[59]

[57] Holmer, 'On Understanding Kierkegaard', *A Kierkegaard Critique*, ed. H. Johnson and N. Thulstrup, 1962, pp. 51 and 53.

[58] Fahrenback, op. cit., pp. 34–35, points out that while the ethical side of the Kierkegaard literature calls for appropriation, it does not do so on authority of Kierkegaard, but on the basis of a genuine confrontation—including, Fahrenbach argues, an intellectual confrontation. We shall see that observation sustained both formally and materially, though it will be made clear that the intellectual moment in the confrontation never attains coercive value.

[59] For the role Kierkegaard recognizes for reason, see above note 53. Collins, op. cit., p. 284, note 21, finds three checks on irrationalism in this understanding: '(a) He admitted the rights of reason in the non-existential fields of the empirical sciences and logic; (b) he allowed to man some moral and religious understanding of the order of existence and subjectivity, a region which is intelligible in its own nature; (c) he championed the omniscience of God and the correlative intelligibility of all aspects of being (which are known comprehensively or "systematically" by God and which will be known by us in a systematic way, when we pass from time to eternity).' In Part Three we will seek to show that these Kierkegaardian affirmations themselves may be seen to reveal the dialectical tension in his thought between the rhythms of diastasis and synthesis. One may find the point being debated illustrated in the question as to whether one may speak of Kierkegaard's anthropology. In a review of *Die Existenzdialektik*, G. Malantschuk takes issue with Diem's denial of an anthropology in Kierkegaard and claims that the anthropology supporting Kierkegaard's work is indirectly expressed for the most part. Malantschuk also argues that Kierkegaard directly affirms the necessity of an anthropology in such passages as *Pap.* V B 53 29, p. 129: 'Psychology is that which we need and above all competent knowledge of the life of man and sympathy for its interests. Thus there lies here a task which must be discharged before there can be any talk about completing a Christian view of life.' G. Malantschuk, 'Sören Kierkegaard's Anthropologi', *Meddelelser Fra Sören Kierkegaard Selskab*, 1954, pp. 20–21.

This defence of a systematic study of Kierkegaard need not be won at the expense of excising Kierkegaard's references to the paradoxical. We have already claimed that Kierkegaard's discourse dealing with mystery and paradox represents the systematic impulse in his thought in two respects.[60] The material verification of that claim must follow in Part Three. It remains for us to observe here that the very concept of paradox includes recognition of the principle of contradiction as a relative but fundamental ingredient.[61] The witness to consistency which the very tension of paradox bears will be seen to parallel internally the insistent movement to interrelate the rhythms of diastasis and synthesis, which calls forth the potentiation of paradox to the point of threatening the meaningfulness of the discourse. Despite the threat, paradox may in the main be said to be in the service of the systematic impulse in Kierkegaard. This service is effectively illustrated in noting that the diastatic tendency so to isolate the human pole as to render faith simply subjective passion is checked by a formulation of paradox which retains and reflects the polar interdependence by providing an objective reality which uniquely fits the quality of the person's highest passion. So Kierkegaard can say of Johannes Climacus: 'That he . . . shows, that the strange thing is that there is a "How" which has the characteristic that once it is precisely given, then the "What" is also given; and that this is the "How" of "Faith". Here surely inwardness at its maximum is shown to be objectivity again. And this is a turning of the principle of subjectivity which, so far as I know, has never before been so carried through or worked out.'[62] While this statement will be exposed to both immanent and transcendental criticism in the course of this book, it seems to us to illustrate how Kierkegaard's references to paradox more reveal than resist the systematic impulse in his thought.

We have noted Kierkegaard's defence of the principle of contradiction against the Hegelian system's monistic confusion of the realities

---

[60] See above, p. 4.

[61] H. Höffding, *Sören Kierkegaard som Filosof* (Copenhagen: Philipsen, 1892), p. 73, makes a suggestion of this sort: 'He too felt a passionate need of understanding. And indeed his whole strong stressing of the paradox, of the irrational, of the sudden jerk that destroys the continuity would be incomprehensible if he did not himself feel a desire for retaining the continuity. His doctrine of truth as a paradox, expresses that this desire has been disappointed.' We shall be arguing that the conclusion which Höffding draws is too simple to express the complex role which paradox plays in Kierkegaard's thought.

[62] *Pap.* X 2 A 299 (*Dru* 1021). Cf. *S.V.* VII, p. 534 (*CUP*, p. 542): 'But with respect to believing (*sensu strictissimo*) it holds good that this "how" is appropriate to only one as its object [italics his].'

of God and man and the relations of thought and existence. We have tried to show that that formal defence of consistency is joined by an invitation to a material systematic study of God and man and that that defence occurs in a body of thought which itself represents such study. Of course the role for such study is a limited one.[63] The order of thought in such a study will reflect the order of existence—but this sentence is not reversible. Thus the transition to Christianity must 'be first felt and then comprehended'.[64] If a certain partial conceptual anticipation of Christian existence and of the transition to that existence is possible, the actualization of that existence still only comes through the individual's inner act of freedom. Professor Holmer surely speaks Kierkegaard's mind when he asserts: 'The distinction between having a passion and having knowledge of the passion is as wide as the distinction between actuality and possibility or the distinction between being ethical or religious and knowing about either ethics or religion.'[65]

One may even say that the distinction is wider than this. For Kierkegaard denies that speech whether in anticipation or retrospection can fully express existential reality.[66] That denial is not surprising to one who recalls Kierkegaard's willingness 'to doubt a little the correctness of the celebrated philosophical thesis that the outward is the inward and the inward the outward'.[67] The inner may defy statement: 'There must yet be something which is so blessed that it does not permit itself to be uttered with words—otherwise, why did those men to whom something really great had been revealed remain mute?'[68] Indeed of the arts of communication systematic discourse may not be the most sensitive to all dimensions of meaning. At times man has to struggle to suggest what he cannot utter. Later in this study we shall note how the words and work of Kierkegaard affirm a projective role for gesture and speech in communication.[69]

The inadequacy of language to convey the wealth of the existential

---

[63] For our preliminary statement of the limitations of this study see above, pp. 4–5.

[64] *Pap.* I A 94.

[65] Holmer, 'On Understanding Kierkegaard', *A Kierkegaard Critique*, ed. H. Johnson and N. Thulstrup, 1962, p. 51.

[66] Cf. Kierkegaard's autobiographical testimony to the fact that he was 'engaged to a Love which infinitely surpasses my understanding'. *Pap.* X 1 A 272. One finds here both a suggestion of the limits placed on communication and a striking example of communication within those limits.

[67] See above, p. 21, note 43.

[68] *Pap.* I A 327.

[69] See, for example, *S.V.* IV, pp. 386–7 (CD, pp. 105–6). For a careful study of

situation may put us on the track of a further limitation which Kierkegaard places on any attempt to state the Christian faith systematically. He views such systematic communication as moving 'from faith to faith'. He can say that 'the meaning lies in appropriation', suggesting perhaps not only that meaning is not communicated apart from existential response, but also that that meaning is itself inclusive of the response.[70] Yet in its inadequacy verbal expression may fail both to reflect the existential moment out of which it speaks and to impel the hearer to translate the possibility language conveys into actuality through action. Perhaps systematic statement is particularly susceptible to the latter failure. If that is so, one can understand Kierkegaard's change: 'It is to get rid of doing God's will that we have invented learning . . . we shield ourselves by hiding behind tomes.'[71] Thus there is mounted a very heavy attack on 'doctrine' (*Laere*) as the symbol for the age's falsification of the existential character of Christianity. But this attack returns us to our earlier observation that such confusion repudiates rather than reflects a systematic use of a reason responsive to the demands of a reality which is too rich to be described in a monistic system.[72] Thus one is not surprised to find that very word *Laere* also used positively to refer to the objective and indispensable structure of the Christian existence.[73] That double usage ought to suggest to Kierkegaard's readers the distinction between the question regarding the systematic character of Kierkegaard's thought and the question regarding a system of existence in the Hegelian sense.[74]

The question of Kierkegaard's relation to systematic thought is

---

this point see Lars Bejerholm, '*Meddelelsens Dialektik*' (Copenhagen: Munksgaard, 1962), pp. 88ff., 110f., and 173f.

[70] *S.V.*, V, p. 175 (*TCS* unnumbered preface). Cf. *S.V.* VIII, p. 117 (*PH*, pp. 27-28.) for a reference to 'understanding for one's self in the inwardness of appropriation. . . . Meaning lies namely in the one meditating and in the understanding of the one meditating on the discourse.'

[71] *Pap.* XI 2 A 376.

[72] Indeed in repudiating that confusion Kierkegaard reveals the persistent systematic tendency in his thought. Thus in sadly prophesying that he would fall into the hands of the professors, Kierkegaard wrote: 'The man in whom the professor is lodged cannot be rid of this tapeworm by any human power, only God can do it, if the man himself is willing.' *Pap.* X 4 A 629 (*Dru* 1269).

[73] Lönning, op cit., pp. 15-16, discusses the two uses of the term and cites extensive textual support for each.

[74] On this distinction see Fahrenbach, op. cit., pp. 34-35. We feel it is precisely this distinction which Hamilton fails to observe in his comparison of Kierkegaard and Hegel. See above, notes 2 and 3.

often identified with the question of Kierkegaard's relation to metaphysics. We have said that we do not understand the basic rhythms to be metaphysical in character, though they seem sometimes to appropriate metaphysical notions.[75] If metaphysics deals with structures of ultimate generality,[76] a deceptive formal resemblance to metaphysical affirmations arises through the fact that these rhythms are present in such great generality in Kierkegaard's thought about reality. While the order of thought may be supposed to reflect the order of reality at this point, it is clear that for Kierkegaard the rhythms reflect patterns of relationship which are dependent on the particular entities constituting the relationship ánd not vice versa. Thus we are removed from the ground of Hegelian metaphysics. Furthermore Kierkegaard would seem more inclined to deny than to affirm the suggestion that the relationship of these entities is descriptive of all reality as such. In making this qualification we are not claiming exemption from metaphysical description for the realities constituting the relationship. But their metaphysical status is not the centre of Kierkegaard's concern and is not descriptive of the structuring of those systematic tendencies in Kierkegaard's reflection which are the object of this study.[77]

5. Pseudonymity and the Stages—Obstacles or Opportunities?

Perhaps whatever success our argument has attained has been won only at the expense of ignoring essential features of the authorship to which it is supposed to apply. What shall a systematic study do when confronted with the pseudonymous character of much of Kierkegaard's work? Even if we for the moment deal only with the formal significance of pseudonymity, we find the problem to be a highly complex one. It is well known that Kierkegaard in the 'first and last declaration' appended to the *Postscript* declared: 'In the pseudony-

[75] See above, p. 6, note 3 and p. 11, note 16.

[76] For such a description of the metaphysical quest see, for example, G. W. F. Hegel, *The Philosophy of Right*, trans. T. M. Knox (Oxford: Clarendon, 1942), p. 228 and A. N. Whitehead, *Process and Reality* (London: Macmillan, 1929), p. 31.

[77] Kierkegaard's works carry strong statements suggesting the complete separation of Christianity from 'philosophy'. So *Pap*. II A 790: 'Christianity will have no dealings with philosophy, even if it will divide with it the spoils; it cannot endure that the king of Sodom should say, I have made Abraham rich.' Cf. *Pap*. II A 239. Such references take aim at a philosophy which, ignoring the Kierkegaardian strictures observed in this section, has usurped the role of faith and now functions as a genuine rival to Christianity (and so may opt to 'divide the spoils'). Such references should not be read as a repudiation of philosophy or metaphysics as such.

mous books there is not a single word of my own: I have no opinion about them except as a third person, no knowledge about their meaning except as a reader, not the remotest private relation to them, as this is after all impossible to have towards a doubly reflected communication.'[78] It would seem to behove his public to respect such explicit reservation, even if one wishes to withhold judgment regarding the value of the works involved.[79]

But the complexity of the problem does not disappear so easily. A good deal of evidence suggests that at least Climacus and Anti-Climacus cannot be separated from Kierkegaard so simply.[80] In a striking entry in his journal from July, 1849 Kierkegaard comments on his relationship to these two pseudonyms: 'The pseudonym [for *The Sickness Unto Death*] is called Johannes Anti-Climacus in contrast to Climacus, who declared himself not to be a Christian.[81] Anti-Climacus is the opposite extreme in being a Christian to an extraordinary degree, but I myself merely strive to be quite simply a Christian.'[82] Such a reference surely invites the reader to regard

---

[78] *S.V.* VII. p. 546 (*CUP*, p. 551).

[79] Thus E. Geismar, *Sören Kierkegaard* (Copenhagen: G. E. C. Gad, 1926–8) I, pp. 136ff., II, pp. 114ff., III, p. 81, and V, p. 50, rejects the pseudonymous writings and turns instead to the edifying discourses as the source for Kierkegaard's understanding of Christianity. So, too, F. Brandt agrees that Kierkegaard 'was only concerned in a literary manner with the points of view stated by the pseudonymous authors', but contends that nonetheless 'the pseudonymous writings are the greatest and most valuable achievement of Sören Kierkegaard', *Sören Kierkegaard. His Life and His Works* (Copenhagen: Det danske Selskab, 1963), p. 26. Apparently the distinction between the two classes of writings is not quite as firm for Brandt as one might suppose from the passage quoted, for he can write 'these words of Vigilius Haufniensis are undoubtedly identical with Kierkegaard's own view', ibid., p. 55.

[80] Some qualification of pseudonymity is already suggested by the fact that Kierkegaard's name appears on the title page as 'responsible for publication' (*PF, CUP*) or as 'editor' (*TC, SD*). Up to the very last Kierkegaard had planned to publish the *Fragments* in his own name (*Pap.* V b 40. 2). See pp. 146–9 in Thulstrup's commentary and Bejerholm, op. cit., pp. 272–3, 295–6. In the first edition of *Training in Christianity* (published 1850) Anti-Climacus says that he has Kierkegaard's permission to include a discourse of Kierkegaard's from the church of Our Lady, and upon the publication of the second edition (1855) he cries out 'take the pseudonymity away' (*S.V.* XIV, p. 81 [*AC*, p. 55]). On the intimate relationship of *TC* to Kierkegaard, see Lowrie, Kierkegaard, pp. 430–7, and *Pap.* X 1 A 410 (*Dru* 936).

[81] *S.V.* VII, p. 7 (*CUP*, p. 19).

[82] *Pap.* X 1 A 510 (*Dru* 936). Cf. *Pap.* X 1 A 517; 'Anti-Climacus has something in common with Climacus, but the difference is in Johannes Climacus having placed himself so low that he even declares himself not to be a Christian and one seems to be able to note in Anti-Climacus that he supposes himself to be a Christian to an extraordinary degree. . . . I considered myself above Johannes Climacus and below Anti-Climacus.'

pseudonymity as a means of distinguishing an objectively accurate
statement of a point of view from a claim concerning the writer's
personal relationship to that point of view. One's response to that
invitation should also be made with caution.[83] Yet that pseudonymity
was a way of saying that the problems under discussion were not
simply Kierkegaard's personal problems does seem to be part of the
truth.

Does that truth apply to the other pseudonyms as well? While
explicit textual evidence of the sort already cited is considerably
more slender, much can be said in favour of an affirmative response.
We do have at least one other reference suggesting that the use of
pseudonymity is intended to affirm that a theme is of universal
interest rather than to disavow that it is of personal interest.[84] One can
also find parallels to the themes of the pseudonymous works in what
appear to be intensely personal passages from the *Papirer*.[85] And one
can observe items in Kierkegaard's biography or aspects of his
personality which could at least have occasioned the use of pseudonyms.[86] What is lacking in an approach composed of such items is a
direct encounter with Kierkegaard's theory—or better, theories—of
indirect communication and its bearing on pseudonymity. That

[83] We touch here the difficult question as to how far (if at all) the content of the
Christian option has been distorted through its presentation in *PF* as a 'project of
thought' over against the 'Socratic' position. We shall be discussing that question
in some detail later and shall also be asking whether the extraordinary character of
Anti-Climacus is simply a matter of the person and not the position itself. On *PF*
as a project of thought, see Emanuel Hirsch, *Kierkegaard-Studien* (Gütersloh:
Bertelsmann, 1930–3), II, pp. 697–8. Hirsch contends that the theoretical viewpoint of *PF* is 'entirely unsuited to grasping a living relation to the God of Grace
in adoration and prayer in the inwardness of one's existence'. Perhaps, but if the
project grasps nothing at all about its alleged subject, it is obviously self-defeating.

[84] See Thulstrup's commentary on the *Fragments*, lxxxv-vi on Kierkegaard's
statement that the author of *The Concept of Dread* (Vigilius Haufniensis)could as
well have been 'Christian Madsen' (John Smith).

[85] See Lowrie, op. cit., pp. 284–90, who settles for the view that the pseudonymous authors represent 'sides' of Kierkegaard, though not the 'whole' Kierkegaard.

[86] Kierkegaard's relation to Regine Olsen is, of course, the example which
comes to mind most quickly. So Collins, op. cit., p. 36, writes of *E-O, REP*, and *FT*:
'These books were his means of communicating with Regine Olsen after their
separation, while Kierkegaard still hoped to become reconciled with her. . . . He
hoped to speak to her significantly without betraying her confidence to the casual
reader.' In support of this suggestion one can cite Kierkegaard's letters from Berlin
to Emil Boesen in which Kierkegaard stresses the need for anonymity and gives
Boesen detailed instructions for his surveillance of Regine, *Breve og Aktstykker
vedrörende Sören Kierkegaard*, ed. Niels Thulstrup (Copenhagen: Munksgaard, 1953)
I, pp. 71ff., 107. It has also been suggested that the Romanticist literary convention
of pseudonymity had great appeal to a writer who was possessed 'by a morbid
reserve which was a specific product of his melancholy' (Lowrie, op. cit., p. 380).

encounter will have to take account of the shift away from pseudo-nymity which characterized the last part of Kierkegaard's authorship and the accompanying re-formulation of the function of pseudonymity. Aage Henriksen provides a useful introduction to the changes in-volved, when he says of Kierkegaard's use of pseudonymity:

> It has two forms, each corresponding to a particular kind of religious tactics; and to make the confusion complete, Kierkegaard calls both kinds indirect com-munication. In his production up to and including 'Unscientific Postscript' indirect communication is contrasted with Hegelian direct communication of objective knowledge, the method being that the narrator, after producing his testimony, destroys himself and leaves the reader deserted with a statement in which qualita-tive contrasts clash. The reader can only save himself from the dilemma by a personal recognition and solution of the problems. In 'The Point of View' the indirect statement is contrasted with the direct preaching, which would lead the hearer to the truth by persuasion. It is interpreted as a method of inveigling him into the truth, by the teacher's pretending to be in the pupil's situation (delusion) and thus achieving personal contact; thereafter he slowly uncovers the truth, so that the learner, absorbed in his interest, with the speed of abandonment, is made to run right into the most decisive precepts of the religion.[87]

We may note that neither of these views places the pseudonymous writings very close to Kierkegaard's own view of life. The Sören Kierkegaard Society has published a very thorough study of the problem by Lars Bejerholm, who is critical of both views.[88] Bejerholm takes aim particularly at an uncritical acceptance of *The Point of View*. He suggests that *PV* was motivated by Kierkegaard's desire to reply to the charge that the Kierkegaard who was no longer to be found on the streets after the Corsair incident in 1846 had grown religious, as old men do, and had lost his aesthetic touch.[89] Kierkegaard responds by writing the aesthetic piece *A Crisis and the Crisis in the Life of an Actress* and publishes it in 1848.[90] He then strikes upon the idea of using this piece to show the unity of his whole authorship—an author-ship which has been characterized by a religious purpose throughout (*PV*). Bejerholm has little trouble in showing that *PV*'s threefold division of the authorship is more tidy than the facts allow.[91] He can also point to Kierkegaard's concession that *PV*'s explanation 'admits a little too much in the direction of consciousness'.[92] Kierkegaard

[87] Henriksen, op. cit., p. 9.
[88] Bejerholm, op. cit.
[89] Bejerholm can persuasively cite Kierkegaard's own remarks at this point: *S.V.* XIII, pp. 521–3 (*PV*, pp. 10–13).
[90] *Pap.* IX A 175, p. 84 (*Dru* 795); *Pap.* IX A 228.
[91] For the schema, see *S.V.* XIII, p. 521 (*PV*, p. 10); cf. Bejerholm, op. cit., pp. 207–303.
[92] *S.V.* XIII, p. 562 (*PV*, p. 73).

counters this concession by an appeal to the activity of divine providence.[93]

Bejerholm is perhaps less persuasive in handling those points where *PV*'s explanation does seem to fit the facts—as, say, Kierkegaard's practice of publishing simultaneously pseudonymous works and edifying discourses in his own name. That practice does not, of course, *require PV*'s explanation, but it does suggest the need for some explanation fuller than an anecdotal description of Kierkegaard's biography. It seems to us that Bejerholm's persistent interest in the personal basis for pseudonymity could lead him to a view which would not only speak to the matter of pseudonymity but also deal with the apparent conflicts in the related problem of indirect communication. Bejerholm notes that Kierkegaard says that the course of the authorship traces the course of his personal development.[94] Perhaps that development did involve genuine participation by Kierkegaard in the alternatives the authorship identifies.[95] Perhaps that development was such that it gave birth to a thought which could both stress qualitative contrast between the alternatives and yet significant points of interconnection. We are suggesting that the rhythms of diastasis and synthesis might be seen here too, rather than only in places where Kierkegaard's discourse is formally devoted to the divine-human polarity. One might even suggest that it is possible to unite a genuine religious interest on Kierkegaard's part and a

[93] *S.V.* XIII, pp. 556ff. (*PV*, pp. 64ff.); cf. *Pap.* X 1 A 283: 'That the pseudonymous, the aesthetic productivity has been used by me as a maieutic, I do not dare say—I cannot say that—but in relation to the world of readers it will be the whole authorship's maieutic in relation to the religious which lay far deeper in my soul; but, as I say that I have used it so, I dare not and cannot say.' Yet Kierkegaard does at times claim consciousness at this point, *S.V.* XIII, p. 562 (*PV*, p. 73); or at least a partial consciousness, *Pap.* X 2 A 89.

[94] So he can say the authorship followed 'my own development' *S.V.* XIII, p. 611 (*PV* 137) and had a 'purely personal meaning', *S.V.* XIII, p. 561 (*PV*, p. 71). Cf. *S.V.* XIII, p. 556 (*PV* 63); 'My existence relation transformed itself, corresponding altogether exactly to the demands in the productivity.' Bejerholm does not necessarily contradict himself in giving weight to these passages, while taking lightly the religious telos their context (*PV*) seeks to give to the whole authorship. But he does seem to us to be rather too inclined to see such passages as themselves weakening *PV*'s argument concerning the telos. We are in the process of suggesting that these possibilities do not exhaust the alternatives. In any case these passages would provide the basis for Berjerholm's scepticism over against *CUP*'s 'declaration'. Bejerholm observes that 'the fact that Sören Kierkegaard thinks that he has succeeded in carrying through completely the fiction of the pseudonyms does not free scholarship from the task of investigating in what degree this actually is the case', op. cit., p. 260.

[95] To this extent Lowrie, op. cit., p. 277, may be right in saying that 'we can perceive that (with the exception of the two books attributed to Anti-Climacus) the pseudonymous works suggest a stage the author has recently passed'.

genuine participation in the pseudonymous identities. The consciousness of the relationship between the two and the very character of
the relationship could themselves be such as to suggest the distinction
between diastasis and synthesis.[96] We find it very difficult to restrict
ourselves to the announced formal discussion of pseudonymity, for
the line of thought we have been following obviously leads us on to
say something about the relationship of the diastasis-synthesis
interpretative structure to Kierkegaard's discourse regarding the
stages on the way of life and beyond that to the actual interrelation-
ships of whatever factual points of view Kierkegaard may be said to
have identified. We withhold ourselves from the latter task until Part
Four. The former concerns us somewhat later in this section.

It should be noted that the contrast between *CUP* and *PV* on the
purpose of pseudonymity is only part of the question as to the significance for our analysis of Kierkegaard's reflections regarding the
relationship between indirect communication and pseudonymity. It
will not do to leave that larger question with the assertion that
Kierkegaard's life and thought reveal the movements of diastasis and
synthesis. Quite specifically, with such an assertion we have not
recognized the shift towards more direct communication in the final
period of the authorship. It may not do to say that the shift is produced by the desire to fulfil the requirement that thought be 'reduplicated' in life. Bejerholm points out that Kierkegaard could—
with current literary conventions supporting him—appeal to the
pseudonyms as 'real' individuals.[97] This reduplication of thought may

---

[96] Kierkegaard himself seems to speak in this direction in a remarkable passage
in which he discusses the apparent contradiction between *CUP* and *PV*: 'Concerning this the following must be said. *Partly*, that what I at that time [*CUP*]
wrote can be quite true, and the later just as true, because I in so many words at
that time was not further in development, had not yet understood myself in the
definitive thought for the whole production, dared not yet once with definiteness
say whether it might possibly end with my finding something which drove me
back from Christianity, while I yet in my religious excitement continued with every
faculty to discharge the task of setting forth what Christianity is. *Partly*, that I
after all even in the writings about my activity as an author do not speak in a
straightforward way about the pseudonyms or identify myself with the pseudonyms,
but merely show their meaning as a maieutic. Finally, that I, after all, add: I now
understand the whole in such a way, that I myself by no means have so surveyed
the whole from the beginning, so little as I dare say that I immediately have
understood that the telos of the pseudonyms was maieutic, since it was at the same
time a moment of poetic outpouring in my own life's development.' *Pap*. X 3 A
258 [italics his]. Cf. *Pap*. X 5 B 145 regarding the idea of the authorship becoming
clear in retrospect.

[97] *Pap*. VIII 2 B 82, 13: The pseudonyms are, to be sure 'only poetic "I"s, but
that is, after all, something'. Cf. Bejerholm, op. cit., pp. 246, 254.

not, then, seem so very different from that attained by the Kierkegaard who wrote the edifying discourses but disclaimed all authority,
asking that the reader pay no attention to him.[98] And surely to the
very last Kierkegaard's speech is indirect in the sense that it leaves
with the individual the act of free judgment and response.[99] Yet
what can be documented in Kierkegaard's authorship is a steadily
rising tide of antagonism to 'impersonal' writing. To be sure, utterances which are not formally pseudonymous may be materially
anonymous—impersonal.[100] But Kierkegaard came to feel that 'a
pseudonym is after all also an impersonal thing'.[101] So it is that even
the half-pseudonymity of TC is removed in the second edition and
that no pseudonyms are used in the attack on the church.[102]

The trend is clear. What one is to make of it is surely less clear. We
discuss below the debate which has raged regarding the relationship
of the attack on the church to the rest of Kierkegaard's authorship.[103]
Here we shall content ourselves with noting that what is clearly added
in the shift is the element of Kierkegaard's personal witness to the
truth of the utterances of this last period. One may, however, read
the significance of that addition very differently. The witness could
be called forth by a concern to grant the reader some help, however
unauthoritative, in the extremity of his genuine uncertainty. Or the
witness may respond to certainties—the certainty of man's depraved
blindness or equally depraved cleverness and the certainty of God's
judgment. Both suggestions—and others—are possible on the basis
of the material at hand from this turbulent period.[104] This question

---

[98] See the stereotyped preface to the discourses, as in *S.V.* III, p. 11 (*ED* I, p. 5).

[99] Bejerholm, op. cit., pp. 207–8, points out that as late as 1850–1 Kierkegaard
could defend the use of indirect communication against attacks by Martensen
(*Pap.* X 5 B 54) and L. Gude (*Pap.* X 6 B 144–61).

[100] *S.V.* XIII, p. 544 (*PV*, p. 45); *S.V.* VIII, p. 96 (*PA*, pp. 58–59). Thus a
pseudonym (though a very special one, see above, pp. 29–30) Anti-Climacus can
accuse the preachers of impersonal preaching. Cf. *Pap.* VIII 2 B 88, p. 183; the
pseudonyms make it possible for the age to hear the 'I' again, 'and a personal
"I"'.

[101] *Pap.* X 2 A 393.

[102] *Pap.* IX A 186. In 1848, with the Corsair incident very much still in mind,
Kierkegaard indicates a plan to issue his journal articles in book form to get
'completely out of journal literature'. Kierkegaard's use of the journal form in the
attack on the church and his invitation to the reader to subscribe to the series which
follows (*S.V.*, XIV, p. 117 [*AC*, p. 91]) hardly seem to us to represent an inconsistency in view of the strong material identification of Kierkegaard with these
articles.

[103] See pp. 39–40 in this section, and pp. 164–71, Part Three.

[104] At this point we have not tried to deal with Kierkegaard's remarks about
the apostle and his unique use of direct (*CUP*) or indirect (*Pap.* X 2 A 147) communi-

defies settlement at this point in our inquiry and even further discussion seems pointless until some attention is given to the substance enclosed in the mystifying veil of pseudonymity: the stages on the way of life.

The structure of the stages seems to delimit the raw material for a study of Kierkegaard's religious thought quite narrowly. Even if one believes that the pseudonymous authors representing the earlier stages in fact represent viewpoints of importance to Kierkegaard's own personal development, one would presumably still have to focus the study on the telos of the personal and systematic development. Surely the prime candidate would seem to be the transcendent Christianity of 'Religion B'. Looking at the problem somewhat longer from this perspective, one finds it natural to ask if what we have called the rhythm of synthesis does not reach merely the preliminary phase of the development—those stages culminating in 'Religion A'. If one wishes to distill the essence of Kierkegaard's intention, one can hardly justify elevating the synthesis ryhthm to equality with the diastatic element in his thought.

We are convinced that matters are not as simple as this line of argument would have us believe.[105] Difficulties arise even within the argument itself. If we wish to say that the development in Kierkegaard's thought is not crowned until the transcendent categories of Religion B are reached, we are yet saying that Religion B is reached within a process of development. That fact would suggest that Religion B itself is not fully characterized by a single-minded attention to the dimension of transcendence. It seems very hard to deny the appropriateness of the category of development. Often that development is stated in psychological terms, paralleling, perhaps, Kierkegaard's own experience.[106] But there are also objective relationships between the stages which sustain the order of subjective development. Those relationships are particularly close between the ethical and religious stages, so that one can well argue

---

cation. Nor have we discussed Kierkegaard's connecting the term indirect communication with the God-Man (*S.V.*, III, pp. 115–35 [*TC*, pp. 122–45]). These questions lead us into the very heart of the substantive analysis of Part Three.

[105] In the next several paragraphs we are indebted to suggestions made by Gregor Malantschuk in personal conversation.

[106] So David Swenson, while arguing that Kierkegaard was beyond 'Or' when he wrote *E-O*, adds: 'But he desired to say what was to be said successively rather than all at once, convinced that one must at least understand what the ethicist in *Either-Or* understands, before one can profitably essay to understand more.' Swenson's introduction to *PF*, xvii-xviii.

that the basic leap is that from the aesthetic stage to the ethical.[107] But even the aesthetic stage is not wholly repudiated, for the self chosen in the ethical stage is the concrete self 'which includes in itself the whole manifold of the aesthetic life'.[108] In choosing that self one also chooses the eternal self and so the absolute who posited that eternal self.[109] It surely does not, then, seem too much to say of these pseudonymous works of the earlier stages: 'The line of thought is pre-Christian, but moves towards the specifically Christian categories.'[110]

[107] So Climacus comments on *SW*: 'There are three stages, an aesthetic, an ethical, a religious. . . . Yet despite this triple division, the book is all the same an Either-Or. The ethical and religious stages stand in fact in an essential relationship to each other.' *S.V.* VII, p. 252 (*CUP*, p. 261). Cf. *Pap.* VI B 41, 10: 'Three stages and yet one either-or'. In support of this view and on the whole matter of the inter-relationship of the stages see Reidar Thomte, *Kierkegaard's Philosophy of Religion* (Princeton, 1948), pp. 97–110 and Emil Brunner. 'Sören Kierkegaards Budskap', *Janus*, 1939, pp. 225–44. See also Hirsch, op. cit. II, pp. 804–5: The manner in which the *Postscript* is usually understood in Germany is roughly as follows: 'Here we have a description of the ethical and religious life devoted solely to the purpose of keeping it entirely distinct from the Christian religious life, and from faith in the paradox. The view could properly be awarded first prize in a competition to see who could say the most stupid thing about Kierkegaard. The *Postscript* is intended to emphasize the principle that everything which calls itself Christianity but does not bear the unconditionality of the ethical, and the depths of religious suffering, and the sense of guilt in itself, is a pseudo-religious aestheticism, a paganism which masquerades as Christianity. The *Postscript* maintains the validity of the ethico-religious "idealism" within which the Christian lies.' As a challenge to this consensus, see Jan Sperna Weiland, *Humanitas Christianitas* (Te Assen Bij: Van Gorcum, 1951), pp. 31–35: 'In this transition [to sin] the developing series of the stages of existence ends and the transcendence of Christian religiousness shows its reality. Here, according to Kierkegaard, is the decisive *aut-aut* in the series of the stages of existence; *here* the roads part in the most decisive way—not between the aesthetic and the ethical, not between the ethical and the religious, but between the two religious structures of *anamnēsis* and "instant" (*atopon*) of Immanence and Transcendence. All the differences between the aesthetic and the ethical-religious stage are at last made unimportant by the fact that they are both "immanent" stages of existence against the transcendent reality of Christianity.' [Italics his.]

[108] Valter Lindström, *Stadiernas Teologi, en Kierkegaard Studie* (Lund: Haakan Ohlssons, 1943), p. 58. Cf. *S.V.*, II, p. 159 (*E-O*, II, p. 148). Cf. *S.V.* II, p. 161 (*E-O*, p. 150) where, understanding the aesthetical as that in a man 'by which he immediately is what he is', Kierkegaard can say: 'With the absolute choice the ethical is, then, posited; but from that fact it does not at all follow that the aesthetical is excluded.' Arild Christensen, 'Der junge Kierkegaard als Schriftsteller-persönlichkeit', *Orbis Litterarum*, 1963, pp. 26–47, is bolder, suggesting that according to Kierkegaard in the enjoyment of irony one can see a feeble anticipation of eternity, reflecting the divine stamp placed on the I.

[109] *S.V.* II, 191–2 (*E-O*, p. 179). See the quotation from Hirsch in note 106 above, and see our discussion of the abiding significance of the ethical, below, pp. 115–8. Cf. also Thomte, op. cit., p. 103.

[110] Thulstrup, commentary to *PF*, lxii. It is this set of objective relationships

We are confident that the mere mention of development and surely our discussion of the development to and including Religion B will evoke a chorus of dissent. Thus H. Diem insists that the stages are not to be seen as a progression but as a circle, which always ends in its presupposition: Christianity as the 'fundamental presupposition of all spiritual being'.[111] It cannot be denied that such dissent finds strong support in Kierkegaard's description of Religion B. That description often does seem to repudiate the possibility of an immanent transition. Hence there arises the problem which bedevils every effort to find such a category of transition. Thus when Michael Theunissen proposes 'Ernst' for this service, he finds Kierkegaard's discourse about the paradox forcing him to the construction that Socratic inwardness is not Christian but conditions the Christian.[112] It is wholly understandable, then, that the objection based on a literal and isolated reading of Religion B should argue that this is a dishonest compromise.[113] If one persists in leaving the developmental conception and the radically transcendent dimension of Religion B in rigid opposition to each other, that objection is sustained, for we shall show in Part Three that on those terms no point of transition to B is available.[114]

One may question, however, whether mute resignation is the fitting mood for contemplating what appears to be a head-on collision in Kierkegaard's thought. Not all Kierkegaard scholars have adopted that mood. Jan Sperna Weiland has argued that in *CUP* Kierkegaard introduces Religion A as an ideal-typical constructive category to make possible the transition which actually is to be referred to divine election.[115] While we do not wish to deny Weiland

between the stages which make it possible for accurate descriptions of the stages to be not so much exaltations of them as movements away from them. See Lowrie, op. cit., p. 232.

[111] Hermann Diem, *Spion im Dienste Gottes* (Frankfurt: Fischer, 1957), p. 73.

[112] Michael Theunissen, *Der Begriff Ernst Sören Kierkegaard* (Freiburg/Munich: Karl Alber, 1958), pp. 127–31.

[113] See Günther Rohrmoser, 'Ernst oder Ironie? Eine Zwischenbemerkung zur Interpretation Kierkegaards', *Archiv für Geschichte der Philosophie*, 1962, pp. 75–87.

[114] It is this conflict within Kierkegaard's thought which has permitted Gerd-Günther Grau, *Die Selbstauflösung des christlichen Glaubens* (Frankfurt: G. Schulte-Bulmke, 1963) to interpret that thought as the 'self-destruction' of Christianity. Grau finds two destructions to be involved at the point we are discussing: (1) a circular one in which the sheer discontinuity affirmed of Religion B returns that religion to an aesthetic moment by virtue of the absence of any continuity, (2) a linear destruction by which a development within a temporal progression advances to the point where all hope for the temporal is lost. We withhold comment to Part Three.

[115] Weiland, op. cit., pp. 115–28.

his constructive preference, this seems a difficult choice to impose on Kierkegaard. The theme of development is simply not created *ex nihilo* with the introduction of the phrase 'Religion A'.[116] And one can point to a great deal both in the earlier stages and in Religion B which should cause one to take the developmental theme considerably more seriously than Weiland does.[117] While we have spoken briefly here to this point, this claim can be fully demonstrated only by our substantive analysis in Part Three. But surely it seems more correct to see Kierkegaard's conception of the Christian's passion as the fulfilment rather than the repudiation of his understanding of the nature of the human spirit set in existence. Hermann Diem rightly underlines this theme by pointed quotation: 'to exist subjectively with passion (and objectively one can exist only in distraction) is in general an absolute prerequisite for being able to have any opinion about Christianity'.[118] But it is simply not clear to us how one can reasonably claim that this structure of spirit and its functions are uniquely Christian possessions. Beyond that, we shall try to show that such material affirmations of Religion B as the transcendence of God and the paradox of the God-Man can be understood as the heightening of analagous affirmations with Religion A.[119]

This line of thought must cut the other way as well, of course. We cannot justify taking our ease in the relative comfort of Religion

[116] Weiland much prefers *PF* to *CUP*. But *PF* too, while branding the state of sin as non-being, acknowledges that 'the non-being preceding the rebirth contains more being than the non-being preceding birth', *S.V.* IV, p. 189 (*PF*, p. 14). Lönning, op. cit., pp. 130. 282 notes that *PF* also offers a preparation for Religion B in its appeal to the paradoxical character of human thought. On the breadth of the developmental suggestion in the authorship, see above, pp. 35–36.

[117] We find it suggestive that N. Söe, who would very much like to see a sharper line between Religions A and B, yet must crticize Fin Jor's book (*Sören Kierkegaard* [Oslo: Land og Kirke, 1954]) for minimizing the line of development. Söe places the blame for the line on the idealistic heritage in Kierkegaard. 'Indförelse i Kierkegaards liv og forgatterskab', *Meddelelser fra Sören Kierkgeaard Selskabet*, 1955, pp. 1–2.

[118] Hermann Diem, *Kierkegaard's Dialectic of Existence*, trans. H. Knight (Edinburgh: Oliver & Boyd, 1959), p. 53 quoting *S.V.* VII, p. 238 (*CUP*, p. 249). Cf. Jörgen K. Bukdahl, 'Indrömmelse, dens plads i Sören Kierkegaards kristendomsfortstaaelse og vaekkelseaktion', *Dansk Teologisk Tidskrift*, 1963, p. 114: 'If one had forgotten what it means to exist as a Christian, so had one also forgotten what it means to exist as a human being. This last must be brought forward.' Collins, op. cit., p. 229, notes a more specific parallel, still on the formal level: 'The Kierkegaardian conception of the absolute equality of all individuals in God's sight is confirmed by the assurance that we can all become equally contemporaneous with Christ.'

[119] Lönning's work is also quite explicit at this point. See op. cit. pp. 152–4 on the paradox, and his article, 'Kierkegaard's "Paradox"', *Symposion Kierkegaardianum, Orbis Litterarum*, 1955, pp. 156–66. Cf. also Price, op. cit., p. 12.

A when Kierkegaard's utterances regarding Religion B are seen to be essentially related to his understanding of Religion A.[120] Yet it does not seem to us to be right to squeeze out of this reciprocity of influence the virtual enthronement of a wholly unaltered Religion B.[121] It seems to us that the juxtaposition should rather suggest to the reader the comprehensiveness with which the developmental conception addresses the data. This would not be to suggest some magic formula by which one can have it both ways. That would be most un-Kierkegaardian. Nor are we suggesting the practical excision of Religion B under the guise of marking it as the telos for the development. But it may be correct to say that the context for the interpretation of Kierkegaard's discourse on Religion B must in the final, if not the first, analysis include the whole scope suggested by the stages on the way of life. To insist on a narrower reading would be to invite distortion.

It is tempting to ask if Kierkegaard explicitly identifies the distorted character of the narrower reading. We have noted his remark that Anti-Climacus represents the extra-ordinary Christian.[122] It is intriguing to ask if what is suggested here is not the degree of individual participation in Christianity but the conception of Christianity itself. Kierkegaard does say that in Anti-Climacus 'the demands of ideality are posited in the maximum'.[123] One might well suppose that the idea of making quantitative distinctions among Christians was not wholly attractive to Kierkegaard. There are, however, references which suggest that Kierkegaard found Anti-Climacus a fitting standard against which to measure himself.[124] If it is difficult to propose Anti-Climacus' work as conscious distortion, one may yet point out that Kierkegaard was aware of the one-sidedness of the viewpoint and sent it forth in the name of a corrective.[125]

[120] Cf. Paul Tillich's comment on the 'structural interdependence' of the three stages which Tillich wishes to understand not as stages but as 'qualities', *Love, Power, and Justice* (New York: Oxford, 1960), p. 31.

[121] This seems to us to be what V. Lindström does, op. cit., pp. 343–8. Leaning heavily on *S.V.* XI, pp. 156–7 (*SD*, pp. 69–70), he finds Kierkegaard elevating the 'ethical-dialectical' viewpoint over the 'purely dialectical' viewpoint.

[122] See above, p. 29, note 82.

[123] *Pap.* X 1 A 548, cf. 546.

[124] So *Pap.* X 2 A 89: 'It judges my life, . . . even if I exert myself' and *Pap.* X 2 A 195 (*Dru* 1000): 'There is to me something so inexplicably happy in the antithesis: Anti-Climacus, I recognize myself and my nature so entirely in it that if another had discovered it, I would have supposed that he spied upon me.'

[125] On this dimension see Bukdahl, 'Indrömmelse, dens plads i Sören Kierkegaards kristendomsforstaaelse og vaekkelseaktion', *Dansk Teologisk Tidskrift*, 1963, p. 115.

It is important to observe that the shift in the authorship to which our discussion of Anti-Climacus introduces us is not the shift from Religion A to Religion B. That change may rather identify a 'Religion C' whose relation to Religion B is no less complicated than that of B to A.[126] Kierkegaard scholarship has found no agreement in analysing or evaluating this shift.[127] We must delay to Part Three any consideration of the question whether a positive doctrine of the church is somehow to be found within the ferocity of the final attack. But we may observe that the line of interpretation which we have proposed does suggest that one should at least try to understand the final period in the context of the whole authorship. We believe that attempt is a helpful one. If one takes the view that the authorship up to the final outbreak already contains at least two rhythms of thought, one will beware of an analysis of the later period which juxtaposes the rhythms chronologically in Kierkegaard's career.[128] On the other hand, we shall not try to deny that an important change occurs in this last period. What we shall seek to show is that this is a change in both the movements of diastasis and synthesis and thus one which can be related to earlier developments in Kierkegaard's work.[129]

---

[126] The phrase Religion C comes to us from Marie Thulstrup, 'Kierkegaards "onde verden"', *Kierkegaardiana*, ed. N. Thulstrup, 1955, pp. 42–55.

[127] Geismar stressed the discontinuity and did not hesitate to add the judgment of value. After 1853 he finds only a steady darkening and Kierkegaard finally becomes irrecognizable (op. cit., V, p. 62; VI, p. 36). Yet in his American lectures, *Lectures on the Religious Thought of Sören Kierkegaard* (Minneapolis, Augsburg, 1937), p. 84, he can say: 'We misunderstand this agitation if we believe that it is a sick man who writes all these articles and pamphlets. These thoughts are not new to Kierkegaard.' This latter line has been strongly defended by G. Malantschuk in his 'Sören Kierkegaards Angreb paa Kirken' in *Kamp Mod Kirken* (with N. Söe) (Copenhagen: Munksgaard, 1956), pp. 38–40.

[128] We feel Valter Lindström's *Efterföljelsens Teologi hos Sören Kierkegaard* (Stockholm: Svenska Diakonistyrelses, 1956), pp. 298–304, reveals this tendency. He does not seem to stress sufficiently the link between the world-denying mood of the final period and the diastatic current in the earlier authorship. Marie Thulstrup, 'Sören Kierkegaards martyrbegreb', *Dansk Teologisk Tidskrift*, 1964, pp. 100–14, shows how the ascetic strand in the Kierkegaard roots in the theme of the opposition between man and God. Thus a certain continuity is in principle established, though Mrs Thulstrup certainly recognizes changes in Kierkegaard's views.

[129] We have suggested above, pp. 34–35, how Kierkegaard's changing conception of indirect communication permits and requires more than one context in order to be adequately understood. We are speaking here not merely of individual instances of continuity or discontinuity in the authorship—as when one observes that in the final period the plea for honesty and inwardness is turned from the professor to the preacher (See Brunner, 'Sören Kierkegaards Budskap', *Janus*, 1939, pp. 225–44). We are speaking of those rhythms of reflection which structure such individual conceptions and chronicle the changes in them.

From all of this it should be clear where we stand on the question of the unity of Kierkegaard's authorship. The debate on that question still finds its lines drawn in the controversy between Valter Lindström and Torsten Bohlin.[130] We do not begrudge Lindström his presumption in favour of unity.[131] But we feel that he consistently defines the unifying principle in such a general way that only a verbal unity is attained.[132] We may seem to be in Bohlin's pathway with

[130] Of the four major documents, we have already cited Lindström's *Stadiernas Teologi* and *Efterföljelsens Teologi* and Bohlin's *Sören Kierkegaards etiska aaskaadning*. The fourth major work would surely have to be Bohlin's *Kierkegaards dogmatiska aaskaadning i dess historiska sammanhang* (Stockholm: Svenska Kyrkans Diakonistyrelses, 1925). If one likes one's polemics made explicit, one should add Bohlin's major response to *Stadiernas Teologi*. That response came in *Kierkegaards Tro*, published only a year before Bohlin's death. Kabell, op. cit., provides a detailed summary of the dispute, and Henriksen offers a shorter English account, op. cit., pp. 141–52. Neither secondary source can provide information about Lindström's *Efterföljelsens Teologi*, which appeared in 1956.

[131] Lindström, *Stadiernas Teologi*, pp. 10–11: 'In the case of apparent contradictions the question must always be put whether a defining of the meaning of the concepts in the judgments which apparently are at variance with each other may not solve the difficulties. In the case of a man of Kierkegaard's standard we must quite simply take it for granted that seemingly opposed tendencies are in some way held together by a general view. Above all, this must be the case with a thinker so thoroughly reflective as Kierkegaard to whom continuity in life and thought and the mutual agreement of these quantities are of decisive importance. A unitary total view must therefore be assumed which forms the background of, and is reflected in, the edifying writings as well as the "aesthetic" production.'

[132] In Part Three we will have occasion to show that Lindström's fundamental theme, 'the unavoidability of the God relation', contains within itself sharply contrasting expressions of the currents of synthesis and diastasis. This is also the trouble with efforts to build the case for unity on such verbal evidence as the frequency of the use of certain phrases. P. Svendsen, 'Opposisjonsennlegg ved cand. teol. Per Lönning's disputas for den teologiske doktorgrad, 5 maj, 1955', *Norsk Teologisk Tidskrift*, 1956, pp. 1–23, notes that in 1854 in writing the foreword to the last discourse he sent out, Kierkegaard used the same text as he did in 1843 in issuing the two edifying discourses which amounted to the introduction to his religious authorship. Svendsen's case is somewhat strengthened by Kierkegaard's comment, *S.V.*, XIV, p. 281 (*SE*, p. 226): 'The text is the first I have used. Later I have often brought it forward. Now I again return to it.' Of course such a remark might as easily be interpreted as a reference to intermediate breaks in the authorship. Yet Kierkegaard did feel that a unity could be found. In addition to the passages citing a unity of purpose which we noted in discussing pseudonymity, see also *Pap.* X 1 A 116: 'The judgment will accordingly come that I have in such a way changed myself a little over the years. In such a way it will come. For me it is just the opposite. I know after all in my inmost being that the authorship has some other kind of continuity, that there is (and especially, after all, with the part of Governance) a totality in the whole, and truly something other to say about it than this empty thing, that the author has in such a way been changed.' Such a passage, for all its warmth, must not be permitted to count against the unity position—yet we expect that it is clear by now that such autobiographical references must be interpreted with considerable caution.

his famous distinction between the 'paradox line' and the 'religious experience line'.[133] While readers who know Bohlin's voluminous writings on Kierkegaard will be able to find several points of agreement, more basic differences will also become clear to them. We feel that Bohlin is often guilty of a quite mechanical separation of the 'lines'. He does not seem alert to the highly complex interpenetration of the rhythms. Related to this is his failure to appreciate the independent thrust of the christological motif in Kierkegaard. Rather than viewing the paradox as a line marking a deplorable metaphysical debt to Hegel, we find in Kierkegaard's discourse at this point the reflection of both movements in his thought and an independent source of counter influence as well.

It may be evident now, too, that the two movements in Kierkegaard's thought with which we are concerned are not to be parcelled out to Religion A and Religion B. We shall make clear that both movements may be discerned in each stage. Even if the reader should limit us to Kierkegaard's explicit discussion of Religion B (against Kierkegaard's intention—we have argued), we should still have to speak of diastasis *and* synthesis. In speaking of these two currents of thought, then—and of the third—we are speaking of a structure which may be found in all of Kierkegaard's thought. And since those rhythms never exist in total isolation from each other we may speak of a unity in Kierkegaard's thought. It is manifestly a restless unity. But we are convinced that the tension in Kierkegaard's thought does not derive from a repudiation of the systematic impulse but from commitment to affirmations which resist reduction to a single centre, when structured by his pre-eminent talents for reflection. While we shall not spare him criticism for inconsistency, we yet affirm that he is an eminently systematic thinker: 'When one sees a man carrying a great number of fragile objects stacked one above the other, one is not inclined to wonder that he walks uncertainly and is every moment clutching after equilibrium; whereas if one does not see the stack, he may smile.[134]

If this is the understanding of the authorship which lies behind our study of Kierkegaard's thought, all his self expression must be

---

[133] Lönning, op. cit., p. 143, effectively points out that Bohlin has abundant company in his discovery of two lines in Kierkegaard. The contrasts include subjective existentialism vs. New Testament Christianity, man's duty to believe vs. supernatural disclosure, personal freedom vs. traditional Christianity. We believe that our analysis is comprehensive enough to make clear how the material of the authorship is so structured as to make possible all these viewpoints.

[134] *Pap.* IV B 1, pp. 105–6 (*DO*, p. 104).

regarded as potential source material. That applies equally to material written late or early, published or private. It does not follow, of course, that all sources will be equally useful or that all have been drawn from with equal adequacy. Yet the scope of our sources must be sufficiently broad and deep to permit the product to claim for its subject the religious thought of Kierkegaard as a systematic thinker.

6. *The Purposes of such a Study and its Place*

Much about what this book attempts to do should have been made clear now by our statement of intention and by the preliminary steps we have taken in this chapter to fulfil that intention. The reader will know in what sense a systematic analysis of Kierkegaard is the goal and will have some idea of the main lines to be followed in making that analysis. But what is the sense of such a study? That is, what purposes might it serve if it were done well?

(1) This sort of analysis could make a contribution to the many-sided study of Kierkegaard which clearly continues to spread, if not deepen. Indeed if this study does not make such a contribution in any sense, it is doubtful that any extrinsic purposes are served by it—or at least any purposes beyond the personal interest of the author. Thus the heart of this book is the substantive analysis of Kierkegaard's thought. This sort of systematic analysis could be helpful both to the specialized student of Kierkegaard's work and to the reader who comes to that work with a more general background. This study might come to aid the less specialized reader by providing a conceptual schema which could lend order to his encounter with the perplexing diversity in the Kierkegaardian authorship.[135] Order is not the *summum bonum*, and the discerning reader will, of course, use the schema with caution to ensure that the schema does in fact lead him into Kierkegaard's work. The more specialized and even the 'expert' reader might find help in a study which invites him to step back from his detailed work to see a larger portion of the canvas in a perspective which—it is hoped—casts more light than shadows over the special province of his concern.

(2) This sort of analysis could render some service to those concerned with the relationship of systematic thinking to religious thought. We have argued that Kierkegaard's work represents an

---

[135] It might even, though less importantly, help him to find his way through the vast maze of secondary literature by showing him how many (surely not all) of these interpretations are possible, if partial, ways of viewing the complex structure of Kierkegaard's thought.

attempt to reflect on the life of man in a way which is both internally self-consistent and responsive to the complexity of the reality with which it deals. As such that work is inviting to the person concerned to understand both the formal and material aspects of the systematic moment in religious thought.

(3) Those very qualities which make Kierkegaard's thought an interesting subject in itself lead many who meet him to broaden their interest in him. So it is, perhaps, that the early quite localized study of this man has given way to the attempt to place his work in the context of the history of thought. That effort in turn aids the attempt to understand Kierkegaard's work itself, since it broadens the context needed for any understanding and may in fact materially correct that context. Yet there is a reciprocity of influence, as many readers come to the conclusion that at least one exception challenges the vaunted homogeneity of nineteenth-century theology. Still, the point regarding Kierkegaard's exceptional character has been made so forcefully that one wonders if the other note of Kierkegaard's authentic citizenship in that century may not need to be sounded the more loudly today. We are not, of course, dealing with absolute alternatives for one outcome of such relational study might be a revised estimate of the theological era which nourished Kierkegaard. This type of study is under way. Our effort to sketch the matrix of Kierkegaard's thought claims no formal uniqueness, then, but does seem to us to offer a new approach by relating the study consistently to the conceptual schema employed in our analysis.

(4) The major emphasis in the area of relational study is indicated by the title of the American series in which this study appears: Kierkegaard is a 'maker of modern theology'. Thus in Part Four we add a suggestion of the 'legacy' of Kierkegaard. In doing so we speak again of Kierkegaard's significance as a systematic thinker. We would not add another (necessarily but hopelessly brief) chapter to the wealth of specialized studies of Kierkegaard's relationship to contemporary thinkers. We do hope to provide a discussion which reveals the pattern in those relationships. We are aware, of course, that citation of parallels does not amount to a demonstration of indebtedness. Even autobiographical testimony can well be treated with caution. Yet study of parallels suffices, if our goal is the clarification of the meaning of modern theological tendencies, rather than sure knowledge of their historical sources.

(5) It may be the case that Kierkegaard's thought so 'lies in the air' today that one cannot understand contemporary theology unless

one understands Kierkegaard.[136] While this claim seems inflated, at least until one inquires into the sense of 'understand' involved, we do find the parallels very striking and believe it probable that Kierkegaard's influence has been both widespread and deep-going. We are, however, also convinced that not all of the legacy of Kierkegaard has been appropriated. In making this study we believe that we identify a potential source for the constructive task of contemporary theology. The major part of our concern in Part Four is to explore that potential in relation to contemporary theological tendencies. In doing this we exceed the bounds of description and analysis and we should offer some statement concerning the criteria supporting our proposal. While we believe Kierkegaard would accept these criteria, not all of his thought passes their tests. We have already tried to show that Kierkegaard accepts the validity of the principle of contradiction in life and thought.[137] We may speak of a body of thought being consistent in two other respects—consistent with the main lines discernible in the affirmations of classical Christianity, and consistent with that human consensus descriptive of the life of man in this world.[138] It will become clear that we are functioning with a relatively inclusive definition of the former consensus and a relatively sceptical assessment of the latter one. We may, of course, also be functioning with other criteria which in fact materially determine the meaning of some or all of those which we have explicitly proposed. Denials on our part at this point would not—and should not—deter the reader from the exercise of his own judgment.

It may be possible to discern a certain correlation between these criteria and the rhythms of diastasis and synthesis, though the correlation would seem to be more a matter of emphasis than a matter of one-to-one correspondence. Both the rhythms and the criteria lead into the vision of the Christ which stands at the centre of Kierkegaard's thought. In Part Four we observe the movement toward that centre and also the movement out from it. Thus we shall be asking what is implied both methodologically and substantively for theological reflection which moves out from this centre. That process of questioning will include putting in question the very process of

[136] The contention is Lönning's, op. cit., p. 7.
[137] See above, pp. 17–28.
[138] Niels Thulstrup ('The Complex of Problems Called "Kierkegaard"', *A Kierkegaard Critique*, p. 294) proposes that one may criticize Kierkegaard in terms of fidelity to the New Testament and consistency as measured by the principles of formal logic. We believe that both of these suggest what we have in mind by respect for the human descriptive consensus.

'moving out', and so will return us to the concern expressed above in paragraph (2).

A final word may be added to those already expressed about the relation of this book to the massive literature surrounding Kierkegaard. Surely another work about Kierkegaard is not a self-evident necessity, even if the material it regurgitates once represented a useful contribution. This book's claim to follow a fresh track, and thus its hope to earn a place in the Kierkegaard literature, is based on two points. We may state these points here in relation to English language studies of Kierkegaard, since those studies will be those most readily accessible to many readers and our dialogue with the secondary literature up to this point has stressed sources in other languages.

The dominant systematic interest of this study already distinguishes it from the wider portion of books in English about Kierkegaard. We refer to the essentially expository treatments of Kierkegaard's life and thought. These works serve a useful introductory function, though that function has narrowed as the primary sources have found their way so steadily and rapidly into English in the last thirty years. If one moves beyond exposition to analysis, one finds two classes of books. The one is the 'Kierkegaard and' type of study in which Kierkegaard finds himself juxtaposed to such figures as Pascal, Nietzsche, Jaspers, and Bultmann. The other class presents detailed analyses of specific themes—Heywood Thomas's *Subjectivity and Paradox* is a good illustration.[139] Both of these tasks continue to have great importance. We have not made these tasks ours in this work, however. But we believe that the broad scope claimed for our analysis not only distinguishes this study from those more specialized ones, but also makes it possible for it to serve them.

The other point distinguishing this study from at least the great majority of English language studies of Kierkegaard is its willingness to hear the rhythm of synthesis alongside that of diastasis in Kierkegaard's thought. One might expect to find a parallel tendency in the considerable Roman Catholic literature on Kierkegaard.[140] It is true that many of the affirmations made within the synthesis movement receive strong expression in such a study as James Collins's *The Mind of Kierkegaard*.[141] Collins's work, however, also illustrates the limitations of the parallel, for he is very pointedly concerned to study

---

[139] Thomas, op. cit.

[140] See the summary statement of this literature in H. Roos, *Sören Kierkegaard and Catholicism*, trans. R. M. Brackett (Westminster, Maryland: Newman, 1954).

[141] Collins, op. cit.

Kierkegaard in relation to Thomist thought. That concern clearly influences his Kierkegaard interpretation, not the least so because of the complex blend of diastasis and synthesis to be found in the edifice by which Collins means to take Kierkegaard's measure.[142] We believe our criteria (and so this study) to be more congenial to Kierkegaard's concerns. In another class entirely are the works of Catholic scholars—such as Marcel—who undertake a creative reduplication of Kierkegaard's concerns. We defer discussion of this class to Part Four's discussion on that part of Kierkegaard's legacy which manifestly has been appropriated.

We have tried to make clear what we seek to do in this work and that that doing is formally both possible and appropriate. We have inevitably in this process of clarification begun the 'doing' itself. Yet the major part of that lies ahead. As Vigilius Haufniensis put it: 'This was the task of the introduction. The introduction may be correct while the deliberation itself . . . may be entirely incorrect. Whether that is so remains to be seen.'[143]

[142] Our analysis in Part Three will provide us with the opportunity to note that the Thomist blend (as represented by Collins at least) differs significantly from the pattern of interpenetration of diastasis and synthesis in Kierkegaard's thought.

[143] S.V. IV, p. 296 (CD, p. 21).

PART TWO

II

THE MATRIX FOR KIERKEGAARD AS A
SYSTEMATIC THINKER

1. *Hegel and Beyond*

KIERKEGAARD'S RELATIONSHIP to Hegel represents so central
a point of orientation for a study of the matrix for his thought
that we find no sufficient reason for launching our discussion
from some other point. In underlining the importance of the relationship to Hegel we are not trying to claim that orthodox Hegelianism
was the dominant threat Kierkegaard found confronting him in
Denmark. That claim is often made in works out-of-touch with the
Danish background for Kierkegaard's thought.[1] Yet it appears that
the circle of genuine disciples did not stretch far and that the only
prominent figure exemplifying unqualified devotion to Hegel was
the playwright, J. L. Heiberg (1791–1860).[2] Heiberg had studied
under Hegel and his *Om Philosophiens Betydelse for den naervaerende Tid*[3]
offers a classic Hegelian statement of the relationship between
theology and philosophy which illumines Heiberg's participation in
the Danish controversy concerning the principle of contradiction.[4]
While facts may not support statements about a reign by Hegel in

---

[1] So Collins, *The Mind of Kierkegaard* (Chicago: Henry Regnery, 1953), pp. 99–
100: 'Intellectuals in Denmark . . . took Hegel's aesthetics and philosophy of
religion as a permanent gain, as a secure framework which only needed to be
altered in minor ways and filled out in detail.' Perhaps one could try to support
this kind of claim by appeal to such a figure as H. N. Clausen (1793–1877), who
spoke in retrospect (*Optegnelser om mit Leveneds og min Tids Historie*, ed. Joh. Clausen,
[Copenhagen, 1877], pp. 210ff.) of Hegel's terrorizing the spiritual life of the time
and of the fanaticism of his followers in the later 1830s. Clausen's comments need
to be understood in relation to his own concern to combat Hegel. Along with
Clausen one may name F. C. Sibbern (1785–1872)—and we shall even add H. L.
Martensen (1808–84)—as important Danish figures who sought to criticize Hegel.
It does not seem right, then, to say (Collins, op. cit., p. 100) that only P. M. Möller
(1794–1838) lent support to Kierkegaard's 'lonely dissident voice'. Other Danes
shared Kierkegaard's concern formally, and to some extent even materially.
[2] See N. Thulstrup's methodical discussion of the Danish background, *Theologische Zeitschrift*, 1957, pp. 200–27.
[3] Prosaike Skrifter (11 vols., Copenhagen: C. A. Reitzel, 1861–7) Vol. I.
[4] See above, p. 18, note 33.

Denmark, his centrality for Kierkegaard still stands. That is so both because Kierkegaard's vision reached beyond Copenhagen, and because many of the tendencies he did oppose there found in Hegel their essential presuppositions, if not their historical origin or their announced *telos*.[5] There is, of course, nothing novel in affirming the importance of Hegel for the understanding of Kierkegaard, but we shall have occasion to point out that beneath the formal consensus lies sharp diversity in the analysis and assessment of the meaning of Hegel for Kierkegaard. In any case it is clear that the relationship to Hegel does not exhaust even the negative side of the matrix for Kierkegaard's thought. We shall have to look elsewhere later.

In Part One we indicated that our work also in this part would receive structure through the interpretative schema which we believe to be basic in Kierkegaard's thought. And we have already made a considerable suggestion about how that structuring finds its shape as regards Hegel in our comments under the heading *The Systematic Impulse and the Critique of the 'System'*.[6] We may now elaborate on the assault both by an independent inspection of the target and by a study of the weaponry Kierkegaard selected from an arsenal stocked by his own experience and reflection and that of other men. In discussing this relationship and others involved in the matrix for Kierkegaard's thought, it will be important at times to cite the sources in some detail in order to correct caricatures which commonly pass as photographs of the figures involved.

We have claimed that 'for Kierkegaard the System represents a mass of confusion because it fails to distinguish sharply between precisely those identities which constitute the polarity structuring his thought'.[7] If that statement is descriptive of Kierkegaard's protest, it is not difficult to find material in Hegel's thought which it addresses. The passion for unity runs very deep there. It would probably be incorrect to identify the primary ingredients for that union as God and man, though we shall see that both Hegel's early theological writings and his later more celebrated philosophical works provide material for such an identification. Yet the classic terms 'the one' and

---

[5] N. H. Söe, *Fra Renaessancen Til Vore Dage* (2nd ed., Copenhagen: G. E. C. Gads, 1948), p. 193, in speaking of an Indian summer for Hegelianism in Denmark in the 1840s, may be referring to this sort of indirect influence.

[6] See above, pp. 17–28.

[7] See above, p. 20. Kierkegaard began reading Hegel's first collected edition while he was working on his dissertation. On the whole we may assume a better knowledge on Kierkegaard's part of the completed system than of Hegel's youthful writings.

'the many' offer themselves more naturally as components whose citizenship in Hegel's thought is beyond contest.[8] On the one hand, Hegel acknowledges the reality of multiplicity: 'If then we cast a glance over the World's History generally, we see a vast picture of changes and transactions; of infinitely manifold forms of peoples, states, individuals, in unresting succession. . . . On every hand there is the motliest throng of events drawing us within the circle of its interest, and when one combination vanishes another immediately appears in its place.'[9] Hegel is suspicious of any viewpoint which compromises the full reality of the many.[10] That very suspicion leads him to reject a position which posits the universal apart from the particulars and so 'invests the finite with the character of an absolute'.[11] Such a universal, set apart from the particulars, itself becomes a part.[12]

Even if stating the relationship between the one and the many by means of static juxtaposition did not violate both relata, the goal of union would rest on bare assertion in such a formulation.[13] What is needed is a uniting truth so concrete that 'whilst it gives a bond and principle of unity, it also possesses an internal source of development'.[14] It is well known that Hegel finds that principle of dynamic union in

[8] W. T. Stace (*The Philosophy of Hegel* [London: Macmillan, 1924], p. 79) and J. H. Stirling (*The Secret of Hegel* [Edinburgh: Oliver & Boyd, 1898], p. 746) stress the role of the notions of the one and the many in Hegel's thought.

[9] G. W. F. Hegel, *The Philosophy of History*, trans. J. Sibree (rev. ed., New York: Willey Book, 1944), p. 72.

[10] Such a compromise is involved in the position taken by the exponents of 'immediate intuition', G. W. F. Hegel, *The Phenomenology of Mind*, trans. J. B. Baillie (2nd ed., London: George Allen & Unwin, 1910), pp. 70–74, 126–30. Cf. Hegel's reference to 'the sapless abstract of immediate knowledge' in *The Science of Logic*, translated from *The Encyclopedia of the Philosophical Sciences* by William Wallace (2nd ed., Oxford: Clarendon, 1892), p. 125. It is this line of thought in Hegel which makes it possible for Sören Holm (*Sören Kierkegaards Historiefilosofi* [Copenhagen: Bianco Lund, 1952], p. 17) to chastize Kierkegaard for failing to see that Hegel attempts to recognize genuine uniqueness.

[11] Hegel, *Logic*, p. 137. So in *The Philosophy of Right*, trans. by T. M. Knox (Oxford: Clarendon, 1942), pp. 112–3, Hegel suggests that monasticism absolutizes the physical by isolating it.

[12] Hegel, *Logic*, p. 23: 'When the universal is made a mere form and coordinated with the particular, as if it were on the same level, it sinks into a particular itself. Even common sense in every-day matters is above the absurdity of setting a universal *beside* the particulars'. [Italics his.]

[13] Hegel, *Phenomenology*, p. 79: 'To pit this single assertion, that "in the Absolute all is one" against the organized whole of determinate and complete knowledge . . . to give out its Absolute as the night in which, as we say, all cows are black—that is the very naïveté of emptiness of knowledge.' Cf. ibid., pp. 78, 81; *Logic*, pp. 225, 228; *Right*, p. 230.

[14] Hegel, *Logic*, p. 24.

the 'absolute notion'.[15] It is less commonly pointed out that Hegel's determination of the notion as the process of negation does bring him beyond bare juxtaposition of the one and the many. In citing contrast and opposition one is not falsifying the claim of unity, but verifying it, for the unity claimed is that all 'existence consists really in transmuting each determinate element into its opposite'.[16]

Hegel is quite ready to meet the objection that the unity he has won is an unreal one composed of the non-being of the distinctions between particulars rather than of their positive substances. Such an objection has failed to recognize 'the positivity of negativity'.[17] That failure has its roots in an understanding of particulars as essentially static atoms of reality. In his *Logic* Hegel marks the way out of this delusion. Since 'on the one hand the limit makes the reality of a thing; on the other it is its negation',[18] it may be said that the finite 'as something does not meet the nature of the other as if it had not affinity to it, but, being implicitly the other of itself, thus undergoes alteration. Alteration thus exhibits the inherent contradiction which originally attaches to determinate being, and which forces it out of it own bounds.'[19] Thus we are not left with a collection of entities united only in the juxtaposition of mutual distinction or negation. Rather it becomes evident that each 'entity' is itself a process of relating—i.e., an instance of negativity.[20]

The way is now prepared for Hegel to point out that as an instance of negativity the particular entity reveals itself to be the very whole itself, for 'every function and "moment" of the notion is itself the whole notion'.[21] He appeals to the living character of process to bear

[15] Thus in the *Phenomenology*, p. 208, Hegel speaks of the 'absolute notion which may be called the ultimate nature of life, the soul of the world, the universal life-blood, which courses everywhere, and whose flow is neither disturbed nor checked by any obstructing distinction, but is itself every distinction that arises, as well as that into which all distinctions are dissolved; pulsating within itself, but ever motionless, shaken to its depths, but still at rest'.

[16] ibid., p. 517; cf. pp. 542, 552, 766–7, 778–81, 793; *History*, p. 27.

[17] Hegel, *Right*, p. 222. Cf. *Phenomenology*, pp. 722–3; *History*, pp. 21–22.

[18] Hegel, *Logic*, p. 173.

[19] Ibid. Cf. *Phenomenology*, p. 208, on the givenness of disruption, and p. 293, for the application of this point to external objects.

[20] N. Thulstrup, 'Kierkegaard og den filosofiske Idealisme', *Kierkegaardiana*, ed., N. Thulstrup, 1962, p. 103, lays particular stress on this point: 'It becomes a matter of great significance that there is developed a dynamic concept of being in distinction from the static concept which dominated in ancient and medieval thinking.' Thulstrup notes further that Hegel's dynamic concept of being 'influenced his famous theory of movement in logic which furthermore is identified by him—characteristically enough—with metaphysics and ontology in the older sense'.

[21] Hegel, *Logic*, p. 292. Cf. *Phenomenology*, p. 468.

the weight of such an assertion: 'it is true only of objects, of things lifeless, that the whole is other than the parts; in the living thing, on the other hand, the part of the whole is one and the same as the whole. . . . What is a contradiction in the realm of the dead is not one in the realm of life.'[22] In this way the foundation is laid for the seemingly boundless expanse of triads which Hegel's works bestow upon the reader. For if each entity as negativity is the whole, it must in turn reveal the 'moments' comprising the whole.

We have now followed the drive in Hegel's thought for unity a good part of its course: the unity of particulars becomes clear to one as the particulars show themselves to be moments in a process; the unity of the process is the unity of the notion whose content is negativity. This last point introduces still another stage in the drive. The oneness of the many lies in negativity not only because negation is the driving force uniting all particulars, but also because the whole world of particulars is the product of the self-negation of the notion in its purity. Pure negativity negates itself and yields particularity as the other.[23] Yet that other as negation is keyed to the logic of the notion.[24] Hence 'genuine actuality is necessity; what is actual is inherently necessary'.[25] Indeed while the moments are logically distinct, 'the course which these

---

[22] Hegel, 'The Spirit of Christianity and its Fate', *Early Theological Writings*, trans. by T. M. Knox with an introduction and fragments trans. by R. Kroner (Chicago: University of Chicago, 1948), pp. 260–1. In a strict sense the reference to the 'lifeless' must be taken to be rhetorical, for all is living for Hegel—see note 19 above.

[23] Hegel, *Logic*, p. 377: 'In the advance of the idea, the beginning exhibits itself as what it is implicitly. It is seen to be mediated and derivative, and neither to have proper being nor proper immediacy. It is only for the consciousness which is itself immediate, that Nature forms the commencement or immediacy, and that Spirit appears as what is mediated by Nature. The truth is that Nature is the creation of Spirit, and it is Spirit itself which gives itself a pre-supposition in Nature.' Cf. *Phenomenology*, pp. 118–19. It is this process which the doctrine of creation symbolizes: 'Merely eternal or *abstract* Spirit, then, becomes an other to itself: it enters existence, and, in the first instance, enters *immediate* existence. It creates a World. This "Creation" is the word which pictorial thought used to convey the notion in its absolute movement.' [Italics his.] ibid. p. 769.

[24] It is this line of thought which gives content to the oft-quoted Hegelian dictum 'what is rational is actual and what is actual is rational', *Right*, p. 10 (Cf. *Logic*, pp. 258–9: 'So far is actuality, as distinguished from mere appearance, and primarily presenting a unity of inward and outward, from being in contrariety with reason, that it is rather thoroughly reasonable, and everything which is not reasonable must on that very ground cease to be held actual.' Cf. *History*, pp. 9–10.) It is to be observed that the word 'is' in the dictum does not posit the abstract identity which Hegel himself elsewhere ridicules (*Phenomenology*, p. 777). Rather the proposition expresses the concrete correlation between negativity as unity (the rational) and negativity as many (the actual).

[25] Hegel, *Right*, p. 283.

traverse . . . is not to be pictured as a temporal sequence',[26] for 'the moments of the whole . . . have, because they are moments, no existence separate from one another'.[27]

Kierkegaardians will already be impatient and cannot, perhaps, be asked to withhold longer the response: 'There you see, the "System" has nothing to do with contingency and time!' But it ought to be noted that Hegel is not rendered mute by this charge. Whether his response is adequate is another question, of course. He notes that if negativity as unity is forced to negate itself to have itself, the resultant negation must be truly 'other' than the unity. If unity expresses necessity and the existence of the moments in each other, its other must represent 'contingency', the 'accidental', and the separation of the moments.[28] So 'it is necessary that the finite . . . should be definitely established as accidental, because accidentality is the concept of the finite'.[29] We can, then, be expansive in the sphere of the finite, for it is 'reason itself which requires us to recognize that contingency, contradiction, and show have a sphere and a right of their own, restricted though it be, and it is irrational to strive to resolve and rectify contradictions within that sphere.'[30]

While the world of particularity is real, its reality is negativity which in turn moves back into the one: 'The alienation will be found to alienate itself, and the whole thereby will take all its contents back into the ultimate principle it implies.'[31] The continuity of negativity in this process manifests a unity, but a unity in which the otherness linked with the temporal passage is preserved. If we associate

[26] Hegel, *Phenomenology*, p. 689.
[27] Hegel, ibid.; cf. *Right*, pp. 35, 233.
[28] Hegel, *Logic*, p. 88; *Phenomenology*, pp. 320–1; *History*, p. 79.
[29] Hegel, *Right*, p. 209.
[30] ibid., p. 137. Cf. *Phenomenology*, pp. 799–800. For more detail see on the accidental, *Logic*, pp. 26–28; *Right*, pp. 80–81; on purpose, *Right*, p. 229; *Phenomenology*, p. 298; on contingency, *Logic*, pp. 80-81, 264–5; *Phenomenology*, p. 719.
[31] Hegel, *Phenomenology*, p. 517. In the *Logic* (p. 181) Hegel tries to explain how the same principle which posits the many in turn dissolves the many: 'The One forms the presupposition of the Many; and in the thought of the One is implied that it explicitly make itself Many. The self-existing unit is not . . . void of all connective reference; it is a reference, as unity of the some and the other, it is a connexion with itself, and this connexion, be it noted, is a negative connexion. Hereby the One manifests an utter incompatibility with itself, a self-repulsion; and what it makes itself explicitly be, is the Many. . . . It would be wrong, however, to view the process of repulsion as if the One were the repellent and the Many the repelled. The One, as already remarked, just is self-exclusion and explicit putting itself as the Many. Each of the Many, however, is itself a One, and in virtue of its so behaving, this all-round repulsion is by one stroke converted into its opposite,—Attraction.'

negativity with thinking, we may speak now of a thinking reflecting upon itself. That state may well be described as 'self-consciousness', since 'this is exactly . . . the way self-consciousness is constituted. It distinguished itself in like manner from itself, without any distinction being thereby established.'[32]

We have now sketched the basic affirmations underlying the System which drew Kierkegaard's fire. It may be appropriate, however, to bring this discussion somewhat closer to Kierkegaard by relating it more directly to the categorical schema which we have found to be central in his thought. Our examination of Hegel's thought makes it possible to understand how Kierkegaard could find in the System a confusion which blurs the identities of God and man. Clearly—for Hegel—'God, far from being *a* Being, even the highest, is *the* Being.'[33] That is, the counter 'God' can best be taken to refer to the very process of reality itself. Such a God is surely not essentially other than man.[34] One needs to add that for Kierkegaard man's reality is fully as much undermined in this process. Kierkegaard could not settle for the suggestion that 'the particular individual is incomplete mind, a concrete shape in whose existence, taken as a whole, one determinate characteristic predominates, while the others are found only in blurred outline'.[35] What is missing in such a suggestion is any acknowledgement of the mystery of human freedom. For all his discourse regarding contingency, Hegel's final principle of explanation for all events lies in the logic of the notion.[36] That will not do for Kierkegaard. If both God and man are violated in this procedure, one will not expect a better result in the description of

[32] Hegel, *Phenomenology*, p. 297; cf. *Logic*, p. 374: 'This unity is consequently the absolute and all truth, the Idea which thinks itself.'

[33] ibid., p. 210.

[34] Hegel, *Phenomenology*, pp. 81, 782.

[35] ibid., p. 89. Cf. ibid., pp. 91, 776–77; *Right*, p. 25.

[36] ibid., p. 17: 'By dint of obscuring the difference between the historical and the philosophical study of law, it becomes possible to shift the point of view and slip over from the problem of the true justification of a thing to a justification by appeal to circumstances, to deductions from presupposed conditions which in themselves may have no higher validity, and so forth. To generalize, by this means the relative is put in place of the absolute and the external appearance in place of the true nature of the thing. When those who try to justify things on historical grounds confound an origin in external circumstances with one in the concept, they unconsciously achieve the very opposite of what they intend.' Cf. Hegel's 'The Positivity of the Christian Religion', *Early Theological Writings*, p. 171, for a specific application of this distinction in the sphere of religion. The *Logic*, pp. 268–9, also gives a theological form to the point: The other may indeed be 'new', 'but God knows what He wills, is determined in His eternal will neither by accident from within nor from without, and what He wills He also accomplishes irresistibly'.

their relationship. Hegel may seem to speak in praise of religion in saying that it is religion which glimpses the true unity of negativity and so represents the whole sphere of temporal passage sensing its return to unity. But religion's vision is only figurative, for it objectifies the reconciling agency in a single individual.[37] By thus excluding his own activity the religious man shows himself to be still caught in the distortions of the finite.[38] So one awaits the 'fullness of time'[39] and the sending of the Holy Spirit.[40] Of this finitude's representational Christ prophesies: 'When ye cease merely to see the divine in me and outside yourselves, then will the divine come to consciousness in you also, because you have been with me from the beginning, because our natures are one in love and in God.'[41] In that moment, in the clear conceptual power of absolute knowledge, spirit has reached the sphere of thinking[42]—the notion has closed with itself.

We need to examine more carefully Kierkegaard's assault upon this structure, and we can do that best by noting the allies he chose for himself. Other men were also restless with Hegel.[43] We can well begin the more careful study of Kierkegaard's attack by setting it in relation to the work of another Dane who was troubled by some of the same points in the System which disturbed Kierkegaard. We speak, surprisingly perhaps, of none other than Hans Lassen Martensen (1808–84), and his famous proposal to 'go beyond Hegel'. It is legitimate to note that that proposal moves Martensen in the direction of Kierkegaard in intention, even if it must be added that the proposal issued in a body of thought which tended to eclipse Hegel and form the more immediate target for Kierkegaard, from whom it

[37] Hegel, *Phenomenology*, pp. 760–1.
[38] ibid., p. 685; cf. in the *Early Theological Writings*, p. 176 ('The Positivity of the Christian Religion') and p. 267 ('The Spirit of Christianity and its Fate').
[39] Hegel, *Logic*, pp. 78–79.
[40] Hegel, *Phenomenology*, p. 794.
[41] Hegel, 'Spirit of Christianity and its Fate', *Early Theological Writings*, p. 272. Cf. p. 273: 'The culmination of faith, the return to the Godhead, whence man is born, closes the circle of man's development. Everything lives in the Godhead, every living thing is its child, but the child carries the unity . . . undisturbed though undeveloped in itself. It begins with faith in gods outside itself, with fear, until through its action it has separated itself more and more; but then it returns through associations to the original unity. The child now knows God, i.e., the spirit of God is present in the child, issues from its restrictions, and restores the whole. God the Son, the Holy Spirit.'
[42] Hegel, *History*, p. 69: One has then transcended religion and reached philosophy, which is the consciousness of the form strictly proper to thought. In philosophy 'thought becomes thinking reason'.
[43] See note 1, p. 51 above.

thus drew the sharper criticism. Kierkegaard had had first hand contact with the target, as Martensen had been his tutor in theology at the University. It was also the translation of Martensen's thesis into Danish in 1838 which provoked the Danish debate on the principle of contradiction which Kierkegaard followed with such great interest.

Martensen's thought shows the influence of his exposure to such diverse minds as Baader, Schelling, Schleiermacher (through the Danish romanticist and free thinker F. C. Sibbern), Eckhart, and Böhme. Yet the relationship to Hegel forms a central point of orientation in his thought.[44] While retaining Hegel's passion for unity,[45] Martensen objected to what he felt to be the material blurring of the identities of God and man in the System.

Holding that 'in the act of creation God brings forth that which is not God, that, the essence of which is different from His own essence',[46] Martensen spurns pantheism as a position which worships a 'derived absolute',[47] confounds ethics by losing the category of personality,[48] and chains God in an 'omnipresence of necessity.'[49] He would stress the personality of God[50] and so understands the plurality present in that personality as to free God from any Hegelian need of the world for self-understanding. God's love was satisfied in the Trinity[51] in which God reveals himself to himself eternally,[52] so that one can say: 'It must have been possible for God not to have created.'[53]

The diastatic withdrawal from the Hegelian confusion of God and

---

[44] N. Thulstrup devotes some space to Martensen's complex relationship to Hegel in *Theologische Zeitschrift*, 1957, pp. 200–27. See also Skat Arildsen, *Biskop Hans Lassen Martensen* (Copenhagen: G. E. C. Gads, 1932).

[45] So in his autobiography, *Af mit Levnet* (3 vols., Copenhagen: Gyldendalske Boghandels, 1883), p. 23, Martensen claims: 'There must be a view of the world and of life in which everything that has meaning in existence (*Dasein*)—nature and spirit, nature and history, poetry and art and philosophy, harmoniously unite to form a temple of the spirit in which Christianity is the all-governing and all-explaining centre.'

[46] H. Martensen, *Christian Dogmatics*, trans. from the author's German edition by W. Urwick (Edinburgh: T. & T. Clark, 1898), p. 114.

[47] ibid., p. 82.

[48] ibid.

[49] ibid., p. 94.

[50] ibid., p. 452; cf. H. Martensen, *Christian Ethics*, trans. by C. Spence (Edinburgh: T. & T. Clark, 1888), p. 132.

[51] Martensen, *Ethics*, p. 73.

[52] Martensen, *Dogmatics*, p. 105.

[53] H. Martensen, *Jacob Böhme*, trans. by T. Rhys (London: Hodder & Stoughton, 1885), p. 111.

man also marks Martensen's discourse regarding man. He argues for the freedom of the human will,[54] and insists that the authentic distinctness of man from God must not be classified as sin. The shadow of sin first passes over man when the distinctness of creation claims self-authenticating character.[55] Furthermore Martensen repudiates the suggestion that evil is a necessary negative principle of motion for the dialectic of redemption. With specific mention of Hegel and Schleiermacher he argues:

> But so far from evil being necessary to the process of development, it is involved in the very idea of evil to be at once a false antagonism and a false reconciliation of antagonisms; to be an untrue dialectic and an untrue solution; consequently its influence is to hinder and *disturb* all true development. Evil cannot be regarded as an immanent feature of the idea of the world, but must, on the contrary, be treated as an *interruption* of the course of its immanent development. Evil is a *false extreme* and must not therefore be confounded with the antitheses or oppositions which are grounded in the nature of the idea. . . . Evil is not involved in the conception of individuality, but is rooted in the perversion of the conception of individuality.[56]

Martensen's efforts to preserve the reality of man even and especially before God climax in his resistance to universalism[57] and in the retention of individuality for those who do enter the Kingdom of the Father: 'Even in the life of the redeemed we cannot conceive that the relation of contrast between God, the Creator, and the creature, will be entirely removed, because it is involved in the relation of the union.'[58]

Much of the substance of the line in Martensen's thought which we have been following could be taken for Kierkegaard's critique of Hegel, if Martensen had only matched Kierkegaard's hectic eloquence. But this line of thought in Martensen is checked by another which breathes the intoxicating air of the System. It is this second and more comprehensive line which would mark Martensen essentially as Kierkegaard's antagonist, even if we lacked the dramatic historical clash occasioned by Martensen's eulogizing Bishop Mynster as 'a witness to the truth'.

Thus, retreating from the diastatic tendency we have observed, Martensen uses Hegelian imagery in describing God's relationship to

---

[54] Martensen, *Ethics*, p. 118; *Dogmatics*, pp. 215–6.

[55] ibid., p. 190: 'Evil is essentially the cosmical principle in so far as this belies its character as created, and in false independence opposes itself to the true and holy world principle, who is the Son.'

[56] ibid., pp. 164–5 [Italics his]; cf. ibid., p. 295.

[57] ibid., pp. 474f.

[58] ibid., p. 329.

the world: 'What the outward world, what nature, what other persons are for us, to wit, the condition of our own self-consciousness—the Son and the objective world which arises before the Father in and through the Son (*di'avtov*) are for the Father,—to wit, the condition of his own identity.'[59] The independence of God rooted in his triune self-fulfilment yields to a process of erosion, for '. . . if Spirit is to exist in life and power and luminous manifestation, it must hold within itself its other, its contrast. . . . But the contrast of Spirit is nature, the unconscious, but nevertheless self-moving, instinctively working principle. Only when there is in God an eternal Nature can we know him as the absolutely perfect spirit.'[60]

The distinctness of man's identity is threatened by such a line of thought and the threat becomes reality in Martensen's discourse concerning the Christ. The Christ does not come as divine response to human sin, for the enveloping of all reality in the divine self-disclosure provides the context for understanding even sin. Hence it is not only the case that God still loves the sinner essentially, though he cannot do so actually.[61] It also holds true that sin—in the modest meaning indicated—is seen to be necessary: 'If divine likeness was not to be a mere gift, but rather a self-acquired attribute of humanity, it was necessary that the parasitical condition should come to an end.'[62] Martensen may appear to stress human freedom in such a passage, but in the last analysis the correct context of explanation lies in the doctrine of divine development which defines the role of human freedom: 'We must . . . distinguish a twofold activity in the Godhead. The one activity proceeds forth from God, establishes and sustains created life in a relative existence apart from God; and this is exactly the conception of an all-creating, all-sustaining, all-enduring logos-energy. The other activity leads back to God, and makes perfect, transforming the relation of contrast into one of union,

---

[59] ibid., p. 109; cf. pp. 108–9: 'Looking on the heavenly image of the world as it arises out of the depths of his own nature, God sees the image of his own essence, his own Ego in a second subsistence. The heavenly ideal world, which is born out of the depths of God . . . would not be a system, if the birth of this heavenly ideal had not been at the same time the birth of God himself as the Logos. . . . When therefore we say that God knows himself as a Father, we say that he knows himself as the ground of the heavenly universe which proceeds eternally forth from him, solely because he knows himself as the ground of his own outgoing into this universe, in which he hypostasizes himself as Logos.'

[60] Martensen, *J. Böhme*, p. 111.

[61] Martensen, *Dogmatics*, p. 303; cf. p. 302: 'The Atonement did not produce a change in the essential relations of God to the world.'

[62] ibid., p. 155.

that God may be all in all: this is exactly the conception of the Christ-energy.'[63] On the other hand, if one seeks to hold that the correlation of sin and human freedom is meaningful even in relative independence of the context of divine development, the consistent orientating of christology within that context will require one to say that Christ would have come, even had there been no sin, since 'altogether apart from sin, the union of the human race with God is involved in the idea of the perfection of the world'.[64]

This context permits Martensen to speak in glowing terms of Christ as the mediator between God and creature[65] and the head of the new humanity.[66] But it also raises some serious difficulties for him, if he is concerned to relate his work to the classical Christian witness. We may identify three such difficulties: (1) However much one may plead the external indivisibility of the works of the Trinity, the Hegelian triad still presses for a distinction somewhere which places the movement of unification in the third person. Martensen's thought does yield to that pressure.[67] In order to accommodate the desire to speak of the Son as the principle of union, then, one is required to emphasize the breadth of the movement of reunification so that which the Son establishes in principle the Spirit may apply in specificity.[68] (2) The attentiveness with which the biblical material

[63] ibid., p. 329.

[64] ibid., p. 261; cf. ibid., pp. 147, 268 and J. Böhme p. 149. Martensen's difficulties in distinguishing clearly between Creation and the Fall are, of course, part of his Hegelian legacy. In the *Phenomenology*, p. 775, Hegel writes: 'In the statement, that the Divine Being from the beginning empties Itself of Itself, that its objective existence becomes concentrated in Itself and becomes evil, it is not asserted but implied that *per se* this evil existence is *not* something alien to the Divine nature. Absolute Being would be merely an empty name, if in very truth there were any other being external to it, if there were a "fall" from it. The aspect of self-concentration really constitutes the essential moment of the self of Spirit.' [Italics his.] So also *History*, p. 79, notes that the phrase 'by nature evil' applies in that 'it is to this state of inward breach that the whole finite action of thought and will belongs'. *Logic*, p. 57.

[65] For Martensen, Jesus Christ disproves the theory that the real and the ideal can be reconciled only in thought, for he represents the perfect unity of real and ideal of nature and history, of fate and liberty (*Dogmatics*, p. 246), and so he becomes in actual existence what he essentially was in his pre-existence, the mediator between God and creature. (ibid., p. 237.)

[66] ibid., p. 309; cf. p. 37, through him mankind receives the principle of the new creation.

[67] ibid., p. 107: 'Is it possible for us . . . to think that God could have been from eternity conscious of himself as a Father, if he had not from eternity distinguished himself from himself as the Son, and if he had not been as eternally one with the Son in the unity of the Spirit?'

[68] ibid., p. 330. Hegel's works offer similar formulations: see above, note 41 and *Phenomenology*, p. 794: 'This unification has, however, already taken place by

and Christian history focus on the suffering of the Christ becomes embarrassing to one for whom all history essentially comes under the rubric of divine development. (3) Why should this historical figure, Jesus of Nazareth, be uniquely identified with the principle of union? Even on Hegelian grounds, Martensen needs to find a different sort of basis for uniqueness than the sinlessness of Jesus as accomplished fact provides. That is so since the Christ would have come (and presumably could have been said to be unique), even had there been no sin. It is not clear how this particular union of spirit and nature can claim any *a priori* uniqueness, since Martensen's very Hegelian treatment of the doctrine of creation permits every man to claim essential representation within the principle of opposition ordered by the second person in the Trinity. Martensen, of course, does claim uniqueness for the Christ.[69] If one thinks of the Christ's uniqueness as lying in the revelation of the Father, Martensen's evolutionary schema creates further difficulties. Thus, while Martensen wishes to accord a certain uniqueness and systematic priority to the apostolic age,[70] he stresses the need for an inner canon held by the individual relatively independently of Scripture and church.[71] He adds that the light, once received in faith, shines with independent vigour and focus[72]—an independence in which an Hegelian increase is likely hidden. This difficulty is already suggested by the fact that for Martensen all history is revelatory of God[73] and man's inner being is particularly so.[74]

---

implication, and has done so in religion in the return of the figurative idea into self-consciousness, but not according to the proper form, for the religious aspect is the aspect of the essentially independent and stands in contrast to the process of self-consciousness. The unification, therefore, belongs to this other aspect, which by contrast is the aspect of reflexion into self, is that side which contains its self and its opposite, and contains them not only implicitly or in a general way, but explicitly or expressly developed and distinguished.' That is, the work of the Spirit is not so much to glorify Christ, as to universalize him.

[69] We are told that Christ was unique (*Dogmatics*, p. 129), creative (ibid.), the 'sum' of all creation (ibid., p. 272), but are never told how it is possible for him to be unique. The *Dogmatics* argues around the point repeatedly and the *Ethics* (pp. 245f.) can manage only an argument from 'Christ's wide influence', which seems manifestly too weak when measured against the need.

[70] ibid., p. 113.

[71] Martensen, *Dogmatics*, pp. 26–27, 41.

[72] ibid., pp. 58–59.

[73] Thus ibid., p. 122, suggests that we view time as 'the form in which the teleological development of creation is accomplished; in which the various momenta, which in the idea constitute one inner undivided unity, necessarily enter on partial and progressive existence'.

[74] ibid., p. 80, suggests that an investigation of both our knowing and our

The third point offers a particularly useful comparison to Hegel. While Martensen manifestly wishes to 'go beyond' Hegel's forthright denial of essential mediatorial significance to the historical Jesus,[75] his thinking does not manage such an advance and may indeed have seemed to Kierkegaard to be the more dangerous for the appearances it acquires in the attempt. With Hegel at least one knows where one is. That is also the impression one gets in studying that other key point of attack for Martensen and Kierkegaard—human freedom. In this life we may speak of freedom, but it is surely one 'bracketed' by divine sovereignty: '. . . the manifold wisdom of God is revealed in the fact that these movements and complications of freedom *must* unavoidably manifest the eternal counsel of God and *must* work together for its accomplishment.'[76] As for the issue of this life, Martensen's writings provide all or very nearly all the pieces needed to complete the universalistic pattern,[77] and make it very hard for the reader to take seriously his denials of this position. And if one asks again in summary of the doctrine of God—that third systematizing force in Kierkegaard's thought—one comes to realize that for Martensen the counter 'God' has been appropriated in Hegelian fashion to designate reality itself. While one may not speak of God as 'the Being',

---

morality leads back to God for 'that eternal something without the presupposition of whose existence, human thought is an insoluble riddle, is the thinking energy, the true God, who pervades all spirits, leads them to wisdom and scatters all deception and mere seeming. And the obligation which we feel we are under to fulfil the law written in our hearts, is in its deepest roots an obligation to obey the personal Will, the Holy Being, who speaks to us through our conscience, and thus reveals himself as the invisible One, in conjunction with whom we know what we know.' The theme of the conscience as a co-knowing with God is already present in Martensen's dissertation from 1837. Cf. also *Dogmatics*, p. 6, and *Ethics*, p. 20.

[75] See above, pp. 57–58. The *Phenomenology*, p. 784, also provides an explanation of the origin of the religious delusion: 'Since this unity of Essential Being and Self has been inherently brought about, consciousness has this idea also of its reconciliation, but in the form of an imaginative idea. It obtains satisfaction by attaching, in an external way, to its pure negativity the positive significance of the unity of itself with essential Being. Its satisfaction thus itself remains hampered with the opposition of a beyond. Its own peculiar reconciliation therefore enters its consciousness as something remote, something far away in the future, just as the reconciliation, which the other self achieved, appears as away in the distance of the past.' In Martensen's case, on the contrary, one may note not only the desire to affirm the uniqueness of the Christ (note 69 above), but also the wish to link the Christ of the heart with the Jesus of history (*Dogmatics*, p. 240).

[76] ibid., p. 215. [Italics his.]

[77] There is no reality to the Devil beyond the world of man (ibid., p. 198); dualism itself exists only in time (ibid., pp. 362–3); no absolute fall from grace is possible because the Spirit sows an incorruptible seed (ibid., p. 398); finally God in love possesses some way of over-ruling the obdurate (ibid., pp. 367, 374).

God is held to be beyond the contrast between the ideal and the actual[78]—a formulation which is no less effective in repudiating plurality in the name of piety.

Martensen's writings are, thus, cut through with the contradictions born of his effort to criticize a System which yet basically informs and structures his thought. That contradictory character could be demonstrated in much further detail,[79] but our primary interest lies after all with Kierkegaard. It should be clear by now, though, that Martensen was by no means the simple disciple of Hegel he is often made out to be. The violence of the clash between Martensen and Kierkegaard should not obscure for us the significant measure of common critical concern present in their relationship to Hegel. Whether Kierkegaard also shares some of Martensen's debt to Hegel will concern us later in this section. In any case it is certain that the critical concern in Martensen never wins the effects it does in Kierkegaard. That is in large part due to Martensen's failure to grant it weapons with sufficient fire power to damage the System's impressive fortress. Kierkegaard did find such weapons. We need now to show that they were not created *ex nihilo*, but were in the main available to him in the world which formed the matrix for his thought.

[78] Martensen, *Ethics*, p. 64. We add a remarkable quotation from the *Böhme* book, p. 76: 'God as the absolute personality—who in the *teleological cycle* of eternity, where *beginning and end coincide*, is his own efficient cause, his own final cause, and who possesses in himself all the means required for manifestation,—is the only self-intelligible being.'

[79] This contradiction could be followed through Martensen's deliverances concerning, and employment of, theological method—a matter which has been implicit in our whole discussion. One can note that Martensen often essays a confessional stance, as when he frankly concedes (*Ethics*, p. 113) that the first sin is inexplicable. (But see above, pp. 61–62.) Yet the romance of speculation lures him: 'The dogmatic comprehending is most closely an explicative comprehending—an unfolding of the "given" in the view, a development of its inner relationships. But the explicative comprehending contains in itself the tendency to the speculative comprehending, which does not stop with merely presenting the relationships in the given, but also asks about possibility and basis, does not only say *ita*, but also *quare*. The thorough explication will not be able to do other than to develop such thought contradictions, such antimonies, which crave a mediation of the concepts. . . . *The speculative rests precisely upon getting the contradictions in the unity of the ideas* . . . the basic form for dogmatics as the theistic theology is *ita* not *quare*. . ., yet it will be impossible to separate the explicative and speculative comprehending by a fast and inflexible boundary. Every *ita* contains a hidden *quare*, which in a thorough explication cannot do otherwise than come forward and invite to *this higher type of comprehending*.' Our translation from *Den Christelige Dogmatik* (Copenhagen: Reitzel, 1849), pp. 79–80.

2. In the Greek Style

We have already sketched the main lines of Kierkegaard's protest against Hegel and Martensen and have suggested that far from revealing a hypersensitivity to peripheral disagreement, that protest shows the issue to have its roots in the irreducible character of the fundamental polarity structuring Kierkegaard's thought.[80] Kierkegaard may have found sustenance for that body of thought, and so support for its protest, in many quarters. We have taken note of his appeal to the Aristotelian principle of contradiction without which the meaning of this and every polarity dissolves.[81] Kierkegaard was a close student of Aristotle's works and may very well have drawn from him in the material formulation of the polarity.[82] Arild Christensen has argued that Kierkegaard's principle of individuation with its distinctions between men, beasts and God is Aristotelian in character.[83] In any case Climacus' discussion of the becoming which issues from the individual's choice makes clear that Kierkegaard found at least a corroborating parallel in Aristotle's discussion of 'kinesis' as the movement of transition from possibility to actuality.[84] Climacus notes that it is this understanding which shows that the reach of the Hegelian logic far exceeds its grasp: 'The transition from

[80] See above, pp. 11–28, 57–58, 60–65.

[81] See above, pp. 25–45. In Aristotle see *Posterior Analytics*, I 3 72 b, and *Metaphysics*, 1005 b 35f.

[82] Niels Thulstrup, 'Kierkegaardian Studies in Scandinavia', *Theology Today*, October 1955, pp. 308–9, suggests that despite the long period during which Kierkegaard studied Aristotle's writings with real enthusiasm, 'generally Kierkegaard seems to have been guided by Tennemann's large history of philosophy written from a Kantian point of view. He used other secondary sources, e.g., Hegel's famous historical lectures, too.' On the relationship of Kierkegaard to Kant, see below, pp. 80–81, 84–85.

[83] Arild Christensen, 'Sören Kierkegaard's Individuationsprincip', *Dansk Teologisk Tidskrift*, 1953, pp. 216–37, finds four probable points of influence: (1) the distinction between the relations example-species and individual-race, (2) man's sublimity in his participation in society (Aristotle) or connection with the whole race (Kierkegaard), (3) the higher sublimity of man's freedom, (4) the exclusion of both animals and God from the elevating relationship described under (2) above—either on ground of their respective lowliness or self-sufficiency (Aristotle), or on ground of their respective absence of spirit or unsynthesized perfection of spirit (Kierkegaard).

[84] Cf. Aristotle, *Physics* (London and New York, 1929), III I 201 b: 'It is clear that motion (*kinesis*) must be the realization of the specific potentiality in question and of the subject only *qua* seat of movement, and a thing is moving just as long as it is actually in this particular way, and neither before nor after.' (Trans. by P. Wicksteed and F. Cornford for the Loeb Classical Library.) See above, pp. 18–21, and below, pp. 106–8.

possibility to actuality is, as Aristotle rightly teaches, "kinesis", a movement. This does not permit itself to be expressed or understood in the language of abstraction, since that language simply cannot give movement either time or space, which presuppose movement or are presupposed by it.'[85] Climacus has other warm words of recognition for Aristotle which suggest a commonality in the analysis of the principle of motion itself with a clear emphasis on the dominance of the practical reason being particularly noticeable.[86]

Much of this material was available to Kierkegaard in somewhat different form in the work of Trendelenburg, of whom Kierkegaard said in 1847: 'There is no modern philosopher from whom I have had so much profit as Trendelenburg.'[87] In Trendelenburg Kierkegaard could find an attack against Hegel based on the logical question involved in the construction of the System: 'Never, in the history of philosophy, did the logical question assume so much importance as at present. Whereas, formerly, the attack had been directed against "the speculative theology" flank, it now approaches closer to the centre, which supports the whole—the *Logic*. The contest regarding the logical question is a contest for the existence of the system. All the consequences which have developed themselves from Hegel, stand or fall with it.'[88] Trendelenburg asserted that, for all its claims to be presuppositionless, the System could never get started, 'since it is impossible for the human mind to accomplish absolutely the required abstraction'.[89] The best one can manage is not the exclusion, but the 'silent co-operation' of the 'first condition of its [the mind's] activity, the condition of the designing fantasy'.[90] This is—for that matter—the better bargain for the System since in that co-operation it wins more than the appearance of a presuppositionless beginning

---

[85] *S.V.* VII, p. 296 (*CUP*, p. 306). Cf. *Pap.* IV B 117, p. 290; B 118, 7. On Kierkegaard's use of Aristotle's apparatus at this point, see Reidar Thomte, 'New Reflections on the Great Dane', *Discourse*, 1963, pp. 149–53.

[86] Cf. ibid., p. 269 (ibid., p. 278): 'Abstract thought is disinterested, but for an existing individual to exist is his highest interest. The existing man has therefore constantly a *telos*, and it is of this *telos* that Aristotle speaks, when he says (*de anima* III, 10, 2) that *nous theoretikos* is different from *nous praktikos tō telei*.'

[87] *Pap.* VIII A 18 (*Dru* 636). In this passage Kierkegaard laments the fact that when he was in Berlin he did not take advantage of the opportunity to hear Trendelenburg lecture. He had studied Trendelenburg's works since 1844.

[88] Adolf Trendelenburg, 'The Logical Question in Hegel's System', *The Journal of Speculative Philosophy*, ed. Wm. Harris, trans. T. Davidson, 1871, pp. 349–59, 1872, pp. 82–93, 163–75, 350–61; passage cited is from 1872, p. 91; cf. 1871, p. 350.

[89] ibid., 1871, p. 358.

[90] ibid.

for its logic in pure thought. It gains also the appearance of movement:

> . . . it was plainly apparent, that, even in the first step, the principle of all external phenomena was presupposed, the concept of *local* motion. The aid of this form-giving intuition was indeed kept hidden, but it aided mightily; and if it was once admitted, there continually arose from it new sensuous vehicles, without which, pure thought would not move from its place. Where pure thought haughtily claims to produce from itself, there this openly despised, yet secretly received principle—there the silently accompanying action of motion reflecting the images in the space of the imagination lends it the logical forms which it could never have produced from itself. By means of this foreign but hidden service, the productions of pure thought receive a sensuous freshness, without which they would have been less than fleeting shadows.[91]

These accusations will seem quite familiar to the reader who comes to Trendelenburg by way of Kierkegaard.[92] To them Trendelenburg adds in *Logische Untersuchungen* a careful scrutiny of the concepts of negation and identity, showing that they cannot perform the duties assigned them by the System, but consistently depend on the issue of the individual's intuition.[93]

Trendelenburg's exposure of the logical errors in the System drew Kierkegaard's praise, but that praise was qualified by Kierkegaard's judgment that in other areas of substantive criticism Trendelenburg fell short.[94] We have in mind particularly criticism related to the divine-human polarity. We have said that Kierkegaard may have found some help in Aristotle at this point—particularly with refer-

---

[91] ibid., [italics his]. For Kierkegaard's endorsement of this critique, see *S.V.* VII, p. 258 (*CUP*, p. 267). Iwan Iljin, *Die Philosophie Hegels als Kontemplative Gotteslehre* (Bern: A. Francke, 1946), has discussed Hegel's system in terms of a struggle between speculative and empirical elements. He too finds empirical data intruding into what is alleged to be the province of pure thought. He further suggests that Hegel tries to find a way out by arguing that even if all cannot be seen to be logical, it is teleological. See also N. Thulstrup's review of Iljin's work in *Meddelelser fra Sören Kierkegaard Selskabet*, 1949, pp. 1–7.

[92] See, for example, *S.V.* VII, pp. 90ff. (*CUP*, pp. 101ff.), on the 'dialectic of the beginning'. Kierkegaard's target within the System is the same, though he mounts the attack somewhat differently, since he lays stress on the point that a presuppositionless beginning would be to begin with the immediate. He points to the process of abstraction from existence which is needed to determine what is the immediate, and notes: 'Only when reflection is halted can the beginning occur, and reflection can only be halted by something other than itself, and this other is something wholly other than the logical, since it is a decision', (ibid., p. 92 [ibid., p. 103]). Kierkegaard and Trendelenburg agree concerning the essentially parasitical character of 'pure thought'.

[93] Trendelenburg, 'The Logical Question in Hegel's System', *The Journal of Speculative Philosophy*, 1872, pp. 82–84. See our discussion above, pp. 51–58.

[94] *Pap.* V A 74 notes that Trendelenburg lacks the category of the 'leap'.

ence to the human pole. But it is to that other Greek that we must look if we are to understand the resources which nourished Kierkegaard in his reflections concerning the individual.

For Kierkegaard, Socrates both states and symbolizes the plight of the man who faces honestly the fact that reality cannot be reduced to the monistic simplicity sponsored by the System. The fundamental dualism characterizing reality means that Hegel's identification of the real and the ideal is a fantasy. Socrates' 'ignorance' is real wisdom in comparison to the vaunted certainty of the System's knowledge. If one will claim the ideal one does so not by objective observation and impersonal reflection, but by a free choice borne by an inner passion. The matter of immortality provides Kierkegaard with an illustration:

Let us consider Socrates. Nowadays everyone dabbles in some proofs; one has many proofs, another fewer. But Socrates! He puts the question objectively in a problematic manner: if there is an immortality. Was he then a doubter in comparison with one of the modern thinkers of the three proofs? Not at all. On this 'if' he stakes his whole life, he dares to die, and he has ordered his whole life with the passion of the infinite in such a way that it might be found acceptable—*if* there is an immortality. . . . The Socratic ignorance was thus an expression, held fast with the entire passion of inwardness, for this, that the eternal truth relates itself to an existing individual, and that it must therefore remain a paradox for him so long as he exists; and yet it may be possible that there was more truth in the Socratic ignorance in Socrates than in the whole System's objective truth, which flirts with the demands of the time and adapts itself to *Privatdocents*.[95]

Surely the fast disappearing temporal moment, beset by all the uncertainty and ambiguity of existence, seems too fragile to link the individual with the prodigious weight of eternity. In Kierkegaard's language the temporal moment is 'incommensurable' with the requirements placed upon it. Kierkegaard believed that the Socratic irony had expressed all of this before him. That belief is suggested as early as 1841 in Kierkegaard's dissertation. Kierkegaard may permit Climacus to chastise the young magister who as a 'positive theological candidate in our time cannot restrain himself from instructing Socrates in a note that this negativity was only to a certain degree true'.[96] But the *Postscript's* appeal to Socrates reaffirms rather than

---

[95] *S.V.* VII, pp. 168–9 (*CUP*, pp. 180–1), [italics his]. For Kierkegaard's comments on his own use of the category of the individual against the System, see *S.V.* XIII, p. 604 (*PV*, p. 129) and *S.V.* XI, pp. 194ff., (*SD*, pp. 133ff.).

[96] *S.V.* VII, p. 71 (*CUP*, p. 83). This is the kind of passage which lends support to Jens Himmelstrup's contention (*Sören Kierkegaards Opfattelse af Sokrates* [Copenhagen: Busck, 1924]) that the dissertation reveals an Hegelian distaste for Socrates' failure to assume his positive duties towards the state. Himmelstrup feels that *CUP's*

rejects the analysis in the dissertation, which held against Hegel that irony was an essential principle with Socrates, who is to be seen as representing infinite and absolute Negativity.[97] It is not surprising that in seeking to awaken his slumbering 'positive' age Kierkegaard found great inspiration in the simple wise man who could distinguish between what he knew and what he did not know: 'The only analogy I have for myself is: Socrates; my task is a Socratic task, to revise the determination of what it is to be Christian: I do not call myself a Christian (keeping the ideal free), but I can make clear that others are that even less than I. . . . It is in an abyss of sophistry that "Christendom" lies, far, far worse than when the Sophists flourished in Greece.'[98]

It should not seem strange that Kierkegaard also appeals to Socrates in the selection of methods to be employed in the discharge of his task. Socrates' refusal to claim authority or to receive fees for his disturbing service as a teacher attracted Kierkegaard. More fundamentally, Kierkgaard hails the maieutic method of Socrates which recognizes the freedom of the learner as well as the relativity of the teacher.[99] Kierkegaard's praise would, of course, have been self-contradictory, had he then submitted himself to a literal reproduction of the Socratic method, rather than using it as a model from which

---

picture of Socrates as an existential thinker reflects quite another understanding of Socrates.

[97] See the sixth thesis in the dissertation. Hirsch, op. cit., Vol. II, pp. 586–602, seems to be right in arguing against Himmelstrup that there is a clear line connecting the Socrates of the dissertation with the Socrates of the later works. The disagreement between the two scholars is not total, for Himmelstrup is also aware of the anti-Hegelian purpose of the dissertation (op. cit., p. 299), and Hirsch acknowledges that the contra-Hegel dissertation itself bears a strong resemblance to Hegel in the matter of several points of interpretation regarding Socrates—for example, his role as a 'world historical figure'. (op. cit., pp. 592–4.) On this point, cf. also Kabell, op cit., pp. 223–43 and Bejerholm, op cit., pp. 313ff.

[98] S.V. XIV, p. 352 (AC, p. 283). This is not to say that the analogy reached him only directly from Socrates. Kierkegaard himself cites Hamann as confirming the example of Socrates, S.V. VII, p. 487 (CUP, p. 495), and with good reason—see, for example, Hamann's Sammtliche Werke, ed. Josef Nadler (5 vols., Wien: Herder, 1949–ㅤ, Vol. II, pp. 73ff., (cf. ed. by Friedrich Roth, [8 vols., Berlin: G. Reimer, 1821-43]), Vol. II, pp. 35ff.). Still Socrates was the great example (S.V. X, pp. 239–40 [CDi, pp. 245–6]). This point concerns Kierkegaard's own understanding of his relationship to Socrates, and so holds true quite apart from the question of the objective adequacy of Kierkegaard's Socrates scholarship. Himmelstrup (op. cit., pp. 267f.) is particularly critical of the scholarship involved in the first part of the dissertation.

[99] On this point and on the whole relationship, see the helpful chapter, 'A Danish Socrates' by David Swenson, Something About Kierkegaard, ed. Lillian M. Swenson (2nd rev. ed., Minneapolis: Augsburg, 1945), pp. 34–70.

he fashioned his own distinctive method of indirect communication.[100]

The Socratic concentration on existence provides an analogy to the faith which is the only way to the truth for the individual—not, as the age was being told, an inferior way. This use of Socrates strikes at targets other than Hegel himself. Both the rationalistic critic and the orthodox defender of the faith err by seeking to settle their issue on objective intellectual grounds.[101] Indeed one may well say that it is essentially such oblivion to the situation of the existing man which qualifies the preaching of the day for the sharp criticism it wins from Kierkegaard.[102] Emil Brunner—in trying to find some continuity between the attack on the church and the critique of the System—has stated the matter well: '[What is Kierkegaard's target at this point?] It is precisely orthodoxy or the orthodox misunderstanding of Christianity, that "confidence" which the true believers have stored up as a sort of life insurance policy for time and eternity and which introduces a situation of comfortable rest and self-satisfaction at that point where the highest tension and suffering ought to rule. The copy has replaced the original. . . . And a copy is infinitely cheaper than an original and can therefore be distributed in an unlimited degree. In other words: faith as a mass phenomenon instead of the decision of the individual.'[103]

[100] On indirect communication, see above, pp. 30–35. On Kierkegaard's adaptations of the Socratic method, see Bejerholm, op. cit., pp. 191, 313–14. Bejerholm notes that Kierkegaard sometimes criticizes features of the method used in the Platonic dialogues—as in *S.V.* VII, pp. 236–7 (*CUP*, p. 247). Bejerholm also notes (op. cit., p. 197) that Kierkegaard was exposed to contemporary parallels to the Socratic method (notably in Möller and Sibbern), and that he had studied the defense for the use of the dialogical form in philosophical communication made by the German philosopher, K. F. Solger.

[101] For the young Kierkegaard's criticism of both, see *Pap.* I A 72 (*Dru* 16). F. J. Billeskov-Jansen, *Sören Kierkegaard Vaerker i Udvalg med indledninger og tekstforklaringer* (4 vols., Copenhagen: Gyldendal, 1950), IV, p. 224, comments: 'With "orthodoxy" Kierkegaard is thinking of that form for Christianity, which he knew from his home and from Mynster's preaching; with "rationalism" of that Christianity he met at the university, especially with Professor H. N. Clausen, whose lectures in dogmatics he had attended in the winter term, 1833–4, and in the summer term, 1834.' Clausen (see above, p. 51, note 1) was perhaps the most influential man in the theological faculty at the time.

[102] Kierkegaard does at times contend that the preaching of the day omits such an essential Christian theme as suffering—*S.V.* XIV, pp. 36, 72–73, 196–7, 259–60 (*AC*, pp. 26, 50, 163, 219). Yet his more frequent contention is that no concern is shown to bring what is preached into life—ibid., 37–38, 132, 239–40 (ibid., pp. 27, 108–9, 201–2). This is true even of the healing Gospel:—ibid., p. 6 (ibid., pp. 5–6). Cf. Bukdahl, 'Indrömmelse, dens plads i Sören Kierkegaards kristendoms-forstaaelse', *Dansk Teologisk Tidskrift*, 1963, p. 121.

[103] E. Brunner, 'Sören Kierkegaard's Budskap', *Janus*, 1939, p. 242.

3. *Beyond Socrates and on to Christianity*

'It is true that he was no Christian, I know that; but I am certainly convinced that he has become one.'[104] So does Kierkegaard, in marking his debt to Socrates, measure his advance beyond him. There is, after all, nothing uniquely Christian present in the Socratic concern with the individual in existence. Indeed Walther Rehm has argued that Kierkegaard's appropriation of Socrates is rooted not in his Christianity, but in his essential romanticism.[105] James Collins, who is not intent to excise the theological matter from Kierkegaard's thought, has noted Kierkegaard's evident early interest in the romanticists and has identified some likely points of attraction:

In them, he perceived a strong counteractive force which might save the age from becoming completely Hegelian. Their emphasis upon all that is strange, mysterious, uncharted, and nonconceptual in human experience seemed to open a gaping breach in the side of the impregnable System, and to make room for values which found no place in that imposing structure. Above all, Kierkegaard found congenial the Romantic notion of 'Lebensanschauung', a life-view which must be achieved by each individual as his inalienable task, rather than passively ingested in ready-made textbook form. Against the vaunted objectivity of dialectical philosophy, he opposed this need for subjective activity and personal assimilation and transformation of experience under leading principles, which can stand the test of life's demands.[106]

Kierkegaard's advance beyond Socrates—and in some sense against romanticism—is made on theological terrain. Since that is the case, that advance reflects the structures of reflection which we have identified as basic to Kierkegaard's religious thought. The role of the diastatic rhythm at this point is the more easily and most often seen. Kierkegaard would correct romanticism's loss of balance by juxtaposing to its immersion in the individual an active and independent interest in God. One may suppose that that interest found its form within a matrix too. Kierkegaard could well have found support in Hamann for this diastatic effort to transcend the Socrates whom he claimed as his example. We have already noted the supporting role which Hamann's 'reduplication' of the Socratic ignorance played for Kierkegaard.[107] We need now to make clear that this

---

[104] *S.V.* XIII, pp. 541-2 (*PV*, p. 41).
[105] Walther Rehm, *Kierkegaard und der Verführer* (München: Hermann Rinn, 1949).
[106] Collins, op. cit., p. 23. If one requires the witness of a registered professional theologian, no less a figure than Brunner has identified Kierkegaard as a late child of Romanticism. See his article, 'Sören Kierkegaard's Budskap', *Janus*, 1939, p. 225.
[107] See p. 70, note 98 above.

witness to the primary of faith is uttered not from a romanticist exaltation of the individual who eludes systematic thought, but from a theological position, which could be critical of such exaltation as well. The romanticist may easily forget that our very existence is from God. But 'this fact . . . is the secret nature of the human soul, its importance and dependence on its maker . . . the greatest secret is disclosed when God breathed upon his pictured work.'[108] It follows, then, that 'our own existence [Dasein] and the existence [Existenz] of all phenomena outside of us must be believed, and can in no other manner be determined. . . . What one believes therefore has no need to be proved, and a proposition can be proved just as irrefutably for that very reason, without having to be believed . . . faith is no work of reason, and can therefore succumb to no attack by it; because Faith comes to pass as little by argumentation as does taste and sight.[109] Even these brief passages suggest the merit of Gerhard Niedermeyer's characterization: 'In the centre of his thinking stand the concepts: I and God, the individual self and the absolute (God) are polarly separated from each other.'[110] Thus Kierkegaard's praise of Hamann is not the least surprising.[111]

We are suggesting that Kierkegaard reacted against romanticism as a view of life which so immerses itself in man as to lose sight of the distinctness and freedom of God. Kierkegaard had occasion to watch that process of immersion at close hand, for a mild form of romanticism was an influential force in the Danish theology of his time. Bishop Mynster (1775-1854) provides a striking example of this tendency. In his massive work *Betragtninger over de christelige Troeslaerdomme*[112] Mynster understands religion as a force which corresponds to human striving and creates harmony within the self. In such religion both human effort and the divine gift may be readily acknowledged and no breach is found between that religion and Christianity.[113] It is not strange that such views, coupled with their apparent consequences in the life of the Danish people, called forth from Kierkegaard a strong and sometimes violent witness to the freedom of God. That

[108] Hamann, op. cit.. I, p. 15 (Roth ed., I, p. 64).
[109] ibid., II, pp. 73f., (Roth, II, pp. 35f.).
[110] Gerhard Niedermeyer, *Sören Kierkegaard und die Romantik* (Leipzig: Quelle and Meyer, 1910), p. 63.
[111] For a fuller discussion of this side of Hamann, see Albert Anderson, 'Ignorance and Enlightenment: A Study in the Religious Philosophy of J. G. Hamann (1730–88)', Harvard (unpublished thesis), 1964.
[112] 2 Vols. Copenhagen: I Deichmann, 1846.
[113] See N. Thulstrup's comments on Mynster's position, 'Kierkegaards Verhältnis zu Hegel', *Theologische Zeitschrift*, 1957, pp. 200–26.

witness would also exercise its cutting edge against a moralism which reduced God's rule to the requirements of a rigid moral order. Such a target could be found, for Kant had been a significant voice in Denmark since about 1790.[114] In Part Three we shall be examining Kierkegaardian themes which voice this witness—such as the 'teleological suspension of the ethical'.

The *Postscript* invites the judgment that the diastatic separation of God and man drew some of its categories from Lessing. We are concerned at this point particularly with the third of the theses 'possibly or actually attributable to Lessing': 'Accidental historical truths can never be proofs for the eternal truths of reason. . . . the transition by which one would build an eternal happiness on historical testimony is a leap.'[115] Lessing, of course, made an altogether different resolution of the problem—turning to the inner logic of Christ's doctrines, which marks them as necessary rational truths.[116] Yet the distinction between the temporal and the eternal is useful to Kierkegaard and he can rightly appeal to Lessing at this point, even if he does so by way of Strauss.[117]

The methodological implications of this distinction were also available to Kierkegaard in Schelling. Kierkegaard was a member of the distinguished audience which heard Schelling's Berlin lectures in the winter of 1841–2 on *Die Philosophie der Mythologie und der Offenbarung*.

[114] Hal Koch, *Danmarks Kirke Gennem Tiderne* (Copenhagen: De Unges, 1939), pp. 106–7, characterizes Kant's role as a 'John the Baptist': 'His critical philosophy broke down the age's naïve trust in reason and natural religion, but at the same time Kant called to account the no less naïve utilitarian morality of the time.' Koch points out that while 'Kant's thinking was not Christianly stamped', yet it 'actually became for many a station on the way to a positive Christianity'. Koch singles out A. S. Orsted (1816–72) and H. G. Clausen (1759–1840) as prominent instances of Kant's influence.

[115] *S.V.* VII, p. 74 (*CUP*, p. 86). In 1777 in *Uber den Beweis des Geistes und der Kraft* Lessing had distinguished between historical truths as accidental and truths of reason as necessary. On the relationship to Kierkegaard, see N. Thulstrup's introduction to *PF*, xlix–lxv.

[116] This was the line taken by Lessing in 1780 in *Erziehung des Menschengeschlechts*. Hans Leisegang, *Lessings Weltanschauung* (Leipzig: Felix Meiner, 1931), pp. 63f. stresses the essentially monistic character of Lessing's thought. He further suggests (ibid., pp. 117–26) that the 'Erziehung' discussion actually masks an 'Entwicklung' concept, in which Lessing looks ahead to an ever increasing revelation of the reasonableness of the faith.

[117] Kierkegaard owned the Danish translation of Strauss's dogmatics prepared by his friend Hans Bröchner. In citing Lessing Kierkegaard follows the citation in the Bröchner translation rather than that available to him in the Lessing edition he owned. See *Pap.* V B 1, 3, p. 53. For further detail on this point, see Billeskov-Jansen, op. cit., IV, p. 154, and N. Thulstrup, 'Theological and Philosophical Kierkegaardian Studies in Scandinavia, 1945–53', *Theology Today*, 1955, p. 301.

In those lectures Schelling contended that the negative philosophy of Hegel could deal only with the possibility of a thing. He sought to formulate a 'positive philosophy' which would deal with the reality of a thing. Several writers—including, notably, Paul Tillich—have tried to link Kierkegaard with that positive philosophy, despite Kierkegaard's biting expression of disinterest in Schelling's lectures.[118] That effort seems rather ambitious, unless one closes one's eyes to the strong ties binding the late Schelling's thought to his earlier 'Identitätsphilosophie'. The positive philosophy affirms as its starting point 'the necessarily existing One'. To be sure, Schelling joins Kierkegaard in rejecting the ontological proof. But he then parts company with Kierkegaard: 'I can quite definitely not take as a departure point the concept "God", in order to prove God's existence, but I can take as a point of departure the "only existing", and just the opposite prove that the undoubtedly existing one is God.'[119] We have, of course, Kierkegaard's explicit attack in *PF* against such a line of argument.[120] Beyond that one may say that for Kierkegaard the whole appeal to a *necessarily existing* one is a confusion of categories—indeed the very categories which supported Schelling's methodological attack on Hegel in which Kierkegaard joined.[121]

---

[118] See, for example, Paul Tillich, 'Existential Philosophy', *Journal of the History of Ideas*, 1944, pp. 49–59; Wolfgang Struve, *Die neuzeitliche Philosophie als Metaphysik der Subjektivität—Interpretation zu Kierkegaard und Nietzsche* (Freiburg: K. Alber, 1948) and Thomas, *Subjectivity and Paradox* (Oxford: Basil Blackwell, 1957), pp. 51–54. *Pap.* II A 31 makes clear that Kierkegaard had read Schelling as early as 1837. For his biting criticism in letters of February, 1842, to his friend Emil Boesen and his brother Peter, see *Breve og Aktstykker vedrørende Sören Kierkegaard*, ed. N. Thulstrup, nos. 69 and 70. While Schelling 'talked nonsense endlessly' and 'quite unbearably', and while Kierkegaard felt 'I am too old to attend lectures, just as Schelling is too old to deliver them', yet he felt he owed one thing to Schelling —namely, 'never in my life have I had the urge to travel, as I really have it now'.

[119] F. W. J. Schelling, *Sämmtliche Werke*, ed. by K. F. A. Schelling (Stuttgart and Augsburg: J. S. Cotta, 1856–61) second division, Vol. III, p. 159.

[120] Schelling holds that all of existence testifies to its Lord as the necessarily existing one, or—in Climacus' words—'there is between the God and his works an absolute relation'. Climacus counters: 'True enough, but which are the works of the God? . . . From which works do I derive the proof? It is from the works as ideally interpreted, i.e., such as they do not immediately show themselves to be. But in that case it is not from the works that I derive the proof, but I merely develop the ideality which I have presupposed . . . but what is that other than to presuppose that the God is present (*er til*).' (*S.V.* IV, pp. 207–10 [*PF*, pp. 31–33].) On the use of the phrase 'the God' ('*Guden*') see the introduction Niels Thulstrup has prepared for the *Fragments* (Princeton, 1962). On the terms Kierkegaard uses concerning the 'existence' of God, see below, p. 102, note 11.

[121] For a summary of that attack see Fahrenbach, *Die gegenwärtige Kierkegaard Auslegung in der deutschsprachigen Literatur von 1948 bis 1962* (Tübingen: J. C. B. Mohr, 1962), pp. 61–67.

The distinction with which we have been concerned in the thought of Lessing and Schelling is appropriated by the diastatic current in Kierkegaard's thought in its insistence that the identities of God and man be kept separate. That appropriation is clear in the decisive centre of the advance beyond Socrates propelled by the diastatic movement. We have in mind here not merely *PF*'s advance from the 'Socratic' recourse to the truth in recollection to the Christian witness to the God-Man who contributes not only the truth but the condition for its appropriation as well.[122] If one restricts oneself to that statement of the advance, one fails to deal adequately with Socrates who 'is constantly departing from it [the principle of recollection], because he will exist':

> By holding Socrates to the proposition that all knowledge is recollection he becomes a speculative philosopher, instead of what he was, an existential thinker, who understood that the essential thing is to exist. The proposition, that all knowledge is recollection, belongs to speculation, and recollection is immanence, and speculatively and eternally seen, there is no Paradox. But the difficulty is that no man is speculation, but the one who speculates is himself an existing individual, subject to the demand of existence; there is no merit in forgetting this, but a great merit in holding it fast, and this is precisely what Socrates did. To accentuate existence, in which is contained the determination of inwardness, is the Socratic position; the Platonic, on the other hand, pursues recollection and immanence. In this way Socrates is basically farther advanced than all of speculation . . .[123]

Furthermore there is a sense in which the principle of recollection does apply for Kierkegaard. He sought not to convey knowledge about Christianity—his age's lack lay elsewhere.[124] But if one inquires into the substance of the faith which needs to be brought to new life in individual existence, one finds an advance beyond Socrates borne by the diastatic rhythm. We refer, of course, to the material specification of the object of faith. We shall be looking at this in detail in Part Three. We need do no more here than to note that the categories employed in the description of the God-Man, the offence, the Paradox, surely sustain the judgment that: 'The Socratic ignorance is as a witty jest in comparison with the seriousness of the absurd;

---

[122] In his introduction to *PF*, lvi, N. Thulstrup states succinctly the connection with the contemporary target: 'Hegel's thought is only a variation of Idealism and of the position of its founder, Plato, that men possess the truth and only need to become conscious of it. Plato held that this evocation of the truth takes place by recollection; Hegel held that it takes place with the help of the dialectical method.'

[123] *S.V.* VII, p. 173 (*CUP*, pp. 184–5).

[124] Cf. Bejerholm, '*Meddelelsens Dialektik*' (Copenhagen: Munksgaard, 1962), pp. 313–4.

and the Socratic existential inwardness is as Greek light-mindedness in comparison with the exertion of faith.'[125]

It may be noted that the diastatic tendency in Kierkegaard's thought finds active expression in his bitter criticism of Grundtvig.[126] Seeking to find an objective basis for faith and reforms, Grundtvig appealed to 'a faith and a confession which—as the Christian—has our own experience, our father's experience, and through almost eighteen centuries the experience of millions, as well as a miraculous historic witness in its favour'.[127] This appeal would already be open

[125] *S.V.* VII, p. 176 (*CUP*, p. 188). It is at least as clear for Kierkegaard that 'what Schleiermacher calls "Religion" and the Hegelians "Faith" is at bottom nothing but the first immediate condition for everything—the vital fluid—the spiritual atmosphere we breathe—and which cannot therefore with justice be designated by those words', *Pap.* I A 273 (*Dru* 78). Torsten Bohlin, *Kierkegaards dogmatiska aaskaadning i dess historiska sammanhang* (Stockholm: Svenska Kyrkans Diakonistyrelses, 1925), p. 380, finds the real target to lie elsewhere: 'It is actually not Hegel, but instead Jacobi, against whom Hegel has turned himself, who has defined faith as the "immediate", in that he . . . asserts that all proofs expressly presuppose an immediate "knowing" in and through which the object is revealed to the consciousness without any reference to the thinking process.' If Bohlin·is right, the dialectical character of Kierkegaard's relationship to other thinkers is again illustrated, for Jacobi drew praise mingled with censure: 'I do not deny that Jacobi has often inspired me, though I see very well that his dialectical skill is disproportionate to his noble enthusiasm; but he is the eloquent protest of a noble, uncorrupted, loveable spirit against the systematic confinement of existence, a victorious consciousness, and an enthusiastic struggle for the principle that existence must have larger and deeper significance than the couple of years in which one forgets oneself in reading the System.' *S.V.* VII, p. 211 (*CUP*, p. 224). This diastatic posture in matters of methodology provides the context in which Hamann's passages proclaiming a radical breach between faith and reason would appeal to Kierkegaard. Lowrie, *Kierkegaard* (London: Oxford, 1938), p. 166, cites such a passage from Hamann: 'A man who lives in God stands therefore in the same relation to the "natural man" that a waking man does to one who is snoring in profound slumber—to a dreamer—a sleep-walker. . . . A dreamer may have images more vivid than a man who is awake, may see more, hear and think more than he, may be conscious of himself, dream with more orderliness than a waking man thinks, may be the creator of new objects, of great events. Everything is true for him, and yet everything is illusion. . . . The question is whether it might in any way be possible for a waking man to convince a sleeper (so long as he sleeps) of the fact that he is asleep. No.' Cf. *Pap.* I A 237, X 4 A 505, XI I A 149, 218.

[126] So, for example, *S.V.* VII, p. 34 (*CUP*, pp. 44–45): 'No one could surely wish to have Grundtvig on his side, who definitely wishes to know where he is, and does not wish to be where there is an alarm, especially when the alarm is the only more specific determination of where one is.' Cf. *Pap.* VI B 235, p. 293.

[127] N. F. S. Grundtvig, *Kirkens Gjenmaele, Vaerker i Udvalg*, ed. Georg Christensen and Hal Koch (10 vols., Copenhagen: Gyldendal, 1941–8), II, p. 324. For a more cautious statement see *Skal den Lutherske Reformation Virkelig Forsaettes* (*Vaerker*, III), p. 270: 'So long therefore as one cannot point out some other church fellowship with a different confession of faith than ours, that represents itself as the original Christian church, and possibly can be that . . . just so long is the oral, audible, public, official confession of faith our church fellowship declares at

to attack on Socratic grounds. It is, however, wholly excluded when one realizes that the Paradox stamps its consequences with its own character. For Kierkegaard Grundtvig's fatal error could be followed through in detail in the relationship between the human and the Christian in this position. Grundtvig's interest in mythology as the true temple of a people's spirit,[128] and his famous cry, 'Man first, then Christian',[129] were vulnerable to attack from the diastatic position. Indeed one feels that the diastatic element in Kierkegaard's thought is not only dominant in the Grundtvig critique, but that it is so to such an extent that significant points of commonality are obscured.[130]

---

baptism the most valid and unmistakable historic witness that can be given regarding what Christians straight from the beginning and up to now have believed.' This passage makes clear that Grundtvig's primary argument is that it cannot be denied that the faith expressed in the baptismal confession defines true Christianity unless 'one will not believe his own eyes'. (Kirkens Gjenmaele, p. 337.) Grundtvig recognizes that the question of determining the truth of true Christianity is a separate question (ibid., p. 346) and acknowledges that there is a dimension of 'secrecy' in this process. (Skal den Lutherske Reformation Virkelig Forsaettes, p. 235.) Yet there is a discernible momentum in his literalistic appeal to the very words of the confession as taught by Jesus which tends to obscure the distinction. On this appeal, see Johannes Knudsen, Danish Rebel (Philadelphia: Muhlenberg, 1955), pp. 100f., who stresses the influence of Wolffian logic in the argument. See also Hal Koch, Grundtvig, trans. Llewellyn Jones (Yellow Springs, Ohio: Antioch, 1952), pp. 93–94.

[128] Grundtvig, Nordens Mythologi, Vaerker, IV, p. 54. Grundtvig holds that fidelity to the spirit housed in the temple of the people's mythology will lead to a clarification of history and of the concept of man. (ibid., pp. 9, 19–20.) That very work of clarification at other times is referred to the divine Spirit at work in Jesus—see Grundtvig's Om det philosophiske Aarhundrede, Vaerker, II, p. 178. Henning Höirup, 'Grundtvigs Gedanken über Christentum und Volk', Grundtvigstudier (Copenhagen: Nordisk, 1952), pp. 74f., has tried to state the connection by suggesting that Christianity has no language of its own, but uses the language of the people. Part of the difficulty in working out the connection comes not from the intrinsic complexity of the subject, but from the effusively metaphorical character of Grundtvig's comments. So in Nordens Mythologi, p. 21, we are told that we are to see the world of the spirit 'with Nordic eyes, but in the light of Christianity'.

[129] See Koch, op. cit., pp. 156–7, for the famous poem on this theme. Cf. Grundtvig, Folkelighed og Christendom, Vaerker, V, p. 251: 'First we must be Danes, just as all human beings must first be living, before it avails to speak to them either about the temporal or the eternal God.' Again in fairness to Grundtvig it should be noted that this theme is not without its corrective in his work. Thus Grundtvig explicitly notes that Danishness saves no one (ibid.) and emphasizes the distorted character of man's humanity: 'human nature by the Fall is so disturbed that all real healing is impossible . . . baptism [is necessary as] an actual bath of regeneration, wherein the believing one is reborn'. Nordens Mythologi, p. 26; cf. pp. 56–57.

[130] Notes 127 and 129 above make clear that Grundtvig is a far more complex figure than the diastatic current makes him out to be. It is striking that Grundtvig

By now it would seem to be incontrovertibly clear that the diastatic rhythm is the one which charts the movement of Kierkegaard's thought beyond Socrates and more emphatically beyond those views judged by it to be inferior to the Socratic position. Yet perhaps the diastatic rhythm does not trace the advance by itself. Indeed in isolation it may even threaten to bring the reader full circle to a 'theological' romanticism.[131] Edo Pivcevic understands Kierkegaard to be attempting an 'inversion' by which the prerogatives of the romantic 'I' are given to God. The attempt is unsuccessful, for its motive power derives from romanticism, which will permit no absolute negation of the I. It is this dialectic which lies behind the theme of the absolute qualitative difference between God and man—man never reaches the deity he seeks.[132]

While Pivcevic's thesis may be overly ingenious in some of the details involved, it does provide a perspective from which something in Kierkegaard's thought can be seen. It is doubtful that it is possible to show that it is an incomplete or even an incorrect view, if one fixes solely on the diastatic strand in Kierkegaard. Within that strand one could, of course, have recourse to the God-Man who surely does not simply signify the separation of God and man and who in the very signifying of the separation seems to elude and frustrate Pivcevic's

---

also appeals to the principle of contradiction (*Skal den Lutherske Reformation Virkelig Forsaettes*, p. 257) against the mystical principle of indifference. Despite apparent areas of agreement, Kierkegaard was critical of Grundtvig as early as 1835. (*Pap.* I A 6ff.). Grundtvig in turn came to regard Kierkegaard as a demonic protest against the power of the Holy Spirit in the communion of believers and against the power of the Sacraments. That is, he reacted to the diastatic strand in Kierkegaard's thought. This is the context usually accepted for a study of the relationship of the two men. Thus Henning Höirup's emphasis on the strong contrast between the two assumes a total negation of the church's reality on the part of Kierkegaard. In 'Grundtvig and Kierkegaard: Their Views of the Church', *Theology Today*, 1955, p. 341, Höirup writes: 'For Kierkegaard the Church is a numerical concept and not a Christian concept, a psychological definition with an inferiority complex.' For a less negative view of the relationship, see Sören Holm, *Grundtvig und Kierkegaard* (Kopenhagen-Tübingen: Nyt Nordisk-Katzmann, 1956).

[131] This is Rehm's charge, op. cit., p. 620: 'The conquest of romanticism and the liberation from it were thus at the deepest level nothing other and more difficult than its translation and transformation in the sphere of the paradoxical-religious, and therewith perhaps only an apparent conquest and an apparent liberation; more precisely and in Kierkegaard's sense, a repetition, a metamorphosis and potentiation of the romantic essence, of its aesthetic concepts and its striving after the unconditioned to a higher stage, within the Christian categories.'

[132] Edo Pivcevic, *Ironie als Daseinsform bei Sören Kierkegaard* (Gütersloh: Gütersloher, 1960), p. 66. See above p. 37, note 114 for Gerd-Günther Grau's analysis of the circular self-destruction of Christianity involved in Religion B.

analysis. But we shall show in Part Three that by itself the diastatic christological motif constantly approaches the twin precipices of cognitive meaninglessness and psychological impossibility. And one no sooner gets a firm hand on the figure of Christ in this strand than one feels the pull of Kierkegaard's thought back towards the rhythm of synthesis.

That does seem the right direction to move if one wishes to follow Kierkegaard's progress beyond Socrates. If the Hegelian confusion must be faulted because it exalts and idealizes man, that critique bears testimony not to an absent God, but to one whose presence and activity measure man and man's measurement of himself.[133] In attacking romantic irony as inferior to Socratic irony in its lack of seriousness, Kierkegaard is drawing on resources available in a doctrine of creation which sees the self not as boundless subjectivity but as a self set in relation to God and to men.[134] This understanding

[133] Bernard Meland, *The Realities of Faith* (New York: Oxford, 1962), preface, understands this idealization as a 'response to the scientific outlook dating from the seventeenth century. In a word, the mechanization of nature gave rise to an idealization of man and of the human equation. In this idealization of man, realism concerning the nature of our human existence went out of our mode of thinking and living; and, with it, a responsiveness to saving realities that are not of man's making.' A later reference (p. 87) adds specification: '. . . under the spell of the Newtonian image, the facilities for exact thought and prediction became so perfected that it became literally impossible for nineteenth-century man to distrust his human powers and ideals. Reality for Western man thus became the human equation writ large.' Meland stresses that the correction comes about through an emphasis on the dimension of distance. We are pointing to the presence of a God who so impinges upon man as to make him aware of the distance to which Meland refers.

[134] Niedermeyer, op. cit., p. 51, well summarizes the analysis of romanticism which is involved in this attack: 'Reality is given to the individual in two ways: as a gift [*Gabe*] and as a task [*Aufgabe*]. Irony is essentially critical of the latter. Its philosopher (Schlegel) as well as its poet (Tieck) is critical. One does not criticize the old classicists, one does not—like Kant—criticize the consciousness, one criticizes reality itself. For the individual, then, reality is given as his history. For irony history has really no validity . . . all history becomes myth.' Himmelstrup, op. cit., pp. 107–8, finds a development within Kierkegaard's thought from such irony to the Socratic seriousness: 'In the dissertation ethical seriousness was only possible within a totality. Therefore irony, which separated the subject from the totality, was without seriousness. After the category of "the individual" is constituted, seriousness is really first possible with the individual. . . . The ethical passion in the concept of irony does not mean, then, a changed understanding of the "totality's" relation to irony—but means precisely the individual's subjective inwardness, as the highest expression for ethical seriousness. . . . Irony, Kierkegaard's and the Socratic irony—it was, of course, through Socrates, irony determined in a new sense—loses with Kierkegaard that mark, which—if I may express it thusly—is the "classic" in the concept of irony: transparency.' We rather feel that Himmelstrup overstates the contrast at both points in the authorship. Arild Christensen, 'Der junge Kierkegaard als Schrifstellerpersönlichkeit', *Orbis Litterarum*,

does permit one to link Kierkegaard positively with Socrates as well as with the ethical concern of Kant.[135] Yet it leads beyond these figures as well. It surely will not do to try to account for that advance by retreating to the influence of romanticism on Kierkegaard. If, for example, Kierkegaard does add material specificity to the formal ethic of Fichte, that corrective is made available to him not through a romantic immersion in the self, but through a Christian encounter with a living God.[136] The negations issuing from Kierkegaard's pen are the product of a positive relationship—thus may we indicate the role of the rhythm of synthesis in the advance beyond Socrates.

Part Three will show that this emphasis on the role of the rhythm of synthesis is not dependent on a bare analysis of the logic of the advance attempted, but finds rich material expression in the substantive thought of Kierkegaard. Here we may add that Kierkegaard's appropriation of the diastatic resources available to him was itself a critical one. In his very praise of Hamann, for example, Kierkegaard inserts a remarkable qualification: 'I will not conceal that I admire Hamann, while I gladly admit that his thought's elasticity lacks balance and his supernatural tension self-control, assuming he tried to work more connectedly.'[137] The synthesis strand in Kierkegaard's thought provides precisely such balance and self-control for the diastatic current.

It would seem unlikely that Kierkegaard's roots in his time are reflected only in the diastatic rhythm in his thought. Such is not the case. Even those sources to which Kierkegaard appealed in building the diastatic argument against 'Socrates' may well have presented him with material of quite another sort. Hamann does extol the primacy of faith, but he finds that faith to be nourished by the very conditions of our creaturehood: 'Faith is one of the natural conditions of our faculties of knowledge and the fundamental impulse of our

---

1963, pp. 26–47, has studied the work of Kierkegaard through the dissertation, and introduces qualifications of the impression received from Himmelstrup. Christensen not only emphasizes the presence of the divine stamp upon the 'I', but also stresses the importance of developing the 'given', which in its uniqueness represents the call of God. This theme of the individual-in-relationships is surely a major theme in the later Kierkegaard as well. See Valter Lindström's *Stadiernas Teologi, en Kierkegaard Studie* (Lund: Haakan Ohlssons, 1943), *passim*.

[135] See Fahrenbach, op. cit., p. 68.

[136] For the emphasis on romanticism see Hirsch, *Kierkegaard-Studien* (Gütersloh: Bertelsmann, 1930–3), II, pp. 470–7. One may say that the static deliverances of moralism recognize neither the freedom of God, nor the placement of man in time.

[137] *S.V.* VII, pp. 210–1 (*CUP*, pp. 223–4).

souls; since every universal proposition rests upon good faith, and all abstractions are and must be arbitrary, the most celebrated thinkers of our time upon religion divest themselves of their premises and middle terms, which are necessary to the demonstration of rational conclusions. The basis of religion lies in our whole existence, and outside the sphere of our powers of knowledge, which all taken together compose the most accidental and abstract mode of our existence.'[138] Similarly, the first, second, and fourth of the theses 'attributable to Lessing' emphasize man's striving in the uncertainty of existence. That striving is not aimless and hopeless subjectivity, but is bent towards, and presumably in some sense nourished by, the truth.[139]

To speak of the continuity of the synthesis strand with Kierkegaard's time invites discussion of the claim that Kierkegaard's debt to idealism is far deeper than he would have us believe. We have noted the suggestion that Kierkegaard's dissertation reveals an Hegelian influence in the analysis of Socrates.[140] The plausibility of that suggestion and even the presence of praise for Hegel's talents[141] do not amount to a demonstration of the indebtedness claimed. For what is being claimed is a far more internal and fundamental influence of idealism in Kierkegaard's thought. An imposing array of scholars, names like Drachmann, Bohlin, Hirsch, and Holm join to sponsor this claim, even though they assuredly differ in detail. When one addresses such an audience, it will not do for the theologian to

---

[138] Quoted by Pfleiderer, *The Philosophy of Religion* (London: W. Blackwood & Sons, 1886), Vol. I, p. 199. On Hamann's use of Bruno's '*coincidentiae oppositorum*' as a qualification of existence and his consequent stress on faith, see Niedermeyer, op. cit., pp. 63–64. Both terms in Bruno's phrase are important to Tage Schack *J. G. Hamann* (Copenhagen: Tidehvervs, 1948), pp. 99–100, in his analysis which emphasizes Hamann's 'faith in a real, though hidden, connection in existence' and yet notes that the contradictions in existence bar reason from reaching the coincidence.

[139] Cf. Lessing's recognition in the *Duplik* (*Werke*, Maltzahn ed. [12 vols., Leipzig, Stuttgart; 1853–7] Vol. X, p. 53), that 'not through the possession, but through the pursuit of truth, do his [man's] powers increase . . . possession makes us quiet, insolent, proud'.

[140] See above, p. 69, note 96.

[141] Open admiration, combined with irritation over the presumption of Martensen's advance, is revealed in a diary reference from 1845 (*Pap.* VI B 54:12): 'I cherish a respect for Hegel which occasionally is puzzling to myself; I have learned much from him, and I know very well that I yet—when I again turn back to him—can learn more and more from him . . . his philosophical knowledge, his amazing learning, his genius's glance, and all other good that can be said about a philosopher, I am in spite of a certain disciple, willing to recognize—no, yet not to recognize, that is too distinguished an expression—willing to admire, willing to let myself be taught by.'

utter a bare denial.[142] And the evidence at hand is not sufficient to clothe any total denial.

One may wish to understand the idealistic influence to be present in the selection and emphasis of certain themes in the total Christian witness. That would seem to be plausible enough, since the defender of the faith need not fire in all directions in order to repulse a very particular enemy.[143] More critically, one may suggest that the weapons themselves are taken from the enemy's arsenal and that such equipment is unfortunately not neutral in the warfare of the spirit. This is, of course, the line taken by A. B. Drachmann and Torsten Bohlin.[144] Henriksen well summarizes Bohlin's approach:

> To Hegel Christianity meant the reconciliation of the finite and the infinite; he regarded the figure of Christ as a manifestation of the essential identity of the divine and the human. This speculative interpretation of Christianity was regarded by Kierkegaard as an extreme danger to the true faith, and he tried to destroy it by energetically asserting the absolute qualitative difference between God and man. He conceded to Hegel that Christ in himself combined the infinite and the finite, but denied that this fact could be accepted as an expression of a theoretical reconciliation. On the contrary, he declared that the unity of the eternal and the temporal in Christ is the paradoxical fact to which faith is unconditionally bound and which constitutes its fundamental difference from speculative thinking. In order to secure more favourable conditions for aiming a death blow at Hegel's conclusion concerning the nature of Christianity Kierkegaard, however, took over Hegel's premises. His polemics against Hegel's attempt to adopt a metaphysical view of Christianity actually rest on the Hegelian categories and metaphysical distinctions (finite-infinite, temporal-eternal, nature-spirit).[145]

[142] Cf. Johannes Slök, 'En Studie i Kierkegaard Erkendelsesteori', *Dansk Teologisk Tidskrift*, 1941, pp. 50–51: 'Their [Hegel and Kierkegaard's] thoughts have nothing to do with each other, their intentions are wholly different, their points of departure, their interests, their methods, their setting, all is different. It is not, then, a case of two philosophers who have developed opposite thoughts about the same problem. It is rather a case of two individualities who have thought widely different thoughts about widely different problems.'

[143] So Weiland, *Humanitas Christianitas* (Te Assen Bij: Van Gorcum, 1951), pp. 88–90, argues that Kierkegaard eloquently emphasizes the gospel's offensiveness to the Greeks, but that that about the gospel which repulses the Jews is not heard so clearly, if at all.

[144] Drachmann argued: 'Christ must be God, not because he has himself said this, but because otherwise Christianity becomes meaningless, when it demands that we shall learn of Christ. That which is demanded is meaningless, because it conflicts with the Socratic principle that the one man cannot teach the other anything. In other words: the decisive Christian determination is developed in connection with the Socratic; and it is Christianity which has to order itself in accord with the Socratic, not vice versa.' Quoted in Kabell, *Kierkegaardstudiet i Norden* (Copenhagen: H. Hagerup, 1948), pp. 219f.

[145] Henriksen, *Methods and Results of Kierkegaard Studies in Scandinavia* (Copenhagen: Munksgaard, 1951), p. 145.

For Bohlin that way lies disaster: '*But this involves, that however strongly Kierkegaard has asserted Christianity's irrational character against the intellectualism in Hegel's view of religion, yet irrationalism with him encompasses a marked intellectualistic element.* And this is the reason why not even Kierkegaard, in spite of his strong emphasis on the historical revelation, could avoid spiritualizing that revelation, certainly not like Hegel to a general Christ-principle, but to a paradox, in which man knows himself to be absolutely separated from God.'[146]

Drachmann and Bohlin have often been repudiated, but it is not clear that they have been decisively answered. Nor do we attempt to silence their charges in this work. We have said that Bohlin's work seems to over-simplify matters and that his analysis of Kierkegaard's christology fails to recognize the theological sources and significance of the God-man strand.[147] Yet Part Three will show that Kierkegaard does at times employ metaphysical notions which link him with idealism. And that use does bear its fruit, though the judgment of value ought not be too quickly added. But we wish to emphasize that it is in large part the diastatic rhythm which supports this process of appropriation. It is the momentum gained in the violent severance of God and man that threatens such Christian themes as the resurrection and the church.[148] The demonstration of this claim must fall to Part Three. We are, of course, not speaking here of a

[146] Bohlin, op. cit., pp. 435-6, [italics his]. Climacus invites reflection on the possibility of such distortion by conceding that his project of thought involves 'an accommodation to a less exact usage'. Yet the distortion is not so great as to be self-defeating to the project. Thus in *CUP*'s 'first and last declaration' Kierkegaard says that 'my name as editor was promptly placed on the title page of the *Fragments* (1844), because the absolute importance of the subject in reality required the expression of dutiful observance, that there should be named a responsible person to accept what reality might propose', *S.V.* VII, p. 546 (*CUP*, p. 552). On the possibility of distortion in *PF*, see above, p. 30, note 83.

[147] See above, pp. 41-42. This appears to be the sort of line taken by N. Thulstrup in his introduction to *PF*, xli-xliv. He severs Kierkegaard from Platonism by underlining Kierkegaard's role as a confessor of the Christian witness that truth is a person and not a viewpoint to be compared with other viewpoints. Such a response to Drachmann *et alia* recognizes what we have referred to as the relative independence of christology as a separate force in Kierkegaard's thought. Yet we should have to add that in the explication and even in the statement of this witness Kierkegaard does offer a body of thought which can be compared with Platonism. An acknowledgement of this qualification still leaves open the question as to whether Kierkegaard appropriated Platonic categories in that process of statement and explication.

[148] On the resurrection see Hermann Diem, *Kierkegaard's Dialectic of Existence*, trans. W. Knight (Edinburgh: Oliver & Boyd, 1959), p. 191; on the church see Anna Paulsen *Sören Kierkegaard* (Hamburg: Friedrich Wittig, 1955), pp. 111, 257, 435 for a critique of the absolute subjectivity of faith in Kierkegaard's view. Both writers blame the influence of idealism.

comradeship of intention with idealism. It is rather shown to be the case that if one wishes to combat Hegel one does so more effectively by discriminate criticism than by seeking a complete reversal. The diastatic quest for such a reversal strangely seems less to break out of the Hegelian circle than to carry one through its course and leave one somewhere near the master once again.

It has been argued that the resources for Kierkegaard's attack on Hegel were quite consciously drawn from other quarters in the spacious expanse of idealism. E. Brunner has tried to link the Kierke-gaardian movement to Religion B with the Kantian recognition of the limits of reason. His argument moves rather quickly from the limitation of reason through the practical question of the value of reason to ethical ground and on again to the crowning theme of radical evil.[149] We frankly boggle over the identification of epistemological limitation in the knowledge of the real with ethical violation in the performance of the ideal. It is no doubt possible to find something which characterizes both Kant's noumenal world and Kierkegaard's God, but one wonders if the commonality is sufficient to support Brunner's argument. If one has managed to convince oneself that this unified development can be found in Kant, one will finally have to regard the optimistic strand in Kant as betrayal of the logic which should have led him to the extrarational solution, the 'God in time'. Furthermore, Part Three will show that quite apart from Religion B, significant differences exist—notably in the area of ethics.

We are wholly convinced that an understanding of the nature and possible origin of these differences is not to be won by proposing still another philosophical source—idealistic or otherwise.[150] They refer us rather to the distinction between philosophy and theology, for they involve the knowledge of God (and so of the world) which the theologian believes he possesses. Of course one might say—putting it very badly—that Kierkegaard was not only interested in God, but also in man. There are *two* poles within his thought. Here one may

---

[149] Emil Brunner, 'Das Grundproblem der Philosophie bei Kant und Kierke-gaard', *Zwischen den Zeiten*, 1924, pp. 31–47.

[150] I. H. Fichte is perhaps most often mentioned. Fahrenbach, op. cit., p. 67, can call him 'Kierkegaard's real idealistic partner'. Cf. Collins. op. cit., p. 109 and Hirsch, op. cit., II, p. 508. From 1837–9 Kierkegaard had read Fichte's *Zeitschrift für Philosophie und spekulative Theologie*, and does have praise for Fichte, *Pap.* II A 31, 204. However, one comes away feeling that once again the two thinkers share an aversion to Hegel, but not the positive basis for the aversion. Even Hirsch, who is generally quite impressed with the positive side of Kierkegaard's relationship to idealism, cannot find in Fichte anything which parallels the sin-grace structure in Kierkegaard (Hirsch, op cit., II pp. 527–9).

believe it possible to discern the idealistic trail again. For one can note Kierkegaard's discourse about the union of the finite and the infinite in man, and then propose that this student of subjectivity in quest of unity is an idealist after all. Indeed he is more specifically a modern one, because his thought is not theocentric, but humanistic.[151] One may, of course, define idealism as one wishes, but Spinoza's observation that all description is by negation would seem to still hold true even in our advanced age. It is doubtful whether drawing the idealistic circle so large says anything of significance about its occupants. Indeed significant differences tend to be blurred by such a procedure. We are convinced that the differences are not to be located by noting that Kierkegaard had an additional interest in God. We have already stated the principle of the interdependence of the poles of God and man in his thought and Part Three will demonstrate this interdependence in detail. The self has its reality from the hand of God and its free choice of itself is a willed acceptance, not an unlimited creation of self.[152]

We lack sufficient justification to carry further the effort to uncover likely sources for, or even to illumine the defining matrix of, the theological dimension of Kierkegaard's advance beyond Socrates—particularly if our concern is with the strand of synthesis within that dimension. The most dramatic instances of Kierkegaard's consciously taking a position towards the theological resources available to him fall nearer the diastatic tradition.[153] Kierkegaard's relationship to Luther has understandably been a topic of great interest.[154] No interpretative consensus concerning the relationship is at hand, however, as might be expected, given the combination of praise and censure Luther receives in Kierkegaard's writings. The fundamental

151 The proposal in this form comes from Wilhelm Anz. See his *Kierkegaard und der deutsche Idealismus* (Tübingen: J. C. B. Mohr, 1956), and his 'Philosophie und Glaube bei Sören Kierkegaard', *Zeitschrift für Theologie und Kirche*, 1954, pp. 50–105. For a detailed critique see N. Thulstrup, 'Kierkegaard og den filosofiske Idealisme', *Kierkegaardiana*, 1962, pp. 88–105.

152 See above pp. 80–81, note 134 and Fahrenbach, op. cit., pp. 60–61.

153 See, for example, M. M. Thulstrup's study of the possibility of influence from the early church on the world-denying turn in the late thought of Kierkegaard, 'Sören Kierkegaards martyrbegreb', *Dansk Teologisk Tidskrift*, 1964, pp. 100–14. In his personal library Kierkegaard had access to Ignatius of Antioch, Clement of Rome, Justin Martyr, Polycarp, and Tertullian as well as to Hefele's *Patrum apostolicorum opera* and F. Böhringer's *Die Kirche Christi und ihre Zeugen*. See *Katalog over Sören Kierkegaards Bibliotek*, ed. N. Thulstrup (Copenhagen: Munksgaard, 1957), pp. 32f.

154 See Diem, op. cit., pp. 159ff., and Lönning, op. cit., *passim*. See also Jaroslav Pelikan, *From Luther to Kierkegaard* (St Louis: Concordia Publishing House, 1950), pp. 117–8.

role of the divine-human polarity in the thought of both men underlies more specific points of commonality—as in the understanding of
faith.[155] Possibly the degree of commonality may have been obscured
because different situations required very different expressions of
convictions held in common by these two great spirits.[156] Yet the
element of contrast in the situations can be overstated. In a sense
the distinctive stress of this study on the synthesis strand in Kierkegaard's thought constitutes an effort to correct such overstatement. As
such it may parallel the tendency of recent Luther scholarship not
only to affirm Luther's reliance upon an existing Christian order,
but also to accentuate the essential catholicity of his thought.[157] It
appears probable, nonetheless, that Kierkegaard's exposure to
Luther—as distinguished from Lutheran dogmatics—was both late
and sketchy, so that in describing this relationship we at best are
identifying parallels, rather than tracing indebtedness.[158]

Perhaps the relative paucity of the material suggesting dramatic
sources for the synthesis rhythm is related to the very character of
that rhythm. In Part Four we shall investigate the suggestion that
while the diastatic impulse is surely the more dramatic of the two
which concern us, it is essentially parasitic. Yet the full-bodied
presence of the synthesis strand in Kierkegaard's thought is noteworthy, given the natural appeal the diastatic rhythm would possess
for anyone seeing the perils of the age through Kierkegaard's eyes.
That presence would seem to suggest that we are dealing in this
strand with something of great intrinsic importance to Kierkegaard.
That suggestion should also remind us that we do wrong if we sort
out mechanically a number of apparent relationships and then offer
an educated guess as to the probable process of assembly. The
freedom of the thinker is very evident in Kierkegaard's case. That

---

[155] As an illustration, see *Pap.* VIII A 465: 'the truth for thee' is Luther's
category—and clearly Kierkegaard intends to make it his as well.

[156] See Johannes Slök, 'Kierkegaard and Luther', trans. A. Rousing, *A Kierkegaard Critique*, ed. H. Johnson and N. Thulstrup, pp. 85–102. Slök suggests that
while Luther and Kierkegaard agree that an inner determination is necessary to
determine the character of man and so of his work, Luther can appeal to the
existing order to give structure for the expression of this inwardness, and Kierkegaard cannot.

[157] As an example of this tendency see Jaroslav Pelikan, *Obedient Rebels, Catholic
Substance and Protestant Principle in Luther's Reformation* (New York and Evanston:
Harper; London: SCM Press, 1964).

[158] See N. Thulstrup, 'Theological and Philosophical Kierkegaardian Studies
in Scandinavia, 1945–1953', trans. Paul L. Holmer, *Theology Today*, 1955, pp.
310–1, and Thomas, op. cit., p. 48. It is generally agreed that Kierkegaard knew
principally the sermons of Luther.

holds true as well of his apparent appropriation of the diastatic resources, as we have seen.[159] The mention of the reality of the individual who with relative freedom develops within a matrix introduces another element of that matrix. We refer to Kierkegaard's personal history, and it is to that which we must devote the final pages of this chapter.

4. *The Crucible of the Self and its History*

We have already spoken in Part One of the degree to which a biographical-psychological study of Kierkegaard may be helpful in understanding his works.[160] It was clear there that our convictions in this matter leave us well behind some of the more ardent practitioners of this art. Of course Kierkegaard's prediction that his life would be much studied may be taken to suggest the subject's willing submission to this discipline.[161] Yet it seems excessive to claim that 'because his works are so largely autobiographical, no interpretation of them can be intelligible which is not essentially biographical'.[162] Perhaps such a statement seems too strong particularly because it may seem to imply that the life behind the thought essentially refuses admission to the systematic impulse. We are convinced that is not the case. Indeed the only claim to uniqueness which these closing pages of Part Two can make is that the discussion of the biographical dimension to the formation of Kierkegaard's thought is undertaken with immediate and persistent reference to the systematic structure of that thought. The reader will judge whether we are right in our confidence that the reference is not arbitrary.

We have seen that it is the diastatic rhythm which stands out the more dramatically when one views Kierkegaard in relation to the intellectual matrix of his thought. The diastatic impulse commands the observer's immediate attention both in Kierkegaard's appropriation of materials available to him and in his repudiation of other such materials. The student of Kierkegaard's biography is likely to come away with a similar first impression. We may delay asking why this is so and whether this impression is a trustworthy guide until we have addressed the material itself.

To speak first of Kierkegaard's father is not simply to submit our

---

[159] See above p. 81, note 137 and pp. 76–77, note 125.
[160] See above, pp. 14–17.
[161] Indeed he wrote, *Pap.* VIII A 424: 'Some day not only my writings, but especially my life . . . will be studied and studied.'
[162] Lowrie, op. cit., ix.

discussion to chronological order, since this figure remains central for Kierkegaard through his entire life. In this figure the analogy to and momentum towards the diastatic tendency in Kierkegaard's thought is most impressive. Michael Pedersen Kierkegaard was nourished by the spiritual resources available to a lonely youth on the bleak Jutland heath. Höffding may seem ludicrous in his attempt to interpret Kierkegaard's thought by tracing the influence of the melancholy he finds to be characteristic of the people of west Jutland.[163] We shall see in Part Three that at times Kierkegaard himself seems to grant nature no role whatever in the shaping of the self. Yet he could write in quite another spirit: 'The heath must be singularly well qualified for the production of strong spirits. Here all lies naked and exposed before God, and there is no place for the many distractions, the many nooks and corners where consciousness can hide itself and from which it is often difficult for serious persons to recapture their dispersed thoughts. Here consciousness must be shut up within itself tightly and decisively. "Whither can I flee from thy presence?" can truthfully be said here on the heath.'[164] At least the hard life on the heath provided ample occasion for a sensitive child to utter a curse against this earth's maker. The influence here may, of course, be more subtle than one at first supposes, for the bitterness of life on the heath makes probable not only the act of cursing God, but also the interpretation of it.[165] In any case the God M. P. Kierkegaard claimed to know represented no silky release from the rigours of life in that barren place, but rather a reaffirmation of them. This was a God who imparts sense to theological talk of aseity and transcendence. More than that—the divine sovereignty finds its sounding board in human sin. This God means judgment rather than fulfilment to man's

[163] Höffding, *Sören Kierkegaard som Filosof* (Copenhagen: Philipsen, 1892). For a critical discussion of Höffding's work, see Henriksen, op. cit., pp. 30–39.

[164] *Pap.* III A 78 (*Dru* 338).

[165] Kierkegaard himself wrote of the boy who cursed God—'and the man was not able to forget this when he was 82 years old', *Pap.* VII A 5 (*Dru* 556). According to Barfod, the first editor of the *Papirer*, the elder brother Peter as an old man offered the following elaboration: 'But the memory of this curse in his childhood never left the boy, the man, the patriarch—and seeing that God's grace from that very moment showered temporal blessings upon him, so that instead of tasting the divine wrath he was overwhelmed with riches, marvellously gifted children, universal esteem—then solemn anxiousness and dread gripped his soul most deeply. God *did* exist, and *he* had cursed this God—was not this the sin against the Holy Ghost which never can be forgiven? It was for this reason the old man's soul continued in anxious dread, for this reason he beheld his children condemned to the "silent despair", for this reason he laid upon their shoulders in tender years the sternest requirements of Christianity—for this reason he was a prey to temptation and in constant conflict of soul.' Quoted in Lowrie, op. cit., pp. 21–22 [italics his].

ambition. One must say that it was to the melancholy service of this austere faith, rather than to some countering counsel, that the father's impressive dialectical skill and power of imagination were bent.[166]

There seems little reason to doubt that this ominous legacy reached Sören Kierkegaard.[167] Of the multitude of Kierkegaard's testimonies to his melancholy a single passage may be cited: 'An old man, who himself was prodigiously melancholy (just how, I will not record), has a son of his old age, upon whom all this melancholy falls as an inheritance—but who at the same time possesses sufficient elasticity of spirit to be able to hide this, while at the same time, and precisely because his spirit is essentially and eminently sound, his melancholy cannot acquire a mastery over him, though the spirit is completely unable to cast it off, can at the most succeed in bearing it.'[168] It seems unlikely that all such passages reflect merely the dark coloration of Kierkegaard's retrospection in the final bitter period of his authorship. That suggestion would be more impressive if one did not find in the negations of that final period much which possesses continuity with Kierkegaard's earlier thought. In all probability this childhood was an uncommonly dark one. Yet we may well be sceptical of the effort to find the direct cause for the sombre material in Kierkegaard's thought in this personal melancholy.[169] The course of the human spirit's ponderings is not traced so easily, for one could as well suppose that Kierkegaard's melancholy would lead to his embracing some form of the cheerful religious escapism which would not have been

---

[166] See *Pap.* IV B 1, p. 111. (*DO*, p. 110) for a highly autobiographical description of the melancholy of 'Johannes Climacus'' father: 'That the father, humanly speaking, was something out of the ordinary was the last thing he would learn in the paternal house. Once in a while, when an old and tried friend visited the family and entered into a confidential conversation with the father, Johannes would hear him say, "I am good for nothing, cannot accomplish anything, my one wish would be to find a place in a charitable institution". That was not a jest, there was no trace of irony in the father's word, on the contrary there was a gloomy seriousness in it which alarmed Johannes. That was by no means an observation carelessly uttered, for the father was capable of proving that the most significant man in the world was a genius compared with him.'

[167] On Kierkegaard's youth see V. Amundsen, *Sören Kierkegaards Ungdomsliv* (Copenhagen: Gyldendal, 1912), and Sejer Kühle, *Sören Kierkegaards Barndom og Ungdom* (Copenhagen: Aschehoug, 1950).

[168] *Pap.* VII 1 A 126. Cf. *Pap.* V A 33 (*Dru* 483), VIII A 126, and *S.V.* XIII, pp. 564ff. (*PV*, pp. 75ff.).

[169] Siegfried Hansen, 'Die Bedeutung des Leidens für das Christus bild Sören Kierkegaards', *Kerygma und Dogma* 1956, pp. 1–28, finds Kierkegaard trying to justify his suffering by an appeal to the New Testament which actually distorts the biblical witness. Hansen places the blame with Kierkegaard's melancholy. Cf. Lowrie, op. cit., p. 538. We have seen above, p. 30, note 86, that Lowrie finds the explanation for Kierkegaard's use of pseudonymity in his introversion.

far from him to seek. At the very least this 'explanation' of the darker side of his thought must be supplemented by taking notice of the fact that this boy was not left to find a faith which would fit his emotional predilection. And the faith he was taught was that stark religion of the father with precious little accommodation to the supposed tenderness of a child's mind.[170] Again passages abound and they cluster around a single theme:

It was related to me when I was only a small child, and as solemnly as possible, that the mass spat upon Christ, who yet was the truth, that the *crowd* ('they that passed by') spat upon him and said, 'Hold thy peace'. This I have treasured deep in my heart (for though there have been moments, yea, hours, when that has been for me as if forgotten, yet have I constantly returned to this my first thought), and so, the better to treasure this under the most opposite outward appearance, I have hidden it in the deepest recesses of my soul; for I was fearful lest it might early escape me, lest it might trick me and become like a blank cartridge. This thought . . . is my life, . . . and though I were to forget everything, yet would I not forget, just as I up to now have not forgotten for a moment, that they told this to me when I was a child, and the impression it made upon the child.[171]

It should be remembered, too, that depravity was not something merely to be ascribed to 'them', for Kierkegaard lived out his days under a compulsion to do penance for sins which were most personal and even secret in character.[172]

Thus do the elements assemble to form a pattern which fits the diastatic design very readily. That pattern can be traced with equal persuasiveness in Kierkegaard's relationship to the other central

[170] It is of interest here to interrelate Kierkegaard's biography and his comments on 'childish Christianity'. On the one hand Climacus criticizes parents who take the path of accommodation: '. . . they would lead the *innocent* child to God or Christ. But is that Christianity, where the point after all is precisely that it is a sinner who has recourse to the paradox?' *S.V.* VII, p. 515 (*CUP*, p. 524). [Italics his.] But he adds later: 'If, on the other hand a child is not permitted, as it ought to be, innocently to play with the holiest of things, if the existing child is forced violently into decisive Christian determinations, such a child will suffer much. Such an upbringing will either plunge the child into despondency and dread, or provoke lust or the dread of lust.' (ibid., p. 523 [ibid., p. 532].) Cf. *S.V.* XIII, p. 564 (*PV*, p. 76): 'As a child I was strictly and seriously brought up in Christianity, humanly speaking, brought up in a crazy way.' Climacus' conclusion is not surprising: 'The age of childhood (directly understood) is therefore not the true age for becoming a Christian.' *S.V.* VII, p. 523 (*CUP*, p. 531).

[171] *Pap.* X 1 A 272. See above, p. 14, note 23, and *S.V.* XIII, pp. 565ff. (*PV* pp. 77ff.). Cf. also *S.V.* XI, pp. 59–61 ('HM' in *PA*, pp. 81–85).

[172] See V. Christensen, *Sören Kierkegaard, Det Centrale i hans Livsyn* (Copenhagen: G. E. C. Gads, 1963), who notes the presence of the penance motif as early as 1839 (*Pap.* II A 250). On the brothel experience see P. A. Heiberg, op. cit., and Heiberg's *Et Segment af Sören Kierkegaards religiöse Udvikling* (Copenhagen and Christiania: Gyldendal, 1918). Cf. also Lowrie, op. cit., pp. 134–6.

figure in his life. It is in fact the very elements which we have identified which seem to show their power in the breaking off of the engagement to Regine. In some respects this relationship is shrouded to an unusual degree in mystery. One may feel that mystery is deepened rather than dispelled by Kierkegaard's reflections on this theme, since no unified interpretation makes its way through his remarks. Yet some things are reasonably clear and they fit the diastatic pattern we have been tracing. Kierkegaard's conviction that his melancholy and guilt blocked the way to Regine[173] itself reflects a diastatic disbelief that such matters can be brought befoŗe the other or surmounted by God.[174] So, too, it is the mark of the penitential life in the service of God that it separates the self from that one to whom it stands most intimately related.

This dominance of material suggestive of the diastatic tendency in Kierkegaard's thought shows itself to be less solid under closer scrutiny. In the study of Kierkegaard's life, as in the study of Kierkegaard's thought, the viewer's immediate enthralment with the diastatic gives way to the acknowledgement of the strong presence of synthesis. A broken engagement still speaks of a deeply significant human relationship—and in Kierkegaard's case of a relationship which was very far from being a closed matter. Even in the pain of withdrawal the self witnesses to the essential worth of that which it denies itself: 'My sin was that I did not have faith, faith to believe that with God all things are possible. . . .'[175] To take leave of the beloved in such a mood and to seek to do so in such a way as to protect and shelter her is a very different thing from a righteous repudiation of human association.[176]

173 *Pap.* IV A 107 (*Dru* 444): 'But had I explained myself, I must have initiated her into terrible things, my relationship to my father, his melancholy, the dreadful night which broods in the inmost depths, my wildness, lusts and excesses, which yet perhaps were not so heinous in the sight of God.' In a clearer reference to the sense of guilt Kierkegaard speaks of enduring the separation as 'bearing what I regard as God's punishment upon me'. *Pap.* III A 159 (*Dru* 377).

174 Hirsch, op. cit., I, p. 93, particularly argues that it was not Kierkegaard's guilt, but his inability to reveal that guilt to Regine which led to the break. This point gains in credibility when one notes Kierkegaard's contention that marriage is impossible without reponsibility. *E-O*, II; *Pap.* III B 39.

175 *Pap.* III A 166 (*Dru* 383). Cf. *CD*'s emphasis on the good of disclosure—the breaking up of the shut-in-ness ('*Indesluttethed*', German: *Verschlossenheit*) of the demoniacal (*S.V.* IV, pp. 386ff. [*CD*, pp. 105ff.]). We discuss this theme in the next chapter.

176 Cf. *Pap.* X 5 A 149: 'To get out of the situation as a scoundrel, a scoundrel of the first water if possible, was the only thing there was to be done in order to work her loose and get her under way for a marriage. . . .' One can also witness to the presence of the synthesis strand by noting that Kierkegaard's renunciation

Kierkegaard's relationship to his father also carries material within it which is suggestive of the synthesis strand in his thought. A persuasive case can be made for the suggestion that a revelatory act of confession on the part of the old man so healed the breach between him and his son that the son could follow the course marked out in *E-O*: 'He repents himself back into himself, back into the family, back into the race, until he finds himself in God.'[177] At this point Kierkegaard's own life provides a parable which challenges the diastatic argument that a self's relationship to God can be isolated from its relationship with its fellow men. With his extraordinary degree of self-awareness Kierkegaard could speak of this: 'I learned from him what father-love is, and thereby I got a conception of the divine father-love, the one unshakable thing in life, the true Archimedian point.'[178]

The rhythm of synthesis in Kierkegaard's thought thus finds a more congenial setting in his life than one supposes to be the case after a first reading. Yet Kierkegaard's own reflections about his life seem to take a turn in the direction of the diastatic tradition late in his life. Thus the note that the severance of the relationship to Regine is required in the service of God more than maintains itself over against the reading of this separation as an act of weakness. That service is no longer seen to be of an exceptional penitential sort, but becomes normative for all Christians. We have discussed briefly the shift in the final stage of Kierkegaard's authorship[179] and Part Three will clothe materially our contention that this stage by no means reveals a total triumph of the diastatic tendency. Yet that tendency surely seems to be ascendent in the last stage of Kierkegaard's thought and his readers have understandably been in quest of biographical material which might at least have served as stimulus or occasion.

The best candidate surely seems to be the Corsair incident of 1845-6. We have Kierkegaard's comment from 1847: 'It is an instance of God's grace to a man when precisely in the experience of

---

was incomplete. The early pseudonymous writings are all concerned with the possibility of being reunited with Regine, but express that concern in pseudonymous form to avoid a public discussion of the matter. On this point, see Bejerholm, op. cit., pp. 281-2.

[177] *S.V.* II, p. 194 (*E-O* II, pp. 180-1). Lowrie suggests that the revelation of the father's failings brought the strictures of his upbringing into focus for Kierkegaard. See Lowrie, op. cit., pp. 180-3 and Hirsch, op. cit., I, pp. 46ff.

[178] *Pap.* III A 73 (*Dru* 335). Jörgen Bukdahl, *Sören Kierkegaard og den menige mand* (Copenhagen: Munksgaard, 1961) would add that from his father Kierkegaard learned an appreciation for the common man.

[179] See above, pp. 33-35, 39-42.

adversities he shows that he is so fortunately constituted that like a rare musical instrument, the strings not only remain intact through every new adversity but he acquires in addition a new string on the string-board.'[180] The specific character of the change noted also seems made to order: 'They have treated me scurvily, disgustingly, a national crime has been committed against me, a treachery by the contemporary generation. But for me it has been profitable, indescribably. For I was melancholy, infinitely melancholy—this is where I have been helped. For in my melancholy I still loved the world—now I am weaned from it.'[181] More particularly it seems that the affair left Kierkegaard with severe distrust, bordering on hatred, for men gathered in a group—and for the group's representative, the press.[182] Thus the individual as the object of Kierkegaard's concern becomes so very nearly the isolated subject set over against and apart from God and society in the diastatic mode. Kierkegaard's personal reaction and the accompanying shift in his thought would seem inexplicable, were it not for the preparation one finds for them in his earlier life and thought and for the restraining counterforces which hedge them in to the very end.

This shadow which is cast over the final stage of Kierkegaard's life deepens in the bitter conflict with the church. One may feel that we here trace the consequences of the self's development rather than discern the causes of that development. One easily gets the impression that the initiative is Kierkegaard's in so disturbingly a complete sense that the attack borders on fantasy at times. Yet it must be recalled that Kierkegaard had long known the church he now attacked. Throughout many years the tide of his unrest built up to the final onslaught.[183] In order to be understood the onslaught, then, calls for a context wider than itself. The struggle with the church was clearly not a matter of personalities. Kierkegaard had warm feelings

---

[180] *Pap.* VIII A 128 (*Dru* 664); cf. *Pap.* X 1 A 138, X 2 A 251.

[181] *Pap.* VIII A 515 (*Dru* 726).

[182] See *Pap.* VII A 107 (*Dru* 593), X 1 A 131, 135 (*Dru* 886). In the last passage Kierkegaard laments the fact that the simple classes did not stand with him in the Corsair affair. He is not uncertain as to where to place the blame: 'God knows that I am not bloodthirsty and I think I have in a terrible degree a sense of my responsibility to God; but nevertheless, I should be ready to take the responsibility upon me, in God's name, of giving the order to fire if I could first of all make absolutely and conscientiously sure that there was not a single man standing in front of the rifles, not a single creature, who was not—a journalist. That is said of the class as a whole.' See above, pp. 33–35 on anonymous writing, and Swenson's 'A Danish Thinker's Estimate of Journalism', op. cit., pp. 186–207.

[183] G. Malantschuk's 'Sören Kierkegaards Angreb paa Kirken' in *Kamp mod Kirken* is particularly helpful in tracing this development.

for Mynster and deliberately delayed his attack until Martensen's succession to Mynster's bishopric was secure. It was a struggle of principle. We have in this part of our work suggested briefly the character of the thought which drew Kierkegaard's fire. That thought —surely as exemplified in Mynster[184]—does not seem to require a total negation of Kierkegaard. Whether the negation is total can only be determined by looking to the body of thought from which the attack issued. From such an investigation we may also expect an answer to the question whether the battle with the church radically departs from whatever structure is discernible in the earlier authorship. We have attempted in Part One to identify, at least formally, basic structural tendencies in Kierkegaard's thought and in Part Two have found the categories of diastasis and synthesis helpful in understanding Kierkegaard's matrix in life and thought. We must now see whether the rich tissue of the thought formed in this matrix can be persuasively fitted on the skeleton without violence to its very life.

[184] To Kierkegaard Mynster 'expresses the purely human ideal in a more masterly way than I have ever beheld it', *Pap.* IX A 240. Beyond that in Mynster Kierkegaard sought—and to some extent found—an ally against the threat of Hegelianism—see above, p. 18, note 33.)

PART THREE

THE THOUGHT OF KIERKEGAARD AS A SYSTEMATIC THINKER

III

THE DISCLOSURE OF THE RHYTHMS
OF REFLECTION IN KIERKEGAARD'S
DESCRIPTION OF GOD AND MAN

KIERKEGAARD'S DISCOURSE on God and man encompasses significant strain within itself. One may, of course, bear witness to a unity of intention and urge that attentiveness to that unity should inform the exegete in all his work. Yet some respect must be shown for the evident meaning of particular units of material, especially since it is not clear that the unifying intention is available to us or even that it was actual for Kierkegaard.[1] The individual units of material do not combine to yield an elegant structure with ease and without remainder. Yet there is structure in this discourse. Much of the strain with the discourse derives from Kierkegaard's commitment to convictions which impart rhythms to his reflection of such a sort that the unity of his thought is threatened. This threat is the more explicit because Kierkegaard consistently senses so keenly and expresses so directly the implications of particular convictions for wider theological reflection. Thus Kierkegaard's systematic bent itself plays a major role in the preparation of the feast of frustration which awaits at least a certain sort of systematician who turns to Kierkegaard.

That systematic bent is not only shown by the fact that Kierkegaard offers consistent developments of thought within such strands as we have called diastasis and synthesis. He is not content to let these rhythms lie alongside of each other in his thought. Moreover, he shows himself to be fully aware of the tendency by which each rhythm would be driven by the other to ever more extreme positions. His thought illustrates a third way of relating the rhythms. It is this third alternative that we try to suggest by the use of the unshapely word 'interpenetration' in the subtitles of several subsequent sections of this work. If one pattern of reflection cannot win from Kierkegaard

---

[1] On the possibility of a unity of intention or any other unity in Kierkegaard's works, see above, pp. 28–43.

a repudiation of the claims of the other, it will not ignore those claims but seek to take them within itself, even though the categories and language involved may be alien ones. This process characterizes a very great deal of Kierkegaard's thought and need not be described only formally. Furthermore, the process is so complex that our description of it must strike the reader as at best a kind of artificial mathematical puzzle, until we follow the course of the interpenetration as it is embodied in the rich tissue of Kierkegaard's actual words. The reader may still judge our claims no more favourably, but we cannot ask him to wait longer for the presentation of the evidence.

1. Diastasis *in the Description of God and Man*

Kierkegaard's authorship is a celebration of God's glory. His works may do other things from time to time, but they always sing in praise of the Most High. Yet this doxological strain finds strikingly different forms of expression. Indeed the differences are so great that it is a very real question whether the unity of the one praised can maintain itself. That question will not be lost from view if we begin our analysis of Kierkegaard's discourse regarding God by turning our attention to a central theme in the doxological current: the independence of God. God is not in need of an other in order to understand himself: 'There is only One who wholly knows himself, who in and for himself knows what he himself is, that is God; . . . who is in and for himself.'[2] Indeed we should not assume that there is some independently existing other whom God must either need or not need, for in the portion omitted from the passage just quoted Kierkegaard says of God: 'He also knows what every man in himself is, for that he is is precisely one with being before God. The man who is not before God is not himself either, for that one can be only by being in the One who is in and for himself.'[3] The proposition stating man's dependence cannot be converted. Kierkegaard will not compromise God's independence by confining him within the limits of the subject-object distinction: 'God is pure subjectivity, perfect, pure subjectivity. He has no objective being whatever in him; for everything that has such objective being comes thereby into the realm of relativities.'[4]

[2] *S.V.* X, p. 45 (*CDi*, p. 43).
[3] ibid.
[4] *Pap.* XI 2 A 54. It is clear that one cannot take Kierkegaard to be identifying some element which can be objectified in neither man nor God. Efforts have been made to read such a passage as an exaltation of the 'I-Thou' relation. That misses the point, for neither Kierkegaard not Buber claims that man is pure subjectivity.

These witnesses to the independence of God carry us to the charge that Kierkegaard's discourse at this point is hopelessly entangled with metaphysical categories which defy rather than serve his intention. We have noted the classical statement of this criticism by Torsten Bohlin.[5] Malcolm Diamond revises the charge slightly and grants it more current theological language, but he remains every bit as willing as Bohlin to judge Kierkegaard unfavourably:

> The technical difficulties that Kierkegaard discovered in traditional apologetics were rooted in his assurance that thinking is limited by a radical dichotomy. In opposition to the Hegelians, he was convinced that all talk of God apart from Christ could only be carried on in timeless categories; and the ones he used were more appropriate to geometrical discourse than to the living God of the Bible. Many of the tensions that we find in his thought derive from his violent contrast of the divine, represented by such terms as infinity-necessity-eternity, with the finitude-possibility-temporality that characterize human existence. Kierkegaard insisted that the divine and the human realms could never be joined in rational terms and he rejected traditional apologetics for moving illegitimately in one of two directions; either it introduced change into the Divine which by its nature is changeless, or it sought to crown the temporal order with the mantle of eternity. Because of his use of static metaphysical categories in describing God, the God of Kierkegaard's philosophical reflections was more like Aristotle's Unmoved Mover than like the God of the Bible.[6]

There is no gainsaying the fact that the analysis involved in such a statement does find supporting material in Kierkegaard's authorship The diastatic disengagement of God and man appeals particularly to a distinction between the temporal and the eternal. While contingency characterizes the temporal,[7] which is 'precisely the different, the manifold',[8] change is to be denied God,[9] for one is 'fully and absolutely right in asserting that seen eternally, . . . there is no either-or'.[10] As generalization held to be descriptive of whole spheres of reality, these statements would seem to be better classified as metaphysical than as religious. The diastatic impulse appears intent on saying that no single set of metaphysical principles applies to both God and man. One may prefer to say that the metaphysical quest for universally descriptive generalizations is frustrated by the diastatic current. Yet

---

[5] See above, pp. 83–84, notes 145–6.

[6] Malcolm L. Diamond, 'Kierkegaard and Apologetics', *The Journal of Religion*, April, 1964, p. 123.

[7] See, for example, *S.V.* IV, pp. 281–4 (CD, pp. 9–12).

[8] *S.V.* IX, p. 81 (*WL*, p. 67).

[9] *S.V.* X, pp. 55–56 (*CDi*, pp. 54–55).

[10] *S.V.* VII, p. 261 (*CUP*, p. 270). Cf. *S.V.* IV, p. 32n (*PF*, p. 32n) for the distinction between factual and ideal being. Underlying all these differences is the final change which faces all men—death; see *S.V.* VII, pp. 137–47 (*CUP*, pp. 147–58).

one must say that at least the psychological effect the severance seeks to produce is heightened by an explicit retention of the premises of universality.[11] But the *telos* for the use of these categories clearly seems to lie in the severance. Thus even when Kierkegaard's discourse would seem to bring God and man together by speaking of their relationship—as in the doctrine of creation—these distinctions cause the note of metaphysical contrast to be heard: 'God does not think, he creates; God does not exist (*existerer*), he is eternal. Man thinks and exists (*existerer*), and existence (*Existents*) separates thought and being, holding them apart from each other in succession.'[12]

We shall not seek to excise this type of material from Kierkegaard's thought. But we are concerned to point out that it is wrong to find in this material the major theme of Kierkegaard's discourse on God and man. There are two reasons why it is wrong to do so, and they involve

[11] In any case we encounter here a forthright rejection of Whitehead's principle that one's God must be the exemplification of, rather than the exception to, one's metaphysical principles. See A. N. Whitehead, *Religion in the Making* (New York: Macmillan, 1926), pp. 70–71. Indeed the rejection obtains materially, for it is precisely the 'processive' character of reality which Kierkegaard denies to God. All things are present to God (*Pap.* X 1 A 362), and 'it is the perfection of the eternal not to have history, and it alone is present (*er til*) and yet has absolutely no history'. (*S.V.* IV, p. 239 [*PF*, p. 62].) See also the passage quoted next in the text. On Kierkegaard's use of Danish terms to denote the 'existence' of God, see Reidar Thomte, 'New Reflections on the Great Dane', *Discourse*, 1963, pp. 144–55. Thomte makes a good case for his argument that a strong pattern of references attributes 'existence' to God in the broad sense of 'Tilvaerelse' (*at vaere til*) (German: *Dasein*). He notes that this term 'is used of the existence of God, of the whole perceptual world, of man, as well as of the circumstances in which he is placed'. According to this same pattern of usage, *Existents* is used in connection with the particular individual's existence with the association of striving and becoming. 'Existence' in this sense is denied God, reflecting the turn of the diastatic rhythm to which we are pointing. It is, however, attributed to the Christ, (See *S.V.* IV, p. 213 [*PF*, p. 36]), so both measuring the paradox of the co-existence of the divine and the human and marking the advance beyond co-existence to which we refer below in chapters five and six. Professor Thomte further observes that 'the term "Tilblivelse" is a real problem because it is used of transitions in nature, in history, in "Dasein", as well as of the transitions in "existence". . . . What is needed is a term that is as neutral as possible, in the sense that the term does not in itself denote that into which the transition takes place.' Thomte favours Swenson's 'coming into being' over Hong's 'coming into existence'. It is unfortunate, however, that in order to keep the special sense of 'existence' intact, the translator is forced to make 'being' work overtime. Thus Swenson translates 'fra ikke at vaere til, til at vaere til' as 'from not-being to being'. (*S.V.* IV, p. 237 [*PF*, p. 60].) In support of this translation Kierkegaard's sketch for the *Fragments* may be cited: 'Tilblivelsen er jo ogsaa en Forandring. Denne Forandring er jo fra ikke at vaere til at vaere'. (*Pap.* V B 15, p. 77.)

[12] *S.V.* VII, p. 287 (*CUP*, p. 296). Cf. above, p. 66, note 83, for Arild Christensen's discussion of the relationship to Aristotle in the theme of God's unsynthesized perfection.

the twin rhythms of Kierkegaard's reflection. Holding ourselves, first of all, to the rhythm of diastasis, we point to Kierkegaard's really quite remarkable awareness that the metaphysical distinction did not lie at the heart of the matter: 'If the difference is infinite between God, who is in heaven, and you, who are on earth: the difference is infinitely greater between the Holy and the sinner.'[13] Here the authentically religious character of the diastatic rhythm makes itself known. Furthermore, it is clear that the severance of God and man is not intended to dissolve all relatedness, but precisely to create the distance involved in the encounter between God and man. Indeed Kierkegaard warns against a view in which 'God becomes so endlessly exalted that there is absolutely no real relationship at all between God and the individual man'.[14] He was aware that the stress on the abyss separating God and man could be made 'for the sake of getting permission to live just as one wants to, in a worldly view of life, or else for the sake of leading a religious still-life without incurring any danger'.[15] For Kierkegaard, on the contrary, speech about the abyss witnesses to a God whose presence is real in judgment. Even judgment is far from exhausting the *telos* of the diastiac rhythm: 'The greatest distance, greater than that from the farthest star to the earth, greater than human art can depict, is the distance from God's grace to God's wrath, from the Christian to the heathen, from being saved in bliss by grace to "an eternal perdition from the face of the Lord", from looking to God to seeing from the abyss that one has lost God.'[16]

In the passage just quoted we encounter the material embodiment of the principle we stated formally above: that the rhythms of diastasis and synthesis find their focus—and to some extent even their form—in the christological centre of Kierkegaard's thought. It is the power of the christological motif within the diastatic current (rather than a collection of scattered sayings about God) which supports and even requires our remarks in the preceding paragraph regarding the intention and character of that current and the severance it secures. It should now be evident, too, that our chapter divisions do involve a

[13] *S.V.* XI, p. 258 ('HP', *CDi*, p. 368).
[14] *Pap.* X 1 A 59.
[15] ibid. Cf. Valter Lindström, *Stadiernas Teologi* (Lund: Haakan Ohlsson, 1943), p. 113.
[16] *S.V.* X, pp. 72–73 (*CDi*, p. 72). Cf. Emanuel Hirsch, *Kierkegaard-Studien* (4 vols. in 2, Gütersloh: Bertelsmann, 1930–33), II, p. 923: 'The qualitative difference between God and man is this, that only God is the Lord; but as the Lord he proves himself to me through judgment and forgiveness.'

measure of distortion in that they separate—though they do not isolate—themes which are constantly interwoven in Kierkegaard's thought. We may only hope that this intermediate exercise in abstraction will provide the reader with a useful guide as he returns to the living body of Kierkegaard's thought.

It should now be clear that the metaphysical characterizations employed by Kierkegaard and attacked by not a few of his readers are conscripted in the services of a religious concern to testify to the sovereignty of God in his judgment and grace. Those characterizations do permit him to make the point emphatically that there is 'an infinite difference of quality' between God and man.[17] Kierkegaard will deny the possibility of a common denominator for God and man in order that he may deny man access to the endless round of intellectual evasions of God's claim. Professor Pelikan, in commenting on the sentence 'subjectivity is the truth', has stated the relationship as follows:

Christian truth was subjective not in the sense that the individual's subjective judgment decided what was true and what was not, but in the sense that all standards and criteria of objective knowledge collapsed before the Holy, for the mind could not enclose or grasp Him. In other forms of knowledge, the initiative might come from the inquiring and investigating mind; but in the knowledge communicated by revelation, the initiative was of God, who disclosed His fatherly heart to give himself by re-establishing His fellowship. When the mind sought to create proofs of Him or propositions about Him in which it could believe, He stopped being the Thou of faith and became merely an It. Then there was no more revelation. For once the Holy had become an object of intellectual apprehension, and faith in Him the acceptance of propositions about Him, the relation between God and man had left the personal, existential dimension within which alone revelation and faith had any meaning.[18]

17 See, for example, *S.V.* XII, p. 27 (*TC*, p. 31).

18 Jaroslav Pelikan, *Fools for Christ* (Philadelphia: Muhlenberg, 1955; London: SCM Press, 1959 [title: *Human Culture and the Holy*]), p. 22. This use of the theme of the absolute subjectivity of God witnesses again to the fact that there are *two* poles in Kierkegaard's thought. Hegel himself could speak of *God* in much the same fashion. So in 'The Spirit of Christianity', *Early Theological Writings*, trans. T. M. Knox (Chicago: University of Chicago, 1948), p. 266, Hegel says of faith in God: 'This faith is characterized by its object [*Gegenstand*], the divine. Faith in a mundane reality is an acquaintance with some kind of object [*Objekt*], of something restricted. And just as an object ([*Objekt*] is other than God, so this acquaintance is different from faith in the divine. . . . Faith in the divine is only possible if in the believer himself there is a divine element which rediscovers itself, its own nature, in that on which it believes, even if it be unconscious that what it has found *is* its own nature. . . . Hence faith in the divine grows out of the divinity of the believer's own nature; only a modification of the Godhead can know the Godhead.' [Italics his.] Kierkegaard's knowledge of the two poles in their interdependence does not permit him to draw this conclusion regarding man.

One must still question whether the metaphysical categories clustering around a Platonic concept of eternity are well suited—or even adaptable—to the service for which they are intended. That question invites our consideration of the prominent line in Kierkegaard's christology which offers the Christ as God's proposal 'to do away with the absolute difference in absolute likeness'.[19] We shall confront this line in a later chapter and shall also note then the difficulties it involves. But now we must give our attention to material of another sort in Kierkegaard's discourse concerning God and man. We refer to material carried by the rhythm of synthesis towards which we have most assuredly moved in noting the checks present within the diastatic rhythm. It is this material which provides us with the second reason for differing with those who find metaphysical contrast to be the major theme in Kierkegaard's discourse on God and man.

2. Synthesis *in the Description of God and Man*

One does not have to reach beyond the rhythm of diastasis in order to find incredible the suggestion that Kierkegaard's witness is to the 'ontologically sovereign I'.[20] But our judgment upon such a proposal is based on more than the fact that Kierkegaard sees God and man turned towards each other even at the point of their greatest distance from each other. It is based in a more complete sense on the fact that Kierkegaard does so speak of God and man as to bring into question the very measurement of the distance between them reported by the diastatic rhythm. In looking at this material, which constitutes the synthesis rhythm, we also find the most persuasive reasons for rejecting the suggestion that Kierkegaard's thought logically leads to the twin perils of theoretical solipsism and practical egoism.[21] Perhaps if one attends only to the most extreme expressions of the diastatic impulse one will doubt that Kierkegaard can account for the self's knowledge of the other 'without presupposing either an impossible physical identity of the two or an equally impossible conflation of the two in an idealistic dialectic'.[22] If one reflects upon the synthesis rhythm in his thought, however, one soon comes to see that John Wild is right in finding the so-called 'problem of the external

[19] *S.V.* IV, p. 214 (*PF*, p. 37).
[20] For the proposal of Wilhelm Anz to this effect, see above, p. 21, note 44.
[21] On those perils see James Collins, *The Mind of Kierkegaard* (Chicago: Henry Regnery, 1953), pp. 153–7.
[22] ibid., p. 156.

world' to be alien to Kierkegaard's thought: 'Understanding is not the product of a mind-thing isolated from the world. It is rather a guiding phase of actual existence. Feeling and understanding are not locked up within a substantial container. They are rather out-stretchings of the human subject, ways of being in the world. They are not separated from, but an essential phase of, my existence. Life and awareness vary together in mutual interdependence.'[23]

If the charge of solipsism could be sustained, Kierkegaard would be contradicting himself in trying to say anything about Man as such. As it is, he defies the limits of solipsism, believing himself to have real knowledge of things and selves about him. There is some basis for holding that he appeals to a doctrine of categories to give ontological support to that knowledge.[24] Thus, too, Kierkegaard can offer his reflections concerning the individual to his contemporaries as something more than a purely private matter.

There is, to be sure, an irreducible dimension of solitariness to the self. We have already spoken of Kierkegaard's rejection of the thesis that the inner is the outer and the outer the inner.[25] The moments of decision which come to be constitutive of the self are radically private and defy predictability. The *Postscript* recognizes this privacy by observing that the production of one's own ethical reality is not a function of thought, just as the thought with which one reaches out to others does not fall in the sphere of ethics.[26] Thus Climacus can say that we do not help others ethically.[27]

[23] John Wild, 'Kierkegaard and Contemporary Existentialist Philosophy', *A Kierkegaard Critique*, ed. H. Johnson and N. Thulstrup (New York: Harper, 1962), p. 32. Wild seeks to show how 'Kierkegaard's attack on the mind-thing theory of Descartes, and his penetrating studies of mood, feeling, and thought as they actually operate in the act of human existing have now been developed by his followers, the existential phenomenologists, into a radically novel *field conception* of man' (italics his). ibid.

[24] *S.V.* VI, pp. 284–5 (*SW*, p. 280): 'I force myself with every power to hold my life to the categories. . . . This is what I will, what I demand of everyone whom I admire, of everyone I am in any real sense to recognize, that by day he should only think of the categories of his life, and dream of them by night.' On the significance of the categories for Kierkegaard, see Lars Bejerholm, '*Meddelelsens Dialektik*' (Lund: Haakan Ohlsson, 1962), pp. 60–63, and Hermann Diem, *Kierkegaard's Dialectic of Existence*, trans. Harold Knight (Edinburgh: Oliver and Boyd, 1959), pp. 31–37. There was widespread interest in Kierkegaard's time in the doctrine of categories. Bejerholm discusses this theme in the work of Paul Möller, J. L. Heiberg, and F. C. Sibbern. Kierkegaard expressed interest in the doctrine as early as 1842–3 (*Pap.* IV C 63 and 90) and that early interest was confirmed by his study of Trendelenburg (see above, pp. 67–69).

[25] See above, p. 21, note 43.

[26] *S.V.* VII, pp. 276, 283, 293 (*CUP*, pp. 285, 293, 302).

[27] ibid., p. 312 (ibid., p. 321).

But this freedom of the individual has meaning only within the inheritance bequeathed to him by reality exterior to and impinging upon the existential moment of decision. In that decision one makes contact with the lives of others and one's own past life.[28] It is this conditioning of the act of choice to which Kierkegaard bears witness, when he says: 'Therefore courage is required for a man to choose himself; for at the same time when it seems that he isolates himself most of all, at that same time he becomes absorbed most of all in the root by which he is connected with the whole.'[29] The correct term is conditioning, not determination, for the self faces alternatives. In this sense the *Postscript* designates all reality beyond the immediate self as possibility in relation to that self.[30] But that heritage of possibility cannot be ignored. It 'restrains' the individual, as the *Postscript* observes.[31] Thus it is the case that 'the individual, however freely he may develop, can never reach the point at which he becomes absolutely independent, since true freedom on the contrary consists rather in freely appropriating that which is given, and consequently in being absolutely dependent through freedom'.[32] The phrase 'absolutely dependent' must be understood to be saying that all the material for the actualizing choice is given, but not that the act of choice itself is given, for one is 'absolutely dependent *through freedom*'.[33]

In turn, the moment of decision contributes to the heritage of

----

[28] *S.V.* II, pp. 205–6 (*E-O*, II, pp. 192–3).

[29] ibid., p. 193 (ibid., p. 181). Cf. Lindström, op. cit., p. 49.

[30] *S.V.* VII, p. 271 (*CUP*, p. 280).

[31] ibid., p. 263 (ibid., p. 272). Thus *Pap.* II A 558 (*Dru* 316) can suggest that one can study the future by studying the past.

[32] *Pap.* III A 11 (*Dru* 323).

[33] *SD* discusses this relationship by describing an infinite movement of the self away from itself (to possibility) and a finite (integrating) movement back to itself. (*S.V.* XI, pp. 143–54 [*SD*, pp. 44–65].) Per Lönning, '*Samtidighedens Situation*' (Oslo: Land og Kirke, 1954), pp. 33–37, 42, 46, provides helpful comments on the relationship under discussion. Lönning does endorse Johannes Slök's statement (*Forsynstanken* [Hjörring: Expres, 1947], p. 94) that Climacus minimizes the element of necessity, while Anti-Climacus maximizes it. While the relationship surely is stated differently in different works, this comment seems to oversimplify the material. As far as Climacus is concerned, we have already noted that *CUP* recognizes the element of restraint. Furthermore, we shall see that *TC* poses a threat to the significance of the historical for the Christian moment of decision. For a detailed expression of Kierkegaard's personal quest for a satisfying integration of the heritage of possibility-necessity bequeathed to him, see the famous Gilleleie reference, *Pap.* I A 75 (*Dru* 22). Emil Brunner, 'Das Grundproblem der Philosophie bei Kant und Kierkegaard', *Zwischen den Zeiten*, 1924, pp. 31–47, finds the involvement of the self with the other(s) to be suggested in the very term Kierkegaard so often uses: interest (*Interesse*)—'being in the middle'. Cf. *S.V.* VII, p. 270 (*CUP*, p. 279) on the moment suspended between possibility and reality.

influence impinging upon other moments of decision. This is the point *The Concept of Dread* is making in describing the formula 'each man himself and the race' as both a given state and a task:

> It is so that at every moment the individual is himself and the race. This is man's perfection, seen as a state. At the same time it is a contradiction; but a contradiction is always the expression for a task; but a task is movement; but a movement towards that same thing as a task which first was given up is an historical movement. Hence the individual has a history; but if the individual has a history, so has also the race. Every individual has the same perfection; precisely for this reason the individuals do not fall away from one another numerically, any more than does the concept of the race become a phantom. Every individual is essentially interested in the history of all other individuals, yea, just as essentially as in his own. Perfection in oneself means therefore perfect participation in the whole. No individual is indifferent to the history of the race, any more than is the race to that of any individual. While the history of the race goes on, the individual regularly begins afresh, because he is himself and the race, and hence in turn his is the history of the race.[34]

We should note that Kierkegaard applies this analysis of becoming very readily to human history, but only very guardedly to natural change. The tendency of 'neo-orthodox' theologians to drive a hard line between nature and history may very well be related to their interest in Kierkegaard: 'Nature does not lie in the moment. . . . Nature's security has its basis in the fact that time has absolutely no meaning for it. Only in the moment does history begin.'[35] Kierkegaard does offer himself as a 'philosopher of life' and seems to share the disinterest in nature which marked the Socrates in whom he found his great example.[36] Yet again matters are not that clear. Climacus observes that 'it is nature's perfection that it nevertheless has a hint of a history (namely this, that it has come into being [*er bleven til*], which is its past; that it is present [*er til*] is its present)'.[37] If it is true that Kierkegaard regarded '*the* problem of freedom and motion' as

[34] *S.V.* IV, p. 301 (*CD*, p. 26). Cf. ibid., p. 342 (ibid., p. 65). See *S.V.* XIII, p. 349 for an early statement of the view that one is given inner qualities and dispositions and therewith the task of developing them. Here Kierkegaard stresses the twin movements of falling back into the self and giving the self to the world. The *Postscript* offers another phrasing: 'Human existence has Idea in it, but it is yet not a purely ideal existence. . . . as existing, man must surely participate in the Idea, but he is not himself an Idea.' (*S.V.* VII, p. 285 [*CUP*, p. 295].) Cf. *S.V.* VIII, pp. 199–200 (*PH*, p. 153).

[35] *S.V.* IV, pp. 358–9 (*CD*, pp. 79–80). Readers who are familiar with Walter Lowrie's translation of *CD* will note that 'instant' for *Oieblikket* is replaced by 'moment', a change which corresponds to the choice made by the Swensons in other works.

[36] *Pap.* IV B 177, 290.

[37] *S.V.* IV, p. 239 (*PF*, p. 62). See above, p. 102, note 11.

'perhaps one of the most difficult of all problems',[38] one could suggest that the distinction between the two dimensions of the historical may not be as great as sometimes supposed. We clearly lack in Kierkegaard any full application of the analysis of becoming to the world of nature. Yet one may feel that such an application could have been open to him. His distinction between dialectic and pathetic transition and his emphasis on the affective element in qualitative transition support that suggestion.

We have seen that synthesis rhythm in Kierkegaard's thought concerning man identifies the charge of solipsism as an incredible one. That rhythm leads one to reject just as emphatically the suggestion that an egoistic tendency is implicit in Kierkegaard's thought. Such a suggestion might already have trouble maintaining itself in the face of the strongly social concept of the self which we have identified in the preceding paragraphs. It is clearly impossible to find the suggestion a responsible one, when one confronts Kierkegaard's reflection on the theological character of the self. Walter Lindström has, perhaps been the most insistent of the Kierkegaard scholars stressing the theme of the 'unavoidability of the God relation' in Kierkegaard's thought.[39] Lindström has not had to coerce the material in order to produce the theme, though one might wish for a closer statement of the different ways in which this theme finds expression.

Malcolm Diamond provides a port of entrance to a study of the theological character of the self by his emphasis on the inevitability of the reference to the 'constituting power': 'Of the greatest significance is the fact that God, the creator and sustainer of the universe, is inevitably an element of the mind by virtue of the fact that man, as a contingent being, is aware of the fact that he cannot constitute himself, that is, he cannot bring about his own existence, nor is the environment in which he finds himself capable of constituting itself. God then is, psychologically speaking, an inevitable constituent of selfhood as the self thinks about both itself and the world. Thus to think properly about reality a self, any self, must imagine God at least as Creator.'[40] We need to make clear that much more is involved at this point than the identification of a verbal answer to an intellectual

---

[38] See Gregor Malantschuk, *Kierkegaard's Way to the Truth*, trans. Mary Michelsen (Minneapolis: Augsburg, 1963), p. 79. [Italics ours.]

[39] Lindström, op cit. He finds this theme to be that which unifies Kierkegaard's discussion of the stages on the way of life. Cf. Per Lönning, 'Kierkegaard's "Paradox"', *Symposion Kierkegaardianum, Orbis Litterarum*, 1955, pp. 156–66.

[40] M. Diamond, 'Kierkegaard and Apologetics', *The Journal of Religion*, April, 1964, pp. 129–30.

puzzle.[41] Kierkegaard would bear witness to a far warmer, more living dependence: [As an arrow speeds to its target,] 'so man as created by God is aimed at God, and cannot find rest before [he finds it] in God.'[42]

The Augustinian analogy is open to distortion. Kierkegaard is not saying that the flight of the human self to God is an unhindered one. The quest for God impinges upon the self in the course of its experience —whether that be experience of success[43] and power,[44] or of death.[45] The natural world waits to tutor the man who comes to know God.[46] Yet it is by no means sure that man will come to know God aright: 'He is in the creation, everywhere in the creation, but he is not there directly; and it is only when the solitary individual turns within himself (thus only in the inwardness of self-activity), that he becomes attentive and is in position to see God.'[47]

But perhaps this way of speaking is unfortunate. Most often Kierkegaard seems to be saying that what is uncertain is the outcome of man's encounter with God, not the event of the encounter. Man's very selfhood is 'before God'. So it is that he longs for God, and so it is that God is present in that longing.[48] Yet does the uncertainty persist, for the God who is present is no mere cosmic prescription for human need. Those impatient to bring down fire from Feuerbach upon the Kierkegaardian analogy to the Augustinian *inquietum ist cor nostrum* have need to pause. The God man meets is the Lord, the Royal Coachman. It is he who drives, and not the horses, and Kierkegaard adds: 'Surely there is for a man a shudder like the shudder of death when Thou doest take the power from him, in order to be the power

---

[41] Indeed one wonders if much of the heat to be found in Kierkegaard's ridiculing of those who would come to God's aid with three proofs does not derive from the certainty of the God-man encounter as it is phrased in the rhythm of synthesis. This is not to deny that the severance of God and man sponsored by the diastatic current contributes much to that ridicule too.

[42] *Pap.* VIII 1 A 601. Cf. *S.V.* V, p. 98 ('MN', *ED*, IV, p. 36): While one may try to hide one's need of God, 'with the deeper knowledge of the self one learns precisely that one needs God'.

[43] *S.V.* III, p. 304 (*ED*, I, p. 104).

[44] ibid., pp. 306–7 (ibid., pp. 106–7).

[45] *S.V.* IV, pp. 161ff. (*ED*, III, pp. 126ff.).

[46] For Kierkegaard's famous reflection on the lessons to be learned from the birds and the lilies, see *S.V.* VIII, pp. 246ff. ('WLF' in *GS*, pp. 165ff.) ; from the sea and the stars, see ibid., pp. 272ff. (ibid., pp. 202ff.)

[47] *S.V.* VII, pp. 204–5 (*CUP*, p. 218).

[48] So *S.V.* X, p. 263 (*CDi*, p. 267): 'I can wish myself away from the world's vanity and corruption, and if the wish does not avail, yet does the heart's longing after the eternal avail to carry me away; for in the longing itself *is* the eternal present, just as God *is* in the sorrow which is sorrow *unto* God' [italics his].

in him . . .'[49] Yet in introducing this very passage Kierkegaard declares that the strong hand of the Master is man's greatest need and he goes on to say: '. . . oh, but if even animal creatures understand in a later moment how good it yet was for them that the royal coachman took the reins, which at the first caused them to shudder and against which they futilely rebelled—should not then a man be able quickly to understand what a good deed it is towards a man that Thou doest take the power and doest give life?'[50] What such passages make clear is Kierkegaard's understanding that the human self is so shaped as to require some master—verily the one he finds in God.[51] This is the unquiet rest of God which satisfies the self!

We need to look longer at the claim which this God places upon man and we need to do so soon. But we can pause to gather together the threads of the discussion thus far. The placement of the self's life in the social matrix makes the charge of solipsism an unreal one. So, too, the unavoidability of the God relationship—as understood by Kierkegaard—turns his thought away from any tendency to practical egoism. Indeed just as the self's social relationships are seen to be constitutive (though not exhaustive) of its reality, rather than accidental to it; just so 'it really is the God-relationship which makes a man a man'.[52] And Kierkegaard adds the judgment of importance: 'The gradation in the consciousness of the self, with which we have concerned ourselves up to this point, is within the determination: the

---

[49] S.V. XII, p. 369 (SE, p. 106). So S.V. IV, p. 158 (ED, III, p. 122): one may see the finger of God in life all right, but the man 'who is troubled about himself really understands it right . . . and he sees constantly the finger of God *pointing at him*. [Italics ours].

[50] S.V. XII, p. 370 (SE, p. 106).

[51] So for Kierkegaard the gospel too becomes a glad message by virtue of its strict, unconditioned character. See S.V. IX, pp. 356ff. (WL, pp. 303ff.) and S.V. XII, pp. 207–8 (TC, pp. 221–2). We approach here the discussion of the law-gospel dialectic in Kierkegaard—a topic which concerns us in a later chapter. We are aware that the royal coachman image is not without difficulties. To a large extent those difficulties seem to derive from the fact that the rhythms of diastasis and synthesis blend in Kierkegaard's use of the image. Yet we feel the contribution of the image which we have identified can be isolated in the interest of serving the concern of this section. We discuss the blending of the ryhthms and the problems involved in that blending later in this chapter.

[52] S.V. VII, p. 206 (CUP, p. 219). A highly poetic passage from E-O states the point more fully: 'So when all has become silent around one, solemn as a starlit night, when the soul becomes alone in the whole world, then there appears before it not a distinguished man, but the eternal Power itself. Then it is as if heaven opens, and the I chooses itself or, more rightly, receives itself. Then the soul has seen the highest, that which no mortal eye can see, and which can never be forgotten; then the personality receives the accolade of knighthood which ennobles it for eternity.' S.V. II, p. 160 (E-O, II, p. 149).

human self, or the self whose measure is man. But this self gets a new quality and qualification in that it is the self directly in the sight of God. This self is no longer the merely human self, but is, what I (hoping not to be misunderstood) would call the theological self, the self directly in the sight of God. And what an infinite reality does not the self receive by being conscious of being directly in the sight of God, by becoming a human self whose measure is God.'[53]

In meeting God man confronts his creator. For Kierkegaard the doctrine of creation does not merely—or even chiefly—concern itself with the origin of the time-space continuum. He who discusses the doctrine of creation speaks of man's—his own—present dependence upon the living God. That dependence is not adequately stated if one starkly juxtaposes the self and its God. Creation rather involves the rich manifold of the concrete relationships which forms the matrix for the self. So it is that God can and does make himself known to man within the very tissue of that actual daily life: 'The divine can well enough move under the earthly conditions, and it does not require the annihilation of the earthly as the condition for its appearance, just as God's spirit revealed itself to Moses in the bush which burned without being consumed.'[54]

We have said that the encounter with God does not cause the self to slumber in some kind of spiritual contemplation, but summons it to action. To discuss the ideal to which man is called in meeting God is to return again to the description of the individual-in-community. The structure of the self's free interaction with the legacy of possibility impinging upon it from the other(s) is not suspended when the self makes the movement of obedient faith. Faith is 'a form of the will',[55] which imparts continuity to the life of the self. Thus God does not call a self to cloister itself from everything but the punctiliar privacy of an existential decision in which it must somehow find its substance. Rather 'a man's eternal worth lies precisely in this, that he can get a history; the divine in him lies in this, that he himself, if he will, can give that history continuity'.[56] This assertion accepts the descriptive observation that 'a life must have continuity in order for it to have any meaning'.[57] It also exceeds that observation, how-

---

[53] S.V. XI, p. 191 (SD, pp. 126–7).

[54] Pap. II A 351.

[55] Pap. IV B 87, 2.

[56] S.V. II, p. 224 (E-O, II, pp. 209–10). Cf. ibid., p. 206 (ibid., p. 193): 'He who lives ethically has, to recall an earlier expression, memory of his life. . . .'

[57] ibid., p. 176 (ibid., p. 165).

ever, by moving in the direction of a material specification, of the ideal—a matter which concerns us in the next chapter.

The structures of the relationship between self and other(s) are not commandeered by God for service to an ideal which ignores or repudiates the parties to the relationship. As a very young man Kierkegaard sought 'something which hangs together with the deepest roots of my existence, whereby I grow, as it were, into the divine'.[58] Later he could speak more formally of the ethical ideal: 'I choose the absolute, and what is the absolute? It is myself in my eternal validity. I can never choose something other than myself as the absolute, for if I choose something other, I choose that as a finite thing, and thus I do not choose it absolutely.'[59] Such a passage well states the problem of psychological impossibility which is posed by a deontological ethic. But it does not commit itself to the logic of humanism. We have said, after all, that the God relationship is constitutive, though not exhaustive, of man's selfhood. The ideal possesses an imperative as well as an indicative character: 'Since he [the ethical subject] has not created himself, but has chosen himself, duty is the expression for his absolute dependence and his absolute freedom in identity with each other. The particular duty he will teach himself . . . and yet he will again here be autodidact, as well as theodidact, and vice versa.'[60]

The call to the ideal does not, then, ignore or repudiate the reality of the self. 'But what, then, is this self of mine? If I were to answer in the first moment, if I were to give a first expression, my answer is: It is the most abstract of all things, and yet at the same time is in itself the most concrete of all things—it is freedom.'[61] The concreteness of the self, its 'immediacy', is manifestly not evil. Again the ethicist puts the matter well: 'The ethical, then, will not make the individual into another man, but it will make him himself; it will not annihilate the aesthetic, but it will clarify it. In order for a man to live ethically it is necessary for him to be so radically conscious of himself, that no accidental feature escapes him. The ethical would not obliterate this concretion, but it sees in it its task, it sees this as that upon which it must build and as that which it must build.'[62]

[58] *Pap.* I A 75 (*Dru* 22).
[59] *S.V.* II, p. 192 (*E-O* II, pp. 179–80).
[60] ibid., pp. 242–3 (ibid., p. 226).
[61] ibid., p. 192 (ibid., p. 180).
[62] ibid., p. 227 (ibid., p. 212). Cf. ibid., p. 235 (ibid., p. 219): 'He who has ethically chosen and found himself, has himself as he is determined in all his concreteness. He has himself as an individual, who has these talents, these passions, these inclinations, these habits, who stands under these outer influences, who in one direction is affected thus, in another thus.'

More yet is involved in ethical concreteness, 'for the self which is the aim is not merely a personal self, but a social, a civic self'.[63] So the reality of the other(s) is recognized in the call to the ideal. One may assuredly point out that the ethical act is surrounded by the reality of the other(s). So Lönning writes of the situation of contemporaneity: 'Thus the situation signifies on the whole an occasion for taking a position in an ethical or Christian sense, and this consists in that the one who shall take the position clarifies his relationship both to that which shall be the object of his taking the position, and to the environment, which on the basis of his taking a position, will take a position towards him. The situation is at one time the presupposition for a positive relationship to that towards which one takes a position and conditioned by that positive relationship.'[64]

One might suppose that even a more fundamental involvement is in sight, if one recalls the description of the self's relationships as constitutive of its reality. One's inclinations at this point are strengthened by the fact that Kierkegaard's constructive statement of the personal and social dimensions to ethical concreteness represent so clearly an application of his descriptive analysis of the individual-in-community. 'He [the ethical subject] has, then, himself as the task for an activity by which he as this definite personality takes hold in the relationships of life. Here his task is not to cultivate himself, but to exert an influence, and yet he cultivates himself at the same time; for . . . the ethical individual lives in such a way that he constantly moves from one stage to the other. . . . From the personal life he moves to the civic, and from this to the personal. The personal life as such was isolated and therefore imperfect, but as he [the ethical subject] through the civic life moves back to his personality, the personal life reveals itself in a higher form.'[65]

Such passages as the one just quoted invite one to wonder if Kierkegaard does not give place to the other(s) not only in the context and goal of the ethical act, but even in the actualizing energy of that act itself.[66] That speculation will not seem bizarre, if one does not suppose Kierkegaard to posit a rigid separation between the com-

---

[63] ibid., (ibid., p. 220).
[64] Lönning, op. cit., p. 46.
[65] *S.V.* II, pp. 235–6 (*E-O* II, p. 220).
[66] Kierkegaard can write: 'If a man has faith, he has truly not by that faith deprived others of something, on the contrary, . . . he has worked for all others. In that time when he worked for himself in order to receive faith, he worked for all others. For the entire race, and every individual in the race is a sharer in the fact that one has faith.' *S.V.* X, p. 121 (*CDi*, p. 121).

munal and personal moments in the life of the self.[67] Yet rather little specific material is available to probe on this point, and it seems better to defer our discussion of it to the chapters dealing with Kierkegaard's christology.

All of this material on the relationship of God, self and other(s) adds up to a very imposing body of discourse in Kierkegaard's work. We do not deny, of course, that there is material of another sort as well, Indeed we began this chapter by discussing Kierkegaard's description of God and man as it appears in the diastatic current. We would concede, too, that much of the material we have cited does not breathe the fine air of the heights scaled in 'Religion B', but we would quickly refer the reader to our discussion in Part One of the interrelatedness of the stages, of the rhythms of diastasis and synthesis, and of the stages and the rhythms.[68] Our study of Kierkegaard's christology will confront us with the task of determining the meaning and assessing the significance of the Kierkegaard witness that the way to the Father is through the Son and the Spirit.[69] But it does not seem wrong to ask of the reader the willingness to give at least a preliminary hearing of the rhythm of synthesis. After all, men laying claim to the name Christian have spoken of the Logos of creation and of a Creator Spirit.

Jan Sperna Weiland well represents that sizeable band which seems to bypass all such discourse:

> The *prima philosophia* is characterized by the fact that all anthropology is theology and that anthropology is the foundation of all theology, that all self consciousness is at the same time the consciousness of God. There is no room here as yet for christology. But when this identity of self consciousness and consciousness of God has vanished and when, on account of the consciousness of sin, no immediate relationship to God can be found and when man no longer has contact with God in his inwardness, but only with himself and his sin, then there is room for christology, for belief in Christ as Mediator between God and man.[70]

Even if one permits such a reduction of christology to soteriology, the logic of the passage is far from invincible. One might think it possible that the salvatory significance of the Christ first wins a real hearing when a man is most aware of God. That is, one could imagine that that awareness would include a consciousness of man's unac-

---

[67] See, for example, *S.V.* II, p. 83 (*E-O* II, p. 76) on the interpenetration of the universal and the particular.

[68] See above, pp. 9, 28–43.

[69] See Lönning, op. cit., pp. 159–60.

[70] Jan Sperna Weiland, *Humanitas Christianitas* (Te Assen Bij: Van Gorcum, 1951), p. 34.

ceptability or that the awareness would acquire that character in the encounter with the Christ.[71]

These questions must be deferred to later chapters when they can be discussed in the light of a reasonably full statement of Kierkegaards christology. All that can well be done here is to observe—as we have—the massive testimony in the authorship to the interrelatedness of God, man, and fellow man. It should be noted that even the strong medicine of the *Fragments* assumes the doctrine of creation and seeks to distinguish creation from fall.[72] Here, too, it has seemed correct to point to Kierkegaard's conviction that man knows God's claim. Or, to state that conviction in more formal theological vocabulary, we may say that the law is revealed to man apart from and before his encounter with the historical figure, Jesus of Nazareth.[73] We cannot discuss here how the figure of Christ comes to be related to the individual's existing knowledge of the law. We shall, however, want to look much more closely at that existing knowledge. Thus the next chapter includes sections in which we discuss the formal and material determination of the ideal. In both cases we find opportunity to observe the interpenetration of the rhythms of synthesis and diastasis. Before turning to that discussion, however, another task remains to us in examining the description of God and man within the synthesis strand in Kierkegaard's thought. It is not a minor task, for what we shall seek to do is to illumine the role which the synthesis rhythm plays in Kierkegaard's doctrine of God.

We have noted that the diastatic impulse leads Kierkegaard to the point of denying that any metaphysical principles can be formulated which characterize God as well as man. In so far as his thought reflects the rhythm of synthesis, on the other hand, he tends to move in the direction of applying the analysis of self and other won from his study of man to his reflection regarding God. Such an application permits—even requires—him to speak of that theme so central to a

[71] Lönning, op. cit., finds Kierkegaard affirming both the givenness and the growth of that consciousness. He finds Kierkegaard speaking of a fall from pure *eros* and a struggle back towards that purity. Divine *agape* collides with that human struggle. If the reader wishes even now at least some token statement acknowledging specifically that consciousness of need does exist apart from the encounter with Jesus of Nazareth, he may see *S.V.* XII, p. 394 (*JY*, p. 129).

[72] See *S.V.* IV, pp. 184–5 (*PF*, pp. 10–11) and above, pp. 37–38, especially note 116, on the two states of non-being.

[73] We may add here still another form in which this conviction gains expression: Kierkegaard's understanding of conscience. See *S.V.* IX, p. 357 (*WL*, p. 304): 'For what is conscience? In conscience it is God who regards a man, so the man must now in everything regard God.' Cf. ibid., pp. 130ff. (ibid., pp. 110ff.).

diastatic thinker: the solitariness of God. And it does not follow that God knows solitariness, privacy, independence only in the sense that man does. Yet the human self's irreducible freedom does provide an analogue to God's independence. One can even add the bolder word: Kierkegaard seems willing to ask if there is not some sense in which man's dependence finds an analogical reality in God.

Kierkegaard's affirmation that the divine in man 'lies in this, that he himself, if he will, can give . . . [his] history continuity' has already told us something about man.[74] One may wonder if that affirmation does not also speak of God. What might it say, if having a history and gaining continuity in it involves the self in response to the reality of the other(s) impinging upon it? Kierkegaard's works render this question more than abstract speculation. Even in affirming the sovereignty of God Kierkegaard can move towards a statement of the significance of the world: 'It is so impossible that the world could continue to exist without God, that if God could *forget* it, it instantly would dissolve.'[75] It is particularly the ethical-religious dimension of Kierkegaard's thought which brings him to say that God—far from 'forgetting the world'—makes man's reality a matter of ultimate importance. Already in his dissertation Kierkegaard could say that a man who develops those talents which are God's gift to him will have reality for God himself.[76] And at the end of his life—despite his despair over man's stupidity and sin—he yet would speak only of God 'helping him in so far as God can help with what only freedom can accomplish'.[77] Within the authorship marked by those boundaries he did not try to stress the seriousness of human life without stating as well the ultimate basis for that seriousness: that man's life has meaning for God. Thus he holds: 'This it is that God cannot take away from a man: the voluntary. . . .'[78] The words of Climacus are no less bold: 'Dare, therefore, says the ethical, . . . dare to become a particular individual, of whom God demands everything ethically, without your being relieved of the necessity of being enthusiastic; behold that is the venture! But then you will also have won this that God in all eternity cannot get rid of you. . . .'[79]

Perhaps it should not surprise us that Kierkegaard speaks so pointedly throughout his authorship of the meaning of man before

[74] See above, p. 112.
[75] *Pap.* II A 622 (*Dru* 129). [Italics his.]
[76] *S.V.* XIII, pp. 351-3.
[77] *Pap.* XI 2 A 439 (*Diary* 239).
[78] *S.V.* X, p. 182 (*CDi*, p. 187).
[79] *S.V.* VII, p. 122 (*CUP*, p. 133).

God, for he was a man who himself lived out his days under orders:
'And how strange it is that from my earliest time (that is to say, in
my youth after my father's death) when I was independent and there
was no question of seeking a settled occupation, when I went about
in deep melancholy and regarded myself as the most miserable of all
—how strange it is that even then I prayed every morning that God
would give me strength for the work "which Thou Thyself wilt assign
me". When I now think about that I wonder how in the world it
occurred to me to pray in this way! And yet how true it has turned
out to be that I have done a work which God himself assigned to
me.'[80]

To articulate the interrelatedness of God and man is much nearer
the centre of Kierkegaard's concern than to contemplate the origin of
that interrelatedness. Yet some scattered suggestions are available to
one asking the question of origin. An early comment from the *Journals*
expresses the positive orientation which underlies much of the later
work: 'The relation between Christianity and Gnosticism is most
significantly indicated in the relationship between the two definitions
at which they arrived: Christianity at the *Logos*, Gnosticism at the
"Name" (Christ was the name of the invisible God); the latter is in
an eminent degree abstract, just as the whole of Gnosticism was an
abstraction, which is why they could never arrive at a creation filling
time and space, but were really forced to regard creation as identical
with the fall.'[81] We have already mentioned the doctrine of categories
which was current in the Danish thought of Kierkegaard's time and
which he at least in part adopted.[82] That doctrine was often so stated
as to give the categories a measure of significance for God, too, by
incorporating them within the 'divine fullness'.[83] May it be that in
affirming Christ as the Logos of God—not merely the name—
Kierkegaard is attributing a priority of some sort to a field of possibilities which come to be actualized in creation through the Logos 'in
whom all things hold together'? Of course 'the inference from essence
to existence is [still] a leap'.[84] But at least at times Kierkegaard
wishes to say that the leap celebrated in the doctrine of creation is a
possible one and indeed one positively willed by God. Thus he does
not ask us to believe that creation signifies the birth of relatedness or
the inception of life for God. Rather he speaks of the Trinity as the

[80] *Pap.* IX A 69 (*Dru* 774).
[81] ibid., II A 237 (ibid., 214).
[82] See above, pp. 67 and 106–7, note 24.
[83] See Bejerholm, op. cit., pp. 60–69 on Sibbern's view at this point.
[84] *S.V.* VII, p. 27 (*CUP*, p. 38).

'community of love',[85] thus adding structure to his assertion that of all qualities attributed to God, only love is attributed substantively, not adjectively.[86] Here too, perhaps, lies the clue to and the structure for Kierkegaard's positive doctrine of creation, for he is confident that 'love is the source of everything'.[87]

In a remarkable note in *The Concept of Dread* Kierkegaard addresses our interest while commenting on the special attention the school of Schelling paid the theme of the consequences of sin in the created world: 'With Schelling himself there is often enough talk about dread, wrath, anguish, suffering, etc. However, one ought always be a little suspicious of such, in order not to confuse the consequence of sin in the creation with what it also designates in Schelling, states of mind and feelings in God. With these expressions he designates—if I dare say so—the creative birth pangs of the Deity.'[88] Kierkegaard did dare say so. After noting more fully Schelling's discussion of 'the sufferings of the Deity trying to create', he warns against treating the matter ironically: 'That one should not do; for a vigorous and full-blooded anthropomorphism is worth a good deal. In fact, the fault is another one, and one can see here an example of how strange everything becomes, when metaphysics and dogmatics are corrupted by treating dogmatics metaphysically and metaphysics dogmatically.'[89] One may take Kierkegaard to be urging a distinction between the acceptibility of a descriptive metaphysical analogy and a dogmatic employment of the analogy which would raise description to the level of explanation.

CD's note has stated explicitly for us the view that analogies drawn from human life can be applied meaningfully and correctly to God. Kierkegaard's works undertake this task and the analogies employed cluster around the central theme of love. Kierkegaard could state the point formally as well: 'Sin is the only thing of what can be predicated of man, which in no way—neither *via negationis* or *via eminentiae*—can be affirmed of God.'[90] To say that man's freedom and dependence is

[85] *S.V.* IX, p. 148 (*WL*, p. 125).
[86] *Pap.* II A 418 (*Dru* 274). Cf. ibid., III A 73 (ibid., 335), where Kierkegaard contends that the 'one unshakeable thing in life' is 'divine fatherly love'. What God is in himself underlies what he is for us.
[87] *S.V.* IX, p. 206 (*WL*, p. 174).
[88] *S.V.* IV, p. 329 (*CD*, p. 53).
[89] ibid., p. 330 (ibid.). Cf. *S.V.* XI. p. 233 (*SD*, p. 202), for Kierkegaard's comment on this advanced age which has rejected all anthropomorphisms.
[90] *S.V.* XI, p. 231 (*SD*, p. 199). The reader will perhaps be aware that this sentence occurs in a context emphasizing the 'yawning qualitative abyss separating God and man'. Yet the meaning cited for the sentence is not lost, as it becomes

analogous to something in God is not, of course, to deny that there may be some sense in which God is without human analogy. We can approach that sense by noting Kierkegaard's persistent witness to the unchangeableness of God.[91]

The counter 'unchangeable' could refer to static immobility. Kierkegaard is fully aware of this possibility and indeed attracted by it: 'In so far as all philosophy is in a position to conceive of the relationship of the divine to the human, Aristotle has already expressed it felicitously, when he says that God moves all things, but is himself *akinētos*. (So far as I can remember Schelling pointed this out in Berlin.) It is really the abstract concept of unchangeableness, and his influence is therefore a magnetic charm, something like the sirens' song. Therefore all rationalism ends in superstition.'[92] We have seen that the diastatic impulse—despite this disclaimer—does appear to press into its service metaphysical characterizations of this lineage. When Kierkegaard denies change to God as an anthropomorphism, he may be expressing this orientation.[93] On the other hand, it is barely possible that it is only this particular anthropomorphism which is being faulted. Such a critique could reflect Kierkegaard's witness to the unparalleled uniqueness of God. In any case Kierkegaard does affirm such uniqueness of God in relation to the notion of unchangeableness. God's unchangeableness is not that of death, but that of life, of utter self-consistency, of fidelity to a telos. It is—if we may put it so—the unchangeableness of ever 'willing one thing'.

That this is Kierkegaard's meaning is made clear by his assertion that God is 'moved and in infinite love moved by all things'.[94] *How* it is Kierkegaard's meaning is far less clear. That is, it is not clear exactly how the uniqueness is attained. We make two suggestions at this point: (1) The advance to this uniqueness is a religious one. Thus when the age is attacked for having 'removed the deep qualitative chasm from the distinction between God and man', the charge is not descriptive inaccuracy, but ethical and religious transgression. In

---

clear in this passage that the *theological* context for the diastatic utterance making up this *literary* context in fact reveals the rhythm of synthesis.

[91] See above, p. 41, note 132.

[92] *Pap.* IV A 157.

[93] *Pap.* VIII 1 A 143.

[94] *S.V.* XIV, 283 ('UG', *SE*, p. 277). Cf. *S.V.* VII, p. 375 (*CUP*, p. 387), where Climacus contends that as distinguished from a conception of God who 'himself unchanged, changes all', 'the religious lies in the dialectic of the intensification of inwardness, and hence in relation to the conception of God suggests that he is himself moved, changed'.

Kierkegaard's words, it is blasphemy.[95] (2) Kierkegaard's witness to the uniqueness of God's unchanging love is not a combination of an *a posteriori* judgment based upon a collection of instances ever incomplete and a prediction possessing a very high order of probability. It is a word of faith concerning the givenness of love for—and in—and of— the God man meets. Perhaps a passage from the *Fragments* best states the point. Climacus tells us that God is such that 'no occasion can so serve as an occasion for him that there is as much significance in the occasion as in the resolve'.[96] So it is that the language of Aristotle can be pressed into service by the man claimed by grace: 'He must move himself . . .'[97] Kierkegard's prose sings: 'But if he moves himself, and is not moved by need, what other than love can it be that moves him? For love does not find the satisfaction of its need outside itself, but within itself. His resolve, which stands in no equal reciprocal relation to the occasion, must be from eternity, even though when realized in time it becomes precisely the moment. . . .'[98]

The reader may contend that it is precisely the diastatic impulse which governs this passage from the *Fragments* and that only a verbal acknowledgement of either love or movement is to be found here. Our reply will have to be: it may be so. Yet there are grounds for holding that Kierkegaard intends in these matters something which well exceeds verbal recognition. He writes: 'God has only one passion: to love and to want to be loved. That which has pleased him is to go through with men existentially all the modes in which one can be loved, to go through loving.'[99] And he adds: '. . . seriousness lies precisely in this: that loving and being loved is God's passion, almost as if—infinite love!—he were himself bound in this passion, in the power of the passion so that he could not cease loving, almost as if it were a weakness, while it is indeed his strength, his omnipotent love, in such a degree is his love not subject to change.'[100] This passion is

[95] *Pap.* VIII 1 A 414 (*Dru* 712). A wider portion of the passage is relevant to our discussion: 'The fundamental confusion of modern time (which branches out in logic, metaphysics, dogmatics, and the time's whole way of life) lies essentially in this: that one has removed the deep qualitative chasm from the distinction between God and man. From that fact there has arisen in dogmatics (from logic and metaphysics) a depth of blasphemy which heathenism did not know (for heathenism knew what blasphemy is, but it is just this which has been forgotten in our time, in the theocentric time) and in ethics a brash unconcern or, more accurately, no ethics at all.'
[96] *S.V.* IV, pp. 193-4 (*PF*, p. 18).
[97] ibid. (ibid.).
[98] ibid. (ibid.).
[99] *Pap.* XI 2 A 54.
[100] ibid. (ibid.).

God's strength and the strength of his passion is his uniqueness. This passion bespeaks God's need. Kierkegaard does not hold back from that: '. . . if God gave no sign, how could man ever come to think that the blessed God could need him?'[101]

Dizziness easily afflicts the mind confronted with such reflections as these. The right way out of all these words given to the independence-dependence of God may, of course, be to say that Kierkegaard has lost himself, his argument, and his reader in a hopeless mass of self-contradiction. This is not the only way out, however, and ought not to be grasped too quickly in dealing with a writer possessing the great precision of thought owned by Kierkegaard. We may do better by distinguishing between an eternal dimension to the love of God and the temporal expression of that love. On the one hand the independence of God is seen in the freedom of the resolve to love. On the other the dependence of God is found in the active and reactive participation of his love in the life of the world.[102] This suggestion does not split God in half, for it is the eternal God of love who loves so unfailingly in this world of space-time. Yet the expression of that love is keyed to his resolve which is ever sure. That may be part of what Kierkegaard has in mind by saying that 'existence (*Tilvaerelse*, German: *Dasein*) itself is a system—for God',[103] because God is 'he who is outside of existence (*Tilvaerelse*, German: *Dasein*) and yet in existence (*Tilvaerelse*), who in his eternity is resolved for eternity, and yet includes existence (*Tilvaerelse*) within himself'.[104] That is, the

---

[101] *S.V.* IV, p. 203 (*PF*, p. 28).

[102] So *S.V.* XII, pp. 75–77 (*TC*, pp. 81–82): God experiences sorrow or joy over man's response. Kierkegaard clearly states that the alternatives of response have meaning for God. See *S.V.* IV, p. 200 (*PF*, p. 25): 'O, to support heaven and earth by the fiat of an almighty word, so that if that word were absent for the smallest fraction of time, all would collapse—how easy that is compared to bearing the possibility that the race might be offended, when one, moved by love, has become its saviour.' See also *S.V.* IX, pp. 65–66 (*WL*, p. 53): heaven rejoices with the glad and sorrows with the sad.

[103] *S.V.* VII, p. 97 (*CUP*, p. 107).

[104] ibid. (ibid., p. 108). See above, page 102, note 11. 'Existence' does seem a better choice than 'being' to register the contrast carried in *Tilvaerelse* in this and the proceeding reference from the *Postscript*. 'Life' might be suggested as a third alternative, but that choice would narrow the reference too much. 'Existence' may be accepted, so long as it is noted that the passages do not blur the distinction between *Tilvaerelse* and *Existents*. The context makes that clear: 'Whenever an existence (*Tilvaerelse*) has been relegated to the past, it is of course complete, has acquired finality, and is in so far subject to a systematic apprehension. Quite right—but, for whom? That man, who is himself existing (*existerende*), can surely not gain the finality outside existence (*Tilvaerelse*) which corresponds to the eternity into which the past has entered. . . . On the contrary, the fact that he is existing (*existerende*) signifies the claim of existence (*Existents*) upon him. . . .' (ibid.

pattern of God's response to the other(s) is primordially complete ('in his eternity . . . resolved for eternity'), while man's resolve must ever be made anew.[105] A fuller point of continuity between these two dimensions of love may be found by asking if the thou(s) sought out by God's choice in the theatre of time have some reality for the eternal resolve itself. It may be right to suppose that the triune community of love provides the means for affirming both that divine love finds completeness prior to participation in this world of time-space and that the divine love's interaction in history is with creatures who find their origin and their present cohesive centre in the eternal *Logos* of God.[106]

Difficulties of at least two sorts appear. On the one hand the reader may bristle with substantive objections to the adequacy of this line of theological construction. On the other, he may wish to contend that the construction—whatever its merits or demerits—is simply not present in Kierkegaard and that the attempt to identify it with him is—at best—a futile guessing game. This second objection is the more serious one at this point in our work. We do not feel these reflections represent an arbitrary imposition of alien categories upon Kierkegaard's works. Yet they surely do more than report what he has said, and it may well be that they reveal the fault of over-systematization. In any case this train of reflection can best be set aside until we discuss the legacy of Kierkegaard in Part Four. At that time it will be in order to face the substantive criticism too. Even here, however, we

---

[ibid.]) Again the broad usage of *Tilvaerelse* provides the continuity sustaining the contrast between God and the individual man. While the contrast retains a note of metaphysical difference, that difference serves the concern of the whole passage to illumine the individual's ethical-religious situation. It is clear that Kierkegaard wishes to stress the challenge the existential situation carries for man. It is not wrong to emphasize the constancy of God as an additional positive ingredient.

[105] See ibid., pp. 158-9 (ibid., pp. 170-1), where Climacus makes clear that it is just for this reason that reality is never a system for an existing individual, i.e., because the pattern of his relationship to the other(s) is always to be decided anew.

[106] This line of reflection outlines a possible response to Collins's charge against Kierkegaard, op. cit., pp. 150-1: 'After admitting a certain likeness between man and God, however, Kierkegaard is faced with the need to explain their difference. Unfortunately, he locates this difference in something other than the very perfection which founds their likeness. He designates sin as the principle of difference, since man derives sin from himself and his own activity. This leaves two things unexplained: how the rest of the created universe is distinguished from God, and how the divine mode of being is set off from that aspect of human being which is perfect, in a natural or supernatural way. A metaphysical theory of participated being would begin by pointing out that, by *deriving* its being from God, the temporal existent is unlike God, even in that respect in which they are alike: *tanta similitudo, major dissimilitudo*' [italics his].

wish to acknowledge that Kierkegaard's discourse in these matters is frought with tension, if not beset by direct contradiction. We shall be speaking very soon of the interpenetration of the rhythms of diastasis and synthesis in Kierkegaard's determination of God's ideal for man. Before doing that we pause to note a particular course which Kierkegaard's thought at times takes in the effort to let his convictions address each other.

3. The Juxtaposition of Synthesis and Diastasis in Kierkegaard's Description of God and Man

We speak consciously at this point of juxtaposition rather than of interpenetration. The convictions carried by the one rhythm are seen to be turned towards those reflecting the other rhythm and are formulated so as to take account of the other convictions. Yet the 'taking account' is more a matter of phrasing than of modification of the essential meaning involved. One gets the impression of separate currents of thought, stable and set within themselves, now acquiring an additional dimension of relatedness, but not one which disturbs the essential course of the reflection involved. Yet another complication can be discerned, and it is such that one might choose to speak of a kind of intepenetration. We refer to the fact that the body of discourse on which our comments in this section are based seems to involve the apportionment of the poles in the divine-human polarity between the rhythms of diastasis and synthesis. Specifically, the diastatic rhythm seems in control of the doctrine of God, while the description of man reflects the rhythm of synthesis.

This highly abstract description can be warmed by some reference to the flesh of the literature itself. Climacus provides us with a start in his statement that 'the more specifically historical coming into being (*tilblivelse*) comes into being (*bliver til*) by a relatively free-working cause, which again definitely points to an absolutely free-working cause'.[107] The mind may hesitate over the apparent combination of relative human freedom and absolute divine freedom, but Kierkegaard greets the challenge with evident enthusiasm in a truly remarkable journal reference, which deserves to be quoted in full:

The whole question of God's omnipotence and goodness and its relation to evil (instead of the distinction that God works good and only permits evil) can perhaps be explained quite simply in this manner. The greatest act that can be performed for any being, greater than any end to which it can be created, is to

[107] *S.V.* IV, p. 240 (*PF*, pp. 62–63). See above, p. 102, note 11.

make it free. In order to be able to do that omnipotence is necessary. . . . God's omnipotence is therefore his goodness. For goodness means to give absolutely, yet in such a way that by almightily taking oneself back one makes the recipient independent. From finite power comes only dependence, and only omnipotence can make something independent, can create something out of nothing which endures of itself, because omnipotence is always taking itself back. Omnipotence cannot be involved in any relation to the other, since there is nothing to which it has any relation; no, it can give without giving away the very least part of its power; it can make the other independent. This is what is inconceivable; omnipotence can not only bring forth the most imposing of all things, the world in its visible totality, but it can create the most delicate of all things, a creature independent before the omnipotent one. Omnipotence can lay its hand so heavily upon the world and yet can make its touch so light that the creature receives independence.—It is only a miserable and worldly picture of the dialectic of power to say that it becomes greater and greater in proportion as it can compel and make things dependent. Socrates knew better; the art of using power is to make free. . . . Creation out of nothing is once again the expression of omnipotence for being able to make things independent. It is to him who made me independent, while he nevertheless retained everything, that I owe all things. If in order to create man God had lost any of his power, then he could not have made man independent.[108]

This beautiful and exasperating passage makes clear that a highly practical interest controls Kierkegaard's discussion in these matters. Kierkegaard intends and believes that his work will matter to the individual who seeks to find his way amid the ambiguities of existence. Not the least of those ambiguities is the experience of apparent evil. Yet a clear word reaches the Christian: his suffering is from God.[109] Kierkegaard senses the threat to the unity of God, but insists that we confront here a 'doubleness' of the divine nature. The mildness and sternness we meet unite in the one God. One may wonder if recognizing such duality in God is not taking a step large enough to commit

[108] *Pap.* VII 1 A 181 (*Dru* 616). On the complete objectivity and subjectivity of God, which marks his superiority, see *Pap.* XI 2 A 97 (*Dru* 1376). This strand of material in Kierkegaard understandably wins high praise from the Thomist point of view. So Collins, op. cit., p. 246, writes: 'There was no conflict in Kierkegaard's mind between a realistic view of knowledge and the transcendence and perfect actuality of God. This suggests that the empiricist proponents of a finite deity have been proceeding on a false alternative. Kierkegaard sought to make return both to realism *and* to a theistic view of God as infinite and transcendent.' [Italics his.] It may be too much to say that Kierkegaard sensed *no* conflict at this point. See *Pap.* II A 752 (*Dru* 204), where he acknowledges that 'the fact that God could create free beings over against Himself is the cross which Philosophy could not carry, but remained hanging from'. In any case Kierkegaard's thought is constantly pulled away from this naked juxtaposition of divine omnipotence and human freedom.

[109] See *Pap.* XI 2 A 130, p. 141, where Kierkegaard openly declares: 'That the Christian must suffer does not come from the devil. And precisely here does the highest exertion of spirit begin in relation to the Christian—that suffering comes from God.' Cf. *Pap.* X 4 A 487.

one to a course which resurrects again the problem of God's unity. Yet Kierkegaard clearly believes that his statement of the matter does give a word to the man of faith, though surely that faith is a strenuous one.[110]

One may feel that the rhythm of synthesis is hardly granted equal time in these last formulations we have offered as suggestive of the juxtaposition of the rhythms. Yet Kierkegaard in an amazing act of self-awareness recognizes that the pulse of synthesis beats faintly at best in these formulations, and that recognition is such that it serves to honour rather than dismiss the claims of the rhythm of synthesis. Thus Kierkegaard acknowledges that man's experience in this world does not provide him with the data necessary to sustain the heady diastatic utterances concerning God which we have cited. Man's knowledge of the world, his understanding of himself—as they are seen in the rhythm of synthesis—are not repudiated, but they do call forth comment from the diastatic impulse controlling the doctrine of God:

> But in the heavens, my hearer, dwells the God who can do all things, or more accurately, he dwells everywhere, even though men do not note that; 'Yes, if Thou, O Lord, wert an impotent and lifeless body, like a flower that fades; if Thou wert like a brook that flows past; if Thou wert like a building that decays in time; then men would take note of Thee, then Thou wouldst be a fitting object for our low and brutish thoughts'; But now it is not so, and it is precisely Thy greatness which makes Thee invisible; for in Thy wisdom Thou art too far removed from the thoughts of a man that he should be able to see Thee, and in Thy omnipresence Thou art too near for him to see Thee; in Thy goodness Thou doest hide Thyself before him, and Thy omnipotence makes it so that he cannot see Thee, for then he would become nothing! But God in the heavens can do all things, and man nothing at all.[111]

It is difficult to see how a diastatic doctrine of God could confront more directly an understanding of man moulded by the rhythm of synthesis without substantive compromise of the concepts involved.

---

[110] *Pap.* XI 2 A 130, pp. 141f.: 'When a man shall conceive of a nature as unadulterated love, then the most fearful exertion for his mind and his soul is that that love should in one respect be cruelty. Behold, this doubleness man has not been able to bear, and so he has made the following division: God is love—from him comes all good . . . all the evil, all plagues, etc., are from the devil.'

[111] *S.V.* V, p. 92 ('MN', *ED*, IV, pp. 25–26). Cf. *Pap.* X 1 A 605 (*Dru* 949): 'For the Christian, God is surely lodged in the creation, but as an invisible mark, just like the watermark in paper.' Cf. *Pap.* III A 38 (*Dru* 326), where Kierkegaard rejects the notion of God's divisibility as implied by a literal reading of the omnipresence he wishes to affirm of God. On the hiddenness of God as the mark of his omnipresence, see *S.V.* XIV, pp. 286–7 ('UG', *SE*, pp. 230–1), *S.V.* VII, pp. 204–5 (*CUP*, pp. 217–8).

The same process of juxtaposition lies behind Kierkegaard's statement that man is indeed made in the image of God, but that we face here an 'image of opposites'.[112]

At times the diastatic control of the doctrine of God seems at the point of giving ground in a more significant way. It is hard to fix precisely the systematic citizenship of the suggestion that God is by his own choice temporarily conditioned, but may choose to revoke this situation at any time. Kierkegaard offers such a formulation when he lets the logic of divine love compromise the witness to omnipotence:

O wonderful omnipotence and love! A man cannot bear that his 'creations' should be something directly over against him; they should be nothing, and therefore he calls them 'creations' with contempt. But God, who creates out of nothing, who almightily takes from nothing and says 'Be!', lovingly adds 'Be something even over against me.' Wonderful love, even his omnipotence is under the power of love!

Hence the reciprocal relationship. If God were only the Almighty, there would be no reciprocal relation; for the creation is nothing for the Almighty. But it is something for love. Incomprehensible omnipotence of love! For in comparison with this omnipotence, it seems as if one could better comprehend the omnipotence which creates out of nothing (which one, however, cannot comprehend); but this omnipotence (more wonderful than the coming into being of all creation) forces itself, and lovingly makes that which it creates to be something directly over against itself: oh, wonderful omnipotence of love! . . . One speaks of God's omnipotence crushing a man. But that is not so; no man is so significant that God should need omnipotence in order to crush him, for over against omnipotence he is nothing. It is God's love, which even in the last moment shows itself as love by letting man be something over against itself. Woe be to him, if omnipotence turns against him.

Thus love, which made a man to be something (for omnipotence let him come into being, but love let him come into being over against God) lovingly demands something of him. Now that is the reciprocal relation.[113]

Such a passage with its centering on human responsibility before God surely seems to beat with the rhythm of synthesis. Yet the passage does warn of 'omnipotence turning against a man'. That warning's reference to the diastatic current is confirmed by the closing words of the discourse supplying this passage: 'So, then, there is nothing to fear in the world, nothing that can deprive you of your power, and make

---

[112] On this theme, see Lindström, op. cit., p. 107. It is this kind of diastatic countering to which Lindström attends when he criticizes (*Efterföljelsens Teologi hos Sören Kierkegaard* [Stockholm: Svenska Kyrkans Diakonistryelse, 1956] p. 45) Marie Thulstrup for her efforts ('Kierkegaard's "onde verden"', Kierkegaardiana, ed. Niels Thulstrup, 1955, p. 53) to identify a tendency towards a natural theology in Kierkegaard's thought.

[113] *S.V.* X, pp. 132–3 (*CDi*, pp. 132–3).

you totally weak, nothing that can break all your confidence in yourself and make you totally weak, nothing that can bend your earthly courage, and make you totally weak—for the weaker you become, all the stronger does God become in you.'[114]

What can safely be said of such discourse is that the bare juxtaposition of the rhythms of diastasis and synthesis has given way to living interpenetration. That interpenetration also characterizes a major portion of Kierkegaard's reflection on God's ideal for man. The statement of the opposition of God and man in the passage last quoted has introduced us to the topic of the determination of that ideal. It is to that subject that we now turn in chapter four.

[114] ibid., p. 137 (ibid., p. 138). Both passages quoted from *CDi* show the soteriological interest of Kierkegaard in these matters. For a briefer but, if anything, even clearer statement of that interest, see *Pap.* II A 758 (*Dru* 209): 'God creates out of *nothing*, wonderful, you say: yes, to be sure, but he does what is still more wonderful: he makes saints (the communion of saints) out of sinners.' [Italics his.] Later in this book we shall be asking what bearing this interest has for the thinker who seeks to adjudicate the claims of the rhythms of diastasis and synthesis.

IV

THE INTERPENETRATION OF THE RHYTHMS
OF REFLECTION IN KIERKEGAARD'S
DETERMINATION OF GOD'S IDEAL FOR MAN[1]

1. *The Interpenetration of* Diastasis *and* Synthesis *in the Formal Determination of the Ideal*

WE HAVE already introduced Kierkegaard's view that man is confronted with an ideal. The attainment of the ideal is a possibility for man—only that and all of that. Our review of Hegel's thought makes it clear that ethical possibility finds no place in the System. Even if one takes Hegel's interest in the many as seriously as possible, the discernment of the ideal must be deferred to the issue of the world-historical process. If one inquires into the reason lying behind that limitation, one encounters the fact that reality as a whole represents the course of the Spirit. Thus the impediment to ethics is seen to be not merely epistemological, but ontological, for the very distinction between the real and the ideal is obliterated.

Kierkegaard takes the steps necessary to permit the reflective man to resist the System's conclusions concerning ethics. In examining his reflection concerning God's ideal for man, we shall find him affirming the genuine possibility of the ideal. We shall be in the most part concerned to emphasize the positive character of this possibility. But we ought not fail—*vis-à-vis* Hegel and to some extent Kierkegaard himself—to note the limitations intrinsic to this possibility. The epistemological limitation is acknowledged. The discernment of the ideal does not proceed smoothly from the rational analysis of the real. Thus the lengthy argument of the *Fragments-Postscript* against building an eternal happiness on an 'approximation' derives much of its force

---

[1] In addition to the secondary works mentioned in connection with matters of detail throughout the chapter, see on Kierkegaard's whole approach to ethics Elfriede Tielsch, *Kierkegaards Glaube* (Göttingen: Vandenhoeck & Ruprecht, 1964). Tielsch sets Kierkegaard's ethical thought in relation to general value theory and discusses both formal and material dimensions to Kierkegaard's ethics, as well as the connection Kierkegaard discerned between ethics and religion.

from the fact that virtual certainty in the discernment of the real in no sense requires identification of the ideal status of the real discerned. The epistemological relationship reflects the ontological situation. Christianity is 'precisely inwardness', but it is 'not any and every type of inwardness'.² It follows, then, that 'attentiveness is by no means partial to faith, as if faith appeared from attentiveness as a simple consequence. The advantage [in being made attentive] is that one comes to such a state of mind that [the nature of] the decision shows itself more clearly.'³

Possibility is the air which human striving needs if it is to survive. Kierkegaard does indisputably identify the life of the self as one of striving.⁴ He judges Christianity to involve a specification of that striving, not a repudiation of it.⁵ No man honours God's sovereignty by sniping at human responsibility: '. . . man is granted a choice. . . . Man not merely *can* choose . . . he *must* choose . . . for in such a way God holds himself in honour, while he also has a fatherly concern for man. If God has condescended to be that which *can be chosen*, then man also *must* choose—God does not let himself be mocked.'⁶ In fact positions are reversed as far as the question of blasphemy is concerned: '. . . in a certain sense God places himself with the world on the equal line of choice, merely in order that man can choose . . .'⁷ 'It is therefore a deceitful speech if someone will say that God is so exalted, that he cannot condescend to be chosen—for then the choice is done away with . . . that speech which with exaltation would hinder God from letting himself be chosen is blasphemy. . . .'⁸ God, then, does not permit a man to choose, he *requires* him to do so.⁹ 'The strictly religious is one whose life is essentially action'¹⁰ and Kierkegaard will permit no man to appeal

---

² *S.V.* VII, p. 241 (*CUP*, p. 251). Cf. the observation that 'the edifying' is a wider category than 'the Christian', ibid., p. 216 (ibid., p. 229).
³ *S.V.* IV, p. 256 (*PF.* p. 78).
⁴ See above, pp. 102–3, 107–9. See also Per Lönning, '*Samtidighedens Situation*' (Oslo: Land og Kirke, 1954), *passim*, for a discussion of the eros motif in Kierkegaard's thought.
⁵ See above, pp. 110, 111, 113–4.
⁶ *S.V.* VIII, pp. 290–1 ('WLF', *GS*, pp. 228–9). [Italics his.]
⁷ ibid., p. 290 (ibid.).
⁸ ibid., pp. 291–2 (ibid., p. 230).
⁹ Cf. *S.V.* XI, p. 189 (*SD*, pp. 123–4), where Kierkegaard identifies 'the sin of poetizing instead of being, of relating oneself to the good and the true through phantasy instead of being that, that is, existentially striving to be that'.
¹⁰ *S.V.* XII, p. 303 (*SE*, p. 37). This must be understood to be the major point that *SE* is trying to make. That point is well supported elsewhere in the authorship. Thus the action flowing from religion is held to make a discernible—yes, even an

to a Christian status which has no relationship to a Christian striving.[11]

One cannot bring Kierkegaard to retract this line of thought by revealing to him the fact that it assumes the freedom of the human will. The professors may tell us that the voluntaristic emphasis must be neatly filed in the compartment labelled 'Judaism', but the way of the free will is actually wholly as much the Christian way.[12] In *PV* Kierkegaard identifies the principle of genuine, though limited, freedom as his own: '. . . I have never for a single moment in my life been forsaken by the faith that one can what one will—only one thing not, otherwise everything, but not one, to throw off the melancholy in whose power I was . . .'[13]

How may this voluntaristic line of thought be related to the apparent inadequacy of the ethical in Kierkegaard's understanding as structured by the schema of the stages? We shall see later in this chapter that more than one point of view can claim a share in the movement of Kierkegaard's thought beyond (against?) the ethical stage. But if we remain for the present attentive to the rhythm of synthesis we have been following in this section, we can let this question bring into sharper focus the theological character of Kierkegaard's discussion of the ideal. In *CUP* Kierkegaard criticizes the ethicist in *E-O*:

If *Either-Or* had tried to make clear where the irregularity lies, the book would have had to be religiously oriented, instead of ethically, . . . The irregularity is that the ethical self is supposed to be found immanently in despair, that the individual by enduring despair wins himself. He has indeed used a determination of freedom, to choose oneself, which seems to remove the difficulty, . . . When I despair, I use myself to despair, and therefore I can very well by myself despair of all things, but when I do that, I cannot by myself come back. In this moment of decision it is that the individual needs divine assistance, while it is quite right to say that one must first have understood the existential relationship between the

---

obvious—difference in one's life. We discuss this emphasis later in this chapter, but even now we may cite a sampling of its range: *S.V.* X, pp. 214–18 (*CDi*, pp. 221–5); XII, pp. 220–1 (*TC*, p. 235); IV, pp. 374–5 (*CD*, pp. 94–96).

[11] *Pap.* XI 2 A 379: 'When one sees thousands and thousands and millions of Christians, whose lives do not have even in the most distant way the least resemblance to what—and this is the decisive point—the New Testament calls Christians: then is it not strange and confusing, is it not to speak as one would in no other situation, if one says: how poorly or how not at all do the Christians express what it is to be Christian? Would one not in every other situation say: These men are not Christian.'

[12] See *Pap.* X 4 A 656 and X 5 A 5, 14: for Kierkegaard 'I cannot' means 'I will not'.

[13] *S.V.* XIII, p. 565 (*PV*, p. 78).

aesthetic and the ethical in order to be at this point; that is to say, by being there in passion and inwardness, one will surely become attentive to the religious—and the leap.[14]

What one encounters in this passage is Kierkegaard's critique of a self-contained ethic. Indeed *Either-Or* itself sounds this note. In discussing the element of necessity marking the concrete self, Judge William is led to speak of the son repenting the iniquity of the father which passes to him, and he adds: 'His self is, as it were, outside of him, and it must be acquired, and repentance is his love to that end, because he chooses it absolutely from the hand of the eternal God.'[15] Judge William observes that 'from this point a theologian will find a point of departure for a multitude of reflections',[16] but declines as a layman to probe deeper. Yet the presuppositions for such an investigation are given in *E-O*. The point of repentance is not merely that the self is participant in a sinful race, but that in itself it possesses no claim to itself. 'His self is, as it were, outside of him, and it must be acquired.' The self is constituted by being before God, and the ethical choice which actualizes the self is empowered and informed by this living relationship to 'the constituting Power'.

What *CUP* adds to *E-O* is a closer measurement of the difficulty involved in a despairing recognition of the futility and depravity of a self contained striving. Climacus makes abundantly clear as well how difficult it is for man to permit his selfhood and its striving to be constituted in dependence on the divine other. Admittedly the diastatic impulse so influences the report that the continuity with *E-O* is at times nearly wholly obscured. But the emphasis on the theological character of selfhood is present in *E-O*. And what this emphasis with its wide recognition in Kierkegaard's works means for our discussion at this point is not only that God is needed for the self, but also that he is available to that self. Indeed our discussion of the unavoidability of the encounter with God[17] has made clear that 'available' is a miserably inadequate and even distorted way of expressing the actual state of affairs. Kierkegaard speaks not of an established self which may in its many relationships happen to strike up an acquaintance with a God who waits at the service of the self. He witnesses rather to a living God who confronts the emerging self and calls it to true selfhood by claiming it for himself.

---

[14] *S.V.* VII, pp. 217–8 (*CUP*, pp. 230-1). [Italics his.]
[15] *S.V.* II, p. 194 (*E-O* II, p. 182).
[16] ibid., p. 195 (ibid., p. 183).
[17] See above, pp. 109–13.

It may be impossible wholly to disregard the massive witness in Kierkegaard's works to the principle that the self is so 'aimed at God'[18] that the divine call to the ethical ideal is not an external one.[19] But how shall one move from this witness to Kierkegaard's pointed emphasis on the uniqueness of the Christian faith and on the role the historical plays in that faith? In our chapters on Kierkegaard's christology we shall find this question pressing upon us. But some comment is also required at this point. A journal reference offers a distinction which bears directly on our concern with the possibility of the ideal: 'The difference between education in relation to the ethical and the ethical-religious is simply this, that the ethical, as it is, is the universal human, but the religious (Christian) education must first communicate a certain knowledge.'[20] Thus while it is the case with the ethical that 'every man knows it',[21] of the religious Kierkegaard must say 'man as such is not aware of the religious, here there is required first of all a little communication of knowledge—but then there sets in again the same relation as in the ethical'.[22]

These passages make a distinction, but hardly suggest a sharp severance or actual opposition between the ethical and the religious (Christian). A significant formal continuity is secured in that the 'little communication' of knowledge is precisely a first step looking towards the engagement of the self's passion—the very kind of decisive action which the ethical calls for from the individual. The

---

[18] See *S.V.* VII, p. 508 (*CUP*, p. 517); IV, pp. 373–4 (*CD*, pp. 93–94). This aiming of the self is more a witness to God's presence than to his absence—see *Pap.* V B 40, 11, where it is suggested that there are no atheists, though some men surely do not let their consciousness of God control their minds.

[19] In *S.V.* II, pp. 228–9 (*E-O* II, pp. 212–3) Kierkegaard criticizes a view which contrasts the aesthetic life of enjoyment with an ethical life of fulfilment of duty: 'The mistake is this, that the individual is set in an external relation to duty. The ethical is determined as duty, and duty in turn as a multitude of individual propositions, but the individual and duty stand outside of one another. Such a life of duty is naturally very unlovely and tiresome, and if the ethical did not have a far deeper connection with the personality, it would always be very difficult to advocate it over against the aesthetic.' In truth, 'the ethical individual has duty not outside him, but within him'. (ibid., p. 230 [ibid., p. 214].) Cf. *Pap.* III A 5: 'It is a thought just as beautiful as profound and sound which Plato expresses when he says that all knowledge is recollection, for how sad it would be if that which should bring peace to a human being, that in which he can really find rest were external to him . . . and if the only means of consolation, this external knowledge (*sit venia verbo*), with its incessant and noisy din, came to drown out the inward need which never became satisfied.'

[20] *Pap.* VIII 2 B 82, 13.
[21] *Pap.* VIII 2 B 81, 5.
[22] *Pap.* VIII 2 B 82, 13.

formal continuity opens on a material continuity, for the contrasts in these passages between the ethical and the religious are not so put as to state or suggest a repudiation of the ethical. We shall want to ask later if Kierkegaard does speak otherwise of the relationship between the ethical and the religious at other times and within this chapter we shall have to deal with the theme of 'the teleological suspension of the ethical'. On the other hand, we shall also want to ask if only anecdotal significance is to be found in Kierkegaard's application of the Socratic analogy to himself on the strength of the fact that his age did not lack *knowledge* of Christianity.[23]

For now, however, it seems correct to say that the Christian faith in Kierkegaard's view does not entail a rejection of the principle that God's ideal is known to man. And it also seems possible for the Christian to accept the further point that since the knowledge of God's ideal is not to be separated from knowing God, the self faced with the illumining and enobling divine presence can no more plead incapability than ignorance. Until our later concern with christology reopens these questions we leave the matter at this, then, relying on the context provided by our earlier discussion of the relationships between the stages.[24]

It should be clear that in saying that the encounter with God is an enobling one for the self Kierkegaard is not employing a euphemism to conceal the actual displacement of the self. The Christian man may in truth say that 'God in heaven waits for him, willing to help', but he knows too that God will help 'in the way one can help with an examination which yet must have the seriousness of the highest examination'.[25]

We have seen that the theological dimension characterizing Kierkegaard's discussion of the ideal is such that man's authentic fulfilment is seen to lie in response to God's call and only there. Apart from God ennui envelops the self; with God all of time is not enough to tire one: 'One can become glutted with and weary of all that is temporal and earthly, so that it would be torment if it were to continue into all eternity. But he who has an eye for the ideals has in the very moment of beholding them only one prayer to God: eternity. This prayer is heard at once, for ideals and eternity are eternally

---

[23] See above, pp. 69–72.

[24] See above, pp. 35–39.

[25] *S.V.* XII, p. 176 (*TC*, p. 188). Cf. *Pap.* XI 2 A 439 (*Diary* 239). See also *S.V.* XII, p. 303 (*SE*, p. 37); IX, pp. 102–3 (*WL*, p. 87) and *Pap.* III A 26 (*Dru* 324) for the emphasis on the sense of responsibility which accompanies the breaking-in on one of the Absolute.

inseparable.'[26] Other passages read 'immortality' for 'eternity': '. . . for ethically everything culminates in immortality, without which the ethical is only the customary . . .'[27]

It is difficult to know how to take such references. They seem to push us beyond the introduction of the ethical as a standard of importance which lifts ethics beyond positivism. They may witness to the unending lure of the ideal which makes the self restless in its finitude. But another meaning intrudes at this point. Kierkegaard seems to move from saying (1) that one would never weary of a divinely validated pursuit, through saying (2) that the self is never to be denied this pursuit, to saying (3) that the pursuit and the finally attained goal is immortality. A passage from *CUP* blends the first two stages in this movement: 'And to ask about his immortality is at the same time for the existing subject, who asks the question, a deed, which it surely is not for those absent-minded people who once in a while ask about being immortal wholly in general, as if immortality were something one has once in a while and the questioner were such a something-in-general. He asks, therefore, how he is to behave in existence in order to express his immortality, whether he really expresses it, and for the time being he is satisfied with this task, which must, after all, easily stretch to fill a human life, since it shall stretch to fill eternity.'[28] But the third meaning imposes upon the consciousness of the self as its task, 'for immortality is the judgment. Immortality is not a continuous life, not even a life continued perpetually, but immortality is the eternal separation between the just and the unjust; immortality is no continuation, which follows as a matter of course, but a separation, which follows from the past.'[29]

To use 'immortality' to refer both to new life beyond time and to a specific form of that life ('blessedness') may be confusing but it is not self-contradictory.[30] The distinction itself implies that the certainty of immortality applies only to the prospect of some future life. That certainty testifies that God's sovereignty cannot be overthrown or eluded, even if it can be resisted. Thus is man addressed: '. . . you are immortal, and you shall make an accounting before God of how

---

[26] *Pap.* X 6 B 173, p. 276.
[27] *S.V.* VII, p. 145 (*CUP*, p. 156).
[28] *S.V.* VII, pp. 146–7 (*CUP*, pp. 157–8).
[29] *S.V.* X, p. 206 (*CDi*, pp. 212–3).
[30] Gregor Malantschuk distinguishes between these two uses of the term and chronicles the tension created by the convictions requiring the twin usages in his *Kierkegaard's Way to the Truth*, trans. Mary Michelsen (Minneapolis: Augsburg, 1963), pp. 79–97.

you have lived, you immortal one! Precisely because you are immortal you will not be able to escape God, you will not be able to hide yourself in a grave and appear as nothing; and the measure by which you shall be judged by God is this, that you are immortal.'[31]

It is difficult to determine which of the rhythms of Kierkegaard's reflection is in the ascendency in the affirmation of this certainty. At any rate one speaks safely here of an 'interpenetration' of the rhythms of synthesis and diastasis. And we may well use Kierkegaard's discourse concerning immortality as a point of transition to our discussion of the dominance of the diastatic tendency in his discourse concerning God's ideal for man. The recognition of the possibility of actualizing the ideal is central to the synthesis strand which has occupied our attention thus far in this chapter. It seems right, in turn, to link the emphasis on the certainty of an actualization of the ideal with the rhythm of diastasis. Of course, if that rhythm were wholly unqualified, it would repudiate the very notion of an ideal. At least that would be the case in so far as the ideal is defined as having subjective significance for God. Malcom Diamond makes the point well in commenting on the Kierkegaardian analogies of the lowly poor man (*TC*) and the king who loved a poor maiden (*PF*): 'These dramatizations of the Divine-human encounter are magnificent, but deeply moved though we may be by Kierkegaard's excursions into the Divine stream of consciousness, we ought not to let them distract us to the point where we ignore his own strictures against regarding this sort of thing as being in any sense possible. Given the God described by Kierkegaard as infinite, eternal, and necessary, these dramatizations are utterly inconceivable, because such a God cannot yearn for anything.'[32]

Diamond seems to discern rightly the path of an isolated diastatic current swept along in its metaphysical tributaries. But the rhythms of diastasis and synthesis constantly penetrate what appear to be alien territories, and within that process of interpenetration the diastatic tendency presses for recognition of a certainty which would as far as possible reflect the absolutely unconditional sovereignty of God.

This pressure for certainty finds many expressions in Kierkegaard's thought, We are not principally interested in the occasional suggestions that all men's striving will ultimately issue in participation in

[31] *S.V.* X, p. 207 (*CDi*, p. 214).
[32] Malcolm Diamond, 'Kierkegaard and Apologetics', *The Journal of Religion*, April, 1964, p. 127.

the final blessedness.[33] We are far more interested in the direct effects the preoccupation with certainty has on the conception of man's striving towards God's ideal. Those effects appear to be direct, though they could—it would seem—also be secured by following out the implications for this life of the logic of universalism. Indeed Kierkegaard can speak of the man of faith making contact with the Eternal, the ground of the future, and so coming to know that his future is certain.[34] But the pressure for certainty scores gains which are not explicitly related to any articulation of a final universalism. These gains seem to represent varying degrees of penetration—or perhaps we should say domestication—of the concept of the ideal and its requirement of possiblity.

An obvious form that the certainty motif might take would be to deny that God ever in any sense at all lets the task of realizing the ideal out of his hand. Self-dependence masks independence in such a formulation. Kierkegaard does speak at times in this way: 'The Christian sings in praise of only one thing, and does that by obedience that God does all, and that all God does is pure grace and wisdom.'[35] One may recall, too, that in describing his own life Kierkegaard makes reference to an overruling power, Thus, looking back to his becoming an author, he has the impression that it was 'as if there were another power, which from the first moment had been observant . . . and said, as the fisherman says of the fish, Only let it run, it is still too early to pull it in.'[36] Yet one must say that the passages suggesting this formulation are few and often are challenged from within. Thus the hymn of praise to the God who does all is sung by man's obedience and the witness to the overruling power of God is countered in its context by the recognition of human responsibility.[37] Kierkegaard's commitment to human responsibility is simply too great for this expression of the certainty motif to be very attractive to him. The early volumes of the *Journals* do reveal his interest in the concept of predestination, but also record his rejection of that concept: 'From every point of view the concept of predestination may be considered

---

[33] One finds such a suggestion in *Pap.* XI 2 A 244: 'Nevertheless it always seems to me that in spite of the profound nonsense in which we are stuck fast, we shall all, however, be saved.' On this point see Malantschuk, op. cit., p. 95.

[34] On this point see Johannes Slök, 'Das Verhältnis des Menschen zu seiner-Zukunst', *Orbis Litterarum*, 1963, pp. 60–79.

[35] *S.V.* X, p. 88 (*CDi*, p. 87).

[36] *S.V.* XIII, p. 568 (*PV*, p. 82).

[37] Thus the autobiographical reference from *PV* cited above falls within a prayer for strength to do God's will.

as an abortion, for having unquestionably arisen in order to relate freedom and God's omnipotence it solves the riddle by denying one of the concepts and consequently explains nothing.'[38]

If one moves slightly nearer a recognition of human responsibility, one can concede that the encounter between God and man may not yield obedience, but still insist that the principle of motion throughout is divine.[39]

A more subtle but equally substantial penetration of the ideal is represented by a tendency to so elevate individuality as to essentially alter it. Thus one will move from saying that the response to the ideal can only come from the individual to suggesting that that response will always be affirmative. In *Either-Or* the critical point is located as follows: 'As soon as one can get a man to stand at the crossroads in such a way that there is no way out for him without making a choice, then he will make the right choice.'[40] This option finds expression in more than early pseudonymous works. Kierkegaard's *Journals* can repeat this identification of the real and the ideal almost to the word.[41] And in 1851 Kierkegaard could publish the following creed: 'And this is my faith, that however much there may be that is confused and evil and detestable in men as soon as they become that irresponsible and impenitent "public", "crowd", there is just as much that is true and good and charming in them when one can get at them as individuals. Oh and in what degree would not men become—men and lovable, if they would become individuals before God!'[42]

A slightly different possibility available to the writer who would give words to the certainty motif is to grant man both the alternatives of obedience and rebellion, but to deny that the latter possesses any significance for God. Such a God's 'will will be done—though all rise up against him, which for him would signify nothing'.[43] The sovereign subject can cause the significance of rebellion to evaporate before him: '. . . certainly (God) is personality, but whether he will be that over against the individual depends on whether that pleases God. It is the grace of God that he will be personality in relation to you; if you waste his grace, he punishes you by relating himself to you objectively.

[38] *Pap.* I A 5 (*Dru* 2).
[39] Thus in *S.V.* IV, pp. 215–9 (*PF*, pp. 39–42) Climacus emphasizes the passive character of offence.
[40] *S.V.* II, p. 152 (*E-O* II, p. 142).
[41] See Lönning, op cit., p. 251, on this witness from the *Journals*.
[42] *S.V.* XIII, p. 499 (*PV*, pp. 149–50).
[43] *S.V.* X, p. 55 (*CDi*, p. 54). Cf. *S.V.* VIII, pp. 159–60 (*PH*, p. 92).

And in this respect one can say that the world (despite all proofs) does not have a personal God. . . .'[44]

If one wishes to object that the significance of obedience is itself only verbally retained in this formulation, Kierkegaard is prepared to recognize the force of the objection:

Hence I am suspicious of the way one uses the expression 'to serve God'. For one cannot serve God as one serves another monarch who, humanly speaking, has a cause he purposes to attain. No, the only fitting expression for God's majesty is: to worship him. In general one does, to be sure, make the distinction, that in worshipping God one has in mind one's feelings, moods and their expression in word, and in serving God one has in mind one's actions. No, your action is precisely the true worship and it is that when it is freed from all busyness, as if God had a purpose. In worship to forsake all, and not because God must use you as an instrument, no, not in any way, but to forsake all as one having the character of the most unconditioned superfluity and object of luxury—that is to worship.[45]

Behind such a formulation lies a view of the relationship between God and man which holds that 'surely all that exists is nothing in the hand of the Almighty . . . (for) by coming into existence (one) attains nothing more than to be superfluous'.[46] This is strong stuff, indeed, and one may feel that nothing actually remains here of the concern for the ideal. Yet that we are still dealing with a process of interpenetration is made clear by a final remarkable passage: 'It is, then, easy enough to see that the one for whom all is equally significant and equally nothing, easy to see that for him there is only one thing left which can interest him: obedience. This is the absolute majesty.'[47]

We have watched the insistence on possibility and the drive for certainty meet—both in violent collisions and in subtle blendings. The interpenetration of the two rhythms appears in its most striking form, perhaps, in a formulation to which we give the closing paragraphs of this section on the formal determination of the ideal. We refer to Kierkegaard's understanding of the self as a synthesis of the temporal and the eternal. This theme is both frequent and fundamental in Kierkegaard's thought, and has merited the considerable

[44] *Pap.* XI 2 A 175 (*Dru* 1388). Cf. ibid., XI 2 A 54: '. . . from a Christian point of view God is infinite majesty in such a way that nothing in and for itself can engage his attention, but only in so far as it pleases his majesty, from which it follows in turn that the most insignificant thing can engage his attention just as much as what we men would call the most significant. . . .' While a war involving Europe, Asia, Africa, America, and Australia would, 'in and for itself not engage God's attention in the least', 'that a poor man sighs to him, that engages his attention, for it so pleases his majesty, and this touches him subjectively', ibid.

[45] ibid., XI 2 A 133 (*Dru* 1381).

[46] *S.V.* X, p. 85 (*CDi*, pp. 83-84).

[47] *Pap.* XI 1 A 5.

attention scholars have paid it.[48] On the face of things the description of man as a synthesis of this sort would not seem necessarily to witness to the interpenetration with which we are concerning ourselves. The phrase could simply refer to the quest so to live among the relativities of life as to transcend them by imparting to one's life the quality to be found in hearkening to the call of the one who measures all that is relative. Yet manifestly more is involved than that, for the goal of synthesis is seen constantly to elude the self. A draft for *CUP* states the unattainability of the goal:

> From a finite point of view, of course, the continued and merely continued striving towards a goal without ever reaching it is something to be rejected, but if we look at it from the point of view of infinity, life itself consists precisely in such striving, which indeed is the essential thing in the life of one who is compounded of the finite and the infinite. The conception of positive completeness is chimerical. No doubt it is possible that logic has such completeness, though this should be more clearly elucidated than has hitherto been done; but the subject is existing, and is thus in contradiction and thus in becoming, and thus if he exists at all, is striving.[49]

This passage and its celebration of the self's constant striving does not push beyond the limits of the synthesis rhythm. It honours the dynamic element by offering it a central place in a reformulated notion of the goal. But Kierkegaard's thought also shows an inclination so to conceive of the goal that the mere presence of striving marks the self as a failure.[50] Thus the striving is seen to symbolize the state of the self caught between the temporal and the eternal, when those terms are filled with the mutually exclusive metaphysical meanings we have found the diastatic impulse occasionally to enlist. The incom-

[48] Such different minds as Walter Schulz (in 'Existenz und System bei Sören Kierkegaard' in *Wesen und Wirklichkeit des Menschen* [Göttingen: Vandenhoeck & Ruprecht, 1957]), Johannes Slök (in *Die Anthropologie Kierkegaards* [Copenhagen: Rosenkilde and Bagger, 1954]), Gregor Malantschuk (in 'Begrebet Fordoblelse hos Sören Kierkegaard', *Kierkegaardiana*, 1957, pp. 43–54), and Wilhelm Anz (in *Kierkegaard und der Deutsche Idealismus* [Tübingen: J. C. B. Mohr, 1956]) agree on the centrality of the theme. Of course the agreement may not be as impressive as it appears on first sight, for we shall find that the theme encompasses great diversity within itself. Lönning, op. cit., p. 136, argues that time and eternity as such are of no interest to Kierkegaard. Lönning is surely right that Kierkegaard's concern is with the factual existence of one 'composed' of the temporal and the eternal. This is not to say, however, that no independent determinations of the temporal and the eternal are brought to bear on the analysis of the existent self.

[49] *Pap.* VI B 35.

[50] Günther Rohrmoser, 'Ernst oder Ironie?—Eine Zwischenbemerkung zu Interpretation Kierkegaards', *Archiv für Geschichte der Philosophie*, 1962, pp. 75–87, pleads for an investigation of the concept of perfection which underlies this judgment.

patibility of these components of selfhood yields a development by which the temporal and the eternal elements each claim the totality of the self.[51] One may still hold the discussion formally to the territory of synthesis by insisting that it is the self's task to unite these components. Yet the stage is set for the drive to negate the temporal.[52] We shall see how that drive builds up momentum when we discuss the material determination of the ideal. Again then we will face the question whether the diastatic impulse, swept along by the momentum of the metaphysical distinctions it has recruited, may not have been carried past the measured distance sought as a base for divine judgment. In any case the diastatic rhythm often seems virtually unchallenged in this material. Still we should add here that the power of the synthesis rhythm is felt in the recognition of its plea that the reality of man—and even his worth—be not compromised in the glorification of God.

Thus the process of interpenetration of the two rhythms in Kierkegaard's formal determination of the ideal is never resolved in the total triumph of one. Rather the clash between them at this point throws off the sparks which ignite other areas in his discourse—as, for example, his statements on paradox. We shall be examining the many turnings of Kierkegaard's discourse on that topic in our discussion of his christology, but even now our discussion has prepared us for the central theme: the paradox that man exists before God. A process of thought in which the effort to emphasize the dimension of distance in the divine-human encounter threatens to yield the disappearance of the one pole or the other will have much to say on this theme. And it should surprise no one that such a process of thought will affirm that the contact is born of and borne by God and yet have more than a little trouble with the systematic implications

---

[51] See, for example, *S.V.* VII, pp. 460–2 (*CUP*, pp. 470–1) for a most revealing discussion of the totality of guilt (temporality). Cf. ibid., pp. 366–7, 499–500 (ibid., p. 378, 508).

[52] In his debate with Olesen K. Larsen in *Tidehverv* K. E. Lögstrup has classified Kierkegaard as a pietist because he requires that absolute demands and finite tasks must be *psychologically* reconcilable. We have tried to show that there is a level at which an opposition in principle can be shown. That will become clearer in the next section of this chapter. What remains in doubt is the extent to which an opposition involving actual antagonism is attained on theological ground. We shall be arguing that as far as the substance of Kierkegaard's theological thought is concerned the severance suggesting antagonism never wholly controls. We may be arguing that as far as the substance of Kierkegaard's theological thought is concerned the severance suggesting antagonism never wholly controls. We may be 'always in the wrong' over against God—but how edifying is that thought! The Lögstrup-Larsen debate runs through many issues of *Tidehverv*, but for the identification of Kierkegaard as a pietist see Lögstrup's 'Svar til Olesen Larsen', *Tidehverv*, 1955, pp. 97–109.

of that affirmation. If the stubborn witness to human responsibility still is not silenced one may understand that man's response comes to be seen as an act quite without relation to the other acts of the self. But we have come upon the ground to be covered in the next section and, indeed, in those that follow it.

2. The Interpenetration of Diastasis and Synthesis in the Material Determination of the Ideal

If one asks of Kierkegaard what living flesh these skeletal lines may be found to bear in the actual existence of the self, one receives a response in which one can discern a highly complex process of interaction between the rhythms of synthesis and diastasis. A number of statements are at hand which will bestow a verbal unity on Kierkegaard's discourse at this point. Thus Valter Lindström surely can contend that God's claim is that man shall be conscious of his God-relation, and that that consciousness is to include an awareness of himself as spirit.[53] But both rhythms manifestly possess strong roots in the description of God and man and so can claim an ideal of God-consciousness as their own—and do. Indeed most of the sources for a discussion of Kierkegaard's handling of this topic are characterized by the presence of the dialogue of claim and counter-claim. We do meet again, then, a process of interpenetration of the rhythms. Yet one can discern the ascendency of a particular rhythm from time to time,[54] and we begin our discussion by examining the utterances which seem to reflect most clearly the rhythm of synthesis.

As one follows the course of Kierkegaard's thought as it flows with this rhythm it becomes apparent that Kierkegaard's effort materially to specify God's ideal for man provides the reader with another witness to the essentially systematic character of his thought. Kierkegaard cannot derive the material specification of the ideal from his analysis of God and man without contradicting the recognition of divine freedom and sovereignty which is so central to that analysis. He respects this limitation. But his consistency finds positive expression as well, for his discourse on the material specification of the ideal

---

[53] Valter Lindström, *Stadiernas Teologi* (Lund: Haakan Ohlsson, 1943), pp. 99–100.
[54] This measure of apportionment is what made it possible for Torsten Bohlin in *Sören Kierkegaards Etiska Aaskaadning* (Stockholm: Svenska Kyrkans Diakoni-styrelse, 1918), p. 260, to find that Kierkegaard had 'placed in direct juxtaposition two views which really had to exclude each other'. We will make clear that the separation does not seem as sharp or as final to us as it did to Bohlin.

attaches itself deftly to his analysis of the divine-human relationship through the middle term of the formal determination of the ideal.

The self's dependence on others is descriptively beyond contest. Kierkegaard's theological perspective leads him to add the judgment contained in the title given one of his edifying discourses: man's need of God is his highest perfection. The ideal to which man is called does not ignore or repudiate that need. Rather it satisfies that need. This is clear already at the point of motivation. If 'love' is the ideal, it is so for the self who needs to love: '. . . the expression for the greatest wealth is to have a need; . . . That one in whom love is a need, surely feels himself free in his love, and precisely that one who feels himself wholly dependent, so that he would lose everything in losing the beloved, precisely that one is independent.'[55] This is surely to distingush between self-fulfilment and selfishness. To be sure, there is material upon which one can base the contention that in Kierkegaard it is Kantian deontology that triumphs.[56] We shall find more than a little of such material borne along by the diastatic current. That current, responding to its distrust of the theme of human fulfilment, can even appear to convert the very character of love and so alter its consequences. Yet the synthesis rhythm restrains one who proposes to render love's meaning clear by means of a sado-masochistic grammar: 'To love him who makes one happy, is to a reflective mind an inadequate determination of love; to love him, who in malice made one unhappy, is virtue; but to love him, who out of love, and so through a misunderstanding, but out of love made one unhappy: that is . . . reflection's normal formula for what it is to love.'[57] The link between love and unhappiness *is* based on misunderstanding, and that holds true of lover as well as beloved, for 'the one who cannot love is the most unhappy of all'.[58]

The exhortation to return love, to 'love one another', supplies the ethical recognition of the reciprocity of satisfaction which one would expect of a thinker who views the self's relationships with others as essential to its creaturehood. That reciprocity is not limited to a process by which the subjects involved alternate in entering the fulfilment one finds in loving. Rather the same moment of love enhances both

[55] *S.V.* IX, p. 41 (*WL*, p. 32). Cf. ibid., pp. 14–15, 42, 147–8 (ibid., pp. 9–10, 33, 125) and *S.V.* XII, p. 5 (*TC*, p. 10).

[56] In a remarkable way it is this strand of material which most engages the attention of both Lögstrup and Larsen in their debate in *Tidehverv*, 1955–8. They do not, of course, agree in the value to be placed on this material.

[57] *S.V.* XIII, p. 565 (*PV*, p. 77).

[58] *S.V.* II, p. 146 (*E-O* II, p. 136).

terms in the relationship. Both subject and object benefit, for 'the true riches is surely to make others rich'.[59] Kierkegaard's ethic draws interest on the capital invested in his doctrine of creation: the fact that the self is essentially a social self opens the way to a good which is communal rather than competitive.[60] Genuine self realization does serve the common good. And it does so because man is so essentially related to the other(s) that he both needs to love the other(s) and needs the other(s) whom he loves. Each self knows three needs: to love, the beloved, and to be loved by the beloved.

One must say that it is precisely this social character of selfhood which makes it possible to distinguish between selfishness and self-love. One surely cannot make Kierkegaard out as a champion of all forms of self interest. As surely as the self may essay a denial of its 'necessity'—of its essential relatedness—so surely may it strive after a goal which captures its narrow self interest.[61] *How* that may come about will concern us later. But there is no questioning that Kierkegaard sees that such narrow self assertion can and does happen and that he labels it as sin. The relationship is not wholly different with regard to the self's relation to the divine other. Thus in contrast to the band of ethicists led by Nygren, Kierkegaard has a major place for the self's love for God,[62] though he cannot be accused of failing to recognize man's penchant for turning the divine into the servant of human desire. We have already brought to view Kierkegaard's reflection concerning the legitimacy and limitations of applying the analogy of human love to God.[63]

The self's status as individual-in-community contributes to the settlement of questions other than the one of motivation. Indeed it leads us to the heart of our concern in this section, for it provides the context, if not the basis, for the determination of the content of the ethical act. It is clearly this context to which we must turn to know what love means materially.[64] The social character of selfhood wit-

---

[59] *S.V.* X, p. 128 (*CDi*, p. 128).

[60] So in *S.V.* IX, p. 22 (*WL*, p. 16) we are told that the proper love of self is reached when one adds the word about loving the neighbour 'as oneself', and in ibid., p. 26 (ibid., p. 19) that 'to love oneself in the right way and to love the neighbour correspond entirely to one another, [and] are at bottom one and the same thing'. Cf. ibid., p. 69 (ibid., p. 56).

[61] This must be said to be the point of the warnings in *PH* against willing the good for the sake of reward, or from fear of punishment, or self-assertively, or only up to a point.

[62] On this point see Lönning, op. cit., pp. 115–8.

[63] See above, pp. 118–23.

[64] In *Pap.* VIII A 82, 120 Kierkegaard discusses a plan to hold twelve lectures on 'love, friendship, and charity'. He never got beyond the stage of making

nesses to the essential co-involvement of all men. It is that co-involvement which makes Kierkegaard's talk of the 'universal human' both consistent with other strands of his thought and capable of winning more than verbal recognition within that thought. Manifestly selves must possess something in common if they can stand in relationship to each other. The recognition of that commonality places one on the path leading to the theme of the universal human. That theme does loom large in Kierkegaard's ethics. 'He who lives ethically works to become the universal man.'[65] Or again, this time from the *Journals*: 'The thing is to save as many of the universal human characteristics as possible in an individual life.'[66]

One may wish to object that in making the step from the recognition of the minimal commonality necessary to support a relationship to the affirmation of something 'universally human' Kierkegaard is making a leap at least as large as any he consciously identified. Many students of human behaviour in our time seem particularly disinclined to make that leap. What, after all, would be such universal human characteristics? Presumably one could get a fair hearing for those categories identified in Kierkegaard's description of man.[67] But these categories are precisely *descriptive* categories and if it is in fact they which form the substance of Kierkegaard's ethic we surely seem to have returned to the Hegelian identification of the real and the ideal. If, on the other hand, remaining and/or becoming human is an authentic task, what content is at hand to fill this noble phrase?

Kierkegaard clearly seems to regard the universal human as a task. Yet he does not provide the reader with a formal list of characteristics towards which he must strive. He has much to say of human character, as we shall see, but he does not set a series of substantial models before the self. It seems to us that his thought leads in another direction—back to the discussion of the relatedness of the self. Here lies the meaning of the 'universal human'. The descriptive generalizations concerning man are an elucidation of this relatedness and the norm confronting man is a call for a specific form of this relatedness. If one asks what for, the literature directs us to

---

notes for another series intended to introduce the series which would have had such direct bearing for our concern. Lacking such explicit source material, our inquiry must take the course suggested.

[65] *S.V.* II, p. 230 (*E-O* II, p. 214).

[66] *Pap.* III A 136 (*Dru* 364). On this point, see James Collins, *The Mind of Kierkegaard* (Chicago: Henry Regnery, 1953), p. 294, note 24.

[67] The best candidates would seem to be those identified above on pages 101-2 and 106-8. Thus we exclude the overtly theological categories.

Kierkegaard's concern with communication. James Collins has commented on this concern: 'The ethical ideal is to bring every aspect of an individual's being into conformity with the universal law, so that what is essentially human may be expressed in the individual instance. The presence of a common standard tends to promote an attitude of self-revelation and co-operation among men, as a counterbalance to the inclination to refuse to communicate in thought and conduct with others.'[68] This moves us in the right direction, but the relationship between the universal human and communication seems to us to be far more internal than Collins' description allows. We can get at that connection by offering now a bold forecast of the descriptive argument the next several paragraphs will seek to make good: one is so to live that the inevitable relatedness of selves bears and so becomes the mutual revelation of selves.

Clearly a statement of Kierkegaard's ethics has somewhere to address his concern with communication. That incessant concern is not an excessive and arbitrary preoccupation with methodological adiaphora. Rather 'the goods of the Spirit are in and for themselves communication'.[69] This substantive significance of communication is discussed at some length in *The Concept of Dread*'s difficult analysis of the demoniacal, the dread of the good. We quote only one passage; which well states the thrust of the material: 'Freedom is precisely the expansive. It is in opposition to this that I think one can employ the word "shut-in" *kat' exochēn* of unfreedom. One generally uses a more metaphysical expression concerning the evil, that it is the negating; the ethical expression for this, when one considers the effects in the individual, is precisely the "shut-in". The demonic does not shut itself in with something, but shuts itself in, and therein lies the profundity in existence, that unfreedom does precisely make a prisoner of itself. Freedom is constantly communicating (it will do no harm to take into account even the religious meaning in the term), unfreedom

---

[68] Collins, op. cit., p. 74; cf. note 5, p. 279.
[69] *S.V.* X, p. 122 (*CDi*, p. 122); cf. ibid., pp. 121–6 (ibid., pp. 121–6). This passage discusses in its wider context specifically the goods of faith, hope and love. The consistent theme is that if a man has faith 'the whole race and every individual in the race is participant in the fact that he has faith'. (ibid., p. 121 [ibid., p. 121].) That theme blends the recognition of the supra-individual dimension to the coming to faith and the recognition of the involvement of all in the content of faith. As to the latter point, Kierkegaard says that 'it lies in the goods themselves, in their nature, that their possession is communication'. (ibid., p. 122 [ibid., p. 122].) Here Kierkegaard comes beyond *CUP*'s reference to 'wonderful, inspiring Christian humanity: the highest is common to all men', where the sense seems to suggest the universal potentiality for faith. *S.V.* VII, p. 252 (*CUP*, p. 261).

becomes more and more "shut-in" and wants no communication.'[70]

We may suppose that in this matter Kierkegaard writes of what he knows most personally. We have noted in chapter two his own judgment on his failure to reveal himself to Regine.[71] There, too, we raised the possibility that an act of revelation on the part of Kierkegaard's father played a decisive role in the son's development.[72] Certain it is that the outcome of a later crisis—that of Easter week, 1848—fits the pattern of our discussion: 'My whole nature is changed. My hiddenness and shut-in-ness (*Indesluttethed*, German: *Verschlossenheit*) is broken—I must speak.'[73] Chapter one has traced the increasing momentum of Kierkegaard's attack against the impersonal and the anonymous.[74] While that attack takes on a darker hue under influence from another quarter, in itself it seems wholly consistent with the maxim of Judge William: 'It is the duty of every man to become revealed.'[75]

The attack on anonymity brings into focus an essential point about the nature of the communication involved. The communication proposed is not any and every sort of contact between individuals. Were it that, Kierkegaard would be at the point of identifying the back-slapping gad-about as the ethical paradigm. His works rather provide the basis for classifying the man-about-town type not only as a nauseating boor, but also as a threat to the good itself. Again it is Judge William who states the point so well:

. . . can you think of anything more terrible than that . . . your nature dissolved in a multiplicity, that you actually became many, became like those unhappy demoniacs, a legion, and that you thus would have lost the innermost and holiest in a man, the integrating power of personality? In truth, you should not joke about that which is not only serious, but dreadful. In every man there is something which prevents him to a certain degree from becoming fully transparent to himself; and

---

[70] *S.V.* IV, p. 391 (*CD*, p. 110).

[71] See above, p. 92, notes 175 and 176.

[72] See above, pp. 92–93, notes 177 and 178.

[73] *Pap.* VIII A 640 (*Dru* 747). Walter Lowrie appropriately laments the lack of an adequate English translation. (*CD*, p. 151.) 'Shut-in-ness' is perhaps not much better than Lowrie's 'Shut-up-ness'. Yet this minor change, while still failing to satisfy the standards of conceptual tidiness, does adequately (and somewhat more accurately) suggest the sense and the sparkle of Kierkegaard's language.

[74] See above, pp. 33–35.

[75] *S.V.* II, p. 289 (*E-O* II, p. 269). Cf. *Pap.* IX A 221 (*Dru* 809): 'But the communication of Christian truth must end at last in "witnessing"; maieutic cannot be the last form. For, Christianly understood the truth does not reside in the subject (as Socrates understood it) but is a revelation which must be proclaimed.'

this can be the case in such a high degree, he can be so inexplicably woven into the relationships of life, which lie out beyond his self, that he is almost incapable of revealing himself; but that one who cannot reveal himself, cannot love, and the one who cannot love is the most unhappy of all.[76]

If one prefers the more surgical prose of Haufniensis, passages witnessing to the legitimate and necessary role of 'reserve' and 'shut-in-ness' (*Indesluttethed*, German: *Verschlossenheit*) are available.[77] Against the aesthete Kierkegaard contends that one must find one's own self, including the radically solitary dimension of that self. Against those enamoured with anonymity he contends that one must reveal this true self as far and best as one can.

It is this emphasis on finding and revealing one's own self which reaches expression in the Kierkegaardian requirement of honesty.[78] In a sense this is all God requires of man, but verily God requires all this of man. Perhaps in view of the nature and history of the community or of the self it is too much to call for communication in the grammar of absolute obedience—but honesty is required: 'Far from impatiently and hot-headedly urging someone else impatiently and hot-headedly to attempt to forsake all things, which God perhaps does not demand, does not demand of him, we would extol honesty, which God demands of everyone. . . .'[79]

In this process of communication, which is true to the character of the self, the self's uniqueness is preserved. That is in line with God's creative intent: 'For every man is primitively planned as a self, determined to become himself; and while it is true that every self in its givenness is angular, it follows from that only that the self should be honed *tilslibes*, German: *zugeschliffen*), not that it should be ground off (*afslibes*, German: *abgeschliffen*), not that it, out of fear of men, should altogether give up being itself, or even simply that out of fear of men, it ought not dare to be itself in its essential accidentality (which is precisely that which must not be ground off (*afslibes*, German: *abgeschliffen*) in which one is, after all, oneself for oneself.'[80] Indeed the self is expanded in this process,[81] and Kierkegaard seems willing

---

[76] *S.V.* II, p. 146 (*E-O* II, pp. 135–6).

[77] See, for example, *S.V.* IV, pp. 391ff. (*CD*, pp. 110ff.).

[78] *S.V.* X, pp. 188–90 (*CDi*, pp. 194–6) offers a representative statement of that requirement.

[79] ibid., p. 188 (ibid., p. 194). Perhaps one may apply such a passage not only to Kierkegaard's call for an 'admission' from the church, but also to the changing course of his reflection concerning the break with Regine.

[80] *S.V.* XI, pp. 146–7 (*SD*, p. 50).

[81] See, for example, *S.V.* IV, p. 400 (*CD*, p. 119).

to grant such expansion place as goal in the conscious reflection of the ethical subject.[82]

Kierkegaard's description of the nature of the self would seem to suggest that the process of revelation is a limited one. In so far as there is an irreducible solitariness to selfhood, communication will never be revelatory of the totality of the self. Indeed here we would seem to encounter part of that which distinguishes Kierkegaard's ethic from the Hegelian formula which calls upon the particular to reveal the universal.[83] We have already identified another element of distinction in noting that the revelation is understood as one which occurs with freedom rather than as a process descriptive of all being as such.

The irreducible independence of the self veils the ethical revelation in mystery, not only in the sense that the revelation cannot be total,[84] but also in the sense that whatever revelation does occur will reflect in its material diversity the uniqueness of the selves involved.[85] Thus there arises a situationalist tendency in Kierkegaard's ethical thought. No public criterion seems available by which one self could judge the act of another. My duty may be the universal, but 'on the other hand, my duty is the particular, something for me alone'.[86] Thus 'it becomes impossible for another man to say what my duty is'.[87] We should take note of the fact that this situationalism is grounded in the individuality—that is to say, the freedom—of man.

[82] Arild Christenson discusses the theme of the self facing the task of developing its given qualities and dispositions in his article on the earliest part of the Kierkegaardian authorship, 'Der junge Kierkegaard als Schriftstellerpersönlichkeit', *Orbis Litterarum*, 1963, pp. 26–47. In a letter written in 1835 the young Kierkegaard speaks in such a way of himself. He finds himself in the position of a man who would cultivate his talents 'in a particular direction, that, namely, which is best adapted to his individuality'. *Pap.* I A 72 (*Dru* 16).

[83] It is not to be denied that some striking formal parallels appear when passages are studied without reference to their systematic context. Cf., for example, Judge William's exaltation of marriage as the ethical paradigm by virtue of its openness and publicly declarative character with Hegel's statement (in *The Philosophy of Right*, trans. T. M. Knox [Oxford: Clarendon, 1942], p. 111) that it is the duty of every man to marry.

[84] This point contributes some of the force to the argument of *Fear and Trembling*, though we shall point out that the diastatic current is powerfully present in that work.

[85] Hermann Diem, *Kierkegaard's Dialectic of Existence*, trans. Harold Knight (Edinburgh: Oliver and Boyd, 1959), p. 115, has written: ' . . . the Christian life in faith has to fulfil nothing special but only the universally human, which every man has to express, and so the Christian is not distinguished from other men by the observable results of his struggle'. We are rather pointing to the multiplicity which comes to characterize the obedient response and so block the way to an objective assessment of ethical actions.

[86] *S.V.* II, p. 236 (*E-O* II, pp. 220–1).

[87] ibid., p. 237 (ibid., p. 221).

It does not bear witness to a capricious God but to particularity and change in humankind. Furthermore, the freedom of the other to whom the ethical act is directed suggests that the act's consequences provide no access to an external criterion to guide the self who seeks to act ethically. Thus one would seem to be turned towards an ethic of intentionality. Climacus contrasts this view with the grandeur of the System: 'World-historically I see the effect, ethically I see the purpose; but when ethically I see the purpose and understand the ethical, then I understand at the same time that every effect is infinitely indifferent, that it is indifferent what the effect was; but then I do not see the world-historical.'[88]

We need to add, however, that Kierkegaard does not reduce intention to a naked stream of subjective passion. Though the Christian choice is not to be objectified in an ethical dogma, it is not contentless.[89]

Furthermore, there are grounds for supposing that an interest in consequences and a concern with intentionality are not seen by Kierkegaard as an absolute either-or. He is clearly interested in consequences. The cry for reduplication is not exactly a minor theme in his work. Moreover, he suggests that this reduplication is publicly discernible. That suggestion becomes a firm assumption at least by the time of the assault on the Church: '. . . the Protestant clergymen contrived this deception: that about in this land live true Christians, people who in all silence are true, genuine Christians—yes, after all, we are all true Christians in our hidden fervour, we are all patterns. How charming! If the New Testament should decide what is to be understood by being a true Christian, it would be just as impossible to be a true Christian in all—jovial, enjoyable—silence, as it is to fire a cannon in all silence.'[90]

Admittedly the diastatic current has coloured such a passage, but a significant component still seems to reflect the rhythm of synthesis. It hardly seems unnatural for an ethic of revelation to show some interest in the issue of the act beyond the boundaries of the self. Kierkegaard notes that the call of the ethical ideal does not merely set the self apart in the loneliness of spirit: '. . . the ethical is the breath of the eternal and in the heart of loneliness it is the reconciling

[88] *S.V.* VII, p. 128 (*CUP*, p. 139).
[89] See ibid., pp. 329–30 (ibid., 339–40): 'To suppose that in saying that Christianity is no doctrine (*Laere*) one is saying that it is contentless, is merely a chicane. When the believer exists in faith, his existence has prodigious content, but not in the sense of paragraph material.'
[90] *Pap.* XI 1 A 106, p. 74 Cf. ibid., IX A 414 (*Dru* 843).

fellowship with every man. . . .'[91] In saying this Kierkegaard seems at the very least to invite reflection on the communal character of ethical judgment. Beyond that one may ask if his suggestion about the substance of the self's intention may find in this passage a means of making contact with his emphasis on the discernible difference Christian faith makes in life. It seems plausible that the essential interrelatedness of all men would provide not only the potentiality for a universal Christian community but an actual 'reconciling fellowship with every man'. Within that community the intention of the self could be said to be intelligible, if not directly statable.[92] One might even suppose that the statement of intention in action is discernible to the other, though that which is communicated would surely fall short of either unmistakable intelligibility or coercive force.

We lack explicit textual support to carry this line of reflection further, but we shall resume this discussion in Part Four, when we discuss the possible legacy of Kierkegaard. We have noted in passing that the diastatic impulse seems to colour passages stating that man's response is publicly discernible. That process of coloration is joined by other effects attesting the powerful pressure which the rhythm of diastasis exerts on Kierkegaard's material determination of the ideal. We give the final pages of this chapter to a more careful consideration of those Kierkegaardian affirmations which seem to bespeak the dominance of the diastatic rhythm.

We have seen how the diastatic impulse is intent on the celebration of divine sovereignty. In fixing on the components of distance and difference within sovereignty the diastatic current approaches the point of honouring a sovereign who can have no subjects. At least the existence of an ideal which could form the test of citizenship in this kingdom is threatened. We have noted that threat in the formal determination of the ideal. The logic of certainty intrudes upon the grammar of possibility. Thus at times the process of interpenetration seems to settle in a static juxtaposition rather like the stand-off Kierkegaard's descriptive analysis of God and man occasionally illustrates.[93] Such juxtaposition claims the language of double-truth as its own:

[91] *S.V.* VII, p. 125 (*CUP*, p. 136).

[92] We have mentioned (above pp. 26–27, notes 68 and 69) Kierkegaard's interest in a projective role for gesture and speech in communication and will give more attention to this theme in Part IV. See Lars Bejerholm, '*Meddelelsens Dialektik*' (Lund: Haakan Ohlsson, 1962) pp. 101–18, for comments on this material. See also Arild Christensen, 'Der junge Kierkegaard als Schriftstellerpersönlichkeit', *Orbis Litterarum* 1963, pp. 26–47, for a discussion of Kierkegaard's early interest in mythological statement which 'arouses' the self.

[93] See above, pp. 124–8.

. . . learn from the lilies to understand that nevertheless really, even when it is man who spins and sews, it is God who spins and sews. Dost thou think that the seamstress, if she understands this, will become less diligent at her work and in it, that she will lay her hands in her lap and think: 'If after all it is really God who spins and sews, the best thing for me is to be free, to be freed from this unreal spinning and sewing'? If so, then this seamstress is a foolish little maiden, not to say an impertinent wench, in whom God can have no pleasure, and who can herself have no pleasure in the lilies, and who is no better than that our good Lord should show her the door, and then she will see what will become of her. But this seamstress, our own dear lovable seamstress with her childlike piety, understands that only when she herself sews, is it God who will sew for her, and hence she becomes all the more diligent at her work, for the fact that by constantly sewing she constantly must understand—oh blissful jest!—that it is God who sews every stitch, by constantly sewing she constantly must understand—oh the seriousness of it!—that it is God who sews every stitch.[94]

The beauty of such a passage may win praise from one's ear but its logic riles the mind. Kierkegaard was too concerned with consistency to permit himself many such passages. Rather he finds some form for expressing divine sovereignty *within* the performance of the ideal itself. Set against God's splendour, man is nothing. If one still speaks of God's ideal for man, such speech must none the less recognize human nothingness. Let it be said that just this—the recognition of one's nothingness—is the task: 'It is true enough that God needs no man, just as little as he needs the whole race or everything, which after all in every moment of its being is for him the nothing out of which he created it; but in spite of that the man fights for God who fights the good fight in order to express that God exists and is the Lord, whose explanation shall be unconditionally obeyed.'[95]

We are definitely here in the context of an ideal calling for genuine human response. For 'to understand that a man can do nothing (the beautiful and deep expression for the God relationship)'[96] is difficult

---

[94] S.V. XII, p. 452 (*JY*, p. 192).

[95] S.V. IX, p. 116 (*WL*, p. 98). A transitional formulation would be to hold that human response—as distinguished from movement in nature—is free, but that disobedience is made to serve the divine will; see S.V. XI, pp. 27–28 ('LF', *CDi*, pp. 336–7); S.V. X, p. 55 (*CDi*, p. 54). Here man's activity is granted a preliminary hearing, though it does not speak so loudly as to require one to read the ideal eliciting that activity under the rubric of nothingness.

[96] S.V. VII, p. 332 (*CUP*, p. 342). This is the sort of passage on which K. E. Lögstrup relies in arguing (*Kierkegaards und Heideggers Existenzanalyse und ihr Verhältnis zur Verkündigung* [Berlin: Erich Blachker, 1950], p. 58) that for Kierkegaard the infinite demand facing the individual is to express in existence the fact that 'the individual is capable of nothing at all and is nothing before God'. Such Kierkegaardian passages cannot be understood to be saying that in everything man does, man requires God's assistance. In the passage cited in the text from *CUP* the

and this truth 'cannot be understood once for all'.⁹⁷ So, too, it may be said of one that she gives a 'mighty and true expression of being able to do nothing at all'.⁹⁸ All these characterizations—that the ideal requires effort, constancy, and intensity—witness to a responsible man set before a possible ideal.

This sort of penetration by the diastatic impulse seems significantly present in two of Kierkegaard's most read books—*Fear and Trembling* and *Repetition*. It is fairly evident that the kind of cyclical repetition sought in the first half of *REP* would negate individuality by denying to the self's acts the seriousness gained in the passage of consequences to the future. But it may not be as readily seen that the 'religious repetition' of the book's second half also threatens to undermine individuality. What happens in this repetition is the attainment of the insight that the losses sustained by the religious self come under the category of a trial. One emerges with a faith that trusts God no matter how his actions seem to contradict our standards of what is just and good. This is formally recognized in *FT* in the theme of the 'teleological suspension of the ethical'. The ethical realm would surely seem to be put in practical suspension if true faith in God is the faith that our distinctions and the strivings which they beget are not representative of God—indeed are to be dramatically disobeyed in the act issuing from faith. Such a creed celebrates the insignificance of our understandings and our endeavours—in making that creed our confession we celebrate the insignificance of ourselves.⁹⁹

---

assertion that a human being can do nothing is set over against the affirmation that 'God can do all things'. (See also *S.V.* V, pp. 87–92 ['MN', *ED*, IV, pp. 18–27].) The two assertions taken together cannot make reference to two powers at work in every ethical act. (Though Kierkegaard presents that view fast upon the heels of the passage quoted on p. 152, note 94, from *JY*—see *S.V.* XII, pp. 452–3 [*JY*, pp. 192–3], yet this talk of God as my 'fellow worker' must be distinguished from the line of thought under discussion.) The synthesis rhythm can well support the statement that we do nothing without God, but the relevant ethical question for it is rather what are we to do with God's assistance and under his command.

⁹⁷ *S.V.* IX, p. 344 (*WL*, p. 292).

⁹⁸ *S.V.* XII, p. 256 ('WS', *TC*, p. 268). It is true that the immediate point under discussion in this discourse is that in relation to finding forgiveness man can do nothing at all. Yet we do not misappropriate the passage, for the lesson of the discourse is reinforced by the fact that 'a man, humanly speaking, has no power at all, even in relation to the least thing'. ibid., p. 257 (ibid. p. 269).

⁹⁹ See *S.V.* III, p. 263 (*REP*, p. 157), where it is observed of one who would experience religious repetition: 'In the same moment the whole question about finitude would have been reduced to indifference; the real actuality would have been a matter of indifference.'

It is to be conceded that this penetration is not complete in *FT* and *REP*. More than the form of individuality remains, for Kierkegaard champions the knight of faith who does not simply make the movement of infinite resignation, but even in the act of resigning the finite hopes for the finite by virtue of the absurd.[100] At times that hope for the finite has in mind quite specific changes.[101] Yet the power of the penetration contributes the acknowledged absurdity of the hope as well as its locus—in the act of the repudiation of human significance. Nor does the return to the finite undercut the independent finite-negating significance of the religiously motivated act of resignation, for 'the result (in so far as it is finitude's answer to the infinite question) is in its dialectic entirely heterogeneous with the existence of the hero. Or shall one suppose that it could be proved that Abraham was justified in relating himself as the individual to the universal, by the fact that he by a *miracle* received Isaac? If Abraham had really offered Isaac, would he therefore have been less justified?'[102]

One can also observe that the systematic significance of the 'teleological suspension of the ethical' is a matter subject to contest. One is probably mistaken if one tries to rescue the ethical by reducing the command to be disobeyed to a moral maxim which is merely (?) representative of mankind's best consensus on matters of conduct. The logic of paradox requires a sober attentiveness to the universal, which hardly seems adequately supported by the candidacy of a collective moral common sense. The paradox of Abraham is so painful because it seems to be God himself who so speaks as to contradict himself. That a lesser reading of the 'ethical' will not suffice is also indicated by the fact that a 'suspension' suggests a return. That return marks the suspension as real but limited.[103] It suggests, too, that to read *FT* as a descriptive of an orthodox *ordo salutis* may be to over-

---

[100] See *S.V.* III, p. 70 (*FT*, p. 22): 'It is great to grasp the eternal, but it is greater to hold fast to the temporal after having given it up.' *Pap.* VIII A 649 (*Dru* 753), where it is said of a man who has made the movement of resignation: '. . . then the possibility of faith presents itself to him in this form, whether he now in the power of the Absurd will believe that God will help him temporally'.

[101] While writing these works Kierkegaard still hoped that Regine might become his wife 'in a moment of repetition'; see *Pap.* IV A 107, 108 (*Dru* 444, 445). The text of *REP* was altered when Kierkegaard learned that Regine was engaged to another. As interest in specific changes fades, the hope for the finite becomes a hope for that in which true obedience can find no expression.

[102] *S.V.* III, p. 113 (*FT*, p. 95). [Italics his.]

[103] This is not to deny that the target in *FT* is Hegelianism. The understanding of the universal and particular in Hegel's ethic fits the specifications of the target well. See Hegel, op. cit., pp. 86–107, especially pp. 92–93. Hegel's *formal* description of ethics does not call for total renunciation on Kierkegaard's part.

dogmatize Kierkegaard's intention, even if one can find place within such rubrics for both suspension and return.[104]

Still one simply cannot make out of *FT* a witness to the way in which the essential interrelatedness of God and man in Kierkegaard's thought bears on his determination of the ideal.[105] Such a witness could accommodate a limited situationalism and indeed must do so, as we have seen.[106] But it is the freedom of God, not the particularity of man, which shipwrecks the universal for the author of *FT*. One may say that Kierkegaard's concern is to attack a self-sufficient ethic.[107] But the God upon whom the ethical claim depends is understood in a way which carries direct consequences for man's ethical life. Johannes Slök states the point well: 'What happens in providence cannot be specified, for this is after all God's freedom that acts and this is the presuppositionless and miraculous that enters. Only this can be specified, that the moment of providence is characterized by faith, obedience, and prayer in opposition to the empty succession of time which is man's domain, which is characterized by ethical reflection and planning.'[108]

We have implied that one may appropriately experience some uneasiness over a reading of *FT* which universalizes the argument that the absolute's claim cannot be universalized. Yet this is not

---

[104] N. H. Söe, *Fra Renaessancen Til Vore Dage*, 2nd. ed. (Copenhagen: G. E. C. Gad, 1948), p. 200, in seeking to relate strains from *FT*, *REP*, and *SW*, comments: 'Meanwhile it is strange that none of these three writings lets it become clear that it is the knowledge of sin and repentance which make it impossible to live in an immediate relation to the "universal", and that it is the grace of the forgiveness of sins that gives a man life in the universal anew. But other writings of Kierkegaard show that this is the intention; and so it becomes clear that herewith, most deeply seen, is not sketched an exception's situation for definite individuals, but the way for every man, who as a sinner meets God.'

[105] Gregor Malantschuk, op. cit., p. 42, seems to attempt such a reading of *FT*. He notes that 'the sacrifice of Isaac as an ethical-religious act is demanded of Abraham only this once. Essentially he lives his everyday life within ethical categories. He has faith in the Eternal, and he submits his temporal existence to the eternal claims of the laws of God.' Thus Malantschuk holds that 'Abraham moves from a purely moral position through the ethical and crosses the frontier into the religious'. This construction depends on the ambiguity of the distinctions between the moral and the ethical and between the ethical and the religious. Its imprecision reflects the restlessness of Kierkegaard's thought and seems a fairer report on the text than the effort to freeze the material within a single current of thought. Cf. also, ibid., pp. 25–27, 48, 52.

[106] See above, pp. 149–51.

[107] Cf. Collins, op. cit., pp. 88–98.

[108] Johannes Slök, *Forsynstanken* (Hjörring: Expres-Trykkeriet, 1947), p. 146. Slök rightly identifies the fact that this line of thought does not merely stress the 'how' of ethical action above the 'what', but leaves one quite without any means of attaching some 'what' to the 'how'.

really what is represented in the situationalist ethic we have discussed. The tendency of Kierkegaard's thought which we have been following does not leave the self expectantly awaiting some self-authenticating revelation of God's will for his 'now'. To be sure, the self's activity is to be engaged only by that which God wills. But the God of whom we speak in this connection is precisely that God whose sovereignty is to be wholly unchallenged. The transition from urging that it *must* not be challenged to arguing that it *cannot* be lies near at hand. In either case one will speak of an ethic of the first commandment.[109] But the will's alertness to God's solitary command will become the self's acceptance of all events as deliverances from the hand of God. One may still speak of a concern with the finite, but that concern seems to have been disarmed: '. . . not only does that one not believe who expects nothing at all, but also that one who expects something particular, or who grounds his expectation on something particular.'[110]

Clearly a man of this faith will have nothing special to say. He can well bear the name Johannes de Silentio. Of course another pattern of thought might permit one to distinguish between the solitary dimension of faith and the social expression of faith. One might even suppose that the privacy of the God-relationship in some important way defies verbal expression and endorses silence as man's fitting posture at this point. Kierkegaard might be saying something like that in writing: 'And so it is that God loves silence. He will not have this raising a fuss with other men about one's God relationship. To do that is perhaps vanity . . . or it is done out of cowardice and lack of faith. . . .'[111] But one may be silent for quite another reason too: '*His* is the kingdom;

---

109 Emil Brunner, 'Das Grundproblem der Philosophie bei Kant und Kierkegaard', *Zwischen den Zeiten*, 1924, pp. 31–47, shows the situationalist character of this appeal and its ultimate basis in his defence of Kierkegaard's formalism: 'There are no independent values. They are all grounded in a command which first qualifies them as values. . . . Theologically expressed: what is important is not that which God commands, but whether man has willed to take as his standard of conduct the demand of God—whatever it be; the consciousness of responsibility to him, the "first commandment" is the decisive point.'

110 *S.V.* III, p. 32 ('EF', *ED*, I p. 31). On this discourse see Johannes Slök, 'Das Verhältnis des Menschen zu seiner Zukunst', *Orbis Litterarum*, 1963, pp. 60–79. If one speaks of the human pole this identification of the real and the ideal will mean that 'purity of heart is to will one thing' and '*in truth to will one thing, then, can only mean to will the good*, because every other thing is not one'. (*S.V.* VIII, p. 142 [*PH*, p. 66].) [Italics his.] Cf. *S.V.* XII, p. 441 (*JY*, p. 180); p. 90 (*CDi*, p. 89); and above, p. 138.

111 *Pap.* XI 2 A 142 (*Dru* 1384). One may perhaps find reference to the solitariness of the resolve in *S.V.* XI, p. 61 ('HM', *PA*, p. 84): 'To be resolved is not one thing and to be silent another; to be resolved is precisely to be silent.' Yet one feels in this passage the pull of the diastatic employment of the silence motif.

and therefore thou art to be unconditionally silent in order that thou may not make it disturbingly noticeable that thou dost exist, but may with the solemnity of unconditional silence express that the kingdom is his.'[112] Such an appeal for silence may seem to suggest man's meaninglessness, but it is shaped to fit the stern specifications of the ideal and involves a severe requirement: 'When a horse which the royal coachman drives stands still, that is something wholly other than when a cab-horse stands still; for with respect to the last what is signified is merely that it is not going, which is no art; while with respect to the first case it is so that standing still is an action, an exertion, the highest exertion which is the horse's highest art, and it stands unconditionally still.'[113]

In these several turnings of thought Kierkegaard reaps in ethics what he has sown in dogmatics—particularly in the doctrine of God. When we began our attempt to trace the ascendency of the diastatic impulse in the determination of the ideal, we spoke first of the sovereignty of God. But does a God whose omnipotence is so utterly without qualfication rule? For such a God it will not suffice to set the ideal before man. One must add that 'it is he who disposes'. The principle of motion to the actualization of God's ideal is to be found within God. Thus it is that we are told that to love is to presuppose love in the other, for in so doing one acknowledges God's priority and omnipotence.[114] Whatever human love may mean, it is God's love that matters and so one is not surprised to find that the loving self can ignore not only the sins of the neighbour,[115] but the neighbour himself.[116]

[112] *S.V.* XI, p. 45 ('LF', *CDi*, p. 355). [Italics his.] Cf. ibid., p. 15 (ibid., p. 323); 'God is in heaven, man upon earth; therefore they cannot well speak together.' It is not possible to read Kierkegaard to be saying that one must first be silent in order then to act. Silence may be the beginning, but 'the beginning is not that with which one begins, but that at which one arrives; and man arrives at this backwards. The beginning is this art of becoming silent; for to be silent as nature is silent is no art. And thus in the deepest sense to become silent, silent directly over against God, this is the beginning of the fear of God, for as the fear of God is the beginning of wisdom, so is silence the beginning of the fear of God. And as the fear of God is more than the beginning of wisdom, as it is wisdom, so is silence more than the beginning of the fear of God; it is the fear of God.' ibid., pp. 14–15 (ibid., pp. 322–3). [Italics his.]

[113] *S.V.* XII, p. 389 (*JY*, p. 124).

[114] *S.V.* IX, pp. 202–34 (*WL*, pp. 170–98). The basis for the presupposing of love in the other takes on the hue of individuality when we are told that we make this presupposition since it is certain that God (love) will eventually triumph. But it is hard to resist the conclusion that the contest is basically unreal.

[115] See the two discourses titled 'Love Shall Cover a Multitude of Sins', *S.V.* III, pp. 274–95 (*ED*, I, pp. 61–93), particularly the first. Love can ignore the sins of the other because the victory of love is not won through the kind of real engagement in which knowledge of the other is needed for the struggle.

[116] Per Lönning, op. cit., pp. 178–9, has tried to argue against K. E. Lögstrup

We may pause to offer a preliminary assessment of the line of thought reflecting the dominance of the diastatic rhythm in the material determination of the ideal. We have found the diastatic impulse contradicting its own concern and doing so in such a way that the mind that seeks to follow the diastatic course finds itself mired in self-contradiction. Kierkegaard does not try to mask the difficulty. One is told succinctly: '[Not only the lilies and the birds, but] Thou too art subjected to necessity; God's will is done nevertheless, so strive to make a virtue out of necessity by finding thyself in God's will through unconditional obedience. . . .'[117] One starts down the road towards saying that the good is consciously to accept the inevitable fact of one's absolute dependence. But that path seems hard to follow or even to find. If one is absolutely dependent upon God it is God upon whom the actualization of the ideal depends. There is no possibility of freeing a sliver of reality called consciousness from the absoluteness of this dependence. It is all very well to say that 'to shorten one's sleep at night, and to buy up the hours of the day and not spare oneself, and then to understand that all of this is a jest— yes, that is seriousness'.[118] One might object that one needs to grant the human self fuller place to render this seriousness *psychologically* possible. But, beyond that, one must say that on the terms of this discussion the human self is not granted place sufficient to make such seriousness *ontologically* possible.

Kierkegaard's thought may find its way into self-contradiction at times, but it never makes that state its permanent abode. The drive towards consistency in this case is the more potent because the self-contradiction from which it flees opposes directly the major material concern controlling the diastatic rhythm. As Schleiermacher observes, it is hardly to the point to exalt the Lordship of a God who can have no responsible subjects.[119] The concern to testify to God's reign will

---

that it is precisely man's nothingness before God which is the condition for his love of neighbour. One could well accept that if the reference were to some particular respect in which man was nothing to God. But Lögstrup notes that 'the infinite demand does not have a definite content, over against which the man may deny himself and before which he may acknowledge his nothingness'. (Lögstrup, op. cit., p. 64.) He can also point to the wedge Kierkegaard drives between self and neighbour. On this point see his articles in *Tidehverv*, 1955, pp. 33–43, 52–61, 97–109; 1956, 6–12. See also Theodor Adorno, 'Kierkegaard's Lehre von der Liebe', *Zeitschrift für Religions und Geistesgeschichte*, 1951, pp. 23–38, for a very similar critique of Kierkegaard.

[117] *S.V.* XI, p. 32 ('LF', *CDi*, p. 341).
[118] *S.V.* VII, p. 410 (*CUP*, p. 421).
[119] See Friedrich Schleiermacher, *The Christian Faith*, English translation of the

not settle for contributing a half portion to the self-contradiction noted. It leads one rather to seek out new formulations which will be more faithful to the religious intent of the diastatic impulse. Closest to hand lies the possibility of formulating the idea not as 'becoming conscious of one's nothingness', but as 'becoming nothing' before God. Thus Climacus writes: '. . . this is the miracle of creation, not the creation of something which is nothing directly over against the Creator, but the creation of something which is something, and which in true worship of God can use this something in order by its self to become nothing before God. . . .'[120]

This alternative could be well represented by saying that the ideal for the self is to ground itself transparently in the power that constituted it.[121] One may suppose that we have mistaken the citizenship of this sentence. Surely the synthesis tradition itself affirms the dependence of the self on its Creator. One could add there that obedience testifies to a second dimension of dependence—the self accepts its creaturely dependence not only as descriptive of its past but as prescriptive for its future. But it does seem *very* imprecise to speak of obedience as linking one *transparently* to the *constituting* power. The discussion of the ideal in such terms seems rather to reveal the diastatic impulse and the threat to the ideal with which that impulse is plagued. Here too may belong the note that 'the opposite of sin is not virtue but faith',[122] for it stresses faith's insight in a way which tends to exclude virtue's ethical endeavour.

Difficulties confront this formulation as well. Kierkegaard seems to be counselling self-annihilation. One may doubt that the kind of total self-annihilation required is possible. One can, of course, act upon oneself to destroy the living centre of integrated processes. But it is difficult to see how that by itself would qualify as 'making oneself nothing'. For both 'making' and 'oneself' suggest real action in the self. They require that *something* be made nothing—i.e., that something that is be made to not be. Thus the formula requires reflexive action, so that it is not enough that I cease to be as a living centre of processes, for even the reality which I did have must be negated. We cannot ask that this mean that I did not have being when I had being,

---

second German edition by H. R. Mackintosh and J. S. Stewart (Edinburgh: T & T Clark, 1956), pp. 218–9.

[120] *S.V.* VII, p. 207 (*CUP*, p. 220). Cf. *S.V.* IV, pp. 351–2 (*CD*, p. 74), for Haufniensis' remark that non-being is not nothing.

[121] *S.V.* XI, p. 194 (*SD*, p. 132).

[122] ibid. (ibid.).

for that is to talk nonsense. Rather it must be said that I had being, but that my having had being—my having been—is now negated. That would be concretely true if all the consequences of my activity were to be effectively removed from the temporal process, so that my having been would have no significance for what now comes to be.

This seems to be what is involved in the notion of 'making oneself nothing' before God. The notion is beset by difficulties, even if we do not ask of the possibility of the individual himself effecting such a change. The actualization of such an ideal would be in direct opposition to the character reality is seen to possess in the Kierkegaardian analysis we have already examined.[123] According to Kierkegaard it is precisely the character of the correlation of unity and individuality that the individual's act of freedom becomes part of the heritage of necessity-possibility impinging on other individuals. In his formulation of man as self and race Kierkegaard sets this analysis in an explicitly chronological context. To propose that one exempt oneself from this process of impinging on the other(s) is to propose as an ideal that which cannot be real.

Kierkegaard recognizes this objection in still another turn which his thought takes. We refer to his analysis of the suffering of the Christian man.[124] The diastatic severance of God and man brings the poles of Kierkegaard's thought into radical opposition to each other. We have seen that this opposition at times seems to be regarded as metaphysical in character.[125] We shall encounter evidence supporting that impression in the course of our analysis of Kierkegaard's discourse on the theme of suffering. Yet we may reliably suppose that the essentially religious bent of Kierkegaard's concern is involved in the movement to the relationship of opposition. Indeed the foothold which the opposition motif possessed in Kierkegaard's religious concern very possibly contributed significantly to a situation in which the metaphysical phrasing of opposition became irresistibly attractive.

In any case the reality of opposition may be taken as a fixed point of reference for the Christian.[126] It is not surprising to be told that 'suffering is posited as decisive for religious existence',[127] for—given

123 See above, pp. 105–9.
124 Cf. on this theme Paul Sponheim, 'Kierkegaard and the suffering of the Christian Man', *Dialog*, 1964, pp. 199–207.
125 See above, pp. 100–2.
126 So *Pap*. X 2 A 317: it was certain that Christ would suffer, and it is certain that the Christian will suffer, because the world does not change.
127 *S.V.* VII, p. 246 (*CUP*, p. 256).

the opposition—what else could God's man expect?[128] Surely in this sphere the positive must wear the garb of the negative.[129] Yet matters are not that simple. We have seen that all the glory of heaven does not make clear how a man can use his nature to be rid of that nature. Similarly, suffering is at least partly an identifiable temporal state. As such it seems linked with those forces opposed to God. The individual becomes aware that he is so related to God that he must serve him and that he cannot do so. What is this, but to suffer?

This dynamic is part of the very complex development of thought in the *Postscript*'s discourse on suffering. One starts with the requirement of the ideal: 'In relation to an eternal happiness as the absolute good pathos is not a matter of words but means that this idea transforms the entire existence of the individual.'[130] But one comes to learn that 'even when the individual has triumphed over immediacy, he is still with the victory in existence and thus still hindered from absolutely expressing the absolute relationship to an absolute *telos*'.[131] The role which metaphysical categories play becomes clear when Climacus roots this inability in the successiveness of the temporal process.[132] Thus the view that the absolute should not exhaust itself in the relative[133] comes to mean that it should not express itself there. We have moved beyond the position of *Fear and Trembling*, where the

---

[128] This grim reality was set before Kierkegaard at an early age, if we may trust his retrospection. See *S.V.* XIII, p. 566 (*PV*, p. 78): '. . . I was very early initiated into the thought that conquering is to conquer in the sense of the infinite, which in a finite sense is to suffer.'

[129] See *S.V.* VII, p. 24 (*CUP*, p. 35) on 'the infinite negative resolve which is the individuality's form for the being of God in him'. Cf. ibid., p. 375 (ibid., p. 387). In *S.V.* II, p. 221 (*E-O* II, p. 206) Kierkegaard has Ludwig Blackfeldt say: '. . . I believe in the rightness of the proposition that no man can bear to see the infinite. This once manifested itself to me in an intellectual respect, and the expression for this is ignorance. That is to say, ignorance is the negative expression for the infinite knowledge. And suicide is the negative expression for infinite freedom.' Walter Lowrie, *Kierkegaard* (London: Oxford, 1938), pp. 144–8, cites journal passages of this period that suggest that the use of the name Ludwig gives this passage an autobiographical shading.

[130] *S.V.* VII, p. 335 (*CUP*, p. 347).

[131] ibid., p. 375 (ibid., p. 387).

[132] ibid., pp. 427, 459 (ibid., pp. 439, 469). Cf. *Pap.* XI 2 A 246: Christ brings spirit and when that is linked with the body, one suffers. It is this line of thought which leads Lögstrup (op. cit., p. 84) to suggest that—contrary to the Jewish-Christian tradition (as Lögstrup reads it)—Kierkegaard so understands guilt that the other man, against whom the injustice is done, is wholly excluded from consideration.

[133] *S.V.* VII, p. 351 (*CUP*, p. 363).

ideal act could not be understood.[134] Now that act cannot be performed, much less identified.[135]

Called at the deepest level of his being to a response which that very being denies him,[136] man 'suffers'. That 'suffering' becomes the expression of the ideal: '. . . the action of inwardness is suffering, for the individual cannot make himself over, any such attempt becoming, like imitation, a mere affectation, and it is for this reason that suffering is the highest action in inwardness'.[137] Of course that suffering, in turn, must not be outwardly discernible. The man of faith 'is a stranger in the world of finitude, but he does not identify his difference from *worldliness* by a foreign mode of dress (that would be a contradiction, since in such a way he would be identifying himself in exactly a wordly manner): he is incognito, but his incognito consists precisely in this, that his appearance is wholly like that of the others'.[138]

The moments in this development crowd their way into a single pregnant passage:

This suffering has its ground in the fact that the individual is in his immediacy absolutely committed to relative ends; its significance lies in the transposition of the relationship, the dying away from immediacy, or in expressing existentially the fact that the individual can do absolutely nothing of himself, but is nothing before God; for here again the negative is the mark by which the God-relationship is recognized, and self-annihilation is the essential form for the God-relationship. And this self-annihilation must not be expressed externally, for then we have the monastic movement, and the relationship becomes after all a wordly one; and the

[134] See *S.V.* III, pp. 160–1 (*FT*, pp. 178–9).
[135] For another expression of the advanced position in this development see *S.V.* IX, pp. 140–1 (*WL*, p. 119), where we are specifically told that one cannot identify love from the outside—not even by the opposition it causes. This position could give support to the familiar assertion that Christianity does not want to change the external, but 'to make everything new, while all still remains old'. ibid., p. 139 (ibid., p. 117) and *passim*.
[136] *S.V.* VII, pp. 364–5 (*CUP*, pp. 375–6).
[137] ibid., p. 376 (ibid., p. 388). Hence one does not seek to resolve the tension by dissipating the finite: '. . . if the God-relationship and finitude up to its most minute point (where the difficulty becomes the greatest) are to be held together in existence, then the assent [to the finite] must find its expression in the sphere of religiosity itself . . .' (ibid., p. 411 [ibid., p. 423].) Johannes Slök, 'Tre Kierke-gaard-tolkninger', *Kierkegaardiana*, 1955, p. 100, writes: 'The eternal is not something other than the temporal, but the qualification of the temporal, and to put together eternity and temporality means for Kierkegaard not to become constantly more eternal or constantly less temporal, but to be wholly in the temporal as the reality in which man is held fast by the eternal.' Such a statement can find support in Kierkegaard, but it does not adequately recognize the fact that the temporal and the eternal are so understood as to create the tension expressed in suffering.
[138] *S.V.* VII, p. 356 (*CUP*, p. 367). [Italics his.]

individual must not allow himself to imagine that it can be done once for all, for this is aesthetics. And even if it could be done once for all, because the individual is after all an existing individual, he will again encounter suffering in the repetition.[139]

The great beauty and power of such passages cannot permanently obscure the logical difficulties involved in this line of thought. If the opposition of God and man is so construed as to deny man any expression of God's ideal, an inner expression ('suffering') must not be permitted to slip through on the coat-tails of what at this point is an unessential difference—that between inner and outer. At times Kierkegaard seems willing to argue that God ought to make an inner difference, just because he is so different. So Climacus argues: 'Precisely because there is an absolute difference between God and man, man expresses himself most perfectly when he expresses the difference absolutely. *Worship* is the maximum [expression] for a man's God-relationship and therewith for his likeness to God, since the qualities are absolutely different.'[140] This is to attempt an emotional justification for a logical impossibility. Such a justification could not fully satisfy one as sensitive to logical requirements as Kierkegaard.

We have already seen that no real settlement of the difficulty is to be found in ruling suffering an essential fact and granting to man's attainment only the consciousness of the fact.[141] Rather Kierkegaard's thought tends to move back from the extreme statement of diastatic opposition. One may note this in a tendency to withdraw from the metaphysical formulation of the opposition between God and man. Thus Kierkegaard can criticize Schopenhauer's formula 'to exist is to suffer', insisting that the formula applies only to Christian existence.[142] Even within the realm of religious opposition, one can trace a certain yielding of the diastatic impulse. So the religious man can respond to the demands of finitude (one does go to Deer Park after all),

[139] ibid., p. 401 (ibid., p. 412). The development in suffering which we have traced is that which led Höffding to suggest that it is the degree of tension which determines the height of the standard in the movement through the stages. But it does not follow that the scale of ethical values set up in this way is purely formal or that it is wholly unchallenged.

[140] ibid., p. 358 (ibid., p. 369). [Italics his.] Cf. ibid., p. 423 (ibid., p. 435), however difficult it may be to sustain oneself in suffering, still another difficulty is added: '. . . with God to be able to do it'.

[141] See, for example, ibid., p. 379 (ibid., p. 391): '. . . viewed religiously, all men are sufferers, and the point is to share fully in the suffering (not by plunging oneself into it, but by discovering that one is in it) and not to get away from misfortune'. On the difficulties involved in such a line of thought, see above, pp. 157–8, on becoming conscious of one's nothingness.

[142] *Pap.* XI 1 A 181.

'for he is convinced that God will not leave him in the lurch, but will help him find the right, where the boundary between what is lethargy and what are the limitations of finitude is so difficult to find'.[143] Indeed one can do more than award a certain neutrality to the temporal. While the negative may be the temporal expression for the infinite, the statement of that equation closes with the exclamation, 'happy the man who finds the positive form!'[144] One can even suggest such positive forms without placing one's hope in the prospect of temporal amelioration.[145] These are significant qualifications and ones quite consonant with the diastatic rhythm, though they surely approach those formulations which we have taken as expressive of a rhythm of synthesis in Kierkegaard's thought.

While Kierkegaard's works do reveal a systematic withdrawal in the face of the difficulties confronting the extremes of diastasis, one must say that the principal historical movement from this point is quite other than the one we have traced. We have already discussed the violent world-denying mood of the final period in the authorship.[146] It remains for us to examine the utterances of that period more carefully and to place them in the context of the interpenetration of diastasis and synthesis in Kierkegaard's material determination of the ideal. We shall find the diastatic rhythm still clearly ascendent here, but in a way which suggests that the dialectical tension noted so far in that reign is so relaxed as to yield an almost totally different product in thought. Yet the systematic continuity with the earlier authorship is clearly discernible, if one attends to the commonality which key diastatic motifs impart.

In this shift in the authorship one still moves out from the extreme diastatic conviction that: '. . . this is what Christianity thinks: the external, the true cannot possibly win the applause of the moment, it must necessarily win its disapproval.'[147] But now opposition takes an external form, as the poor, the derided self acquires the hue of ideality. The development is not unchallenged, for the qualification is added: 'Far from Christianity be the foolishness of saying that every one who was insulted while he lived, was therefore on the right path. It says merely that among those who were insulted while they lived,

---

[143] S.V. VII, p. 431 (CUP, p. 443).

[144] S.V. II, p. 221 (E-O II, p. 206).

[145] Kierkegaard's handling of the theme of mercifulness in WL seems to involve such a suggestion. On this point, see Malantschuk, op. cit., pp. 62–63.

[146] See above, pp. 33–35, 39–41, 93–95.

[147] S.V. X, p. 226 (CDi, pp. 232–3).

the true Christian must ordinarily be found.'[148] Yet one notes that the principle that the good will be rejected by this world is not essentially displaced by this qualification. Kierkegaard's perceptive remarks about the 'anxiety of poverty' tend to give way to his confidence that it is easier for a poor man to enter the kingdom than for a rich one to do so.[149] So, too, 'for a good cause' tends to drop out and leave simply 'suffer reproach' as the definition of the ideal. Claiming New Testament support, Kierkegaard invites the Christian to transform suffering and martyrdom from probable or even certain consequences to willed ends.[150]

It may seem that this understanding of the Christian ideal for the self gives the other too large a role, for his opposition is central to the very constitution of the self as Christian.[151] Yet Kierkegaard's thought is highly ascetic in this period.[152] But the drive beneath these contrasting assessments of the contribution of the other is the same sharp rhythm of diastasis. The continuity does not always seem to have been a matter of consciousness. Indeed Kierkegaard can attack monasticism as a substitute for martyrdom.[153] One can make a case historically for the opposite view that monasticism is linked positively with martyrdom through the middle term of celibacy. In

[148] ibid. (ibid., p. 232).

[149] ibid., pp. 57–59 (ibid., pp. 56–58).

[150] The textual evidence supporting the claim that Kierkegaard regarded suffering as the certain consequence of being a Christian is truly massive, and fairly well known. In the *Papirer* alone, see X 4 A 600 (*Dru* 1262), X 2 A 635, IX A 312 (*Dru* 821), and XI A 279. Kierkegaard finds New Testament predictions of martyrdom (in John 16.2 for example) and adds his own. ibid., X 5 A 81, p. 92; X 2 A 317.

[151] This is among the charges K. E. Lögstrup makes in his debate with Olesen Larsen in *Tidehverv*, 1955–8. Lönning, op. cit., pp. 183–4, makes much the same point in conceding that at this point in the authorship the consequences of the ethical demand tend to usurp the place of the demand itself.

[152] Orphic speech concerning the penal colony of this world and a persistent tendency to identify creation and fall characterize the productions of this period. See *Pap.*, XI, *passim*. The passages have often been cited and little good purpose can be served in piling them up again. Lönning, op. cit., pp. 267–79, has collected the principal passages. Olesen Larsen argues that the material of this phase is not really ascetic. One does not withdraw from the world, but retains it so that one can continue to give it up, as one must. (See his articles in *Tidehverv*, 1957–8.) This sentence does express something of the tension the self experiences in the suffering of inwardness. We have noted the difficulties facing that formulation. (See above, pp. 120–5.) Lögstrup identifies those difficulties in another way when he argues that one cannot say that a contentless absolute demand can bring one to alter one's relationship to the material world without bringing one to alter one's relationship to the form of the material world. (This point is also made in the course of the debate in *Tidehverv*, 1955–8.)

[153] *Pap.* XI 1 A 462, X 5 A 123.

any case the systematic link in the diastatic rhythm is secure and comes into prominence in the last period of the authorship, when Kierkegaard employs both martyrdom and asceticism to express the opposition of God and world.[154]

As a testimony to God's sovereign goodness the Christian may say: '. . . Thou didst use men against me in order to help me to love Thee.'[155] Yet fundamentally this testimony has its roots in the opposition of God and man and it is that opposition which empowers the drive in this final period to sever the self from its relationships. The diastatic impulse can sponsor such a severance in the interest of setting the naked self—quite without the distraction or the defence of the crowd— before the claim of God.[156] Indeed the ideal itself at times seems to be defined as attaining the state of being 'unconditionally a stranger in the world, without the least connection with anything or with any single man in the world where everything else is in connection'.[157] Still more is involved in the isolation of the self, however, as Kierkegaard suggests when he notes that one can ask oneself whether the Christian principle of hating oneself is not so anti-social as to render the formation of a community impossible for Christians.[158] That is, if one recalls the constitutive significance accorded the self's relationships, one comes to see this emphasis on withdrawal as a practical

[154] See M. M. Thulstrup, 'Sören Kierkegaards martyrgreb', *Dansk Teologisk Tidskrift*, 1964, pp.100–14. Mrs Thulstrup writes (pp. 105–6): 'Whether it concerns asceticism or martyrdom, Christianity means a destruction of the human.' She also notes an ambiguity in Kierkegaard's thought on the question whether the Christian is to be classified as the object or the subject of the work of destruction. Again the same pattern of difficulties can be discerned beneath the alternative formulations.

[155] *Pap.* XI 1 A 509. Cf. *S.V.* VIII, pp. 85ff., 99 (*PA*, pp. 37ff., 61), where the community provides the negative pole for the struggle of faith.

[156] So *S.V.* XII, p. 433 (*JY*, p. 172): '. . . connection with the world, and with the things of the world, thus also connection with other men, is what makes it so difficult to serve only one Master, and makes this impossible, if the connection is not broken, though love remains'. Cf. *Pap.* XI 3 B 199, pp. 330f. See also Valter Lindström, *Efterföljelsens Teologi hos Sören Kierkegaard* (Stockholm: Svenska Kyrkans Diakonistyrelse, 1956), p. 218.

[157] *S.V.* XII, p. 441 (*JY*, p. 180). This emphasis is not uncontested in the context for it is suggested that one may serve the Master by 'obeying those whom He wills one should obey'. (ibid., p. 437 [ibid., p. 176].) But the systematic identity of the passages under discussion from *JY* is clear, as Kierkegaard's handling of the Virgin Birth doctrine again makes evident. Cf. *S.V.* X, pp. 129-37 (*CDi*, pp. 129–38); XII, pp. 344–6 (*SE*, pp. 80–82); and IX, pp. 100–1 (*WL*, pp. 84–85). See also *S.V.* XIII, pp. 592–3 (*PV*, pp. 110–11) and *Pap.* X 3 A 659 (*Dru* 1161) for the suggestion that God's power over a man becomes less the moment he speaks to another man of God's will.

[158] *Pap.* XI 1 A 190. Cf. Lindström, op. cit., p. 214. See also *S.V.* XII, p. 111 (*TC*, pp. 118–19) on the charge that Christianity is essentially misanthropic.

exercise in 'making oneself nothing'.[159] We are not perhaps so far removed from earlier diastatic strains in the authorship after all, though surely the teleological exception has become normative and the knight's renunciation visible.[160]

If one attends to the rhythm of thought beneath the violent utterances of this last period in the authorship one will be quite prepared for Kierkegaard's contention that it could never occur to a Christian to marry.[161] This statement does not bespeak the mystic's distracting engagement to another love, so much as positive abhorrence: '. . . christianly, it is the highest degree of egoism that because a man and a woman cannot govern their desires another being must therefore sigh, perhaps for seventy years, in this penitentiary and vale of tears, and perhaps be lost eternally.'[162] Racial suicide only states in collective form and principle of 'making oneself nothing' by severing oneself from all relationships.[163]

We have tried to suggest that the utterances of this vitriolic final period have their roots in the rhythm of diastasis and possess

---

[159] From this perspective sociality is at best a concession to human weakness. (*Pap.* IX A 35.) The better course is to kill the longing for society which is natural to man. (ibid., XI 2 A 387.) This line of thought, of course, underlies the shifting assessment of the break with Regine. (See above, pp. 92–93.) What was once seen as one's sin comes to be seen as the virtue of freeing one's self from all earthly expectations. See *Pap.* X 1 A 648, X 4 A 539.

[160] Yet even at this time Kierkegaard did not will visible suffering as a means for bringing about visible social change. He dramatizes this point by delaying the attack until the memorial fund for Mynster and Martensen's succession are secure See *Pap.* XI 3 B 99, p. 158 and Gregor Malantschuk, 'Sören Kierkegaards Angreb paa Kirken', in *Sören Kierkegaards Kamp mod Kirken* (with N. H. Söe) (Copenhagen: Munksgaard, 1956), p. 22. See above, pp. 93–95.

[161] *S.V.* XIV, 254 (*AC*, p. 213).

[162] ibid., p. 265 (ibid., p. 223). Such a passage seems impressed and distressed by how few there are who enter the narrow gate. Yet the conclusion drawn is far removed from the Kierkegaardian insistence on individual responsibility. In seeking to defend such passages, E. Geismar rather reflects the diastatic rhythm than justifies it. See his *Sören Kierkegaard* (6 vols., Copenhagen: G. E. C. Gad, 1926–8), VI, p. 45: 'If one believes that the majority of men are lost—and through many sufferings Kierkegaard had come to feel that must be assumed—it then becomes very difficult to regard the process of procreation with joy.'

[163] While the counsel of racial suicide is consistent with other expression of the rhythm of diastasis, one may yet note that it does acquire a prominence in that Kierkegaard does not urge upon the individual a literal abstinence from food and drink. M. M. Thulstrup, 'Kierkegaards "onde verden"', *Kierkegaardiana*, ed. N. Thulstrup, 1955, pp. 42–54, identifies this exaltation of celibacy as the end point of a series of alterations in Kierkegaard's view of the natural, beginning in *CDi*'s affirmation of the goodness of creation. She also notes Martin Buber's suggestion of a biographical basis for the prominence of the appeal for celibacy: 'God cannot be Regine's rival!' See Martin Buber, *Between Man and Man*, trans. Ronald Gregor Smith (London: Routledge and Kegan Paul, 1949), pp. 171f.

significant continuity with earlier assertations borne by that rhythm. Thus these utterances may not stand apart as sharply as is commonly supposed. Yet one still casts about for some explanation of the shift involved, even if that explanation has a somewhat lighter burden to bear. We have seen that the Corsair incident has represented the most promising candidate to Kierkegaard scholars and to Kierkegaard himself.[164] We have also investigated the possibility that some of the rigour of this final period represents conscious one-sidedness on Kierkegaard's part.[165] If one wishes to emphasize the extraordinary element in the Christian possible (as one might wish to do if it were that element which were being almost totally ignored in one's time), one may well be attracted by the opportunity to dramatize the Christian possible by stressing the separateness discernible in visible suffering. Two final qualifications concerning the production of these caustic pages also deserve mention: (1) that Kierkegaard consciously sought to write in such a way that disciples would be repelled,[166] and (2) that the format and tempo of the battle did not permit him the leisure to grant polish—or possibly, precision—to attack.

These considerations do much to soften the contrast marking this final period, particularly if one bears in mind that the contrast is by no means an absolute one even if one limits oneself to a strict juxtaposition of texts. Kierkegaard may permit himself a new interest in discernible suffering, but he holds that suffering to the logic of impossibility by denying it constructive significance. Suffering may visibly mark God's man, but it does not so change the world as to suggest an alteration of the fundamental opposition of the finite and the infinite. Indeed one is not even attracted by 'earthly goods and profits'.[167] As far as the interest in suffering is concerned, we have shown in Part Two that preoccupation with suffering in some sense

---

[164] See above, pp. 93–94. In addition to the passages cited there, see *Pap.* IX A 64 (*Dru* 770): 'O, it is blessed to dare to say: God knows what I have suffered in this respect. I have suffered for a good cause and because I did (humanly speaking) a good deed in a truly unselfish sacrifice. I dare say this to God's face—and I know more certainly than that I exist, more certainly than all else, because I sense it already that he will answer "Yes, my dear child, you are right in that".'

[165] See above, pp. 39–40.

[166] See *S.V.* XIII, pp. 518–19 (*PV*, pp. 6–8) for Kierkegaard's claim that what men took to be his pride was actually his self-denial.

[167] *Pap.* XI 3 B 99, p. 158. Cf. *S.V.* XIV, p. 71 (*AC*, p. 48), where Kierkegaard insists that he is not after the clergy's daily bread and indeed may very well come to their defence, if this should come to be a point of controversy. Cf. above p. 167, note 160.

was an early and continuing feature of Kierkegaard's life. And in this chapter we have tried to show how the shifting senses given to the suffering of the Christian man reveal the fundamental systematic movement of Kierkegaard's thought.

The discussion of suffering has largely focused the systematic movement of Kierkegaard's thought in the rhythm of diastasis. But we should note that we still deal at this point with the interpenetration of diastasis and synthesis. That is evident not only in the category of the ideal which the diastatic impulse addresses. It may be seen at other points as well. We mention one such point which links the material and formal determinations of the ideal. We refer to the remarkable blend of suffering and joy which Kierkegaard accords the self claimed by God. The blend takes sharply differing forms. One may suffer under the temporal, but even now be blessed by the thought of the joy that awaits one.[168] Or one may permit the logic of satisfaction intrinsic to the ideal to transform even one's assessment of suffering. For the diastatic witness to God's sovereignty suffering must come from God. Perhaps he tests us[169]—in any case his purpose is good and our suffering the sign of his love.[170]

This responsiveness of Kierkegaard's thought to the formal requirement that the self's good lies in God's ideal does not repulse the pressure from the extreme diastatic separation of God and man, but restrains it. It may be blessed to be 'always in the wrong over against God'. One *can* very well transcend in joy the bodily pain of martyrdom, 'but at the same time that the individual suffers religiously he cannot in joy transcend the suffering: for the suffering refers precisely to the fact that he is separated from joy, but at the same time it designates the relationship [to joy]. Thus to be without suffering signifies that one is not religious.'[171] This process becomes particularly clear in a journal passage in which the quest for satisfaction, denied entrance to the temporal, outflanks the diastatic opposition and even so redefines itself as to accommodate that opposition within itself: 'When one is able to endure the isolation involved in being a single individual, entirely without the mitigation of intermediate terms, without the alleviation of any illusion, alone in the endless world and the endless world of men—but out of a million men 999,999 will lose their senses

[168] See, for example, *S.V.* VII, pp. 394–8 (*CUP*, pp. 405–9) for the view that while the happiness comes 'afterward', one may possess it even now in anticipation. For an autobiographical expression of this point, see *S.V.* XIII, p. 568 (*PV*, p. 82).

[169] *Pap.* IX A 358, 326.

[170] ibid., X 4 A 593, XI 2 A 130.

[171] *S.V.* VII, p. 394 (*CUP*, p. 406).

before they attain this isolation—alone before the face of God—then the thing of loving God and being loved by God will appear to him so blessed that for sheer blessedness he must say: O my God, now I have but one wish, one prayer, one desire, one passion, that I may experience suffering, become hated, persecuted, mocked, spit upon, put to death. For if God's love for me were to be expressed in the fact that in a sensual sense I enjoyed good days, that I received this world's goods, if it were thus to be directly expressed—phew, phew, that would be disgusting to me, I should die for shame, I should loathe it like an unnatural lust, feel that it was as disgusting as fat fish with treacle. Behold this is the passion for martyrdom.'[172] The mind's willingness to accept such an arbitrated settlement may exceed the fuller self's capacity. In any case one does witness a counter-movement which pulls back from the diastatic conviction on suffering: 'Thou art love; and when I perceive that the close relationship to Thee (in the pain of that unlikeness of mine) will continue to be suffering, Thou wilt in "grace" permit me, yea, Thou wilt aid me to slip away a little farther from Thee; for this I understand that the closer one comes to Thee, the more suffering there is in this life.'[173]

This last counter-movement ought to remind us that one may criticize Kierkegaard's comments on suffering as freely as one likes, but one ought not to seek to claim that this is all there is to be found in Kierkegaard's characterization of Christian experience.[174] We have seen that Kierkegaard speaks of much more than suffering in his determination of the ideal. No critique of Kierkegaard can claim to be responsible, if it fails to recognize the complexity of his thought.

All the complexity we have encountered in Kierkegaard's discourse concerning God and man is carried into his reflection about the Christ. We shall find his discussion of the God-man responding to those pressures and counter-pressures we have seen to be generated by the rhythms of synthesis and diastasis. We shall also see that Kierkegaard's christology is far more than a reflection of those rhythms. We hope to show how those rhythms are both focused in the christological centre of Kierkegaard's thought and formed by the independent systematic force represented by the witness to the Christ. Neither that focusing nor that forming can cause us to leng-

[172] *Pap.* X 5 A 81, p. 92.
[173] ibid., X 4 A 600 (*Dru* 1262).
[174] For an example of such one-sided reading of Kierkegaard, see Siegfried Hansen's highly critical 'Die Bedeutung des Leidens für das Christusbild Sören Kierkegaards', *Kerygma und Dogma*, 1956, pp. 1–28.

then this chapter. But neither could be intelligibly discussed until the rhythms were permitted to disclose themselves in Kierkegaard's discourse on God and man.

A Transitional Note

In chapter five we begin our analysis of Kierkegaard's utterances concerning the Christ. We give that beginning the title 'The *Actuality* of the Christ'. One might suppose that it would be impossible—or at least irrelevent—to get beyond any beginning deserving so sweeping a title. Yet the phrase suits well the limited and preparatory character of chapter five. This is the case in two important respects:

(1) We have discussed Kierkegaard's handling of the themes possibility-necessity-actuality in his description of man.[175] Kierkegaard's employment of those categories encourages us to distinguish between the actuality of an individual and the issue of that actuality for others. Thus we attempt in chapter five to analyse Kierkegaard's description of the reality of the first-century figure called the Christ, but we defer to chapter six ('The *Efficacy* of the Christ') the task of charting his reflection concerning the 'becoming' of this 'being' for others. This distinction cannot be made absolutely. At least for Kierkegaard the other's actuality is necessity as well as possibility for the self! Yet clarity may be won and an interminably long chapter avoided, if we distinguish between moments which surely are never isolated in the living process of Kierkegaard's reflection.

(2) Our major concern in chapter five lies with the analysis of Kierkegaard's actual statements regarding this actuality of the Christ, not with the task of relating this christology to his wider theological reflection. In discussing Kierkegaard's affirmations concerning the God-Man we shall, of course, again call into service the categories Kierkegaard employed in describing God and man. Near at hand

---

[175] See above, pp. 105–8. It has also been clear that this handling does not go unchallenged (see above, pp. 100–1, 151–60). Similarly, we shall encounter christological material which seems to resist our mode of procedure. This challenge represents a significant voice within the diastatic current, but not a dominant one. Unable to proceed in more than one direction at one time, we take the course which we feel can claim the greatest support within the authorship. (See above, pp. 28–43.) We leave to Part Four the adjudication of whatever dispute may be found to exist between the rhythms of synthesis and diastasis as far as theological method is concerned.

lies the question whether this man's convictions concerning God and man not only supply categories for christological characterization, but also control the use of those categories. That question first finds a full discussion in chapter seven: 'The *Possibility* of the Christ'.

The phrasing of that title correctly holds a hint of the independent character of the Christ encounter. There thus arises the relational task for the student of Kierkegaard's thought, In chapter seven we shall be asking how far and in what ways Kierkegaard's convictions regarding God and man permitted him to speak his mind regarding the Christ he came to know. But the question must be put the other way as well. The encounter with the Christ provides not only a field in which the rhythms of the divine-human polarity may come to focus. It yields a witness which represents a shaping, constructive energy in Kierkegaard's reflection. For Kierkegaard there is this sort of 'actuality' characterizing the Christ and the word about the Christ. In chapters five and six we deal with the material which forms the basis for the christological counter-influence and observe isolated instances of gains scored by that influence. But the larger question of the significance of the Christ for theological reflection as a whole is deferred to the open country of chapter seven. There that question is addressed as it bears on the *description* of Kierkegaard's thought. The bearing of the question for any constructive effort in contemporary theology dominates Part Four, though it underlies as well the conception of the entire book.[176]

[176] See our earlier statement of the relationships between the rhythms of diastasis and synthesis and the christological affirmations of Kierkegaard, above, pp. 11–14.

V

THE FOCUSING AND FORMATION OF KIERKEGAARD'S REFLECTION IN HIS DISCOURSE REGARDING THE GOD-MAN: THE *ACTUALITY* OF THE CHRIST

1. *The Person of the Christ*

THE THEME of the coming together of God and man in the Christ is central to Kierkegaard's christology and to his religious thought as a whole. It is not the case that Kierkegaard would, as it were, add a word about Christ to others he uttered and that he was willing to pay the price of what is perhaps a definitional acknowledgement of the divine and the human in christological formulation. Granted words at all, it is the God-Man of whom he would speak. But he spoke of more than the God-Man, and was far too consistent a thinker to leave these 'speakings' lying unrelated to each other as the products of his mind. We have seen that it is precisely God and man who form the poles for Kierkegaard's wider religious reflection. Just as surely as he would witness to the God-Man, so surely do the difficulties deriving from his determination of God and man surround and penetrate that witness. Yet the apparent intensity of Kierkegaard's christological concern not only yields persistance in witness, but exerts not inconsiderable pressure on the sources of the difficulties themselves. In this chapter and in the two which follow it, we shall see Kierkegaard's christology both focusing and forming the rhythms of his reflection.

However one may settle the analytical question of priority, logical and chronological, it is descriptively clear beyond all possibility of doubt that Kierkegaard affirms the presence of God and man in the Christ. He would say quite starkly: 'To believe is to believe the divine and the human together in Christ.'[1] That affirmation may be sketched rather briefly, since it proceeds along lines now familiar to the reader. Thus Kierkegaard gives content to the assertion that

[1] *S.V.* XI, p. 69 ('HM', *PA*, p. 99).

Jesus was a 'wholly ordinary man'[2] by speech about a capacity for sympathy which derives more from the material relatedness of selves than from their formal possession of a common abstract 'nature'. It is true that Jesus knew experiences of men, because he bore their nature. He himself knew hunger, thirst, suffering and death.[3] Yet still more basic to the human self is its relatedness to others and the one we call Christ was himself bent towards the other. In a striking passage in the *Works of Love* Kierkegaard brings together the Christ's possession of 'human nature' and his living participation in the being of other humans: '. . . He who loved the whole race, our Lord Jesus Christ, yet humanly felt the need to love and be loved by an individual man. . . . He was an actual man and can therefore share in all that is human; he was not an airy form which beckoned in the clouds, without understanding or wishing to understand what humanly happens to a man. Oh, no, he could have pity over the multitude which needed food, and that in a purely human sense, he who had himself hungered in the wilderness.'[4]

We should note explicitly that Kierkegaard does not exempt the Christ from the solidly human experience of temptation. The Christian knows as his Lord one who was 'tempted in all things, yet without sin'.[5] Without sin surely, and yet Kierkegaard makes temptation psychologically plausible by identifying elements in the Christ's experience which may be said to be the seed bed for sin. So he could write in an early journal reference: 'One of the outbursts where the human in Christ comes to the fore most strongly is his word to Judas, "what thou doest, do quickly" . . . this human unrest, this vacillation as the decisive moment approached also found its place, and will be a consolation to many if they remember it in the hour of need.'[6] And the published works include frequent poignant passages attesting the reality of the cry 'My God, My God, why hast thou forsaken me?'[7]

One might seek to find further expression of this intent to affirm the humanity of the Christ in Kierkegaard's frequent dismissal of all

[2] *Pap.* IX A 101.

[3] See, for example, *S.V.* X, pp. 270–1 (*CDi*, p. 273) and *S.V.* IV, pp. 201–2 (*PF*, pp. 24–25).

[4] *S.V.* IX, p. 148 (*WL*, pp. 125–6). Kierkegaard goes on to find an example of the human need to love and be loved in Jesus' relation to Peter.

[5] *S.V.* X, p. 270 (*CDi*, p. 273).

[6] *Pap.* II A 258 (*Dru* 221).

[7] See, for example, *S.V.* VIII, pp. 354, 363 (*GS*, pp. 73, 86); X, p. 271 (*CDi*, p. 273); XI, p. 65 ('HM', *PA*, p. 91), and *Pap.* VIII A 580.

efforts to find data in the life of Jesus which would be suggestive of his deity. Perhaps that quest is better intended than guided. For the major systematic source of the dismissal under discussion seems rather to lie in Kierkegaard's doctrine of God. That will not seem such a strange suggestion, if one recalls the tendency of Kierkegaard's thought to move towards an apportionment by which the diastatic impulse claims dominance in the doctrine of God.[8] A wholly independent God may well (must?) be freed from finding expression in the visible and so becoming an *object* for man's investigation and assessment. This matter will face us most directly in chapter six, when we discuss the efficacy of the Christ.[9]

We should note other indications of the strength of the diastatic impulse in the affirmation of the deity of the Christ. What is implied by the presence of God in the Christ? A total foreknowledge offers a fitting epistemological correlate to the logic of certainty which we have found to be so congenial to the rhythm of diastasis. We are told that 'Christ knew his fate from the beginning, knew that it was unavoidable—he willed it himself, after all he went freely into it.'[10] Neither development nor limitation can find place in such a mind.

Yet mental development and limitation are marks of man's humanity, not his depravity. Indeed there is no conceivable human state which would correspond to the completeness of this divine knowledge. There is a fundamental incommensurability between this God and this man. So it is that Kierkegaard speaks of the intrinsic incognito of the God-Man, for a human being revealing God can

---

[8] See above, pp. 124–8.

[9] Hayo Gerdes, *Das Christusbild Sören Kierkegaards* (Düsseldorf-Köln: Eugen Dietrichs, 1960) notes that Kierkegaard's tendency to deny evidential value to any material stressing Christ's glory brings him into line with contemporary biblical criticism and its tendency to dismiss the legendary material in the New Testament literature. This observation is in a measure correct, but we should be alert to the possibility that the common 'result' may flow from very different sources and so actually 'mean' something quite different in the two cases. It is this possibility of the confluence of markedly different sources which makes plausible Emanuel Hirsch's suggestion (*Kierkegaard Studien* [4 vols. in 2, Gütersloh: C. Bertelsmann, 1930–3], vol. II, p. 883) that the decisive statement in Kierkegaard's christology is taken from John's dialectic of Jesus and the Jews ('they received him not'), but the living concrete colours come from the synoptics.

[10] *S.V.* XII, p. 345 (*SE*, p. 81). Cf. ibid., pp. 172–3 (*TC*, p. 184) for the suggestion that the God-Man, unlike man who is a 'frail creature', 'is in a position at the first moment to know all beforehand, his suffering and the certainty and necessity of his destruction and then yet able to live calmly day by day, devoted to God, who has only all good things in store for him'. Cf. also *S.V.* VIII, p. 338 (*GS*, p. 50) concerning the Christ 'who knew all things, whose thought encompasses all things'.

never become an instance of direct communication.[11] Indeed one may well wonder if one deals here with communication at all, for the incommensurability is so great that Kierkegaard approves Pascal's word that God is hid more deeply in the Incarnation than in creation.[12] The co-presence of this divine and this human does constitute a paradox of the most fundamental order. Of course no one who sets pen to paper with the intent of saying something about Kierkegaard's christology can fail to speak of paradox. But that speech often has carried the surprising suggestion that this theme actually marks Kierkegaard's debt to sources which are fundamentally alien to his own thought.[13] One may already experience surprise upon being told that so prominent a theme has no better claim in a body of thought characterized in so many respects by self-awareness and precision. Our approach to Kierkegaard illumines that surprise and renders its protest explicit by making clear how the paradox motif stands at the juncture of the fundamental rhythms of Kierkegaard's reflection. It is far more to the point to speak of Kierkegaard's paradox as the reflection of his reason (a reason whose distinctions do threaten to become divisions), than to suggest that Kierkegaard is somehow stuck with the paradox and then calls in an illicit irrationalism in its defence.

In some of Kierkegaard's remarks concerning the Christ as Paradox one senses that his thought has reached a kind of plateau from which movement to new ground can be generated only with great exertion. That is, Kierkegaard does at times seem not only intent to assert that God and man meet in the Christ, but content to leave the matter at that.[14] And the God and man who meet are so understood that it is hard to see how one can speak intelligibly of the meeting. The meeting itself tends to become a juxtaposition of realities for which no common

[11] For useful secondary discussion at this point see Per Lönning, 'Samtidighedens Situation' (Oslo: Land og Kirke, 1954), p. 91, on the intrinsic incognito and Gregor Malantschuk, Kierkegaard's Way to the Truth, trans. Mary Michelsen (Minneapolis: Augsburg, 1963), p. 73 on the impossibility of direct communication. This is the dynamic to which Günther Rohrmoser points in saying ('Ernst oder Ironie?—Eine Zwischenbemerkung zur Interpretation Kierkegaard', Archiv für Geschichte der Philosophie, 1962, pp. 75–87,) that irony becomes a theological category in Kierkegaard by virtue of the fact that he introduces the theme of the hidden God.

[12] Pap. X 3 A 626.

[13] J. Heywood Thomas, Subjectivity and Paradox (Oxford: Basil Blackwell, 1957), pp. 103–8, offers a convenient summary of the contentions of Teisen, Drachmann, and Bohlin at this point. See also above, pp. 82–85.

[14] See, for example, S.V. IX, p. 148 (WL, p. 125); XI, p. 69 ('HM', PA, p. 99) and Pap. VIII A 579.

ground is available, save the subjective ground of the believer's passion. We shall explore that ground in chapter six. At this stage in the development of Kierkegaard's thought even attempts to deal with specific aspects of the Christ's person reveal the tendency towards a rather static juxtaposition of the divine and the human, rather than a living internal meeting. Thus, caught between the logic of an *imitatio Christi* appeal linked with the human Christ and the docetism sponsored by a severely diastatic reading of the divine in him, Kierkegaard can write: 'He, who was the truth, and the way and the life, he, who needed to learn nothing, he yet learned one thing: he learned obedience. In so close a relation does obedience stand to the eternal truth, that he, who is the truth, learns obedience.'[15]

Yet Kierkegaard seems unwilling to leave the christological witness with the naked assertion of a paradox which seems to reduce the unity of the Christ to a matter of words. He does not turn his back on his defence of the principle of contradiction.[16] Rather he sets about a restatement of the paradox, though this surely does not entail a replacement of the theme in a larger sense. Thus there arise passages which show that Kierkegaard wishes to affirm some kind of kenosis doctrine.[17] Often one encounters the picture of a kind of daily kenosis. Thus Kierkegaard writes: 'Christ will not be God; with an omnipotent resolve he has forced himself into being an individual man, now he must suffer in an entirely real way the miserable impotence of being a poor individual man with humanity's case at heart—and at every moment it is his free resolve which forces him: he has, after all, the power to break through and be God.'[18]

This formulation honours the central diastatic concept of the freedom of God as fully as any kenosis concept can: 'Thus One chooses an incognito, that shows him to be far poorer than he is. . . . The incognito is his free resolve. He exerts himself to the utmost, using all his inventiveness and intrepidity in order to hold fast to the incognito. He either succeeds or he does not. . . . Oh, self-denial, and on the other hand, oh what an immense strain, for he has after all at every

---

[15] *S.V.* VIII, p. 340 (*GS*, p. 54).

[16] See above, pp. 18–20.

[17] For a discussion of the choices available to Kierkegaard and a contention concerning his selection, see H. Roos, 'Sören Kierkegaard und die Kenosis-Lehre', *Kierkegaardiana*, ed. N. Thulstrup, 1957, pp. 54–60. Lönning, op. cit., p. 161, notes that the most abundant support in Kierkegaard for the pre-existence of the Christ comes through the emphasis placed on the humiliation involved in the earthly state of the Christ—an emphasis which surely moves towards some kenosis position.

[18] *Pap.* X 3 A 118. Cf. ibid. X 2 A 296 (*Dru* 1020), X 6 B 239.

moment had the power to show this true form. Oh, self-denial, for what is self-denial without freedom.'[19]

Still one may perhaps praise God's freedom as fully and yet grant a more secure place to the unfettered humanity of the Christ. Climacus shows the way in language which still reveals some nostalgia for the lure of the uncompromised freedom of God: 'God's servant-form is . . . not a disguise, but is actual; not a parastatic body, but an actual body; and from the hour when he with the omnipotent resolve of his omnipotent love became a servant God has so to speak imprisoned himself in his resolve, and now must go on (to speak foolishly) whether he wills to or not. He cannot then betray himself; he does not have the possibility which is open to the noble king, suddenly to show that he is after all the king—which, however, is no perfection with the king (to have this possibility), but shows merely his impotence and the impotence of his resolve, that he does not actually have the power to become what he wills.'[20]

What seems to have happened in this turn of thought is that the extreme diastatic pressure has been resisted or even repulsed. Such pressure does after all threaten the humanity of the Christ, and Kierkegaard will not compromise on that point: 'He is indeed the God-Man and so eternally different from every man, but he was none the less at the same time a true man, tempted in all things human. . . .'[21] But perhaps the banishment of the extremes of diastasis comes about in the interest also of God—of the God active in the Christ. Having turned away from the metaphysical extremes of diastasis as fitting heralds of the king's reign, one may find it possible to develop an understanding of the Christ which would speak intelligibly of a meeting of God and man in his person.

There are indications that Kierkegaard did take this path which we have seen him to open to himself. God is present in the Christ and his presence is in some sense even open to discernment. After all, the implication of a wholly uncompromising emphasis on the incognito is not attractive: '. . . the whole life of Christ on earth would have been a game, if he had been incognito in the degree that he went through life wholly unnoticed—and yet he was in truth incognito.'[22] Rather, the glory of the Christ shines through his life of humiliation.[23] It seems too little to say that this is simply the glory of an exceptional

[19] *S.V.* XII, p. 121 (*TC*, p. 129).
[20] *S.V.* IV, p. 221 (*PF*, p. 44).
[21] *S.V.* IX, p. 148 (*WL*, p. 125).
[22] *S.V.* XIII, p. 525 (*PV*, p. 16). Cf. *Pap.* IV A 62.
[23] *Pap.* X 4 A 86.

man.[24] Kierkegaard will find God present in the Christ and with characteristic consistency pays the price for that affirmation: '[Just as God's kingdom is not] the absolute unknowable, which would be identical with that it did not exist at all. . . . [so] Christ was not, after all, incognito either, not in the degree that it was never noticed that he was the God-Man . . .'[25] Kierkegaard warns quickly that the communication by which the Christ makes God known is not direct. But perhaps the indirectness of the Christ's revelation of God is analogous to the indirectness grounded in the distinction between the inner and the outer[26] and required by a truth which incites to action.[27]

In speaking of the revelation of God in the Christ we are thrust into Kierkegaard's discussion of the work of the Christ. That will provide a fuller answer to the question of the nature of the divine presence in the Christ and so of the meeting of the divine and the human in this person. Before turning to that, however, we may note that the development of Kierkegaard's christology which we have followed in this section does witness to the *'actuality* of the Christ' for him. The insistence on relating God and man and the movement of his thought beyond a relationship of artificial juxtaposition reveal something more than a mental craftsman's diligent interest in the interrelating of all his concepts under the banner of consistency. These characteristics reveal as well—and far more importantly—the encounter of the writer of the words with the Christ and the consequent concern—passion is not too strong a word—to grant that encounter a central place in his Christian thought and speech.[28] Thus it is that Kierkegaard insists that christology finds its subject matter not in the union of God and humanity, but in that union in an individual.[29] Or, as he put it to

[24] Hayo Gerdes, *Das Christus Verständnis des jungen Kierkegaard* (Itzehoe: 'Die Spur', 1962), p. 49, finds Kierkegaard admitting data suggesting a most extraordinary man, but nothing suggesting deity.

[25] *Pap.* X 6 B 263.

[26] See above, pp. 20–22.

[27] See above, pp. 106–7.

[28] To this extent it seems unfortunate to discuss Kierkegaard's thought as caught between an orthodox-pietistic picture of the Christ present as an alien heritage and his own dialectic of subjectivity, which implies a new view of Christianity. For such a discussion see Gerdes, *Das Christusbild Sören Kierkegaards.*

[29] *S.V.* XII, p. 79 (*TC*, pp. 83–84): 'Offence relates itself essentially to the setting together of God and man, or to the God-Man. Speculation naturally has thought that it could "comprehend" the God-Man—that one can well enough comprehend, for speculation takes away from the God-Man the determination of temporality, contemporaneity, and actuality. . . . No, *the situation* belongs with the God-Man, the situation that an individual man, who stands beside you, is the

himself in a journal reference: first and fundamentally, 'the God-Man is himself the existential'.[30]

2. *The Coming about of the Work of the Christ*

Kierkegaard is fully aware of the consequences which follow from his affirmation of the humanity of the Christ. In speaking of the work of this Christ he reintroduces categories familiar to us from our discussion of the ideal confronting man. This is true of the coming about of the work. The ideal confronting man is a genuine challenge bearing the character of contingency. Now we, are offered a view which affirms the freedom of the Christ's work. Indeed this is no formal acknowledgement, for Kierkegaard gives himself with zest to the theme of the temptation. The Christ knew temptation at every moment in the discharge of his mission.[31] Kierkegaard endorses that assertion with a description whose realism draws directly from the tissue of human life:

. . . he it is who can wholly put himself in thy place, Jesus Christ, who truly learned to know every temptation in that he withstood every temptation.—Is it concern for food, and quite literally in the strictest sense concern for food, so that death from starvation threatens: he too was tempted thus; is it rash daring which

---

God-Man. The God-Man is not the unity of God and man. . . . The God-Man is the unity of God and an individual man' [italics his]. Cf. *S.V.* XI, pp. 226–32 (*SD*, pp. 191–201).

[30] *Pap.* X 2 A 439 (*Dru* 1054). This passage asserts that 'science is an impossibility' for one contemporary with this existential Christ. We are inquiring into the nature of that impossibility. Since the journal passage sets the Christ encounter in the context of Climacus' description of possibility and actuality (see above, pp. 106–7), it seems right to leave open the question whether the immediate impossibility of 'scientific' description of the Christ may give way to some kind of subsequent possibility. We discuss that question further in chapters six and eight.

[31] *S.V.* XII, pp. 343–4 (*SE*, pp. 79–80): '. . . from the very beginning his life is a story of temptation; it is not merely a particular part of his life, the forty days, which is the story of temptation; no, his life (as it also is the story of the passion) is the story of temptation. In every moment of his life he is tempted—that is to say, he has in his power the possibility of taking his calling, his task in vain. In the desert it is Satan who is the tempter, otherwise it is the others who play the role of the tempter, at times the populace, at times the disciples, perhaps also at one time, especially in the beginning, the mighty exerted themselves to tempt him to secularize his calling, his task. . . .' The context of this passage invites the suggestion that the temptation was for Jesus to use the supernatural powers which he had at his disposal. Yet that reading is not required for the secularization of the calling might be supposed to bring a quite natural success, given the circumstances surrounding the activity of Jesus. Even if one does introduce the content of the access to supernatural powers, the reality of the temptation is in no way lessened as a matter of Kierkegaard's concern.

tempts: he too was tempted thus; is it to fall away from God that thou art tempted: he too was tempted thus; he can put himself wholly in thy place, whoever thou art. Art thou tempted in loneliness: he, too, whom the evil spirit led out into the lonely place in order to tempt him. Art thou tempted in the confusion of the world: he too, whose good spirit kept him from withdrawing from the world before he had completed his work of love. Art thou tempted in the great moment of decision, when what is involved is forsaking all: he too; or is it in the next moment, when thou art tempted to regret that thou didst offer all: he too. Art thou tempted when sinking under the possibility to wish that the actuality of danger were nearly present: he too; art thou tempted, when languishing, to desire thy death: he too. Is the temptation this, to be forsaken by men: he too was tempted; is it that—but no, this trial surely no man has experienced, the trial of being forsaken by God; but he was tempted thus. And so in every way.[32]

That the Christ experienced temptation may comfort the Christian; that the Christ resisted temptation rouses him from every false comfort. The *imitatio Christi* appeal draws upon the humanity of the Christ for its power in quite specific ways. Thus the lowliness and poverty of Jesus are held to witness that the relevance of the ideal is not limited to those in positions of esteem and advantage.[33]

The reader will know that this line of thought does not pass unchallenged within the authorship. One would find it challenged, even if no protest could be seen to be forthcoming from Kiekegaard's discourse concerning the Christ. We refer, of course, to the fundamental movement of Kierkegaard's thought to exalt divine sovereignty by stating God's independence in the strongest possible terms. That movement can contribute the postulate of certainty to anyone who would speak of a will of God. That contribution is not such that a distinction between prescription and performance is welcomed as a useful means of clarifying the certainty involved.

We are not limited to *expecting* influence from this quarter on Kierkegaard's christology. In a way that influence finds its most direct expression in the formulation which reduces the work of the Christ to the sheer existence of his person.[34] We shall be discussing this formulation when we speak of the content of the work of the Christ. Even now, however, it should be clear that such a statement of the certainty motif is threatened with the possibility that by simple conversion it may be precisely the contingency of the work which is conveyed. One may suppose oneself to be speaking of the processive character of the Christ's personhood and not of the punctiliar character of his work.

[32] *S.V.* XI, pp. 256–7 ('HP', *CDi*, pp. 366–7).
[33] *S.V.* XII, pp. 214–20 (*TC*, pp. 228–34); IV, pp. 199–200 (*PF*, pp. 24–25).
[34] See, for example, *Pap.* I A 53 (*Dru* 14).

This threat can be handled by taking it within the certainty motif. Speak openly, then, of the processive character of the work, but deny all talk of struggle which mixes badly with the mood of certainty. Or, make contact with other convictions by acknowledging the presence of visible struggle, but bar the way to any struggle as far as the Christ's 'self-understanding' is concerned. Thus one will say: '. . . for the individual Christian there is reserved a suffering by which even the God-Man could not be tried. . . . the God-Man knows in his inmost self and with eternal certainty that he is the truth and he does indeed suffer because as the truth or in spite of being the truth he is persecuted, but he does not suffer at the same time at another point in his inmost being concerning how far he now at every moment himself is in the truth. But this is the case with the individual Christian.'[35] It would surely seem that if the Christ quite literally cannot doubt his indentification with (as) God's truth, any real basis for temptation is denied him.

The line of exploration which we have been following in this section leads on beyond the range of this chapter. One wants to ask, 'If the Christ event is certain, are its effects wholly as sure? (the *efficacy* of the Christ: chapter six).' And then, 'If the event and/or its effect(s) are sure, in what sense can one speak of the event as real? (the *possibility* of the Christ; chapter seven).' We shall come to these questions better equipped if we first inquire more carefully into the content of the event.

3. *The Content of the Work of the Christ*

Again we encounter characterizations of the work of the Christ which bring to mind material made familiar by our discussion of God's claim upon man. One might understandably be reluctant to attribute much significance to the reappearance of the word 'love', for that counter does seem to come to the lips of religious folk with impressive ease. That reluctance could maintain iteslf even in the face of formal likenesses in the usages of the term.[36] But one can hardly

---

[35] *S.V.* XII, p. 182 (*TC*, p. 194). The context does contain a diastatic challenge, for we are told of the individual Christian: 'The blasphemy of wanting to be the truth could naturally never occur to him, before God he is a poor, sinful man, who only very imperfectly relates himself to the truth.' (ibid. [ibid.].) Two equivocations support the challenge: (1) the equivocation between being the truth and being in the truth, and (2) the equivocation between having the truth as a standard for one's striving, and having the truth as an achievement of one's striving.

[36] See, for example, *S.V.* XII, pp. 156–67 (*TC*, pp. 167–79) and *S.V.* III, pp. 275–6 ('LC', *ED* I, pp. 64–65).

fail to be impressed when the material specification of the ideal of love is seen to be descriptive of the Christ's work. The point does not concern something that is less than essential to the work of the Christ. For the work of the Christ is the work of one who 'with his love cannot shut himself within himself, he who out of love gave himself for the world'.[37] And 'this, after all, was Christianity, not that a rich man makes the poor rich, but that the poorest of all makes all rich, both rich and poor'.[38] Surely, then, the Christian may well learn obedience 'from him, who is the way, him, who himself learned obedience and was obedient, obedient in all things, obedient in giving up all things (the glory he had before the foundations of the earth were laid), obedient in doing without all things (even that upon which he could lay his head), obedient in taking upon himself all things (the sin of the race), obedient in suffering all things (the guilt of the race), obedient in submitting to all things in life, obedient in death'.[39]

The relationship between Kierkegaard's discussion of the Christ's self-revealing, self-giving work and his discussion of God's ideal for man simply cannot be reduced to a matter of a verbal analogy. If a child seeks the meaning of the crucifixion scene, one will have to do more than say the crucified man is the Saviour of the world: 'But to this the child will not be able to attach any definite conception; tell him therefore merely that this crucified one was the most loving man who ever lived. . . . Tell the child, that he was love, that he came to the world out of love, that he took upon himself the form of a humble servant, that he lived only for one thing, to love and help men, especially all those who were sick and sorrowing and suffering and unhappy. Then tell the child what befell him in life. . . .'[40] That the commonality we are discussing is not a formal one is made clear when Kierkegaard refuses to limit the self-giving of the Christ's love to his death. Rather that death comes as a further expression of the love which ruled the Christ's every waking moment and which surely seems one with the love to which men are called: 'His love was wholly present in the least as in the greatest . . . it was equally present at every moment, not greater when he breathed his last on the cross than when he let himself be born. . . .'[41]

---

[37] S.V. X, p. 300 (CDi, p. 294).
[38] S.V. XII, p. 143 (TC, p. 153).
[39] S.V. X, p. 88 (CDi, p. 87).
[40] S.V. XII, pp. 163-4 (TC, p. 176). Cf. ibid., pp. 41-42 (ibid., pp. 45-46) concerning the Extraordinary who does not hold people at a distance, but approaches them to be their servant.
[41] S.V. IX, p. 98 (WL, p. 82).

Such love will suffer at the hands of men, for men do not understand it. 'He was, divinely understood, love; he loved in the power of the divine understanding of what love is, he loved the whole race; he did not dare—out of love to give up this understanding, for that would have been precisely to betray the race. Therefore his whole life was an awful collision with the merely human understanding of what love is. It was the ungodly world which crucified him. . . .'[42]

Perhaps men do not understand such love, but they *shall* do so: 'Therefore Christ is in truth the pattern, and therefore he is also the eternally exacting in being a man, because he merely said that he was a man like other men. He makes the divine commensurable to being a wholly ordinary man.'[43] Not that men have not 'known' the law of God before. The Christ comes to be the fulfilment of the call men have heard despite themselves and in this fulfilment the call sounds the clearer: 'No, surely Christ did not come to destroy the law—he himself is the fulfilment of the law, and has thus presented himself as pattern. This is an entirely qualitative sharpening: the fact that there is a pattern who is the fulfilment of the law and whom we must imitate.'[44]

Setting the claim of the *imitatio Christi* appeal in the context of man's knowledge of God's law may seem to bring Kierkegaard far down the path to a mean-spirited moralism. This is in fact not the case. True it is, that man only measures himself rightly when he comes to know the Christ.[45] But the measure and goal the Christ makes known to the self is God. No one can suppose Kierkegaard to be speaking of some process of deification of mortal flesh. But no one who has heard him speak of the constitutive significance of the self's relationships will be surprised by the suggestion that the nature and the destiny of the self are to be understood by inquiring into its relationship to God. And what is God like? We may quote a journal passage a second time: 'God has only one passion: to love and to want to be loved. That which has pleased him is to go through existentially with men all the different modes of loving, to go through loving. He himself naturally takes the roles, then, and arranges everything in relation to this. At one moment he would be loved as a father by his

---

[42] ibid., p. 107 (ibid., p. 90). Per Lönning, op. cit., pp. 152–4, has made available the best brief discussion of this collision.

[43] *Pap.* IX A 101.

[44] *Pap.* X 4 A 366, p. 216. Cf. *Pap.* X 2 A 451, X 3 A 712, and X 4 A 230 (*Dru* 1207). On the law known apart from and before the appearance of Jesus, see above, pp. 132–5.

[45] See Hirsch, op. cit., II, pp. 879–80.

child, at another as a friend by a friend, at another as the one who only brings good gifts, at still another as the one who tempts and tests the beloved. And in Christianity the idea is, if I may say so, to want to be loved as a bridegroom by his bride and in such a way that it becomes a pure testing. At one moment he transforms himself almost into equality with man, in accommodation, in order to be loved in this way: at another, the idea is as spirit to be loved by a man—the most strenuous task, etc. etc.'[46]

In looking in the Christ at the God who loves him man knows who he is. In opening himself in the Christ to the God who loves him man moves towards what he is to become.[47] Man is made in relationships and made for them. An earlier sentence can serve us again; one is so to live that the inevitable relatedness of selves bears and so becomes the mutual revelation of selves. The syllogism shapes itself: love is the fulfilment of the law, the Christ is love, therefore the Christ is authentic humanity. The determination of this humanity is not in man's hand. But, then, the movement to attain that humanity does not originate with him either. A living God has confronted man, powerfully and personally in the Christ, who could not 'shut himself in'. Thus it is in these two respects that Kierkegaard can combine, and even identify, the *imitatio Christi* appeal with the recognition that man is nothing before God.[48]

The preceding paragraph clearly shows how intimately Kierkegaard's christology is related to his discourse concerning God and man. While it makes clear specific arteries structuring the relationship to other sets of affirmations, it does not make clear which way(s) the traffic of influence flows. We shall have something to say about that in chapter seven, but for now we need to note that the traffic plan itself is considerably more complicated than our discussion of

---

[46] *Pap.* XI 2 A 98 (*Dru* 1377). While the diastatic safeguard sounds in the 'almost', one notes that the principle of analogy has scored a more significant penetration in the admission of the desire to be loved 'behind' the divine action which the diastatic impulse manages to check.

[47] That this talk of measure deals with a substantive connection and not an abstract comparison is made clear by Kierkegaard's statement that '*first* in Christ is it true that God is man's goal and measure, or measure and goal'. *S.V.* XI, p. 224 (*SD*, p. 186). [Italics ours.] Cf. *Pap.* X 2 A 643 (*Dru* 1089).

[48] This statement of nothingness does not dissolve the task, but defines it. In a fully identical way, Kierkegaard can be intent on stressing the striving required of the self, but he does not fail to express the state supporting the striving. So in *S.V.* X, p. 46 (*CDi*, p. 44), he can write: '. . . if one is a Christian, one must *have become* that. . . . As a man he was created in *God's* image [*Billede*]; but *as a Christian* he has *God* for a *pattern* [*Forbillede*].' [Italics his.] (The reader is asked to note the pointed correction of the existing translation.)

Kierkegaard's christology has thus far shown. And yet the reader may well have anticipated us, for we have spoken here of *suffering* love and earlier of the complex use of the suffering motif in Kierkegaard. One could well be surprised if the suffering of the Christ revealed only a single strand of meaning.

We may begin our investigation of other strands by noting the presence in Kierkegaard's christology of themes which we earlier found to be linked with the diastatic employment of the suffering motif. Thus the appeal to sever the self from its relationships as a practical exercise in making oneself nothing wins space: '. . . the illegitimate child, without knowledge of any race and without concern for any race, outside of society, born in concealment at midnight behind a bush: thus it was that he let himself be born—from lack of room, just as he indeed also was crucified, because the world had no room for him!—in a stable (for in relation to the despised maiden there was no family connection with a layette in readiness) laid in a manger—if in this case there is to be any talk of connection, it must be with the horses.'[49]

We are familiar with such dark judgments on human 'connection'. What is changed in this statement is that the isolation of the self has been moved from being the goal for the self to being the given state of the self. Such a movement is wholly fitting with the essential dynamic of the formulation: to assimilate the call to the ideal to the exaltation of God as the wholly independent one. Indeed this very moment by which one affirms the ideal status of the real gains another form of expression when Kierkegaard exalts Christ as serving only one master, as if evil could not achieve fully as cohesive an integration as good.[50]

The presence of these themes is symptomatic of pressures which assert themselves in the statement of the Christ's suffering. One comes upon passages in which the major stress is placed on physical pain and external reproach.[51] One moves on to the lesson that it is

---

[49] *S.V.* XII, p. 433 (*JT*, p. 172).

[50] ibid., pp. 433–5 (ibid., pp. 172–4).

[51] See *S.V.* XII, p. 62 (*TC*, p. 69), where Anti-Climacus makes external suffering essential to and very nearly identical with the ideal in speaking of the Christ as a 'lowly man' who expressed 'what God understands by compassion (and the very fact of being the lowly and poor man, when one will be the compassionate, is included in this)'. Cf. *S.V.* X, pp. 126–7 (*CDi*, p. 127). In *S.V.* XII, pp. 156–67 (*TC*, pp. 167–79) Anti-Climacus suggests the basis for this formulation in emphasizing the certainty that men will reject the good. Earlier he wrote (ibid., p. 32 [ibid., p. 37]) that we cannot assume that Christ's rights will be reinstated: 'If one assumes that history is capable of that [reinstatement], one is placing Christ's humiliation in an accidental relation to him . . . instead of recognizing that Christ

an error to wail piously over 'Christ's delicate body which suffers so terribly or . . . the fact that he who was so holy, the purest and most innocent of all, that he had to suffer'.[52] Rather, one ought to see that 'the paradox is that Christ has come into the world *in order to suffer*'.[53] If one traces back the power behind the phrase 'come into the world', one comes to see how the dialectic of suffering is controlled by the opposition of the temporal and the eternal. Thus Kierkegaard imposes a corrective on the emphasis on physical suffering quite apart from the maudlin sentimentality which so easily accompanies that emphasis: '. . . a childish orthodoxy has also gotten the decisive attention directed to the fact that Christ at his birth was swaddled in rags and laid in a manger, in short, to the humiliation involved in his coming in the lowly form of a servant, and it believes that this is the paradox in contrast to coming in glory. Confusion. The paradox lies chiefly in that God, the eternal, has come into existence in time as an individual man. Whether this individual man is a servant or an emperor is neither here nor there; it is not more adequate for God to be king than to be beggar; it is not a greater humiliation for God to become a beggar, than to become an emperor.'[54]

Given the development of thought traced in the preceding paragraph, it will not be difficult for Kierkegaard to say that the whole

---

freely willed to be the lowly one, and although his purpose was to save men, yet he also would express what "the truth" must suffer in every generation, and what truth must suffer.'

[52] *S.V.* VII, p. 520 (*CUP*, p. 529).

[53] ibid. (ibid.).

[54] ibid., p. 519 (ibid., pp. 527–8). Anti-Climacus adds strong support of this note. So in *S.V.* XII, p. 119 (*TC*, p. 127), in discussing the incognito, he finds it to be 'irrelevant in a certain respect whether the individual man is distinguished or lowly', and on p. 38 (p. 43) puts the matter still more strongly: '. . . it is always a humiliation for God to be man, even if he were emperor over all emperors, and he is *essentially* not more humuliated because he is a poor, lowly man, mocked, as the Scripture adds, spat upon' [italics his]. Cf. *S.V.* X, p. 262 (*CDi*, p. 266); XII, pp. 28–31 (*TC*, pp. 32–36); *Pap.* VIII A 275. We touch here the power behind Kierkegaardian formulations which have drawn sharp criticism. Hirsch, op. cit., II, pp. 944–56, concedes that Kierkegaard is quite right in finding the church of his time to be related to the 'world' in a manner different from that characterizing the New Testament confessors of the faith, and ultimately the Christ himself. But the extreme diastatic reading of the opposition of the eternal and the temporal does not permit Kierkegaard to say with Hirsch that the world has changed and that it is not the task of the church to recreate the original antagonism. Cf. Siegfried Hansen, 'Die Bedeutung des Leidens für das Christusbild Sören Kierkegaards' *Kerygma und Dogma*, 1956, pp. 1–28. See also above, pp. 151–71, on the ethical implications of this opposition. In Part Four we shall assess the force of this line of criticism.

life of the Christ is one of suffering.[55] Indeed the way is prepared and the pressure is present for that turn in Kierkegaard's thought in which the reconciling element of suffering slips away, leaving the bare juxtaposition of the eternal and the temporal: '. . . the believer is . . . different from an ethicist in that he is infinitely interested in the reality of another (for example, in the fact that God has really existed)'.[56] Thus it is the same dynamic of thought which permits— requires—one to exalt every moment of the Christ's life as essential[57] and to reduce that life to the coexistence of the eternal and the temporal in a single moment. Little wonder that readers can both praise Kierkegaard for denying the third use of the law status in the Christ's experience[58] and chastise him for reducing soteriology to christology.[59]

If one keeps one's eye on the extreme diastatic statement of the opposition between the temporal and the eternal, one will not be surprised by these turnings in Kierkegaard's thought and the reactions they arouse. One will not expect to find any *discernible* uniqueness in the life of the Christ.[60] And while Christian faith may be said to be faith in this person and not in some doctrine about this person,[61] one will not look for *discernible* consequences flowing from that faith. Perhaps one may contend that a reconciliation of the finite and the infinite in the self is attained through the relationship of this Christ,[62]

---

[55] See, for example, *S.V.* VIII, p. 340 (*GS*, p. 53) and X, p. 80 (*CDi*, p. 78).

[56] *S.V.* VII, p. 279 (*CUP*, p. 288). It is no doubt the *Fragments* which has made this sort of formulation so widely known. See *S.V.* IV, p. 222 (*PF*, p. 44): 'God's presence in human form, yes in the lowly form of a servant, is itself the teaching. . . .' Or still more provocatively on p. 266 (p. 87): 'Even if the contemporary generation had left nothing other than these words: "We believe that in such and such a year God manifested himself in the lowly form of a servant, lived and taught among us, and then died"—that would be more than enough.' Cf. *S.V.* XII, p. 114 (*TC*, p. 122): '. . . the God-Man is the object of faith.'

[57] *S.V.* X, pp. 126-7 (*CDi*, p. 127): 'And his life indeed never expresses anything accidental, [as for example] that he was accidentally poor. No, his life is the essential truth. . . .'

[58] See, for example, Valter Lindström, *Efterföljelsens Teologi hos Sören Kierkegaard* (Stockholm: Svenska Kyrkans Diakonistyrelse, 1956), p. 279.

[59] This represents a main line of criticism in Henning Schröer, *Die Denkform der Paradoxalität als Theologisches Problem* (Göttingen: Vandenhoeck & Ruprecht, 1960), pp. 87, 131f. Cf. Johan B. Hygen, 'Opposisjonsennlegg ved cand. teol. Per Lönnings disputas for den teologiske doktorgrad 5 maj. 1955', *Norsk Teologisk Tidskrift*, 1956, esp. pp. 38-41.

[60] See, for example, *Pap.* IV A 62 and *S.V.* IV, p. 213 (*PF*, p. 36).

[61] See Niels Thulstrup's commentary to the *Philosophical Fragments*, commentary trans. by H. V. Hong (Princeton: Princeton, 1962), pp. 162-4 for a statement of this point.

[62] Walter Schulz, 'Existenz und System bei Sören Kierkegaard', *Wesen und*

but one will not try to point to data deriving from such a reconciliation.

Our discussion of the suffering motif has brought us to the topic of the next chapter: the *efficacy* of the Christ. If one were to summarize the systematic course of the development of the motif as it bears on the theme of the present chapter, one would be tempted to stress the power of a radically diastatic impulse. Yet one can note a countering within the very province of that power. Thus the suffering of the Christ is appropriated as the content of the *imitatio Christi* appeal.[63] In attaining contemporaneity with the Christ the Christian is formed into God's likeness[64] and so as God's man encounters—no, wills—the suffering the God-man once knew.[65] The content of this appeal is clearly diastatic, but the appeal does, nevertheless, represent a withdrawal from the God whose independence requires that no temporal state can be distinctively linked with him. The radical diastatic impulse may try to check this withdrawal: really, only God knows what it is to be humiliated.[66] Or the creed of suffering may give way to an invisible—and thus in empirical terms contentless—looking to God as the meaning of the Christ model.[67]

Again, then, we are forced to speak of the interpenetration of the rhythms of diastasis and synthesis. That is what we encounter in Kierkegaard's discussion of the work of the Christ—and in particular detail in his handling of the suffering motif. Per Lönning rightly points to a final interpenetration of these strands when he identifies the burn-

---

Wirklichkeit des Menschen (Göttingen: Vandenhoeck & Ruprecht, 1957), p. 125: 'But into this existence-without-transcendence God himself enters in Christ and so transforms it into the paradoxical sphere of transcendence. Now man can in faith accept the discord of existence as justified through God's becoming man.' Schulz adds that it is possible to regard 'the Christian as "the final step in the authentic appropriation of existence as existence"', since it supports the existing one in the brokenness of his life and makes senseless the flight from transcendence. Cf. George Price, *The Narrow Pass* (London: Hutchinson, 1963), p. 29: '. . . the secret of the Paradox is that, although it provides no new information about himself, it enables him "to be himself".'

[63] See, for example, *S.V.* XII, pp. 344–51 (*SE*, pp. 80–87). One must say that this appropriation is dominant throughout *TC*.

[64] This very phrase occurs in *S.V.* XII, p. 60 (*TC*, p. 67).

[65] More often one finds the connection obscured by the simple statement that those won by love will be made unhappy, for they will be set in opposition to the world. As a sampling, see *S.V.* IX, pp. 106, 108 (*WL*, pp. 88–91); X, p. 185(*CDi*, p. 191); and VIII, p. 339 (*GS*, pp. 52–53).

[66] *S.V.* XII, pp. 31–32 (*TC*, p. 36).

[67] *Pap.* X 2 A 317: 'Christ as pattern expresses absolutely that which no man is naturally capable of: to hold oneself to God absolutely in all things.'

ing centre of the Christ's suffering as the pain love knows in not being able to make itself understood to the beloved.[68]

4. The Uniqueness of the Christ's Work

Perhaps the terms thus far employed in the discussion of the Christ's works have imposed a distortion on Kierkegaard's intention. We have stressed the relation of Kierkegaard's christology to the rhythms of thought discernible in his discussion of God, man and God's ideal for man. The authorship willingly enough yields material for a discussion of that relationship. Yet one may feel that more should be said of the Christ. We have spoken of the existential actuality of the Christ-event and of the systematic primitivity of the christological witness for Kierkegaard. It remains, however, to ask what there was about the Christ Kierkegaard knew which granted this event such power in his life and thought. We may ask Kierkegaard: 'In what sense(s) is the Christ unique?'

Kierkegaard seems to reply to this question most directly when he speaks of the Christ as saviour: 'So it is not just a matter of course that Christ is the pattern and I merely must be willing to imitate him. In the first place, I need his help in order to imitate him; and in the second place, in so far as he is the saviour and redeemer of the race, I cannot, of course, imitate him.'[69] Such a passage seems to require *some* kind of objective theory of the atonement. In any case such a theory offers itself to Kierkegaard as a way of strongly affirming the uniqueness of the Christ: 'Co-worker with Christ in the matter of atonement you cannot be, not in any possible manner. The guilt is entirely yours; the making satisfaction is entirely his.'[70] One does encounter the language of punishment,[71] merit,[72] and sin-bearing.[73] While it is true that Kierkegaard never offers a fully worked out systematic statement of an objective theory of the atonement, that seems more to reflect the circumstances of his writing and the character of his concern, than to register his essential disinterest in this

---

[68] See Lönning, op. cit., p. 155. This interpenetration is well known from *PF*. See also *S.V.* IX, p. 108 (*WL*, pp. 89–90); on the Christ as 'unhappy love': '. . . to be misunderstood as no other man was ever misunderstood by another man, to be thus misunderstood as Christ was—and then to be love as Christ was!'

[69] *Pap.* X 1 A 132. Cf. X 1 A 134 (*Dru* 887), X 6 B 241.

[70] *S.V.* X, p. 316 (*CDi*, p. 308).

[71] *S.V.* XI, p. 258 ('HP', *CDi*, pp. 368–9).

[72] *S.V.* IX, pp. 364–5 (*WL*, p. 310); *Pap.* X 4 A 419.

[73] *S.V.* VII, p. 209 (*CUP*, p. 222); XII, p. 258 ('WS', *TC*, p. 270).

view.[74] There are simply too many passages which require this pattern to regard it as less than essential to a thinker possessing the high degree of self-conciousness characterizing Kierkegaard.[75] And our approach permits us to see the systematic centrality of the quantitatively impressive at this point.

This formulation of the Christ's uniqueness tends to lay special weight upon the significance of his death. In the discourse from 1850 bearing the title 'The Woman that was a Sinner' Kierkegaard offers a fairly full statement of this emphasis. Perhaps by virtue of his suffering the Christ may be said to bear the sins of the world even during his life, 'yet the outstanding fact is that he is the pattern'.[76] 'But then he dies. And his death changes everything infinitely. . . . Christ's death is the atonement, is the making of satisfaction . . . and it is first when Christ is offered as the sacrifice of atonement, first then, that the comfort is at hand which makes doubting whether one's sins are forgiven as impossible—yes, as impossible, as it is possible; for this comfort exists only for faith.'[77] Of course this stress on the death of the Christ is based in turn on an assumption concerning his person. One may indeed feel that the passage just cited represents a new form of the dynamic by which (in the words of Schröer) soteriology is reduced to christology—or, in stronger terms, the ideal is identified with the real. The death of the infinite gathers all finite lives within itself and reduces them to nothingness. That which is not ideal shall not be real—or that which has lost its reality has won ideality. The mind reels, but may still find the course these words set before it, if it appeals to the perspective made available by the diastatic determination of the ideal.[78]

Perhaps the relationships of the concerns controlling Kierkegaard's thought at this point are not as clear as one could wish. It is clear, however, that the death of the Christ is no martyr's tribute: 'But now as for those who did put the witness to the truth to death or are putting him to death, can the witness to the truth do anything to

[74] Gerdes, op. cit., p. 75, represents those who find Kierkegaard's statements at this point to reflect his uncritical dependence on his 'orthodox-pietistic' background.

[75] For further reference see S.V. XI, pp. 258–9 ('HP', CDi, pp. 258–9); XII, p. 169 (TC, p. 181); IV, p. 305 n. (CD, p. 30n.); and Pap. II A 62, 63 (Dru 116), 64, 187 (Dru 168), 263 (Dru 223); X 1 A 119, 132, 229; and X 5 A 87.

[76] S.V. XII, p. 258 ('WS', TC, p. 270).

[77] ibid., pp. 258–9 (ibid., pp. 270–1). For further discussion of the theme of the Christ's death, see S.V. X, p. 261 (CDi, p. 265); and Pap. X 1 A 132; 2 A 361; 3 A 409, 573, 712; 4 A 499.

[78] See above, pp. 151–71.

take their guilt from them, has his death *retroactive* power? No, only Christ's death had that, for he was more than a man and stands in relation to the whole race. And even if the fact that they became guilty of his death helped them to become attentive to the truth: their guilt remains none the less unaltered, indeed it may then only show itself to be the greater.'[79]

The actuality of the Christ-encounter seems to press forward with independent reflection-shaping force in these statements. Yet its progress moves along certain lines laid down in Kierkegaard's description of God and man. That progress may seem to be won at the expense of other lines in that description. Ethical striving in general and the imitation of the Christ in particular may seem psychologically, if not logically, impossible in the light of the absoluteness characterizing the interpretation of the death of the Christ.[80] The very meeting of God and man, which in some sense seems the essence of the christological witness, may be made to accommodate a diastatic note of opposition. That process of accommodation yields a christological parallel to the anthropological statement that the image of God in man involves not a direct likeness, but the resemblance of opposites. So Kierkegaard writes: 'As a sinner man is separated from God by a yawning qualitative abyss. And naturally when God forgives sinners he is again separated from man by the same yawning qualitative abyss. In other words, if it otherwise might be possible by a converse kind of accommodation to transfer the divine characteristics to the human: in one respect man never in all eternity comes to resemble God, in forgiving sins.'[81]

Kierkegaard's discussion of the atonement and particularly of the death of the Christ does reveal the tendency that an extreme diastatic development may import content which actually turns the christological witness in a direction which seems contrary to its own intention. We have already noted that the diastatic impulse to exalt God's sovereignty by affirming his independence may so define that independence as to leave God a lord quite without subjects. Yet now, as before, we find that the diastatic impulse is not permitted an unlimited control of the development of the material. Indeed it must be said that it is precisely the power of the christological witness

---

[79] *S.V.* XI, p. 75 ('HH' *PA*, p. 111). [Italics his.]

[80] This contention is basic to the argument of Bishop Bohlin's interpretation of Kierkegaard. On the literature involved and for a statement of our attitude towards this position, see above, pp. 41–42, 82–85.

[81] *S.V.* XI, p. 231 (*SD*, pp. 199–200).

(and behind that the sense for the actuality of the Christ encounter) which checks any single-minded diastatic withdrawal. Even within the christological formulations most clearly expressive of the rhythm of diastasis the Christ is still seen to mean that God addresses man. The presence and power of God bore in upon man in the Christ and continue to do so through the witness to the Christ.[82]

This movement of Kierkegaard's thought back to the co-involvement of God and man finds fuller expression in christological affirmations which would speak of the Christ's uniqueness in ways suggestive of the rhythm of synthesis. It may be objected that the atmosphere of intelligibility, coherence, and rationality associated with the synthesis tradition inevitably emasculates the statement of the uniqueness of the Christ. Malcolm Diamond puts the point forcefully: 'He [Jesus Christ] is distinguished from Socrates by an infinite qualitative gulf. In order to formulate this distinction Kierkegaard must describe the God-man in categories that are utterly irrational since any rational framework into which the distinction might be set would render it merely quantitative: a prophet, only more so; a lawgiver, only more so; a philosopher, only more so; a priest, only more so, etc. . . . the clear formulation of the absolute finality of the revelation and redemption in Jesus Christ is achieved by Kierkegaard only through a total sacrifice of meaning.'[83]

Diamond offers us here a heady combination of analysis and criticism, but one may wonder whether the material can be fitted to the severe lines of this pattern. In *CDi* Kierkegaard links the Christ's uniqueness with his gift of life and adds the Christian's testimony: 'For without him it is indifferent whether I live or die, it is an empty way of speaking to say that one has saved my life, when this life he saved for me is yet to be dead. But he is the life, to him I owe life, eternally understood, to him on whom I believe.'[84] The reference here seems to be to a new quality of life, to life 'eternally

---

[82] Critics attentive to the diastatic strain in the christology have claimed that the resurrection and ascension have no 'cash value' for Kierkegaard, that the note of victory in Christian experience is lost. See Schröer, op. cit., and Siegfried Hanson, 'Die Bedeutung des Leidens für das Christusbild Sören Kierkegaards', *Kerygma und Dogma*, 1956, pp. 1–28. We are pointing out that the christological witness even in its most diastatic form does represent a movement back from a severance which threatens to replace concern with the co-involvement of God and man with indifference. There is more to see and say, of course, if one hears other strains than the diastatic sounding in Kierkegaard's christology.

[83] Malcolm L. Diamond, 'Kierkegaard and Apologetics', *The Journal of Religion*, April, 1964, p. 132.

[84] *S.V.* X, p. 240 (*CDi*, p. 246).

understood', to a life that is marked off by its difference from the life that is death. Yet that life seems to be characterized by continuity with life at another level and its distinctness does not seem to involve 'a total sacrifice of meaning'.

We seem to have moved towards rooting the uniqueness of the Christ in the consequences of his work. To know the Christ *is* to know his benefits. If one asks how that work is wrought, other passages are available in addition to those we have linked with an 'objective' theory of the atonement. Again it is *CDi* which provides us with a particularly pwerful passage: 'O, when he wandered about in Judea, then he moved many with his miracles of mercy; but when nailed to the cross he did a still greater miracle, he did the miracle of love, that he without doing anything—by suffering, moves everyone who has a heart.'[85] And the consequences following upon that moving deed of love fall into line with the expectations the synthesis tradition has bestowed on the reader: 'Only as saved by him and with him, when he holds me fast, do I know that I will not betray him . . . he moves me irresistibly, I will not shut myself up in myself with this dread for myself without having confidence in him. . . .'[86]

We have now sampled passages of two sorts which support the debate over whether Kierkegaard held an objective or subjective theory of the atonement.[87] One may ask to be excused from making a choice of these alternatives without resigning oneself to the view that he 'held both'. Each view can find support in Kierkegaard. But one may suspect that here again we will meet the restless unity of Kierkegaard's thought which restrains the tendency of the rhythms of diastasis and synthesis to veer off from each other in direct contradictions. That suspicion is strengthened by the fact that particular passages often yield language suggestive of both views of the atonement. So the very passage which speaks of the cross as the moving miracle of love can declare in the next paragraph that 'his death upon the cross is the sacrifice of atonement for the sin of the world'.[88] One feels compelled to ask if Kierkegaard is not trying to state a view of the Christ's work which gets beyond the hard lines of opposed 'subjective' and 'objective' theories of the atonement and yet in-

---

[85] ibid., p. 290 (ibid., p. 288).
[86] ibid., (ibid., p. 287).
[87] As spokesman for the subjective view, see Hirsch, op. cit., II, pp. 876, 886, and Eduard Geismar, *Luthersk Troslaere i Grundrids* (Copenhagen, 1932), pp. 214f. On the objective view's support in Kierkegaard, see Lönning, op. cit., p. 188, and Lindström, op. cit., p. 55.
[88] *S.V.* X, p. 290 (*CDi*, p. 288).

corporates the essential intention and much of the substance of those views.[89]

The outline of this view include a strong insistence that the atonement does not involve a change in God. 'Making satisfaction is indeed precisely God's counsel from eternity.'[90] Kierkegaard gives the point involved effective expression in the language of prayer:

> Father in Heaven! Thy grace and mercy do not change with the changing times, they do not age with the course of years, as if thou, like a man, wert more gracious on one day than on another, more gracious at first than at last; thy grace remains unchanged, as thou art unchanged, the same, eternally young, new with every day—for thou sayest every day, 'yet today'. O, but when a man gives heed to this word, is gripped by it, and in a holy resolve with seriousness says to himself 'yet today': then this means for him that he desires to be changed on this very day, desires that this very day might rightly become significant for him beyond other days, significant by means of renewed confirmation in the good he once chose, or perhaps even significant by means of [his first] choosing of the good. . . . That word, which when thou, O God, dost utter it is the eternal expression of thy unchanged grace and mercy, that same word is, when a man—rightly understood—repeats it, the strongest expression for the deepest change and decision— yes, as if all were lost if the change and decision did not happen yet today.[91]

This passage suggests that it is God's word which evokes the change in man. The Christ is precisely this word of God addressing man in judgment and grace. Kierkegaard draws upon that conviction in his discourses on the occasion of the holy communion: 'It must be *his* voice thou hearest, when he says: come unto me all you who labour and are heavy laden, hence his voice, which invites thee; and it must be his voice thou hearest, when he says: this is my body. For at the altar there is no talk about him; *there* he is himself personally present, there it is he who talks—if not, then thou art not at the altar. Empirically understood, one can indeed point to the altar and say "there it is"; but spiritually understood, it is nevertheless only really *there*, if thou dost hear *his* voice *there*.'[92] This passage on the communion

---

[89] Lindström, op. cit., p. 55 sees Kierkegaard getting beyond the subject-object distinction and uses language rather like that appearing in the text above. But his statement of the matter seems to flow from the enthronement of a diastatic concept of God as one who is independent of the subject-object distinction. Thus the likeness of his contention to our concern is at least largely formal.

[90] *S.V.* VIII, p. 343 (*GS*, p. 58). In chapter seven we shall see that Kierkegaard's use of the theme of God's eternal counsel is itself far from unambiguous.

[91] *S.V.* X, p. 275 (*CDi*, p. 275). In *Pap.* VII A 143 Kierkegaard stresses that the atonement does not require a change in both members of the relationship involved, and appends a warning against understanding the unchangeableness of God as an abstraction.

[92] *S.V.* X, p. 278 (*CDi*, p. 278). [Italics his.]

speaks of a most real presence and does so in a way quite in keeping with Kierkegaard's understanding of the God-man relationship. For one hears individually, after all, and 'the sacrifice he brought, he did not bring as it were for men in general, nor would he save men, as it were, in general—in that way it simply cannot be done. No, he offered himself in order to save each individually.'[93]

Can one link the word of God speaking in the Christ with the historical mission of Jesus and the language of sacrifice? Perhaps one can do so, if one recalls our earlier discussion of the good of revelation or communication. The Christ makes himself known, and this is to reveal both true God and true man. He so 'utters' himself as to enter the life of the other(s) and this utterance of love becomes salvatory 'to those who receive him'.[94] It will not seem strange that it can be so unless one forgets the constitutive significance of relationships for the self. And such a view will not seem to cheapen the work of the Christ unless one supposes that love is natural, self-revelation simple, and openness to the other(s) a matter of course.[95]

This understanding places the work of the Christ in continuity with the work God summons man to perform. Kierkegaard's works make clear that he wishes to affirm some kind of contact at this point. He will not understand the Christ's sacrifice to be vicarious in the sense that it frees man from living out his days in a set of relationships which have been marked by sin.[96] And while the Christ's death may alter 'everything infinitely', it does not abolish the fact 'that he is at the same time the pattern; no, but his death becomes the infinite comfort, the infinite advance, that the striver begins with—that an infinite satisfaction has been made, that to the doubting, the disheartened there is offered the highest pledge—impossible to find anything more

---

[93] ibid. (ibid.).

[94] See above, pp. 182–6, for a fuller statement of the 'content' of the work of the Christ, so understood.

[95] It is striking that at very nearly the same time that Kierkegaard was developing these themes, Horace Bushnell (1802–76) was offering just such a programmatic statement of the costliness of love as central to the atonement. See his *God in Christ* (Hartford: Brown & Parsons, 1849) and *Forgiveness and Law* (New York: Scribner, 1874).

[96] *Pap.* II A 63 (*Dru* 116): 'This is how I think of the relation between the vicarious satisfaction and man's own atonement for his sins. It is surely true, on the one hand, that sinners are forgiven through the death of Christ; but on the other hand man is not therefore as if by magic torn out of his old relationships, that "body of sin" which Paul speaks of (Rom. 7.25). He must return along the same road he came, while the consciousness that his sins are forgiven him holds him upright and gives him courage, and hinders despair. . . . He goes the dangerous way . . . and will not tempt God or demand a miracle of him.'

reliable!—that Christ has died in order to save him, that Christ's death is the atonement, the satisfaction.'[97] The atonement does not emasculate the striving of the self, it enables it.[98] That striving will know a suffering which may be said both to result from its relation to the Christ and be like unto the Christ's suffering.[99] One may even identify the suffering of love as central to the ideal to which man is called. Kierkegaard writes of a man who long pondered the picture of the crucified one: 'He was indeed aware that there was nothing presumptuous in his longing, as if he could at some moment forget himself to such a degree that he presumptuously could forget that this crucified one was God, the holy—and he a sinner. But wanting to suffer for the same cause unto death, in this there was, after all, nothing presumptuous.'[100]

We come to see the danger of approaching Kierkegaard's thought with rigid water-tight distinctions as the instruments of our understanding. Even before beginning this chapter's discussion of christology, we should have been able to anticipate that it would not do to place the Christ as saviour within the sphere of gospel and the Christ as pattern within the sphere of law.[101] Now we see that it is fully as mistaken to divide the Christ's person by reference to the performance of certain functions. Kierkegaard suggests that in commenting upon the significance of the Christ as pattern for the Christian: 'He believes, that this pattern, if he constantly struggles to resemble it, brings him into kinship with God a second time and into an ever

[97] S.V. XII, p. 258 ('WS', TC, p. 270).
[98] On the death of the Christ helping the Christian in this sense, see also Pap. X 1 A 132. This may be the way in which the thrust of the 'classical' theory of the atonement finds expression in Kierkegaard's thought. Many writers miss that theory—see, for example, Lönning, op. cit., pp. 188–9.
[99] Pap. X 2 A 635; Pap. XI 1 A 7.
[100] S.V. XI, pp. 59–60 ('HM', PA, p. 82). Cf. S.V. XII, p. 166 (TC, p. 178) concerning the individual who from early childhood has pondered the picture of the crucifixion: 'Then when he became older and mature he would not have forgotten the impression of childhood, but he would understand it differently. He no longer wished to strike; for, he would say, in such a way I obtain no likeness to him, the humbled one, who did not strike, even when he himself was struck. No. he wished now only one thing, to suffer approximately as he suffered in the world. . . .' Admittedly these passages sometimes take on a very dark colour. Kierkegaard seems conscious of that in retrospect: 'Very far back in my recollection goes the thought that in every generation there are two or three, who are offered for the others . . . in such a way I understood myself in my melancholy, that I was singled out to this end.' We are trying to trace the lines of the portrait upon which these colours are imposed.
[101] See above, pp. 110–1, and note particularly the way in which the royal coachman image is employed.

closer kinship, that he does not merely have God for a creator, as all creatures have, but *he has God for a brother.*'[102] But quite apart from such explicit textual support one faces here the fact that for Kierkegaard the Christ is precisely the God-Man—that in this one God and man do meet personally.

This indivisibility of the divine and the human in the Christ provides the context within which an answer becomes available to a question which still plagues this discussion. It has been made clear that the Christ is continuous with the structure of human existence and the best in human achievement. In what sense may one still speak of him as unique? The answer lies precisely in the fact that he does bring the full and powerful presence of God in personal address to man. But we are made aware that it is very much to the point to inquire into the characteristics of the God who speaks in the Christ. We have said much of Kierkegaard's description of God. Yet one feels impelled to ask if the power of the christological witness may not bring God into still clearer focus. Indeed the Christ event may in its actuality so bear in upon Kierkegaard that his christological statements come to constitute a corrective over against that description of God with which we have thus far been concerned. That is, this discussion of the actuality of the Christ draws us on to chapter seven's discussion of the 'possibility' of the Christ. Quite literally on the way we inquire into Kierkegaard's analysis of the efficacy of the Christ as a sort of middle term between his actuality and 'possibility'.

102 *S.V.* X, p. 48 (*CDi*, p. 46). [Italics ours.] Harmut Metzger, *Kriterion christlicher Predigt nach Sören Kierkegaard* (Göttingen: Vandenhoeck & Ruprecht, 1964), pp. 83–85, speaks for those who would like so to apportion the person of the Christ that the role of pattern refers to the human and the role of redeemer to the divine. Yet Metzger concedes the difficulty of this project in the light of Kierkegaard's stress on the unity of the person of the Christ. Hirsch, op. cit., II, p. 683, attempts a statement which better honours the unity: 'Christ as God is my redeemer and *even therein* as man is my pattern' [italics ours]. See also Hygen's criticism of Lönning at this point: 'Opposisjonsennlegg ved cand. teol. Per Lönnings disputas for den teologiske doktorgrad 5 maj, 1955', *Norsk Teologisk Tidskrift*, 1956, pp. 23–56.

VI

THE FOCUSING AND FORMATION
OF KIERKEGAARD'S REFLECTION IN HIS
DISCOURSE REGARDING THE GOD-MAN:
THE *EFFICACY* OF THE CHRIST

1. *The First Component: The Contingency of the Effect*

IF MAN is free and responsible, he will himself be very much involved in whatever effects the Christ event wins in the world of men. Kierkegaard's analysis of the structures of necessity-possibility-actuality[1] does make room for a kind of efficacy in events prior to and even apart from the response of the subject. One may speak of a necessary effect or a necessary ingredient in an effect. But when one has spoken so, one still has much more to say, if one intends adequately to state Kierkegaard's meaning in this matter. Our analysis of Kierkegaard's affirmation of the freedom of the self has placed in view the basis for this further dimension.

Kierkegaard will not yield to the theologian's temptation to forget what he knows about man when he speaks faith's mind about the God-Man's meaning for man. There is, of course, material concerning the efficacy of the Christ which seems to bypass (i.e., repudiate) Kierkegaard's recognition of human freedom. We shall be looking at that material in the next section of this chapter. It will be clear then, however, that what one finds in this material is not an author turning a deaf ear to all his discourse about man, but rather one hearkening to a strain in that discourse which is sharply different from the one to which we now attend.

The very condition of sin against which the work of the Christ is directed contributes the component of freedom to our discussion. Sin is 'not merely finitude, but in sin there is a moment of freedom and of free finitude'.[2] Speaking of sin instead of merely sins may well

---

[1] See above, pp. 105–8.

[2] *Pap.* III A 118. Kierkegaard is even quite prepared to use the word 'synergism' in speaking of this element of freedom. It is Christianity which 'has brought into play the concept of synergism'. (ibid.)

suggest the condition of bondage which results from the wrong use of freedom. But the sinner's liberation still comes about by an enabling word to a centre of responsibility, and not otherwise. Let there be praise for the Christ, then, but let that praise be guided by the fact that his work potentiates man's responsibility, rather than emasculates it. Think what suffering it must bring to the Christ that he the almighty 'who can do all things and in love sacrifices all things, yet—[is] impotent, himself suffering under this impotence, because he is more concerned for thy welfare than thou art and yet must submit to the question whether thou wilt be offended or not, whether, saved by him, thou wilt inherit blessedness or make thyself unblessed and make him as saddened as love can be'![3]

It is clear, then, that while the Christ may draw a man to himself, 'in order in truth to draw him to himself, he will draw him as a free being to himself, and thus through a choice'.[4] One may still ask, however, whether this choice of the Christ departs from the 'normal' process of choice. One can certainly conceive of conditions which would require an affirmative answer to this question. Suppose the self's choice to be the solitary act of unconditioned freedom positing itself. Then suppose the significance of the choice of the Christ to be death for that sovereign self. Under these conditions it would not be clear how the choice of the Christ possibility could be associated logically or psychologically with the human function of choice.[5]

We have shown that many of Kierkegaard's works suggest that this statement of the Christ's efficacy is wholly mistaken. In chapter three we heard Kierkegaard speak of a 'theological' self which bears

---

[3] S.V. XII, p. 75 (TC, p. 80). S.V. VII, p. 24n. (CUP, p. 35n.) notes that even the ultimate certitude of revelation does not bypass the question of appropriation. One recalls Kierkegaard's warning against so exalting the divine 'that there is absolutely no real relationship between God and the individual man' and his suspicion that such an exaltation can be undertaken 'for the sake of getting to live just as one wants to, in a worldly view of life, or else for the sake of leading a religious still-life without incurring any real danger'. (Pap. X I A 59.) Cf. above, pp. 102–5.

[4] S.V. XII, p. 150 (TC, p. 160). Cf. ibid., p. 143 (ibid., p. 153); S.V. X, pp. 115, 259 (CDi, pp. 115, 259).

[5] See above, pp. 159–60, on the difficulties involved in the appeal to make oneself nothing. In a way this statement of the problem underlies the work of Edo Pivcevic, Ironie als Daseinsform bei Sören Kierkegaard (Gütersloh; Gerd Mohn, 1960), in the effort to make irony the central category in Kierkegaard. On the other hand, such a problem provides the challenge which arouses Michael Theunissen's agonizing (Der Begriff Ernst bei Sören Kierkegaard [Freiburg: Karl Alber, 1958], pp. 127–31) over how to incorporate man's relationship to the paradox into a unifying category of 'Ernst' which finds its classic expression in Socrates. See above, pp. 36–37, 79–80.

little resemblance to the sovereign solitary self of the preceeding paragraph's supposition. That chapter, and the next also, suggested that the God who inescapably confronts the self does so as the good for the self.[6] The two points are indeed related. An idolatrous submission to an object wholly alien to the self would in its heteronomous orientation constitute 'the cruellest self-torture'.[7] In a rich passage in the *Christian Discourses* Kierkegaard dissuades the man who would deny the association between the act of faith and the fulfilment of the self's need:

> If a man were to maintain in the most solemn and emphatic terms that he loved God, that God, only God was the object of his love, his only love, his first love—and this man, if one asked him the reason why, were to answer 'Because God is the highest, the holiest, the most perfect being'; and if this man, when one asked him whether he had never loved God for any other reason, whether he now and then did not love God for any other reason, were to reply 'No': then one might well suspect him of being a fanatic, might well warn him in all seriousness to take care lest this fanatic mood might end in presumption. The simple and humble thing is to love God because one needs [*traenger til*] him. Surely it may seem so natural that in order to love God, one must raise oneself to heaven where God dwells: the best and surest way of humbly loving God, however, is to remain on earth. Surely it may seem so lofty a thing to love God because he is so prefect, it seems so much a matter of self-love to love God because one needs him: yet the latter way is the only one in which a man can in truth love God. Woe to the presumptuous man who would dare to love God without needing him! In the relationship between man and man there can perhaps be talk about such a fanatic love; but the prime condition underlying a man's love for God is thoroughly to understand that one needs God, to love him purely and simply because one needs him.[8]

The reader may now expect to be shown that the choice of the Christ self-evidently crowns an unbroken movement to self-fulfilment. He hardly need spend his time awaiting such a demonstration from

[6] See above, pp. 110–1, 142–5. In addition to the passages cited there, see *Pap.* XI 1 A 533.

[7] *Pap.* X 2 A 525 (*Dru* 1072).

[8] *S.V.* X, p. 190 (*CDi*, p. 197). Thus 'the man who most deeply recognizes his need for God loves him most truly. Thous shalt not presume to love God for God's sake; thou shalt humbly understand that thy life's welfare eternally depends on this, and therefore thou shalt love him.' (ibid., pp. 190–1 [ibid.].) Cf. *S.V.* XI, p. 278 ('WS', *CDi*, p. 384). It is this fact of need which underlies *CUP's* transitional category of guilt. Jan Sperna Weiland, *Humanitas Christianitas* (Te Assen Bij: Van Gorcum, 1951) argues that this category is an 'ideal typical' or 'constructive' category which is introduced to bridge the gap between Religion A and B. Weiland contends that no human experience, but only divine election, can bridge the gap between the comfortable immanence of A and the shattering transcendence of B. Guilt is not an artificial construct, however, for the God under whose judgment one stands is the God one needs quite apart from the matter of sin. Of course, whether that judgment and need can manage the sharp assent of Religion B depends on how one measures the incline involved. See above, pp. 28–43.

Kierkegaard. It may be true that the Christian's testimony is that 'there is in life one blessed joy: to follow Christ',[9] but few are they who make that judgment. And it is surely far from Kierkegaard's mind to suggest that the fault of the many who find the broad way is stupidity. Reality is not ontologically weighted in the direction of the good, which is God.[10] Sin is quite literally a possibility and the actualization of that possibility bears the mystery of an act of freedom, but none other.

Choosing the Christ thus entails a risk which marks as genuine alternatives those other possibilities open to the self's striving. Kierkegaard did, after all, write more than occasionally of the Christ as paradox. We shall have much to say on this theme in the next section of this chapter, where the diastatic rhythm comes under close scrutiny, but not all Kierkegaard's talk of paradox belongs there. The discourse on paradox which falls within the present line of discussion denies the choice of the Christ any ontological bias, but not an epistemological basis. It is not self-evident that this Christ will satisfy man's need, but a man in need will hardly fail to notice him. Emanuel Hirsch can well support his assertion that Kierkegaard denies that God is directly knowable in the Christ, but not this 'that Jesus Christ is a sign awaking our attention and putting the question of God to us; not this, that the picture of Jesus Christ above all in his passion is capable even in a purely human sense of bringing the human heart to burn within'.[11] There is something strangely compelling about this Christ, though no man is compelled to follow him against his will.[12]

One's eyes are drawn to this man, but one may very well be repelled by what one sees. The threat is not to the reasoning capacity of the self as such.[13] Yet the struggle of 'offence' may even from the

---

[9] S.V. VIII, p. 316 (GS, p. 20).

[10] Indeed Kierkegaard criticizes Augustine for introducing Plato into Christianity, for this places Christianity in the 'immediate'. Pap. XI 1 A 237, XI 2 A 380.

[11] Emanuel Hirsch, Kierkegaard Studien (4 vols. in 2, Gütersloh: Bertelsmann, 1933), II, p. 932. See above, pp. 178–9, on the sense in which the presence of God is discernible in the Christ. On the need for some occasion for faith see K. E. Lögstrup, 'Christentum ohne den historischen Jesus', Orbis Litterarum, 1963, pp. 101–12. Lögstrup finds this point recognized even in the movement to what we have called the diastatic position: if one cannot find the occasion in the deeds of Jesus, one will find it in the claim to be God. The insistence that Christianity be faced as an 'understood possibility' contributes much of the force to Kierkegaard's critique of infant baptism—see S.V. VII, pp. 321–3 (CUP, pp. 332–3).

[12] S.V. XII, pp. 160–1 (TC, pp. 170–1). Cf. ibid., pp. 47–48 (ibid., pp. 52–53): even those who 'knew him not' knew something of his power.

[13] See above, pp. 23–24, 27. In S.V. IX, p. 103 (WL, p. 86) Kierkegaard even

outset take place in the province of a reason called into service to protect from all challenge the self's way of understanding and being itself.[14] In the disturbingly noticeable Christ God breaks through the defences of the self that has shut itself in—often behind walls made of the concepts and configurations of the reason. In describing this confrontation words like 'paradox' and 'offence' well state Kierkegaard's meaning.

It is well known that Kierkegaard diagnosed conformity to the crowd as one of the more subtle ways in which a self may shut itself in from real relationships. For such a self anything really exceptional will be offensive.[15] Beyond that, men turn the more quickly from one whose exceptional character lies in his devotion to God—a devotion so complete that it illumines by contrast the fraudulent and trivial in the commitments which compose the lives of men.[16] And even this—that the true word about the human condition comes through a man who speaks for one who is not a man—even (especially) this outrages the self shut up within itself.

Perhaps one can synthesize these strands by saying with Geismar that the Christ is the paradox in that he is 'the discontinuous which comes as an absolutely new beginning'.[17] This proposal is attractive in that it seems to take seriously the sharpness of Kierkegaard's

takes the fact that there is no conflict between faith and reason as an analogy by which he will show that there is no conflict between love and the law. Cf. ibid., p. 223 (ibid., p. 188).

[14] David F. Swenson states this point well in a note to his translation of the *Fragments* (*PF*, pp. 99–100): 'Reason' is to be taken as 'the reflectively organized common sense of mankind, including as its essential core a sense of life's values. Over against the "Paradox" it is therefore the self-assurance and self-assertiveness of man's nature in its totality. To identify it with any abstract intellectual function, like the function of scientific cognition, or of general ideas, or of the *a priori*, or of self-consistency in thinking, etc., is, wholly to misunderstand the exposition of the *Fragments*.' Students of Kierkegaard with very different points of view yet converge on this point. Thus see Valter Lindström, *Stadiernas Teologi* (Lund: Haakan Ohlssons, 1943), pp. 325, 328; and Hermann Diem, *Kierkegaard's Dialectic of Existence*, trans. Harold Knight (Edinburgh: Oliver and Boyd, 1959), p. 70. Per Lönning's 'Kierkegaard's Paradox', *Orbis Litterarum*, 1955, pp. 156–66, is a useful summary article with an interesting constructive attempt to find an alternative beyond the lines laid down by the 'against reason—beyond reason' debate. In addition to the passages already cited, see *Pap.* VII A 215, and VIII A 11 (*Dru* 633).

[15] *Pap.* VII 1 A 115.

[16] *S.V.* XII, pp. 81ff. (*TC*, pp. 86ff.); *S.V.* XIV, pp. 297–302 (*AC*, pp. 239–44); *S.V.* XII, pp. 393–4 (*JY*, pp. 128–9). This sentence and the one which precedes it contributed to the construction by which the offence is linked with the break with the 'establishment'.

[17] Eduard Geismar, *Sören Kierkegaard* (6 vols., Copenhagen: G. E. C. Gad, 1926–8) III, p. 71.

language without requiring a revelling in the irrational. Still this way of stating the paradox is neither precise in its own terms nor faithful to the line of thought in Kierkegaard which we are discussing. After all, an 'absolutely new beginning' formally and materially—a Christ who comes wholly without relation to anything else in man's experience—could be as easily described by the man concerned as 'against' his reason, as 'beyond' it. But more importantly, there is material in Kierkegaard's works which would deny that the Christ is such an absolutely new beginning. We have voiced Kierkegaard's conviction that the claim of God is known to man apart from and prior to the career of Jesus of Nazareth.[18] If the Christ encounter were wholly without relationship to the experience of the self, the self might presumably dismiss it as an illusion or fantasy or the like. This the self cannot finally do, for the claim of the Christ has too strong a hold in the reality of the self.

Yet we come back to the fact that sin is ontologically possible— and indeed the note which sounds the clearest in the actuality of the self. For that reason the discontinuous element in the Christ encounter will be the prominent one. This means that the process of appropriation will be a real one. It means as well that the organ of appropriation can be described as set against the reason. At least that will be possible if one understands by reason 'a chaining together (enchainment) of truths, a conclusion from reasons'.[19] For one can then very well conclude that 'belief cannot . . . be demonstrated, proven, or understood . . . and what will this say other than that this is a paradox; for this is clearly the distinguishing mark of the paradox—it lacks continuity, or at any rate only has an inverted continuity, which means that it does not originally show itself as a continuity'.[20]

We are stressing that *this* kind of speech about paradox can be made altogether appropriately within the lines marking the course of the synthesis rhythm. Indeed one may say that the way is prepared for this emphasis on 'Incommensurability' in the very analysis of the self and its relationships. That analysis emphasizes the constitutive significance of relationships. No sovereign subject exists to order the 'foreign affairs' of its relationships. The immediate experience of this self cannot be adequately expressed in verbal form, for 'immediacy has no relationship, for as soon as a relationship is present, the immediacy is cancelled'.[21] Faith is a 'higher immediacy', for here the self affirms a possibility whose contact with and claim upon the self are 'indefinite' in the sense that sin has so dominated the self that God appears a stranger who may well beckon to destruction. 'It does not originally show itself as a continuity.'

The continuity between the possibility posed by the Christ-encounter and the existent actuality of the self is not, then, clear in any irresistibly convincing way, when the self makes the movement of faith. Another continuity seems no more clear—that between the deciding individual and his other(s) in the human community. This relatedness may indeed seem to be even more completely withdrawn from the self's view. Within the line of reflection under discussion Kierkegaard will insist that—all troubles notwithstanding—'this God relationship of mine is the happy love in my life'.[22] Yet 'this love story . . . has the essential mark of the true love story, that only one person can wholly understand it, and there is absolute joy in telling it to one only, the beloved, thus that one by whom one is loved'.[23]

This last passage leads us directly into the notorious problem of Kierkegaard's 'individualism'. We shall not fail to expose to view the basis for this charge and even join in speaking the word of judgment. But in the present context a responsible reading of Kierkegaard needs to point to material in his thought which balances the stress on solitariness and indeed brings that stress within a concept of Christian community.

We may begin at least somewhere very near the beginning by noting that the Christ-encounter does not leave a solitary subject juxtaposed to an abstract sketch of possibility. Rather the encounter is with a person who has gone before one into the possibility he presents. Kierkegaard called often on the Johannine word 'if any man's will is to do his will, he shall know whether the teaching is from God or whether I am speaking on my own authority'.[24] What

---

[21] *Pap.* IV B 1, p. 145.

[22] *S.V.* XIII, p. 556 (*PV*, p. 64).

[23] ibid., (ibid., pp. 64–65). We shall observe later that the context for this passage does include recognition of the communal element.

[24] John 7.17. Thus in *Pap.* X 4 A 349: 'The world has wholly upset Christianity's point of view. In the New Testament, the matter is extremely simple. Christ says "Do according to my words and you shall know." Consequently, there comes first the decisive action. With the assistance of the will, your life comes into collision with all of reality, and then you will find something to think about, rather than doubt, in both the first and the second sense, you will need Christendom, as pattern and gift.' Cf. *Pap.* X 3 A 455: 'Christ who never attempted to prove the

we may fail to note is that the speaker of these words has 'done' them. Kierkegaard states the alternatives in these terms: 'One can put faith first and imitation second . . . one can put imitation first and faith second.'[25]

We said before that the meaning of the Christ is not to be parcelled out with the gospel claiming the saviour and the law the example. We now have encountered a second obstacle to any such apportionment. The strong challenge to imitation which the Christ presents not only sets before the self its true goal, it sustains the movement toward that goal: 'A pattern is to be sure a summons, but what bliss! We already speak of good fortune when we speak about the fact that there is something within a poet which summons him to song; but the pattern makes its demand even more strongly, impels even more strongly every one who sees it, for whom it exists. The pattern is a promise, no other is so sure, for the pattern is after all the fulfilment.'[26]

If one attends to this line of thought one may find less than convincing the charge that there is no place for the Holy Spirit in Kierkegaard's thought. Jan Sperna Weiland writes: 'After earnestly reading Kierkegaard's works one cannot escape the conclusion that not a trace of a trinitarian belief in God is to be found in them. With this it is said at the same time that it is impossible for Kierkegaard to put the question after the "dynamis" and the "energy" of the transition to Christianity in the right way.'[27] The evidence supporting re-

---

truth of his teaching or to provide a foundation for it, used only one proof: "If any man do the will of my Father, he shall know of the doctrine, whether it be of God or whether I speak of myself." Herein is contained the idea that the situation of action is necessary in order to arrive at that point of tension where the decision of faith can come into being; this is a hazardous venture. It is not thus (as some have maintained, reversing the order): first the proof and then the venture (which anyway is a self-contradiction and nonsense), no, first the venture, then the proof comes forward . . .'

[25] *Pap.* X 3 A 454.

[26] *S.V.* X, p. 46 (*CDi*, pp. 44–45). In such a way it can be said that we love one another 'in Christ'. (*Pap.* II A 24.) Perhaps this is what Lindström (op. cit., p. 339) wishes to suggest in insisting that the following of the Christ does not become an imitation of the Christ. For a schematization of this matter through a law-gospel dialectic, see Per Lönning, 'Samtidighedens Situation' (Oslo: Land og Kirke, 1954), pp. 189ff. Lönning draws particularly heavily on *Pap.* X 4 A 459. Even when Kierkegaard links the Christ as gift more narrowly with the atoning death of the Christ, he does not wish to let the appeal to a discipleship of deeds be enervated. See the prayer to Jesus the Redeemer and Pattern, which opens the second part of *JY*. The last sentence of that prayer reads: 'Yet Thou didst leave behind Thee a footprint, Thou the holy pattern of the human race, of every individual, in order that, saved by Thy atonement, they might every instant find confidence and boldness to will to strive to follow Thee.' *S.V.* XII, p. 423 (*JY*, p. 161).

[27] Weiland, op. cit., p. 138.

sistance to this charge is far more than verbal. Take the Kierkegaard-ian sentence: 'There is only one proof for the truth of Christianity: the inner proof, the *argumentum spiritus sancti*.'[28] The mention of the Spirit clinches nothing, of course, for the passage might be read as confusing the third person of the Godhead with the solitary human subject. But if one recalls how Kierkegaard links the 'do and you shall know' principle with the *imitatio Christi* appeal, one can find in such passages testimony to the Spirit who comes to glorify the Christ.[29]

Of course if the presence of the Holy Spirit requires the evacu-ation of the human spirit, Kierkegaard is no trinitarian Christian. An early journal reference already makes that clear: 'According to the teaching of Christianity man is not to be merged into God by way of a sort of pantheistic disappearance, or by the obliteration of all his individual traits in the divine ocean, but through a heightened consciousness. "Man shall give an account of every idle word he has spoken", and although grace washes away sin, the union with God proceeds through personality, purified by that whole process.'[30] And the later works pointedly make clear that becoming a Christian is quite literally a matter of becoming—that the call to enter the Christian possibility is a continuing one and one bearing concrete significance for the actual relationships of life.[31] So, too, the continu-ing involvement of the self bears a darker meaning within itself: 'Therefore it is said that we should work out our salvation with fear and trembling, namely because it is not finished or completed, but a

---

[28] *Pap.* X 1 A 481 (*Diary* 201).

[29] In the passage just cited from the *Papirer* Kierkegaard, having identified the inner witness of the Holy Spirit as the only proof of Christianity, quotes the first part of I John 5.10: 'He who believes in the Son of God has the testimony in him-self.' He comments: 'It is not the reasons that motivate belief in the Son of God, but the other way round, belief in the Son of God is the evidence.' (ibid.) This form of statement affirms that the Spirit's witness is to the Christ and suggests that the conviction is informed (formed?) by the testimony. A diastatic tendency to tele-scope the elements involved in the affirmation of the Christ seems present, however, in the dismissal of evidence of *all* sorts.

[30] *Pap.* II A 248 (*Dru* 220).

[31] On the continuing character of the challenge, see *S.V.* XII, pp. 145–6 (*TC*, p. 156) and VII, pp. 99–100 (*CUP*, p. 110). On the concrete implications of the challenge, see *S.V.* VIII, p. 228 (*PH*, p. 197): The consciousness of one's eternal responsibility before God 'does not demand that thou shouldest withdraw from life, from an honorable calling, from a happy domestic life. On the contrary it is precisely that consciousness that shall sustain and clarify and illumine thy conduct of the relationships of life. Thou shalt not withdraw and sit brooding over thy eternal accounting. By doing that thou dost take new blame upon thyself. Thou willst better and better find time for thy duties and tasks.' *S.V.* IV, p. 374 (*CD*, p. 94) asserts: '. . . to explain how my religious existence comes into relationship to and expresses itself in my outward situation, that is the problem.' Cf. also *S.V.* X,

falling back is possible.'[32] The Christian does know the 'continuity' of fulfilment,[33] but time grants him no respite. As he lives into the future Christianity continues to become possibility for him and to bear the character of challenge.[34]

We have come to see that any tendency in Kierkegaard towards subjectivism or mysticism is checked by his insistence that the individual is confronted with the presence of God in the Christ and that the response to this confrontation bears consequences for the relationships constituting the individual's life. But can this Christian 'individualist' speak in any fuller sense of the role of relationships with respect to the efficacy of the Christ? Quite specifically the question of the status of the Christian community in Kierkegaard's thought requires a fuller analysis in this study. Kierkegaard is, of course, most often portrayed as a critic of the church.[35] Those of

---

p. 280 (CDi, p. 280). It is surely clear, then, that the good which the Christ imparts is received by an individual in existence and bears claims on that existence. This is the background for the power of Kierkegaard's polemic against the 'hidden inwardness' of 'established Christianity'. See S.V. XII, pp. 189-212 (TC, pp. 200–26) and S.V. X, p. 241 (CDi, p. 247). Indeed Kierkegaard implies that we have the good ourselves only as we do the good for others—see especially, S.V. IX, pp. 353–65 (WL, pp. 300–10), on the relationship between forgiveness and 'forgivingness'. It is quite appropriate to add that the works of love, though manifest (S.V. IX, pp. 14–15 [WL, p. 9]), are not identifiable as such by the external observer (S.V. VII, pp. 51, 115–16 [CUP, pp. 63, 127]).

[32] Pap. I A 174 (Dru 61). Cf. Pap. II A 63 (Dru 116). So S.V. X, p. 296 (CDi, p. 290): 'As long as there is life there is hope—but as long as there is life there is indeed also the possibility of danger . . .' Cf. ibid., pp. 17–18, 138–46 (ibid., pp. 16, 139–48). James Collins. The Mind of Kierkegaard (Chicago: Henry Regnery, 1953), p. 291, seems oblivious to the ongoing character of human becoming in writing of the assent of faith: 'Once this assent is made, however, all dispute and doubt are removed. Just as becoming in general removes mere possibility, so the process of believing removes the special form of possibility which expresses itself as the attitude of disputing and doubting.'

[33] See above, pp. 203–5.

[34] One may speak here of a 'third use of the law' in Kierkegard, if one wishes—see Johan B. Hygen, 'Opposisjonsennlegg ved cand. teol. Per Lönnings disputas for den teologiske doktorgrad 5 maj, 1955', Norsk Teologisk Tidskrift, 1956, pp. 23–56. See especially pp. 47–48 for Hygen's contention that Lönning wrongly and unsuccessfully seeks to excise such a 'use' from Kierkegaard's works. Valter Lindström, Efterföljelsens Teologi hos Sören Kierkegaard (Stockholm: Svenska Kyrkans Diakonistyrelse, 1956), pp. 294f. laments that the literature does support Hygen's contention. Yet this form of statement is misleading. We have already suggested that it is most imprecise to deny gospel significance to the Christ as pattern. One can affirm such references to the 'third use of the law', however, if the intent is to assert that the challenge of the pattern in its many dimensions continues to confront the Christian after the 'leap' of faith.

[35] For a recent popular statement of this sort, see John A. Gates, Christendom Revisited: A Kierkegaardian View of the Church Today (Philadelphia: Westminster, 1963).

his readers who have wanted to find him innocent at this point have diligently unearthed biographical occasions for the neglect which is supposed to stretch to cover explicit criticism.[36] Such treatments of the matter still leave unanswered the fundamental question: 'To what extent, if at all, does a positive view of Christian community greet and possibly even instruct the contemporary reader of Kierkegaard's works?' Upon recognizing the diversity in the rhythms of Kierkegaard's thought it becomes possible to point to elements contributing to such a positive view, without denying that not only the Danish church of the mid-nineteenth century, but also any doctrine of the church at all, faces severe attack within Kierkegaard's works.[37]

We really cannot emphasize too strongly the support which Kierkegaard's understanding of the social character of selfhood contributes to an attempt to formulate a view of the Christian community. We cannot here well repeat the material discussed in chapter three, but we may point out again that Kierkegaard roots the relatedness of the self to other men in the relationship of the self to God. If Kierkegaard affirms that God the creator brings into existence selves in relationship, one may doubt that he will argue that the work of God the redeemer wins its effects apart from some kind of Christian community. Furthermore, chapter four made clear that the self's relationships to the other(s) are central not only to the reality of the self, but also to its ideality. That this is true materially, as well as formally, is evident in Kierkegaard's emphasis on communication and revelation.[38]

[36] Thus it may be pointed out that Martensen stressed the triumphant church, or that the attack on Hegel afforded no place for a legitimate stress on community. It is true that Kierkegaard suspects an alliance between the clergy and the professors. Thus *Pap.* X 2 A 357: 'A few years ago the clergy were busy "getting the gown changed so that it almost looked like a professors gown", that was the "scientific" [*Videnskabelige*].'

[37] The tendency to try to get everything in Kierkegaard within some positive view mars the otherwise useful work of Per Wagndal, *Gemenskapsproblemet hos Sören Kierkegaard* (Lund: CWK Gleerup, 1954).

[38] In chapter three above, see pp. 105-9; in chapter four, pp. 143-8, 150-1. If one objects that this argument depends too heavily on an early stage in Kierkegaard's thought with its strongest expression in *Either-Or*, it should be observed that a new edition of precisely that work is issued in May 1849, when the ammunition is being made ready for the final bitter attack on the church. Indeed the very attack itself might make one suspicious of any attempt to describe the late Kierkegaard's thought as wholly individualistic. As E. Geismar has put it (op. cit., I, p. 140): the view that all that matters is one's own salvation does not harmonize well with a concern to publish that view. We shall be asking whether the attack also bears material suggestions of a more positive view of the church. It should also be noted that the sources cited in discussing Kierkegaard's emphasis on communication and revelation as the good are hardly a small or peripheral part of his production (*E-O, WL, CD, CDi, CUP*).

All of this material from other fields of Kierkegaard's concern leads us to expect from him a positive statement regarding Christian community. That expectation is not denied—not even in the attack on the church which is far from being a declaration that the solitary Christian can and must 'go it alone'. The Christian stands in the 'vertical' continuity of the centuries and Kierkegaard could appeal to this historical givenness in his criticism of the Christianity he found before his eyes in Denmark.[39] Nor does he deny in principle all 'horizontal' continuity. His sighting of a goal between barren individualism and supine submission in the mass found early expression: 'How terrible it is when all history vanishes before a morbid brooding over one's own miserable history! Who points out a *via media* between this consumption of oneself by reflections which imply that one is the only man that has ever been or ever will be—and a sorry comfort in a universal human commune naufragium? Yet it is this which a doctrine of the church ought to supply.'[40] Kierkegaard found the contemporary church wide of the mark, however, and sharpened his criticism as the church failed to respond in reform. The attack—one must admit—sharpens to the point of distortion.[41]

It has been suggested that even in his most congenial moments Kierkegaard found it impossible to speak favourably of the church, other than as a *result*.[42] It is true that passages can be cited which insist that the believer's relationship to other Christians must be preceded by the establishment of a faith relationship to the Christ.[43] And at times it seems the communal result follows only in the very remote future—the church in the distance.[44] The futuristic under-

[39] See *Pap*. IX A 264, X 2 A 335, X 3 A 696 (*Dru* 1166), X 4 A 58.

[40] *Pap*. II A 172 (*Dru* 163).

[41] Kierkegaard can speak as if he were quite conscious of the distortion. Already of Anti-Climacus (*TC*) he wrote (*Pap*. X 2 A 366): 'It is the sharpening of an awakening that he sets up, when he says that in the striving church there are only individuals, thus not recognizing the community.' As late as May 16, 1855, Kierkegaard could write: '. . . the establishment has *perhaps* lost . . .' (*S.V.* XIV, pp. 85–86 [*AC*, p. 59].) [Italics ours.] The condition may refer not to the uncertainty of victory, but to doubt as to the identity of the enemy and the depth of the dispute.

[42] See Lindström, op. cit., pp. 188–93 and Hirsch, op. cit., IV, pp. 341–7.

[43] See, for example, *Pap*. II A 579.

[44] Cf. *Pap*. X 1 A 552 (*Dru* 941): 'The "Church" ought really to represent "becoming" the "State" on the other hand "existing" (*Bestaaen*). That is why it is so dangerous when Church and State grow together and are identified. Where the "state" is concerned, even though one or the other of its institutions is not very fortunate—when it is an established reality (*et Bestaaende*) one should be very careful about doing away with it, simply because the "state" is, in idea, "the established" (*det Bestaaende*) and one is perhaps better served by strongly main-

standing of the church is, however, tempered by the recognition of the Christian community as a present reality supporting the individual believer. Early journal references clearly, if rather stiffly, point to the need for the community.[45] Later in his life Kierkegaard can say in retrospect that despite the fact that his God relationship is a love story and so steeped in solitariness, 'it is also a joyous thing to talk to others about it'.[46] And along the way of the authorship he found cause, despite the nature and severity of the perils he sighted, to give content to the affirmation that the individual Christian does not struggle alone, but 'in union with others'.[47]

There is, then, an important sense in which the church does not wait in the wings for the passing of this world of time-space. Is there any sense in which its present existence is not the product of some popular consensus (however slender the minority involved)? If the community is 'more than the sum of individuals', one might suspect that it is not simply the effect of the acts of individuals.[48] Indeed a case can be made for stating the relationship the other way round. Another early journal reference opens the door to such a statement: 'Christ certainly died for all men, and also for me; but that "for me" must be understood in the sense that he only died for me in so far as I belong to the many.'[49] This passage irritates readers of many kinds, but it need not be more disturbing (and must not be less!) than a major theme of Kierkegaard's work. The wider context in this entry speaks of the support the community affords the self and of the

---

taining a less fortunate established thing (*Bestaaende*) than by reforming too soon. In the Church the opposite is true, because the idea is becoming. "Becoming" is more spiritual than "existing"; the servants of the Church ought not therefore to be officials, probably not married, but those *expediti* who are fitted to serve "becoming".' On the motto 'the church in the distance' see the letter of 17 July 1838 to Emil Boesen (*Breve*, pp. 40–42). Cf. *S.V.* XII, pp. 204–5 (*TC*, pp. 217–18).

[45] *Pap.* I A 177 (*Dru* 62): 'It is dangerous to separate oneself too much, to withdraw oneself from the bond of society.' Cf. *Pap.* I A 178: 'Do you not need the leading-strings of the community; can you get along without the support of the go-cart your contemporaries give you?'

[46] *S.V.* XIII, p. 556 (*PV*, p. 65).

[47] *S.V.* XII, p. 205 (*TC*, p. 218).

[48] *Pap.* X 2 A 390. In this entry Kierkegaard contrasts the church with the public which is composed of 'negative individuals, of individuals who are not such, they become so only through the sum'. The church, on the other hand, 'is a sum through the individuals which compose it'. One's suspicion is strengthened rather than stilled by this formulation, since the contrast is not seen to be absolute. Kierkegaard does not say that the Christian community comes to be *only* through the individuals who compose it (though it is 'an essential' factor), or that true individuals become such *only* through a self-originating and self-sustaining action.

[49] *Pap.* II A 223 (*Dru* 192).

commitment to the other(s) required of that self. We should not read Kierkegaard to be denying the individual place in the divine intention, then, but to be describing the process by which that intention is transformed into effect. The Spirit does not fly through the air like a bird.

This point does not depend on an isolated journal passage, though it must be admitted that it never receives a full systematic statement. Many passages come forward to support the claim that the way to the divine other is through the other members of the human community. *E-O* sharpens the description of the man who goes that way: 'He repents himself back into himself, back into the family, back into the race, until he finds himself in God.'[50] And the community is more than a passive pool of resources. In the *Christian Discourses* Kierkegaard speaks of how 'the whole race and every individual in the race is participant in the fact' that a man has faith.[51] Or one may put the matter in a more serial manner: '. . . there is a password which God whispered into Adam's ear and which one generation must pass on to the next and which will be demanded of them on the day of judgment. . . .'[52]

What is involved in this recognition of the dependence of the individual on the community is Kierkegaard's conviction, so fundamental to his view of man, that the self must not and really cannot escape from its necessity—and that the self's relationships compose the material of that necessity. But one may acknowledge the importance of this conviction to Kierkegaard and still insist that it does not manage the movement from anthropology to ecclesiology. We can only reply along two lines: (1) This study seeks to show that the 'movement' involved is not so violent as is commonly suggested

---

[50] *S.V.* II, p. 194 (*E-O* II, pp. 180-1).

[51] *S.V.* X, p. 121 (*CDi*, p. 121).

[52] *Pap.* I A 340 (*Dru* 96). So in *S.V.* VII, p. 523 (*CUP*, p. 532), even while attacking 'childish Christianity', Kierkegaard can affirm that 'the religiousness of childhood is the universal, the abstract, and yet the imaginative-inward foundation for all later religiousness'. This dependence on childhood training is equally important for the philosopher in his proof of God's existence (*Pap.* IX A 119), and for the religious man in his faith that God is love. Of that faith Kierkegaard writes (*Pap.* VIII A 25 [*Dru* 640]) : 'It really absolutely depends on a religious upbringing, on the *a priori* which is won in the fact that it is absolutely decided for one from the earliest time, that God is love. This proof that God is love, rising from an inexplicable impression, an impression which has grown together with one's whole nature from the earliest time: this is really the main point.' Kierkegaard was conscious of such a dependence in his life. So in *Pap.* III A 73 (*Dru* 335) he writes of his father: 'I learned from him what father-love is, and thereby I got a conception of the divine father-love, the one unshakable thing in life, the true Archimedian point.' Cf. *Pap.* IX A 68 (*Dru* 773) and see above pp. 92-93.

by a diastatic reading of diastatic texts in Kierkegaard. (2) There are suggestions of a more specific discussion of the dependence of the Christian individual on the Christian community. We have already heard Kierkegaard speak of the Christ dying for the individual in so far as he is a member of the many. And what 'many'?—that of the human community, to be sure, but also that of the community of the word in which the Christ is re-presented to the individual. Characteristically the severity of TC closes with a prayer which stresses the 'servants of the word'.[53] Kierkegaard's scathing critique of the preaching he heard was powered by a judgment of importance and a vision of a possibility.

Yet, while Kierkegaard does not by any means demean the role of the sermon as 'proclaiming his word and his teaching', he finds especially meaningful the presence of the Christ in the word spoken at the altar on the occasion of holy communion. Then, 'every word is said exactly as it was handed down by the fathers', '*there* he is himself personally present, there it is he who speaks'.[54] This sense of dependence on the word of the apostles[55] should serve to chasten another line of criticism. David E. Roberts speaks for those who appreciate Kierkegaard's emphasis on faith, but find that he 'surely . . . has failed to make clear the relationship between faith and historical fact (as contrasted with the *meaning* of historical fact) . . . he fails to meet squarely the kind of problem that would arise if the high probabilities of historical research went contrary to faith'.[56] Kierkegaard does concern himself with the historical givenness of the revelation,[57] though he surely will not permit an escalation of such concern to an historicism which overleaps the role of the believer's faith.

Kierkegaard has been charged with reducing the faith to an overleaping of another sort. Oscar Cullmann claims that Kierkegaard 'implicitly destroys the redemptive line, inasmuch as he really

[53] *S.V.* XII, pp. 238–9 (*TC*, pp. 253–4). Unable to pray for all the classes of men, Anti-Climacus singles out the ministers of the Word and the simple Christians. The clergy seem to be singled out because they face a special mission and special perils; the simple Christians, lest either the mission or the perils be regarded as *too* special.

[54] The quoted portions of this sentence and the one which precedes it are from *S.V.* X, p. 278 (*CDi*, p. 278). [Italics his.] Cf. ibid., p. 313 (ibid., p. 305).

[55] Cf. *S.V.* VII, p. 527 (*CUP*, p. 535).

[56] David E. Roberts, *Existentialism and Religious Belief*, ed. Roger Hazelton (New York: Oxford, 1959), p. 88. [Italics his.] Cf. Hirsch, op. cit., II, p. 880.

[57] For a slightly different approach to some of the passages we have cited in support of this claim, see Lönning, op. cit., p. 198.

abstracts from it. He emphasizes the necessity of an "overleaping", because otherwise, as our distance in time from Christ's death continues to increase, we would also be removed ever farther from this event's essential meaning, that is, its significance for salvation. But he thereby overlooks the fact that, according to the New Testament faith, Christ now rules invisibly over heaven and earth, and works visibly in and through the Church.'[58] We have shown in this section that Kierkegaard does affirm the church as the community in which the word of the Christ is spoken anew and individuals are brought to faith thereby. That affirmation did not forbid criticism of the institutional church; it required such criticism and—as we have seen—informed it.

This is not to say that Roberts and Cullmann and all the others are fighting mirages in Kierkegaard's thought. There is something which they have seen. We have been concerned to show that their 'seeing' has distracted them from observing those configurations of thought which we have sketched in this section. Having voiced this caution and corrective, we need to look at what these men see. The systematic orientation of that which is to be surveyed with them leads us on to other sections of this chapter.

2. *The Second Component: The Certainty of the Effect*

The line of reflection just traced is countered by one which would reject anything suggesting contingency as far as the efficacy of the Christ is concerned. This component can be discussed briefly, since we have already shown in detail how the certainty motif comes to be associated with a strongly diastatic concept of God.[59] It should be explicitly noted that it is precisely the diastatic movement to enthrone God as the wholly independent one which governs the development of the material with which we shall have to do and thus supports the similarity to our earlier analysis. The mood of this movement can be restated by citing a single passage in which Kierkegaard paradoxically appropriates and repudiates an analogy in order to state the divine independence: 'Precisely because God cannot be the object for man, because God is the subject, precisely for that reason the reverse is absolutely true: when a man denies God he does not harm God but destroys himself; when a man scoffs at God he scoffs at himself. The purer a man is the nearer will he come in his relations with other men

---

[58] Oscar Cullmann, *Christ and Time*, trans. Floyd Filson (Philadelphia: Westminster; London: SCM Press, 1950), p. 168. Cf. ibid., pp. 53n., 76n., and 146f.

[59] See above, pp. 136–42.

to the impossibility of being an object for them. Yet naturally there is in this case an infinite qualitative difference.'[60]

Kierkegaard does not leave his reader speculating over the implications of this diastatic movement for an effort to describe the efficacy of the Christ. For a really purist reading of independence, the very element of distinction posited in the notion of efficacy becomes troublesome. God seems thereby to be linked with the world of change, of 'passing'. Sensitive to this difficulty, Kierkegaard offers a view which moves towards an affirmation of the Christ's ideality, but quite consciously away from a recognition of the troublesome suggestion of efficacy: 'He will not be judged in a human way, according to the consequences of his life, . . . to judge him according to the consequences of his life is blasphemy; as God his life, this that he lived and has lived, is infinitely more decisive than all the consequences of it in history.'[61]

It should be noted that this passage does not really refuse to apply the category of 'efficacy' to the Christ, but rather rules for a distinction by which successiveness, temporality, is excised in the process of application. A total denial of the category of efficacy would violate Kierkegaard's religious intention, for surely the Christ means the power of the totally sovereign one present in life. That is, the extreme diastatic tendency which grants only a disappearing God is here checked not only by the essential thrust of diastasis toward the distance measured by Lordship,[62] but also by the power of the christological witness. Yet there is an apparent attractiveness about a formulation which would affirm the efficacy of the Christ, while so reading that efficacy back into the very constitution of the Christ's ideality as to blunt the sharp edge of successiveness, of distinction. Thus one may welcome a view of the Christ's work as an objective transaction, inevitably bringing benefit to mankind. A journal reference well outlines the thrust of the formulation sought: 'The objective reality of Christ's atonement, independent of its subjective appropriation, is very clearly shown in the story of the ten lepers— They were all of them healed, though only of the tenth, who thankfully returned to give honour to God, is it said: Thy faith has made thee whole. What was it that cured the others?'[63]

All times may be co-present to God,[64] but none are so for man.

[60] *Pap.* VII A 201 (*Dru* 620).
[61] *S.V.* XII, p. 22 (*TC*, p. 26).
[62] See above, pp. 102–5.
[63] *Pap.* II A 263 (*Dru* 223). See above, pp. 190–3.
[64] *Pap.* XI 1 A 362.

Man inescapably lives, moves, and has his being in the time-space process. To leave the sheer act of the Christ and the pulsating reality of that process in stark juxtaposition hardly seems satisfactory. The reader will be familiar with the various attempts to accommodate (that is to say, domesticate) the processive character of human life to the logic of divine certainty. Resistance may be regarded as futile,[65] or even ruled impossible.[66] In either case, while one may have formally retained man's experience of succession, one has materially repudiated his sense of possibility. One may still speak of possibility, but 'the relationship of possibility, which is the inspiration of the ethicist in his joy over God, is God's freedom'.[67]

One does not decisively escape the logic of this position by granting man the possibility of a subjective resistance to a wholly necessary objective compliance. Yet Kierkegaard can write at great length and with striking beauty, giving voice to just such an 'alternative':

In the choice between two masters, it is not so that if one merely chooses one of the two, and then serves that one, regardless of which it is, that one then serves only one master. No, there is only one, who in such a way is master (*Herre*), is 'the Lord' (*Herren*), that if one serves him one serves one master; it is thus clear enough that if 'there is one Lord' only, one does not serve one master, if one does not serve him. Therefore it is not true that he who chose wholly to serve mammon, serves only one master; against his will he is nevertheless in another master's, in 'the Lord's' service. If a man chooses a master other than God, he must hate God, 'for he must either love the one and hate the other', that is, when he loves the one, he must hate the other, but however much he hates God, he still

---

[65] *S.V.* X, p. 55 (*CDi*, p. 54): The Christian believes that 'it is an unchangeable God, who dwells in the heavens, who will have his way,—though all rose up against him, which would signify nothing to him.' The suggestion of futility blends with that of impossibility, when we are told that the Christian's faith also is that this God 'wills obedience'. Cf. above, p. 214, note 60.

[66] To employ a term much linked with the synthesis rhythm in Kierkegaard's thought, it is sure that 'nothing, nothing, can hold out against a lover'. (*S.V.* IX, p. 326 [*WL*, p. 277]; cf. ibid., p. 293 [ibid., p. 249]; *S.V.* XI, p. 134 [*SD*, p. 153].) So in the edifying discourses, love sees no sin because it sees God, who cannot be resisted (*S.V.* III, pp. 273–95 ['LC', *ED*, I]) and faith is sure of victory for the same reason (*S.V.* III, pp. 15–34 ['EF', *ED*, I]).

[67] *S.V.* VII, p. 129 (*CUP*, p. 140). Here it is hinted that the doctrine of predestination may be employed to include rejection of God within the compass of God's activity, while in other formulations that doctrine is seen to address the fact that 'the blessedness which is linked with an historical occasion excludes all those who are outside the condition, and of these excluded ones there are countless who are excluded not by their own guilt, but by virtue of the accidental fact that Christianity has not yet been preached to them'. (ibid., p. 508 [ibid., p. 516].) Kierkegaard says further: 'This discrimination gives the Christian a certain resemblance to one who is fortunate through favour, and when it is so understood selfishly by a Christian, we have the desperate presumption of predestination.' ibid., p. 507 (ibid.)

does not slip free from God's service, and he is still not serving one master. A man's relationship to God in service is not like the relationship between a man and his servant, who can flee from his service, and flee so far that his first master cannot get hold of him, or even take refuge in a relationship so altered that his first master must relinquish his claim upon him. No, that man who chose to serve another master than 'the Lord', no matter how desperate and determined his will, still remains in the service of two masters. And just this self-contradiction is his punishment: to will the impossible; for it is impossible to serve two masters. But it is also the case that only then is it possible to serve one master, when one has chosen *wholly* to serve 'the Lord'.[68]

On these terms a fall from grace is inconceivable. Rather 'the truth of the matter is, that one cannot cease being loving; if one is in truth loving, one remains so; if one ceases to *be* loving, then one *was* not loving'.[69] And yet one *will* be loving—for God's triumph is absolutely sure. Thus does the lure of a universalistic position show its power, for the Christ who would draw all men unto himself is stronger than 'that which would frighten us away'.[70]

If neither an initial resistance to grace nor a subsequent fall from grace is possible, it is difficult to see how the individual could still be free in the sense in which we have seen this word to be used in Kierkegaard's thought. One may say all one wishes about freedom meaning commitment to the good, rather than disengaged subjectivity. But it is not clear how 'commitment' can acquire meaning without reference to a choice issuing from a self confronted with genuine alternatives. Without such alternatives, to be the 'free', the 'committed' self is to be no self—in Kierkegaard's view.[71] The process of reflection we have been following in this section accedes to the force of the objection and moves towards a position in which the triumph of grace represents the annihilation of all decisive individuality. The language of St Paul is available to state the point: 'He is not dead, but living, yes, thou shalt rightly live thyself in and together with him, he shall be and become thy life, so that thou dost not live thyself, dost no longer live thyself, but Christ liveth in thee.'[72]

---

[68] *S.V.* X, p. 86 (*CDi*, p. 85). [Italics his.] Just as in this formulation one retires from the use of the notion of predestination to domesticate the fact of rejection, one abandons it as well as a device for handling the unblessedness of those who simply never encountered the Christ. Instead, still clinging to the form of individuality, one indulges in the speculation concerning the teacher and the learner that 'if they met again in another life, then the teacher would again be able to give the condition to anyone who had not received it'. *S.V.* IV, p. 187 (*PF*, p. 12).

[69] *S.V.* IX, p. 289 (*WL*, p. 245). [Italics his.]

[70] *S.V.* XII, pp. 141–6 (*TC*. pp. 151–6). See above, pp. 136–7.

[71] See above, pp. 106–8.

[72] *S.V.* X, p. 264 (*CDi*, p. 268).

In less conventional religious language, one will speak of trading time for eternity[73] in which one grows away from differentiation and relatedness[74] and from striving for specific goals in God's name.[75]

While this line in Kierkegaard's thought seems willing to accept— even welcome—the annihilation of individuality, the thinker himself could not finally do so. We are speaking, after all, of one of the poles which form the fundamental structure for his thought. That structure was not a temporary encumberance, soon discarded by a developing Kierkegaard. More specifically, we have seen in the preceding section how this affirmation of individuality finds expression when Kierkegaard witnesses to the efficacy of the Christ. A less consistent mind might simply have left these strands starkly juxtaposed to each other. In Kierkegaard's case, however, the strands become the components in a complex set of formulations which represent both the coexistence and the collision of his commitments to contingency and certainty.

3. The Collision and Coexistence of the Components: The Actualizing of the Effects in the Paradoxical Passion of Faith

In the Christ God and man meet. But if the parties to the meeting are understood as utterly opposed to each other, the assertion of their meeting itself will only restate the tension or contradiction character-izing the 'relationship'. To speak of such a meeting as paradoxical is surely not to exaggerate. Kierkegaard did not regard the use of the term paradox in such a case as the intrusion of an alien mode of speech: 'The paradox is not a concession, but a category, an on-tological determination which expresses the relationship between an existing, knowing spirit and the eternal truth.'[76] Indeed perhaps paradox is the term one needs above any other. After all one might suppose any difficulties deriving from the definition of God and man to be heightened by the intimacy of the collision of these components

---

[73] S.V. X, pp. 138–46 (CDi, pp. 139–48). So as one lives eternally, one rids oneself of a concern for the 'next day' (ibid., pp. 76–77 [ibid., p. 75]; cf. S.V. XI, pp. 40–41 ['LF', CDi, p. 350]).

[74] S.V. IX, pp. 86–87 (WL, pp. 71–72). So, too, the emphasis on the absolute sufficiency of God's grace for all man's needs tends to posit withdrawal from the living interdependence of society (S.V. V, pp. 81–87 ['MN', ED, IV, pp. 7–16]; cf. above pp. 166–7).

[75] One simply assumes that God sends the best (S.V. VI, p. 195 [SW, p. 197]) and thanks him even for that which does not seem good (S.V. VII, pp. 147f. [CUP, pp. 158f.]). This represents a kind of anticipation of eternity where there will be no striving (S.V. IX, p. 185 [WL, p. 157]) and faith will be abolished (S.V. VII, p. 19 [CUP, p. 31]).

[76] Pap. VIII A 11 (Dru 633).

in the figure of the Christ. It may be hard enough to give content to the term 'relationship' when that term is set 'between' this God and this man. But all the power of the opposition involved exerts itself against a claim of a 'meeting', surely rendering that claim the more 'paradoxical'.

The later sections of the *Postscript* present this heightening quite directly. The basic formula calls for the juxtaposition of the individual and the eternal. To resist the suggestion that the individuality involved is essentially eternal (and so the conflict false), the qualification is added that one becomes eternal 'in relation to something historical'. To resist the suggestion that this eternal is really just a dimension of the historical, the qualification is added that this historical something is that which can become historical 'only against its own nature'. One can only concede that one is left with a genuine impossibility.[77]

One cannot blunt the edge of this impossibility by a process of approximation. Not only are proofs irrelevant, but anything that would seem to make the object of faith more probable would be a temptation.[78] Thus eighteen centuries can greatly alter our judgment of probabilities in things historical, but can only obscure the issue if the object of faith is an impossibility: the non-historical coming to be in history.[79] If the nature of the man addressed by the paradoxical fact seems to require at least some epistemological occasion for faith in the impossible, let it be the claim of the man Jesus to be God.[80] In

[77] This is, of course, an appeal to paradox quite different from that involved in the first section of this chapter. See above, pp. 203–5. There the emphasis is on the risk of faith and the revolutionary character of obedience, but not on a pure impossibility confronting man. For a discussion of the many sub-distinctions, particularly on the diastatic side of the distinction, see Henning Schröer, *Die Denkform der Paradoxalität als theologisches Problem* (Göttingen: Vandenhoeck & Ruprecht, 1960).

[78] This theme is, of course, very widespread in Kierkegaard's works, but is particularly strong in *PF*, *CUP*, and *SD*.

[79] *S.V.* VII, pp. 35–37 (*CUP*, pp. 46–47). Cf. ibid., p. 3 (ibid., p. 15) and *S.V.* IV, pp. 258–9 (*PF*, pp. 79–80).

[80] Paulus Svendsen, 'Opposisjonsennlegg ved cand. teol. Per Lönnings disputas for den teologiske doktorgrad 5 maj, 1955', *Norsk Teologisk Tidskrift*, 1956, pp. 1–23, contends that one of Kierkegaard's important concerns was to counteract the possible negative effects of biblical criticism and adds ironically that the only trouble with his effort is that it may not be possible to show that Jesus did claim to be God. We are emphasizing that Kierkegaard's formulations at this point have a strong confessional root in the rhythms of his thought, and do not represent an expedient extrinsically directed by apologetic requirements. K. E. Lögstrup, 'Christentum ohne den historischen Jesus', *Orbis Litterarum*, 1963, pp. 101–12, claims that Kierkegaard would not be troubled even if it could be shown that no evidence whatever supports the suggestion that Jesus claimed to be God. Faith

granting such an occasion one moves away from the strict logic of paradox, perhaps, but this is what Kierkegaard seems compelled to do. He notes that while the absolute paradox would call for the existence of the God-Man to be wholly unnoticed (wholly unnoticeable), yet the divine paradox is that he was noticed at least to the point of being crucified.[81] An appeal to miracles may seem at least formally a further withdrawal from the logic of paradox, but such an appeal does preserve materially the contradictory juxtaposition of the divine and the human.[82] While Kierkegaard may seem at times to be saying that the evidence concerning the Christ is inadequate rather than non-existent (no evidence is possible for an impossibility), one must acknowledge that the diastatic impulse is still dominant in the measurement of the inadequacy.[83] The power of the paradox motif as a celebration of the collision also shows itself in Kierkegaard's dismissal of the doctrine of verbal inspiration as offering a false security—again an 'approximation'.[84] Similarly, the presence of contradiction in the content of the scriptures fittingly preserves the dialectic of the meeting of God and man in the Christ.[85]

Nor does understanding follow upon the leap of faith, for faith does not want to 'understand itself in another way than to continue in faith's passion'.[86] Yet one may feel that a kind of verification motif is introduced. Does Climacus not ask of the way to an eternal hap-

---

knows of itself—quite apart from any historical research—that Jesus lived and made this claim. The diastatic impulse does tend in this direction, but its movement is challenged in ways which Lögstrup does not seem to take into account. See above, pp. 204–14. Surely individual differences between works must be acknowledged at this point. Thus *TC* shows a far greater interest in the details of the life of Jesus, than does *PF* (though *TC*'s interest is qualified by a tendency to know in advance what those details ought to be).

[81] *Pap.* IV A 103.

[82] Thus it is that the miracles can be viewed both as a cause of offence and as support for the leap of faith. See Lönning, op. cit., pp. 88–89, on both uses.

[83] One may state this point in a non-christological form by saying that the judgment that man cannot find meaning in history depends on the meaning of 'meaning', and may reflect a diastatic vision of a universal system.

[84] *Pap.* X 2 A 548f.

[85] *Pap.* X 4 A 435, XI 1 A 154, XI 2 A 429.

[86] *S.V.* VII, p. 6 (*CUP*, p. 18). Cf. ibid., p. 196 (ibid., p. 209): 'One generally presents the matter thus: that the improbable, the paradox, is something which faith merely relates itself to passively, it must temporarily be satisfied with this relationship, and little by little things will surely get better—there is even a probability of that! O, wonderful creation of confusions in speaking of faith! One is to begin to believe in the confidence that there is a probability that it will soon enough get better. In that way one gets probability smuggled in and one is hindered in believing; in that way it is easy to understand that the fruit of having believed for a long time becomes that one ceases to believe; instead of, as one should think,

piness? That he does, but the fulfilment or satisfaction is precisely *eternal*, and that is to say that it does not alter the conditions of his striving in this life.[87] Indeed Kierkegaard employs the eternal validity of the fulfilment motif to ridicule any effort to bring the motif to bear in the world of time. God may appeal to 'terror over eternal punishment . . . hope for an eternal happiness', but in doing so he is not saying: 'I will seize upon your person and torture you to death in the most horrible manner, if you do not (watch out now, here it comes) make your life here on earth as profitable and enjoyable as you possibly can!'[88] Despite contemporary theology's romance with the word 'eschatological', Kierkegaard essentially separates time and eternity and so does not materially violate the logic of paradox by speaking of an eternal happiness.[89] That promise *is* 'incommensurable' with the leap of faith—or in more current language, the promise itself is part of the hypothesis and cannot be introduced as evidence for the hypothesis.[90]

---

that one believes the more inwardly. No, faith relates itself self-actively to the improbable and the paradox, self-actively in discovering it and holding it fast every moment—in order to believe.' While the word improbable (*Usandsynlige*) is used rather than impossible (*Umulige*), the context clearly requires the strictest reading of the paradoxical.

[87] Thus Jesus himself first experiences satisfaction and reward in the Ascension, which 'is not a direct continuation of the foregoing, truly not'. (*S.V.* XII, p. 349 [*SE*, pp. 85–86].) And we '*expect* an *eternal* happiness'. (*S.V.* IV, pp. 139ff. ['EE', *ED*, III, pp. 95ff.].) [Italics ours.] So, too, it is 'eternity, which is the true repetition'. (*S.V.* III, p. 254 [*REP*, p. 144]; cf. *S.V.* IV, p. 417n. [*CD*, p. 135n.].) The believer does not give up Christianity, even if it has made him unhappy, for he believes precisely that 'in the end Christianity must make it good to him. In the end, yes that is not little by little, it is much less and yet infinitely much more.' *S.V.* VII, p. 514 (*CUP*, p. 522).

[88] *S.V.* XIV, p. 135 (*AC*, p. 110).

[89] Thus Per Lönning is right in stressing the role the eros motif plays in Kierkegaard's thought. But Valter Lindström, 'Eros och agape i Kierkegaards aaskaadning', *Kierkegaardiana*, 1955, pp. 102–13, can understandably express concern lest that stress be understood to blunt Kierkegaard's discourse on paradox. The eros motif of course involves much of the material dealt with in the first section of the chapter, but it finds a formal expression here as well.

[90] Helmut Thielicke, 'Nihilism and Anxiety', *Theology Today*, October, 1955, pp. 343–54, seeks to show how the eschatological appeal has consequences for this life. The theme of his article is well expressed in its concluding sentences: 'We do not know what will come; but we know Who will come. That means to lose anxiety about the possibilities because one knows the last reality.' (ibid., p. 354.) Cf. Kierkegaard's remarks on 'the expectation of an eternal happiness and the significance this expectation has for the present life', *S.V.* IV, pp. 145–56 ('EE', *ED*, pp. 103–20). Perhaps one 'knows' enough in this present life to make the eschatological appeal less than a pure one. The line of thought we have been following in this section does not permit so full a knowledge, however. In this context we have not sought to discuss the basic question of any appeal—this

On these terms not only the Christ is an impossibility, but faith in this paradox is equally impossible. Faith is a psychological impossibility, for the paradox does not offer itself as a candidate competing with the other goods of this life, but as a source of certain suffering. We have traced the development by which the opposition between God and man comes to characterize God's man in the interpretation of Christianity as suffering.[91] We only need to show now that the same development reaches to include the man who affirms the God-Man: '. . . it is true, so true, and in another sense also so true, when the wise and prudent man in the situation of contemporaneity . . . judges Christ by saying: "*He is literally nothing*"—most certainly true, for he is the absolute. Christianity came into the world as the absolute, not—humanly understood—for consolation, on the contrary, it speaks again and again of how the Christ must suffer, or of what a man must suffer in order to become and be a Christian, sufferings which he consequently can avoid by merely refraining from becoming a Christian.'[92]

---

worldly or other worldly—to verification by fulfilment. A comment on that question falls to Part Four.

[91] See above, pp. 160–8. The suffering is so certain that it can be invoked as a criterion. Thus if I will know that I have lived for others, I will 'know it from the fact that they have derided me'. (*S.V.* IX, p. 84 [*WL*, p. 70]; cf. ibid., pp. 216–34 [ibid., pp. 182–98].) Any success would have to come as a 'special bestowal of providence'. (*S.V.* VII, p. 112 [*CUP*, p. 123].) This dynamic influences the use of the self-denial motif, when Kierkegaard says that success would invalidate true love which is 'the true sacrifice which must be unconditionally without reward'. (*S.V.* IX, p. 116 [*WL*, p. 98]; cf. ibid., p. 331 [ibid., p. 281]; *S.V.* XII, p. 471 [*JT*, p. 213].) This is also what is involved in the Kierkegaardian certainty that the less outward (progress), the more inner (goodness). (*S.V.* XII, p. 367 [*SE*, p. 103]; cf. *S.V.* IX, p. 78 [*WL*, p. 64].)

[92] *S.V.* XII, p. 60 (*TC*, pp. 66–67). [Italics his.] It is striking to note the association of nothingness with suffering—suggestive of the fact that the principle of opposition behind the view that Christianity reaches its true expression in suffering finally requires that no expression at all is possible. (See above, pp. 160–2.) '*He is literally nothing!*' Lönning, op. cit., p. 182, well expresses the tension within the formulation of suffering: 'To relate oneself to Christ means at the same time to suffer pain by being on the world's side against God and by being on God's side against the world.' The Christ himself is in no outward way impressive as a likely bearer of satisfaction. (*S.V.* XII, pp. 400–1 [*JT*, pp. 136–7].) Thus it is not surprising that his followers will surely suffer. (*S.V.* XII, pp. 110, 144 [*TC*, pp. 118, 154].) Kierkegaard explicitly asserts that there is 'no wherefore' for this faith. To make the point that possible advantage is not a 'wherefore', it would be best to preach Christianity in poverty. (*S.V.* XII, p. 405 [*JT*, p. 141].) Thus the fact that the clergy is salaried becomes a sore point. Kierkegaard pleads for an either-or: '. . . *either* there is real renunciation of the earthly, in order with sacrifice to preach Christianity; *or* one assures oneself of the earthly, the temporal but makes then the admission that this preaching is not properly Christianity'. *S.V.* XII, p. 412 (*JT*, p. 149). [Italics his.]

The certainty of this suffering is not to be excluded from the believer's motivation: 'That which distinguishes the Christian narrow way from the common human narrow way is: the voluntary. Christ was not one who sought after earthly goods, but had to be satisfied with poverty; no, he chose poverty; He was not one who longed for human honour and esteem, but had to be satisfied to live in lowliness, or to be misjudged and slandered; no, he chose humiliation. This is the narrow way in the strictest sense.'[93]

But perhaps Kierkegaard's creed was the Pauline 'I consider that the sufferings of this present time are not worth comparing with the glory that is to be revealed to us'.[94] Such faith seems the depth of naïveté and vulnerable in the worst way, unless some foretaste, some earnest of that glory is experienced in the events of this present time. But perhaps that is not so. Or perhaps in some way or other the whole appeal to self-interest can be suspended—transcended—in matters of faith.[95] But even if one should grant that psychological possibility, faith in the paradox stubbornly remains a logical impossibility. How shall a man affirm as true a proposition which is logically self-contradictory? What can it 'mean' to do so?

This problem is the one which leads Sören Holm to characterize Kierkegaard's christology as 'fictionalist'. The paradox of the Christ is a 'pretended or postulated event which never will be able to participate in the being of actuality',[96] and 'the object is to *believe* that this man is God, and to believe it so steadfastly, *as if* he really were that, although as an empirical individual he obviously cannot be that'.[97] It is not easy to slip away from this noose. One does not do so by saying that 'the problem is . . . not how one should find it

---

[93] *S.V.* XII, p. 351 (*SE*, p. 87).

[94] Rom. 8.18.

[95] It is very hard to resist the impression that this is what one strand in Kierkegaard's thought asks the reader to do. That strand is balanced by others, of course, but is not annihilated by them. Nor can it be removed by regarding it as conscious distortion. At least Kierkegaard can claim that, far from pitching things too high, he has 'abated' 30 to 50 per cent of the Christian message. (*Pap.* X 6 B 247). (Since this comment is from the journals it seems more likely that it does candidly report Kierkegaard's understanding of the matter at this time at least, rather than representing a further expression of conscious distortion.) It is this stern message which has caused many to shake their heads over Kierkegaard. Even Karl Barth (who cannot well be accused of tailoring his message to man's preferences) is troubled with the fact that Kierkegaard has failed to express clearly that 'the gospel is the *joyous* message of God's YES to man'. Karl Barth, 'Mein Verhältnis zu Sören Kierkegaard', *Orbis Litterarum*, 1963, p. 99. [Italics his.]

[96] Sören Holm, *Sören Kierkegaards Historiefilosofi* (Copenhagen: Bianco Lund, 1952), p. 116.

[97] ibid., p. 117. [Italics his.]

possible to affirm of one or another event a composition which is self-contradictory in an ontological respect, but where the historical existence's final qualification comes into view'.[98] Chastising those who approach Kierkegaard with a 'Platonic metaphysical schema' does not make clear how one's own approach can avoid a metaphysical commitment of some sort. Furthermore, we have shown that at least some of the terms Kierkegaard employs do seem to suggest a metaphysics so out of fashion today.[99] The contribution of that metaphysics to the characterization of God and man combines with Kierkegaard's acceptance of the principle of contradiction to constitute the paradox which elicits the believer's passion.

Still Holm's 'fictionalist' characterization distorts Kierkegaard's intention, for faith is interested in the question of truth. The believer is not a champion of fantasy, but a confessor of fact—albeit a fact which defies the principle of contradiction. The believer acts 'as if' God and man met in the Christ because he believes they did—and do.[100] Thus offence in the essential sense takes the forms of lowliness and eminence—but in both cases rejects the truth claim involved in the paradox.[101] This is the point too of Kierkegaard's insistence that the absurd is not the meaningless, and that the Christian will use reason to help him believe against the reason: 'So the believing Christian both has and uses his understanding, respects the universal human, does not seek to find an explanation in a lack of understanding if someone does not become a Christian; but in relation to Christianity he believes against the understanding, and also here uses the understanding—to make sure that he believes against the understanding. Nonsense, therefore he cannot believe against the understanding, as one might perhaps fear, for precisely the understanding

---

[98] Johannes Slök, 'Tre Kierkegaard-tolkninger', *Kierkegaardiana*, 1955, p. 93.

[99] See above, pp. 101–3. See also the detailed analysis of Kierkegaard's philosophic categories in the 'interlude' of the *Fragments* made by Charles R. Magel in his (unpublished) dissertation for the doctorate in philosophy from the University of Minnesota, 1960.

[100] Thus it is also a mistake when Günther Rohrmoser, 'Ernst oder Ironie?— Eine Zwischenbemerkung zur Interpretation Kierkegaards', *Archiv für Geschichte der Philosophie*, 1962, pp. 75–87, says that for Kierkegaard faith believes in itself because Kierkegaard's God has no freedom to be direct. Kierkegaard would drive a way between these alternatives by appeal to the paradoxical faith in the paradoxical fact. This is also the line of response required by Gerd-Günther Grau's contention (*Die Selbstauflösung des christlichen Glaubens* [Frankfurt: G. Schulte-Bulmke, 1963]) that Kierkegaard's thought involves the 'historical' self-destruction of Christianity, since it can permit no temporal expression to an eternal reality, when the eternal is by definition the non-temporal.

[101] See *S.V.* XII, pp. 90–101 (*TC*, pp. 96–108).

will discern that it is nonsense and hinder him from believing it; but he uses the understanding so much that he by it becomes aware of the incomprehensible and then he relates himself to this, believing against the understanding.'[102]

We shall argue that the components we have analysed in this chapter finally drive Kierkegaard's thought to a formulation which represents an advance beyond the fact of collision and state of co-existence evident in the material studied in this section. It seems likely that the reality of the Christ event for Kierkegaard was itself the catalyst which moved his reflection to this advance 'beyond coexistence'. Quite apart from that movement and its cause(s), Kierkegaard illustrates eloquently the principle of 'movement at a point'. That is, he dissects and develops the logic of the coexistence of the divine and the human in paradox, all the while abiding by the requirements of that logic. In doing so he exposes to view the more clearly the internal difficulties which bedevil this phase of his reflection concerning the efficacy of the Christ. We need to give these developments further attention, because they not only are stated in the most striking fashion but indeed have struck some of the clearest blows in contemporary theological thought.[103]

In view of the logical and psychological problems facing faith in the paradox, it does seem 'almost an impossibility to keep the learner's confidence alive'.[104] How is faith in the paradox possible? Perhaps the clue lies in the fact that faith is a passion: 'Faith is a miracle, and yet no man is excluded from it; for that in which all human life is unified is passion, and faith is a passion.'[105] Christianity endorses the in-

---

[102] S.V. VII, p. 495 (CUP, p. 504). Cf. Pap. X 2 A 354 (Dru 1033), where Kierkegaard describes how the understanding knows the paradox 'negatively—but not more'. Cf. S.V. IV, pp. 263–4 (PF, pp. 85–86).

[103] Schröer, op. cit., is particularly helpful in tracing the impact of this side of Kierkegaard on contemporary theological thought. In Part Four we comment in more detail on the dominance of the diastatic in the appropriation of Kierkegaard's legacy.

[104] S.V. IV, p. 197 (PF, p. 21).

[105] S.V. III, p. 116 (FT, p. 77). Cf. S.V. VII, p. 144 (CUP, p. 154), where Climacus proposes that 'immortality is precisely the potentiation and highest development of the developed subjectivity'. See also ibid., pp. 157–212 (ibid., pp. 169–224) for the development of this potentiation. Per Lönning, 'Kierkegaard's "Paradox"', Orbis Litterarum, 1955, p. 162, well states the thrust of this appeal: 'In its assumption of the exclusive historical origin of the eternal truth, Christianity enters into an unconditional conflict with any non-Christian understanding of human existence. On the other hand, the subjective passion of faith, required by "that fact" (hiint Faktum, namely: The God in time) is in itself not essentially different from the passion of any other existential relation to the eternal, but just

dividual's quest to synthesize the temporal and the eternal and appropriates the passion that anticipates that synthesis.[106] An analogue to faith becomes visible in the common experience of man. Indeed faith may be spoken of as a 'higher immediacy', whose certainty parallels the indubitable facticity of immediate sense experience.[107] This avenue is attractive because it seems to sidestep the logical problems linked with the paradox: 'They would lead us to believe that the objections against Christianity come from doubt. That is an utter misunderstanding. Objections against Christianity come from insubordination, unwillingness to obey, rebellion against all authority. Therefore in fighting the objections one has up to now been beating the air, because one has fought intellectually with doubt, instead of fighting ethically with rebellion.'[108]

Yet this appeal to passion only reclothes the problems of the paradox motif. One may join Kierkegaard in decrying the absence of passion in a given state of Christendom without claiming that Christianity has a corner on passion. Shall we place no other criterion on the matter of becoming and being a Christian? Kierkegaard at times comes near letting the matter rest at that—notably in the famous reference from *CUP*: 'If one who lives in the midst of Christianity goes up to the house of God, the house of the true God, with the true conception of God in his knowledge, and then prays, but prays in untruth; and if one who lives in an idolatrous land, but prays with all the passion of the infinite, though his eyes rest upon the image of an idol: where is there most truth? The one prays in truth to God, although he worships an idol; the other prays in untruth to the true God, and therefore worships in truth an idol.'[109]

---

the fulfilment and the perfection of it, affirming it through adapting it as its own "pathetic" element. Subjectivity is at the same time both the truth and the untruth.'

[106] *S.V.* VII, p. 164 (*CUP*, p. 176): 'Only momentarily can the particular individual be existentially in a unity of the infinite and the finite, which transcends existence. That moment is the moment of passion.'

[107] This point is of particular importance to Theunissen, op. cit., in his effort to see *Ernst* as the unifying category in Kierkegaard's thought.

[108] *Pap.* VIII 1 A 7 (*Dru* 630). Cf. ibid., 414 (ibid., 712).

[109] *S.V.* VII, p. 168 (*CUP*, p. 178). It is this sort of passage which arouses Schröer's fear that existence is being confused with Christian existence—or, in the language we have used, the real is being identified with the ideal. Schröer finds the cause of this tendency to lie in the fact that Kierkegaard regards the basic paradox to be an ontological one (op. cit., pp. 78–80, 87, 200). We have emphasized the activity of a diastatic religious impulse behind the employment of the ontological paradox.

But Kierkegaard's commitments did not permit him to leave the statement 'Subjectivity is the truth' standing as a final statement of the Christian truth about faith. *CUP* does move on from that thesis to a very precise analysis of the objective paradox which marks man's existence as untruth. As soon as that analysis is readmitted to the discussion the appeal to passion is immersed in difficulties once again. For how shall the subject—for all his passion—attach himself to an alleged objective reality, when attachment to the reality described is both a logical and psychological impossibility? Faith involves a reversal rather than a potentiation of the passion basic to individuality. The passionate quest for the good is turned away by the suggestion that we ought to seek exactly the opposite of satisfaction. The inward dynamic by which man actualizes possibility is repudiated in proposing the actualization of impossibility.

Climacus, conscious of this reversal, attempts to employ a quasi-Hegelian category of negativity to secure the introduction of faith. Since the 'highest potentiation of every passion is always to will its own downfall',[110] reason (equals humanity, individuality, i.e., passion) wills its downfall and becomes faith. This accurately expresses what is required for the introduction of faith, but in no sense makes plausible that introduction. One may state the problem in the terms of Hegel's categories. Hegel may be read to assert that every material expression of negativity is negated. But that negating only occurs through the continuing presence and activity of negativity. What Kierkegaard requires, on the other hand, is that the moving power of the process, i.e., negativity itself, be negated. In a similar way Kierkegaard finds a preparation for the leap to the paradox in the thesis that 'ignorance is the negative form for infinite knowledge'.[111] But one still must face the fact that the paradox as the point of collision seems to threaten the competence of reason in any finite realm at all, not its idolatrous omnicompetence.

Kierkegaard honours these objections and would overcome them, when he writes: 'In relation to love . . . it does not hold true that a man, by determining his How can say what or whom he loves. All

---

[110] *S.V.* IV, p. 204 (*PF*, p. 29).

[111] See the passages quoted above, p. 161, note 129. Emil Brunner, 'Das Grundproblem der Philosophie bei Kant und Kierkegaard', *Zwischen den Zeiten*, 1924, pp. 31–47, attempts a similar argument when—in relating Kant and Kierkegaard—he sees Kierkegaard's God-in-time as both a paradox and a fulfilment of the truth urge. The step from a limited reason to a logical impossibility is blurred in this comparison. It is not clear how a paradox which violates our reason can be said to be the ground for our reason.

lovers have the How of love in common, and the individual must add the name of his beloved. But with respect to believing (*sensu strictissimo*) it holds true that this How is appropriate only to one as its object.'[112] It is hard to find this response persuasive. It seems to try to convert its deficit into capital by pointing to the great exertion which must be at hand if one is to believe the impossible. One may readily agree and add that indeed more is asked than man should (can?) muster.

It does not help to buttress this appeal by linking divine and human subjectivity. To be sure, one can meaningfully relate the act of faith to the solitariness or inwardness of the self set in relationships. But if God is pure subjectivity in the sense that he is wholly unrelated, he cannot become an object for human subjectivity. And if one says that it is just this God who has revealed himself in the Christ, it is not clear how one can trust a revelation whose content seems to be that God cannot (does not?) reveal himself. In such a trust the human subject would turn against its own best bearings. One seems—sooner or later, apart from or in the Christ—required to say more of God. On the other hand, if God is the 'infinitely compelling subjectivity'[113] in the sense that his revelation elicits man's affirmation, then one seems to have moved beyond the proclamation of paradox in the sense in which the term has been used in this section.[114]

Yet perhaps that is not the case. We have in Frithiof Brandt's

[112] *S.V.* VII, p. 534 (*CUP*, p. 542). J. Heywood Thomas, *Subjectivity and Paradox* (Oxford: Basil Blackwell, 1957), p. 15, notes that the structure of paradox is reduplicated in this appeal: '. . . he was able to preserve a delicate balance between what we may call autobiography and public description so as to give a comprehensive philosophical description of faith. This description thus yields a paradox—that faith is something strangely like subjective statements because it is essentially something about me, and yet is never reducible to just this.' It is in this 'reduplication' that Thomas finds the theme and title for his book.

[113] *Pap.* X 2 A 401 (*Dru* 1042).

[114] On this whole matter, see Valter Lindström, 'The Problem of Objectivity and Subjectivity in Kierkegaard', *A Kierkegaard Critique*, ed. H. Johnson and N. Thulstrup; article trans. by Niels Erik Enkvist (New York; Harper, 1962), pp. 228-42. Lindström's basic thesis is stated briefly early in the article: 'If we wish to approach the core of Kierkegaard's philosophy, we must begin by observing that his writings are permeated by an increasingly conscious effort to overcome the difficulties caused by the dualism between objectivity and subjectivity in presentations of Christianity throughout the history of Christian thought. More and more clearly he grasped that it was impossible to arrive at the essence of Christianity by way of the two concepts of objectivity and subjectivity as they had been traditionally defined. On vitally important points his decisive analyses aimed at destroying this false and deceptive distinction in the interpretation of Christianity.' (ibid., p. 230.) Lindström deals persuasively with a great number of specific themes, but hey do not add up to the demonstration of this basic thesis.

words shown that 'to Kierkegaard Christianity was an inhuman religion, for it opposed the instinctiveness of human nature and its natural demands for happiness in this life and demanded completely to the contrary, a dying to the world and a concentration on life after death. All this in addition to being "absurd" from the intellectual point of view.'[115] But why shall one insist that Christianity must be human? Does not Kierkegaard point in another direction when he contends that 'one must be saved by subjectivity, i.e., by God, as the infinitely compelling subjectivity'.[116] Is he not saying that the way out of the morass in which this discussion is mired is to realize that faith is a work of God? If the God of whom we speak in all this is quite literally the infinite, it is inconceivable that the work of faith could be placed in the hands of some other centre of power. And while faith does indeed seem impossible from a human point of view, God 'has in his eternal consciousness the medium which is precisely the commensurability'.[117]

The divinity of faith is suggested not only by a scrutiny of the object of faith, but also by a closer study of the believer's passion itself. Kierkegaard suggests this, even while attempting to cling to the continuity of passion:

To ask with infinite interest about a reality which is not one's own is to will to believe, and this expresses the paradoxical relationship to the paradox. Aesthetically one cannot ask such a question except in thoughtlessness, since aesthetically possibility is higher than reality. Intellectually one cannot ask such a question, since intellectually possibility is higher than reality. Nor is it possible to ask such a question ethically, since ethically the individual's one and only infinite interest is in his own reality. The analogy of faith with the ethical lies in the infinite interest, which makes a believer absolutely different from an aesthetician or a thinker. But then again the believer differs from an ethicist in that he is infinitely interested in the reality of another (for example, in the fact that God has really been present in time [vaeret til]).[118]

That is, the believer's interest in the reality of the other is qualitatively different from the ethicist's quite definite interest in others. In recognizing that difference Kierkegaard implicitly expresses the fact that the real difference is not in the reference to the other, but in the presence of the self. The believer's infinite interest in the other is different from that of the ethicist, since the other acquires for the

[115] Frithiof Brandt, *Sören Kierkegaard* (Copenhagen: Det danske Selskab, 1963), p. 69.
[116] *Pap.* X 2 A 401 (*Dru* 1042).
[117] *S.V.* VII, p. 114 (*CUP*, p. 126).
[118] *S.V.* VII, pp. 278–9 (*CUP*, p. 288). See above, p. 102, note 11.

believer an objective significance independent of subjective appropriation. In so far as one still retains the forms of individuality the process of appropriation must be placed elsewhere than in the believer. The objectivity of the other's significance proposes the answer: the locus of the appropriation is in the other—it is in God.

This line of thought of course brings to mind the project of the *Fragments* with its insistence that man lacks not only the truth but the condition for understanding the truth as well. It is important to move with considerable care in analysing this assertion. Clearly Kierkegaard is referring to more than the fact that a certain passivity is involved in a relationship which yields knowledge. That passivity is balanced by an activity of the self, and it is just this ordinary activity which Kierkegaard would deny a place in the substance of faith: 'The emperor was, after all, immediately knowable and therefore someone could well have known the emperor without the emperor knowing him; but this teacher, of whom we speak, was, after all, not immediately knowable, but could only be known when he himself gave the condition.'[119]

But is Kierkegaard intent to deny any and all activity to the self as far as faith is concerned? The *Fragments* and the wider scope of Kierkegaard's works do not reply to this question with a single voice. Kierkegaard can speak of the communication of the condition as having an inciting function: '"Receiver" is an active word.'[120] Climacus puts the matter thus: '. . . faith is not an act of will, for all human volition constantly has its capacity within the scope of a condition. . . . But if I am not in possession of the condition and that is what we are assuming in order not to turn back to the Socratic principle, all my willing helps not in the least, although as soon as the condition is given, the Socratic principle will again apply.'[121]

At other times, however, Kierkegaard moves towards the kind of formulation familiar to the reader from the preceding section's comments on the irresistible power of grace. In this case one will not merely say that 'it is God who . . . gives it to a man to believe'.[122] One will extend that giving to include everything. The Christian 'accepts all by God's grace—even the grace itself; he understands

---

[119] *S.V.* IV, p. 232 (*PF*, pp. 55–56).
[120] *Pap.* VIII 2 B 81, 7.
[121] *S.V.* IV, pp. 227–8 (*PF*, pp. 50–51). Lönning, op. cit., pp. 196–203, observes that this formulation essentially preserves the structure of the dialectic between the self and the other(s), though in this case the 'given' for the self surely possesses an exceptional character.
[122] *Pap.* X 1 A 59.

that he cannot be without God's grace even in order to pray to him for his grace'.[123] Such an extension surely leaves no room for speech of any individual possessing a responsibility which no one else (man or God) can perform. The life of faith is born out of death.

> Faith is against the understanding; faith is on the other side of death. And when thou didst die or die to thyself, to the world, thou didst at the same time die to all immediacy in thyself, and also to thy understanding. That is when all confidence in thyself, or in human support, or even in God in an immediate sense, when every probability is excluded, when it is dark as in the dark of night—it is after all death that we are describing—then the life-giving Spirit comes and brings faith. This faith, which is stronger than the whole world, which has the powers of eternity, which is the Spirit's gift from God, this is thy victory over the world, in which thou dost more than conquer.[124]

It may seem puzzling to find a pattern of thought which some moments before seemed to rush headlong towards the uncritical elevation of the self's passion now turning towards a very high doctrine of election.[125] But in fact we here encounter the fundamental tendency of diastatic thought to move to a total polarization of God and man. Kierkegaard still holds to both poles and thus, while placing all under God's grace, can nevertheless admonish the Christian to learn to be satisfied with that grace.[126] Still the tendency towards polarization maintains itself and influences the way in which one speaks about both God and man. The results are aften strikingly similar—as may be seen by turning to the notorious problem of the relationship of the efficacy of the Christ to the historical process.

If faith is God's act, it is difficult to see how the realities of the historical process can be importantly involved in that act. For if God is essentially non-temporal, any use of historical processes would compromise his very character. The matter may be put as follows: 'When the believer is the believer and knows God through having received the condition from God himself, then the successor must

---

[123] *S.V.* X, p. 68 (*CDi*, p. 67). So *S.V.* V, pp. 87–93 ('MN', *ED*, IV, pp. 18–27) and *S.V.* IV, pp. 179–80 (*PF*, pp. 5–6) laud God who, unlike man, can beget development and not merely occasion it.

[124] *S.V.* XII, p. 365 (*SE*, p. 101). In a slightly different formulation one may retain individuality in the act of faith, but deny it place in the aftermath of faith. So *S.V.* X, pp. 238–9 (*CDi*, pp. 244–5): 'If someone says to me "But if", that I no longer understand. I understood it once, in the moment of decision, but now I understand it no longer . . . that word "if", which must be first understood before one grasps faith, that word is in turn the word and the thing which faith understands least of all.'

[125] Weiland, op. cit., p. 114, puzzles over the fact that Kierkegaard can seem to be on both sides of the Erasmus-Luther debate.

[126] *S.V.* X, pp. 68–69 (*CDi*, pp. 67–68).

receive the condition from God himself in exactly the same sense, and cannot receive it at second hand; since if he did, the second hand would have to be God himself, and in that case there is, after all, nothing at all to be said of a second hand.'[127]

One might suppose that the church represents such a 'second hand of God' in some sense at least. But 'the one knight of faith can provide no help at all to the other'.[128] It is not merely that the one who offers such help acts as if 'God could not help himself and the individual concerned'.[129] Such help involves more than impertinence —it constitutes opposition to God, for it defies the truth that it is a higher thing to relate to God directly than to do so through the race.[130] Perhaps the communal may be incorporated as a concession to weakness[131] or as a negative pole to challenge individual faith.[132] But fundamentally one must kill the longing for society,[133] 'since it is just this solitariness which is the way'.[134] The only way in which relationships can be granted a legitimate place is by freeing them from the perils of time in an eternal church triumphant.[135]

We are familiar with passages of this type from our discussion of the diastatic statement of the ideal. If God is the sole actor in the birth and life of faith, the logic of self-annihilation central to the diastatic ideal will come easily to hand. So the principle of self-hatred is said to deter the Christian from forming a community.[136] Or, in an alternative formulation, one can speak well of the individual, so long as one does not intrude the reality of the relationships which sustain that individual.[137]

Under the pressure of this dynamic the vertical community fares no better than the horizontal: '. . . what true Christians there are

[127] *S.V.* IV, p. 232 (*PF*, p. 56). Cf. *Ibid.*, p. 184 (*ibid.*, p. 10). See also *S.V.* IX, p. 114 (*WL*, p. 96): each individual gets his orders directly from God, not from 'the others'.

[128] *S.V.* III, p. 120 (*FT*, p. 82).

[129] *S.V.* VII, p. 60 (*CUP*, p. 73). The offerer of help violates the principle that the religious man has to do with himself alone and not with others—see *S.V.* VII, p. 49 (*CUP*, p. 61); *S.V.* X, p. 114 (*CDi*, p. 114); *S.V.* IV, pp. 153–5 ('EE', *ED*, III, pp. 116–18); and *Pap.* VII B 235, pp. 38–39 (*AR*, p. 33).

[130] *S.V.* XIII, p. 572 (*PV*, p. 89).

[131] *Pap.* IX A 315.

[132] *S.V.* VIII, pp. 86–87, 99 (*PA*, pp. 40–41).

[133] *Pap.* XI 2 A 387.

[134] *S.V.* VII, p. 53 (*CUP*, p. 65).

[135] This theme is very strong in *TC*. For a typical reference, see *S.V.* XII, p. 104 (*TC.* p. 217).

[136] *Pap.* XI 1 A 190.

[137] For an earlier discussion of the substance of the preceding two paragraphs in a different context, see above pp. 165–7.

in every generation are contemporary with Christ, have nothing to do with the Christians of former generations, but everything to do with the contemporary Christ'.[138] Indeed once again the community constitutes a genuine obstacle: 'What matters is neither more nor less than a revision of Christianity; what matters is eliminating the 1,800 years as though they had never been at all.'[139]

If the historical community is repudiated, the historical Christ seems just as surely to come under attack. We have, after all, no possibility of non-historical access to figures from the past, for 'every man can be contemporary only with the time in which he lives'.[140] But we are told that the Christ is the great exception, 'for Christ's life on earth, holy history, stands for itself alone, outside history'.[141] We saw earlier that in this phase of the coexistence of contradictory components Kierkegaard's mind grants place to an historical occasion for faith only in the sense of a bare claim of the man Jesus to be God—and possibly to miracles which paradoxically reduplicate that claim. Now it seems doubtful that even this much is retained. First-century folk could presumably cover their ears, as well as close their eyes,[142] for the contemporaneity permitted by sensory perception seems irrelevent. Indeed, more than that, such historical contemporaneity seems impossible, if we are to believe the invocation from *TC*:

> To be sure it is eighteen hundred years since Jesus Christ walked here on earth; but this is after all not an event like other events, which first, when past, go over into history, and then, when long past, go over into forgetfulness. No, his presence here on earth never becomes something past, and thus not something more and more past—if faith is to be found upon earth. And if not, yes then it is in that very moment a long time since he lived. On the other hand, so long as there is a believer, such a one must, in order to become such, have been, and as a believer must continue to be, just as contemporary with his presence as those [first] contemporaries; this contemporaneity is faith's condition, and more closely determined, it is faith.[143]

Climacus draws the conclusion well enough: 'But what does it mean to say that one can be contemporary without yet being contemporary, that one thus can be contemporary, and yet, using this advantage (immediately understood) be a non-contemporary; what does this

---

[138] *S.V.* XII, p. 61 (*TC*, p. 68). Per Lönning, op. cit., deserves much credit for showing this correlation between the horizontal and the vertical so clearly in his analysis of contemporaneity.

[139] *Pap.* IX A 72 (*Diary* 173).

[140] *S.V.* XII, p. 61 (*TC*, p. 68).

[141] ibid. (ibid.).

[142] *S.V.* IV, p. 228 (*PF*, p. 51).

[143] *S.V.* XII, p. 1 (*TC*, p. 9).

mean except that one simply cannot be immediately contemporary
with such a teacher and such an event. . . .'[144]

Surely one senses here that the reference to history involved in the
christological witness is only verbally retained, while the diastatic
concept of an eternal God, who is equally near all times,[145] controls
the settlement of the question of the efficacy of the Christ.[146] Of
course there are forces in the synthesis tradition too which can contribute to this development. We have seen how the diastatic tendency
to reject the community through a polarization of God and the solitary subject can find a point of entry in the dimension of inwardness
which the synthesis tradition attributes to the self. Similarly, the

[144] *S.V.* IV, p. 231 (*PF*, p. 54). One may try to remove some of the force of that
conclusion by adding that 'that which really happened (the past) is not the real,
except in a special sense, as opposed to poetry. It lacks the determination, which is
the determination of truth (as inwardness) and of all religiousness: the *for thee.*'
(*S.V.* XII, pp. 60–61 [*TC*, pp. 67–68].) [Italics his.] The reader will form his own
judgment as to the success of this venture and the related effort to separate 'holy
history' from ordinary history. (ibid. [ibid.]; cf. ibid., pp. 28–29 [ibid., pp. 33–34].)
Kierkegaard's readers veer away from this conclusion. So Roberts, op. cit., p. 88,
'clarifies' Kierkegaard's intention: '. . . he says that even the contemporary of
Christ can grasp the historical only by means of faith, and this is nonsense unless
what Kierkegaard has in mind is the revelatory meaning of the event, not merely
what one can apprehend by means of sensory perception. The contemporary
could be certain that Jesus existed, but he could not be certain, by logical or
empirical means, of His deity.' This more moderate position does find expression
within Kierkegaard (for example, see above pp. 202–5, 210–3), but that should
not blind us to the extremes reached or at least sighted by the diastatic impulse.
Thomas, op. cit., p. 131, seems to acknowledge this when he writes that 'to say
. . . that Christ's life on earth is not a past event . . . is to say that the history
of the words and deeds of a person living during the period 7 B.C. to A.D. 26, which
is the cash value of "the life of Christ on earth" is not history. This is sheer contradiction and nonsense.' But then he retreats: '. . . the assertion that Christ is God
incarnate is not an historical judgment. That is, by this statement we at once refer
to a person belonging to the past and make a judgment that is no more an assertion
about the past than it is about the present—indeed less so. Therefore in a real sense
the assertion is timeless' (ibid., p. 132). K. E. Lögstrup, 'Christentum ohne den
historischen Jesus', *Orbis Litterarum*, 1963, pp. 100–14, is nearer the mark in holding
that for Kierkegaard faith knows of itself that Jesus lived and claimed to be God.
Lögstrup unfortunately does not see the balancing of this emphasis by the synthesis
strand.
[145] *Pap.* XI 1 A 362.
[146] So *Pap.* VII B 235, p. 78 (*AR*, p. 60) makes the assertion that 'the Christian
fact has no history, for it is the paradox that God once came into existence in
time'. This assertion well corresponds to the specification from *PF* that the eternal
has no history. (*S.V.* IV, p. 239 [*PF*, p. 62].) Cf. *S.V.* XII, p. 28 (*TC*, p. 33):
' "History", says faith, has nothing at all to do with Jesus Christ; in relation to
him one has only holy history (which is qualitatively different from history in
general), which recounts the story of his life under the conditions of his humiliation,
together with that he himself said that he was God. He is the paradox which history
can never digest or convert into a general syllogism!'

concern that the self be personally involved in the formative events of its communal history can move towards a spiritualistic loss of history. Thus Kierkegaard writes: 'We humans think: that business with the fall of Adam, that has long, long since been put behind us and forgotten; we are fine fellows: for God that business with Adam happened today. We humans tell ourselves: that about Christ being put to death, that infamy of the human race, it is now eighteen hundred years since that took place, it was long since put behind us and forgotten; now we are fine fellows: for God that about Christ happened today.'[147]

Still, in this turning of thought at the stage of coexistence, we do encounter fundamentally the dominance of the diastatic impulse. While the minority component of human contingency deters any movement to the logic of certainty, strong voices deny the actualizing passion of faith a base in the realm of contingency. And that will mean that one will be hard pressed to speak positively of either the resurrection or the church.[148]

Still the very dynamic of thought which denies place to the church can swing around to speak of a 'second hand of God'. We have in mind, of course, Kierkegaard's statements about the apostle. The apostle is not a genius—he is not one distinguished from other men by his exceptional gifts. Rather 'an apostle is what he is through having divine authority. *The divine authority is the qualitatively decisive factor.*'[149] Furthermore, a good case can be made for saying that Kierkegaard extends this mantle of authority to the contemporary bringer of the word as well: '. . . to the sermon there corresponds a priest, and a priest is essentially what he is through ordination, and ordination is a teacher's paradoxical transformation in time, by

---

[147] *Pap.* XI 1 A 362.

[148] Kierkegaard has been hit very hard at this point. Siegfried Hansen, 'Die Bedeutung des Leidens für das Christusbild Sören Kierkegaards', *Kerygma und Dogma*, 1956, pp. 1–28, makes the rather familiar assertion that without the resurrection the church is both psychologically and exegetically impossible. We have been content to show the systematic connection between these two lacunae in Kierkegaard's thought. This is the context in which Weiland's lament over Kierkegaard's shortcomings (see above, p. 206, note 27) has place. Valter Lindström, 'Eros och agape i Kierkegaards aaskaadning', *Kierkegaardiana*, 1955, pp. 102–12, seeks to reply to such charges (particularly as voiced by Per Lönning, op. cit.) by arguing that Kierkegaard does speak of the exalted Christ and so implies a strong faith in the resurrection. He is right in that contention, but it should be noted that the strand of thought which we are discussing denies speech significance for the existing Christian—it is the lowly Christ who draws all men to himself.

[149] *S.V.* XI, p. 98 ('DIFF', *PA*, p. 144). [Italics his.]

which he becomes in time something other than what he would be through the immanent development of genius, talent, gifts, etc. Surely no one is ordained from eternity, or in a position to remember himself as ordained, as soon as he is born. On the other hand, ordination is a *character indelebilis*. What can that mean but that here again time becomes decisive for the eternal so that recollection's immanental return to the eternal is prevented.'[150]

These statements are strongly worded, and may mislead the reader, unless he knows that they are made in a context in which two principles are basic: (1) The appeal to the authority of the apostle and priest never circumvents the appeal to the authority of the paradox, but reduplicates that appeal, making it current. (2) The appeal to the authority of the apostle and the priest never repudiates the role of the individual hearer in appropriation, but renders that role critical by reduplicating the word the paradox brings, making it current.

(1) It may be the case that 'the sermon operates absolutely, solely through the authority of the Scripture and of Christ's apostles'.[151] But the apostles are Christ's[152] and in the Scripture one hears the voice of 'him to whom, according to his own statement, is given all authority in heaven and on earth'.[153] Thus Kierkegaard offers a parallel to his dismissal of historical evidence for the deity of the Christ in his rejection of anything humanly impressive in the apostle. Rather 'the apostle's call is a paradoxical fact, which from the first to the last moment of his life stands paradoxically outside his personal identity with himself as the definite person he is. A man has perhaps long since come to the age of discretion, when he is called to be an apostle. Through that call he does not get a better mind, he does not get more imagination, more discernment, etc., by no means; he remains himself, but through the paradoxical fact he is a man sent by God on a specific mission. Through the paradoxical fact the

---

[150] *S.V.* VII, p. 232 (*CUP*, p. 244). Cf. *S.V.* XI, p. 101n. ('DIFF', *PA*, p. 149n.).

[151] *Pap.* VIII 1 A 6 (*Dru* 629).

[152] Thus the apostle's relationship to direct or indirect communication is stated differently at different points in the authorship, but the difference derives from the fact that the paradox with which the apostle is essentially linked is related differently at different times to the forms of communication. On the one hand (*S.V.* VII, p. 527n. [*CUP*, p. 535n.]) the apostle alone has the authority which can justify the use of direct communication; on the other hand indirect communication is later seen to correspond to that which is above the human (*Pap.* X 6 B 151. 8, p. 229; X 2 A 147), just as *TC* sees that it is impossible for the God-Man to be direct (*S.V.* XII, pp. 124ff. [*TC*, pp. 132ff.]). On the changing views regarding communication, see above, pp. 30–35.

[153] *S.V.* XI, p. 106 ('DIFF', *PA*, p. 158).

apostle is made paradoxically different from all other men for all eternity.'[154]

Nor will one expect a different situation to obtain with regard to the ordained preacher of the word, for it is true of the paradox that 'however long it may be proclaimed in the world, it remains essentially just as new, just as paradoxical; no immanence can assimilate it to itself'.[155] Thus Kierkegaard can well summarize the relationships involved by saying: 'Christ is himself the sphere of the paradox and the chosen are the derived, who bear the mark of belonging to this sphere.'[156]

(2) The preached word of the paradoxical Christ may bear authority, but the preacher 'who is entirely correct in his discourse must speak in such a way, when he quotes a word of Christ: "This word is from him to whom, according to his own statement, is given all authority in heaven and on earth. My hearer, thou must now consider by thyself whether thou wilt bow thyself under this authority or not, accept or believe the word or not." '[157] True, Kierkegaard surely seems to deny that the hearer's judgment is to be made on immanential grounds. Yet it is hard to see how the individual's experience of self and world can be wholly excluded from the process of judgment, without evacuating all meaning from the phrase 'individual appropriation'. In assessing Adler's claim to revelation, Kierkegaard wrote: '. . . the new point of departure was the difference between the sincere ordinary man and the sincere extraordinary man; the essential human criterion, the ethical, they have both in common'.[158]

While Kierkegaard does not throw much light on the process of

---

[154] ibid., p. 97 (ibid., pp. 143–4).

[155] ibid., pp. 97–98 (ibid., p. 144). Thus the hearer is to accept the word on authority. If he will not do so, he is cautioned: '. . . for God's sake do not go and accept the word, because it is clever or profound or wonderfully beautiful, for that is blasphemy, that is to criticize God'. *S.V.* XI, p. 106 ('DIFF', *PA*, pp. 158–9).

[156] *Pap.* VII 2 B 235 p. 66n.

[157] *S.V.* XI, p. 106 ('DIFF', *PA*, pp. 158–9).

[158] *Pap.* VII 2 B 235, p. 45 (*AR*, p. 36). Cf. ibid., pp. 64–65 (ibid., pp. 50–51) where Kierkegaard offers a carefully balanced statement: 'the extraordinary must be imparted, must be fitted into the existing state of affairs, and the chosen one, the unique one, must, as one says, receive the terrible shock of being a paradox, and precisely through being that he passes on the shock. Dialectically there are two points here; that the shock should qualitatively and decisively really be a shock, and, on the other hand, that the existing state of affairs should as far as possible be spared. Just as little as God is a God of confusion, so little is the elect man called to confuse minds and then to run away. He must love the existing state of affairs and be willing to sacrifice himself.'

judgment involved in individual appropriation, the whole strain concerning the authority of the word, the apostle, and the priest must be seen to be moving back towards a view in which the co-involvement of God and man render that appropriation critical. We have seen that the extremes towards which the diastatic rhythm moves involve a polarization in which the efficacy of the Christ is transferred to a non-historical realization by God or to the equally non-historical subjective passion of man. If Kierkegaard's discourse about the authority of the church bypassed the question of appropriation it would not essentially alter this state of extreme polarization.[159] We have seen, however, that the question of appropriation is importantly addressed in this discourse. The appeal to the word of the Scriptures, the apostle and the ordained preacher represents a decided check on the diastatic tendency to discuss the efficacy of the Christ in non-historical terms. As Kierkegaard puts it: 'Through ordination the Christian *nota bene* stands once again.'[160] He will not, of course, argue that these witnesses to the word produce effects by weight of their number, as if they could make the word more probable. But they do make the word available and so ensure that the quality of that historical word-event—whatever it may be—shall not be lost.

This movement back towards a recognition of the role of the historical process in giving expression to the efficacy of the Christ is a further indication of the instability we have found characterizing the state of the coexistence of the components of certainty and contingency. That instability reports Kierkegaard's sensitivity to the fact that the coming together of these components does constitute a collision. He does not settle for saying 'yes and no' in an indefinite number of ways. It is not acceptable to ever bring God and man together and ever drive them apart and to do so at the same time and in the same formulations. Rather the instability noted seems to develop into what one may term an advance to a position 'beyond coexistence'. Perhaps the advance is less a recognition of the inadequacy of a particular dialectic to meet the formal requirement of

---

159 We noted earlier that only a formal place is open to the individual with regard to the efficacy of the Christ, if the community is denied place. The other side of the coin now becomes clear. Emil Brunner, 'Sören Kierkegaard's Budskap', *Janus*, 1939, p. 241, puts the matter well: 'Precisely this is the church: a society which consists of qualitative individuals, that is to say, of those who under personal responsibility stand before God . . . the church, that is the society of all those who have ceased being the mass, because they have become individuals.'

160 *S.V.* VII, p. 232 (*CUP*, p. 244).

meaningfulness, than a response to the material orientation imparted by the christological witness. In any case the movement of thought we have been following in the last several paragraphs can well serve to introduce us to the character of the advance, as the ground taken does represent the ascendancy of the synthesis rhythm in speaking of the effects of the Christ.

4. *Beyond Coexistence: The Issue of Faith*

From what Kierkegaard wrote it is impossible to conclude whether the withdrawal from the extremes of diastasis (encompassing an advance beyond the coexistence of the components for our discussion) is simply a literary movement away from a position which he never did in fact regard as a balanced statement of Christian truth. He can write persuasively:

> In my presentation severity is a dialectical moment in Christianity, but leniency is just as strongly represented; the first is represented poetically by the pseudonyms, the second personally by myself. Such a mode of presentation is required by a time which has taken Christianity in vain. But it is quite a different thing when a despairing man does not have anything more to say about Christianity than that it is the cruellest self-torture. In order to put an end to coquetry I had to introduce severity—introduced precisely for the sake of giving impetus toward the leniency of Christianity. Thus I have understood Christianity and my task. Had I only understood its frightful severity—then I would have kept silent.[161]

He can portray his function as a deliberately corrective one, and add that 'the next generation will always need an opposition to the corrective'.[162]

Yet we must be aware that this talk of a corrective rests on a particular definition of Christianity and the situation it confronts. The diastatic impulse may penetrate those definitions,[163] neutralizing the significance of any talk of corrective. We have to reckon too with Kierkegaard's claim that he has 'abated' up to 50 per cent of the 'height' of the Christian message.[164] We must accept the fact that Kierkegaard's intentions are not recoverable apart from his works

---

[161] *Pap.* X 2 A 525 (*Dru* 1072).

[162] *Pap.* X 5 A 106.

[163] One feels that such a penetration has occurred when Kierkegaard chastises the clergy for reversing the true order of Christian proclamation. For that order is seen to mean that the requirement is the universal and must be proclaimed, while indulgence is particular and is applied individually by God as a prerogative of his glory. *Pap.* X 3 A 72 (*Dru* 1097).

[164] *Pap.* X 6 B 247. See above, pp. 29–30, 39–40, on the extraordinary character of Anti-Climacus and on Kierkegaard's delight with the appropriateness of Anti-Climacus.

and that his works do not always speak with a single mind, despite the bold efforts of his retrospection to make it appear that they do so.[165] What is clear, if not obvious, however, is that his thought regarding the efficacy of the Christ does move beyond the highly complex statement of the co-existence of the components of certainty and contingency.

Even in those formulations in which the diastatic rhythm dominates another note sounds as well. The Christ suffered all his days, but the Ascension did bring satisfaction and reward.[166] And we do *expect happiness*, despite the tribulations of this present life.[167] In this way one formally honours the principle that 'divinely understood, Christianity is the highest good',[168] while one denies man access to the consciousness which provides the needed commensurability, or one at least points to how dangerous the human path to that good is. More significantly, these formulations centre in the Christ who means that God is present, even if the joy of God is future. Even the most radically diastatic description of the Christ as paradox does not deny the operative presence of God in the Christ.

The believer may come to be certain of that presence. Here the theme of certainty (which is so often the property of the diastatic tradition) functions as a check on the tendency of the components so to collide that no firm ground is set free from the dialectic of paradox. The believer is not both certain and uncertain at the same time. The man outside the circle of faith sees the absurd. But 'naturally it is a matter of course that for him who believes it is not the absurd'.[169] This very certitude means that the tension of faith is retained, but redefined: '. . . the immediate believer cannot remove himself from direct continuity with others, cannot understand that what for him is the most certain thing of all, blessedness, for others is and must be the absurd. . . . This is the tension, the tension of the life of faith, in which one must keep oneself.'[170]

One can even make a case for saying that the dialectic of the paradox itself calls forth from man an affirmation which moves him towards his true humanity. M. Diamond puts the matter so: 'The self that affirms the truth of this paradoxical affirmation in the passionate

---

[165] For a discussion of those efforts, see above, pp. 28–43.

[166] *S.V.* XII, pp. 349–50 (*SE*, pp. 85–86).

[167] *S.V.* IV, pp. 145–8 ('EE', *ED*, III, pp. 103–8). Cf. *S.V.* X, pp. 190–202 (*CDi*, pp. 197–209).

[168] *S.V.* IX, p. 188 (*WL*, p. 161).

[169] *Pap*, X 2 A 592 (*Dru* 1084).

[170] ibid. (ibid.).

subjectivity of faith maximizes the tensions sustained in its imagination and maximises its inwardness. Thus by that same process whereby he enters into an authentic relation to Christian truth the individual achieves his most authentic selfhood, and this intimate connection between personal and Christian authenticity is one reason why, in the face of the absurdity of its central paradox, Kierkegaard chose to affirm rather than to discard Christianity.'[171] One can state the point more concisely by saying that the Christian finds joy in his suffering. Thus the Christ responds to the pledge of discipleship: 'Very well, but I must require one thing more if thou art to remain with me, that thou must maintain that to be thus unhappy with me is nevertheless the highest happiness.'[172]

These formulations of Christian fulfilment do not move beyond the state of co-existence to speak of a satisfaction that is not immediately undercut by its contrary. Yet Kierkegaard does at times offer such speech. It is a God of love who is incognito in the Christ, and who surely risks that the beloved may not understand the incognito. Perhaps divine love must bear the incognito of cruelty,[173] because men do so skilfully speak of God's love in order to cover their desire to go their own way.[174] In the 'moral' attached to the first part of *TC* Kierkegaard both preserves this check against the human tendency to corrupt grace and still sings of the goodness of God:

> But if the Christian life is something so terrible and awful, how in the world can it occur to a man to accept Christianity?' Quite simply, and, if you want that too, quite in a Lutheran way: only the consciousness of sin can force, if I dare put it so (the force on the other side is grace), one into this awful situation. And in that very moment the Christian life transforms itself into pure leniency, grace, love, compassion. For any other point of view Christianity is and must be a sort of madness or the greatest horror. Admission is only through the consciousness of sin; to seek to enter by some other way is high treason against Christianity.[175]

That one enters the kingdom by the consciousness of sin suggests the reality of human need as much as the supremacy of God. And God shows his sovereignty by addressing that need. Here Kierkegaard moves beyond the dialectic of coexistence. He gives that move-

---

[171] Malcolm L. Diamond, 'Kierkegaard and Apologetics', *The Journal of Religion*, April 1964, p. 129.

[172] *S.V.* XII, p. 471 (*JY*, p. 212). See the whole second series of 'Christian Discourses' ('the joy in the fact that . . .'), *S.V.* X, pp. 97–160 (*CDi*, pp. 97–163). Cf. *S.V.* XIV, pp. 355–6 (*AC*, pp. 285–6), where Kierkegaard speaks of his own suffering, but still sees that as a sign of God's love.

[173] *S.V.* XII, p. 127–9 (*TC*, pp. 136–8).

[174] *Pap.* X 4 A 655.

[175] *S.V.* XII, pp. 64–65 (*TC*, p. 71).

ment striking statement in saying that God not only forgives, but actually forgets sins. Surely this statement does not seek to comment on the divine intelligence. It witnesses rather to the divine activity to heal man in the actualities of his temporal life: '. . . the possibility of faith presents itself to him in this form: whether he will believe by virtue of the absurd that God will help him temporally. (Here lie all the paradoxes. So the forgiveness of sins also means to be helped temporally, otherwise it is mere resignation, which can endure to bear the punishment, though still convinced that God is love. But faith in the forgiveness of sins is to believe that here in time the sin is forgotten by God, that it is really true that God forgets.)'[176]

The passage we have just cited was written after the decisive religious experience of 1848, though one can find remarkable parallels to it earlier.[177] Yet this theme does appear to have come home to Kierkegaard with new force in that experience. The theme does carry the suggestion that one flees to grace in order to 'use' grace.[178] God's 'forgetting' sin does not magically remove the consequences of sin in the process of time, but it does assure that the powers of the Creator of time-space are at work against the rule of sin.[179]

In this advance one may still join references to suffering and joy in a single sentence, but one does so to bear witness to the triumph of joy over suffering.[180] We do not deal here with a simple progression within immanence—one enters this joy through the narrow pass of the absurd.[181] Strenuous exertion is required to enter here—a discipline, a renunciation is required.[182] Yet Kierkegaard insists that one must not remain transfixed with the rigours which attend admittance to this new life: 'The way renunciation is usually understood has appeared to me to be an attempt to make God out a foolish

---

[176] *Pap.* VIII A 649 (*Dru* 753).

[177] *Pap.* VIII A 250 (*Dru* 694).

[178] *S.V.* XII, unnumbered preface (*TC*, p. 7).

[179] *Pap.* VII A 141 (*Dru* 606) strongly repudiates the magical understanding. The positive recognition that forgiveness involves a movement away from sin finds its basis in the paradox that man exists before God and that God is concerned with his sin. (*S.V.* XI, pp. 194ff. [*SD*, pp. 214ff.].) For further expression of the recognition so based, see *Pap.* III A 215, VIII A 673 (*Diary* 189), 674, X 1 A 433, 462.

[180] One may stress the suddenness of the change—see the passage from the moral in *TC* cited above on p. 241. Or one may emphasize the reality of the struggle —see *S.V.* VIII, pp. 398–416 (*GS*, pp. 138–69). In any case there is no question concerning the direction in which the thought is moving.

[181] So *Pap.* IV A 108 (*Dru* 445): Faith has hope for this life, but—be it noted—by virtue of the absurd.

[182] See *S.V.* XII, pp. 365ff. (*SE*, pp. 101ff.): The Spirit may bring life, hope, and love; but these gifts reach only the man who has died to himself.

pedant and God's relationship to man an eternal stinginess and perpetual pettiness. . . . But the real situation is entirely different; for renunciation, yea, the delight of renunciation, is precisely a lover's understanding with God.'[183] The absurd luminously marks the fact that one enters this new life by a leap. But one may look back and say: 'There is nothing terrifying about this category of the absurd. On the contrary, it is the category of courage and enthusism. Consider an analogy: love makes one blind. True. It is nevertheless a confusing thing to say that one becomes blind. You can, to be sure, reduce the blindness a little so that one does not become wholly blind. But take care lest in reducing the blindness you reduce also the love. True love blinds completely. And true faith breathes health and joy in the absurd.'[184]

By the passion of faith, then, an understanding with the 'reason' is reached.[185] One need not limit that understanding to general remarks about joy. Rather the advance to the issue of faith makes quite specific contact with the discussion of the ideal which is man's real good. We may recall that Kierkegaard's experience in Easter week of 1848 with the God who forgets sin issued in the cry: 'My whole nature is changed. My hiddenness and shut-in-ness (*Indesluttethed*, German: *Verschlossenheit*) is broken—I must speak.'[186] It seems fair to suggest that the passion of faith permits the revealing word to illumine life and so makes it possible for the believer to order his life and 'speak'.[187]

---

[183] *Pap.* X 4 A 673 (*Dru* 1279).

[184] *Pap.* X 6 B 79. It should be clear by now that this is not to claim that all difficulties disappear. Outward success is not at all sure, for example, but love knows an intrinsic reward. (*S.V.* IX, p. 346 [*WL*, p. 294].)

[185] *S.V.* IV, pp. 215, 220–1, 224 (*PF*, pp. 38, 43, 47).

[186] *Pap.* VIII A 640 (*Dru* 747).

[187] Cf. the remarks of two of Kierkegaard's readers who on other points find it quite possible to criticize Kierkegaard (and who do so from quite different points of view). Weiland, op. cit., pp. 88–90, writes: 'So one is compelled to say that a *Credo quia absurdum* cannot be found in Kierkegaard's works and that his *Credo . . . absurdum* means that belief is an "understanding" and a "knowledge" of the things which are an *absurdum* for the understanding, as it is a stumbling block unto the Jews and foolishness unto the Greeks. Just as the Jews are offended by the Cross, because it means the end of righteousness by the works of the law, so the understanding is offended by the Cross, because it means the end of its autonomy, which considers the Cross as an *absurdum* only . . . the Christian has made the transition; he believes the *absurdum* and it is no longer *absurdum* but the power of God and the wisdom of God (I Cor. 1.24).' And Diamond, 'Kierkegaard and Apologetics', *Journal of Religion*, April, 1964, p. 126, asks if Kierkegaard holds that faith must be blind and totally arbitrary: 'The fact is that once he has defended the passion needed to overcome the objective uncertainty engendered by the central Christian affirmation, Kierkegaard is prepared to use the entire panoply of biblical

This is a significant advance beyond coexistence, as far as the issue of faith is concerned. It is indeed significant enough to cause one to wonder if some revision of the description of the act of faith is undertaken through the momentum gained here. That does seem necessary. Jan Sperna Weiland asks our question: '. . . when the transition to the Transcendence of Christianity is really the way to the Truth, and when this transition is carried into effect by means of a "crucifixion" of the understanding, how can man then still come to this absurd act? . . . what sort of freedom is it by which man comes to crucify his understanding and to want his own destruction?'[188] We have noted that even in asserting the paradoxical character of the Christ, Kierkegaard claims reason as an ally in order that the paradox may not be confused with nonsense. Does he 'advance' to grant reason and/or experience some constructive role in the leap of faith?

One lacks the material for a solid affirmative answer. There is, of course, the appeal to 'evidence' suggested in the first section of this chapter. But there is not a like appeal emerging from the collision of the components discussed in the course of the chapter. If Christianity is to be 'first felt and then comprehended',[189] one could argue that the 'feeling', the passion of faith, in its own way comprehends something in the leap—that the leap is far from blind. If human eros emerges from its collision with divine agape in a corrected form,[190] but still emerges, one might expect a like description of the powers of human judgment. One must say, however, that Kierkegaard does not offer such argument or fulfil that expectation in any extensive way. That fact introduces a further question about the structure of Kierkegaard's thought. If the primitivity of the Christ-event and the power of the christological witness lie behind the 'advance' we have just traced, are there forces which impose the limits on that advance? Or more than that, can pressures be identified which have made impossible the realization of the apparent intention of Kierkegaard's christology? And is there evidence of a counter-influence, moving from the christological witness against those pressures? These are questions about the possibility of the Christ.

---

and theological insights in an effort to show that even though it is utterly implausible, Christianity does illumine life. One might state his position in the following way: "Surrender all pretence to objective certainty and to plausibility, and all these things shall be yours as well," where "these things" may be understood as standing for the cumulative wisdom of the Christian tradition.'

[188] Weiland, op. cit., p. 90.

[189] *Pap.* I A 94.

[190] On this point, see Lönning, op. cit., *passim.*, and especially p. 132.

VII

THE FOCUSING AND FORMATION
OF KIERKEGAARD'S REFLECTION IN HIS
DISCOURSE REGARDING THE GOD-MAN:
THE *POSSIBILITY* OF THE CHRIST

1. *The Impasse in Thought: The Extrinsic Assessment of Christological Possibility*

IT IS the systematic character of Kierkegaard's reflection which permits and requires us to ask of the possibility of the Christ. If his mind had not been the highly disciplined and supremely sensitive instrument it was, this line of inquiry would be at best irrelevant. But because Kierkegaard did value consistency and did essay to see things whole, we can relate his christology to the rest of his thought and be confident that the ground we tread in doing so was not foreign to him. Indeed the material at hand suggests that the 'relating' was far more internal to the development of his thought than subsequent to it. Again we may observe the 'constructive' activity of reflective faith.

Two questions identify the points at which Kierkegaard's intention to affirm the Christ as the God-Man may make direct contact with the rest of his religious thought: (1) Are God and man so understood as to make possible for Kierkegaard discourse concerning a harmonious meeting of God and man in the general sense of an affirmative human response to the divine intention? (2) Are God and man so understood as to make possible for Kierkegaard that more specific form of meeting in personal unity which may be designated as christological? Since we want to know not only *where* contact is made, but also *what* the nature of the contact may be, two other questions will be important to our analysis: (3) Is the christological witness so fashioned as to reflect and incorporate the prospects for that more general harmonious meeting of divine intention and human response? (4) Is the christological witness so fashioned as to reflect and incorporate the prospects for that more specific meeting in personal unity which may be designated as christological? These four questions will guide our discussion in this first section and force us to ask others in the sections which follow.

The reader will not expect us to set aside the categories which have structured our analysis of particulars in Kierkegaard's thought, when we come to the task of relating the particulars. Nor will he be surprised to find that the rhythms of synthesis and diastasis require somewhat (by no means totally) different responses to the questions proposed.

It has already been shown that the synthesis rhythm does attribute to man the freedom which is required for an affirmative answer to question (1). A meeting of God and man in the general sense of an affirmative human response to the divine challenge is made possible by the freedom Kierkegaard understands man to possess. That freedom does not refer merely to man's relationships to things 'below' him. It is explicitly posited in relationship to the ideal confronting man. And to speak of an ideal need not merely be to discourse about human conventions—it may be to identify the divine intention.

Both of these points may be illustrated by making reference to *The Concept of Dread*. While this work is described on its title page as a 'simple psychological-demonstrative deliberation',[1] it is no more *simply* psychological than it is simple. To say that it is 'oriented in the direction of the dogmatic problem of original sin'[2] errs on the side of understatement, for the work cannot be denied theological import. In any case crucial weight hardly needs to be placed on this example. We have seen that the affirmation of human freedom finds wide support in Kierkegaard's thought.[3] Furthermore, the thesis that man is free, rather than being a human fancy requiring correction from a theology informed by God's self-disclosure, is a claim to be made on the basis of the believer's knowledge of God. That affirmation is a celebration of the God who creates: 'Every man stands once, at the beginning, at the crossroad—this is his perfection and not his merit; where he stands at the conclusion (for at the conclusion it is impossible to stand at the crossroad) is his choice and his responsibility.'[4] And this affirmation of freedom envisions the movement from the mood of confession to the moment of obedience: '. . . when eternity says "thou shalt love", it assumes the responsibility for guaranteeing that it can be done.'[5]

---

[1] *S.V.* IV, p. 275 (*CD*, p. 1).
[2] ibid. (ibid.).
[3] See above, pp. 106–8, 130–4. The sources cited there are *CUP*; *SD*; *CD*; *CDi*; 'WLF', *GS*; *SE*; *TC*; *PV*; *E-O*; and *Pap*.
[4] *S.V.* X, pp. 25–26 (*CDi*, p. 23).
[5] *S.V.* IX, p. 44 (*WL*, p. 35). Cf. ibid., p. 79 (ibid., p. 65): '. . . eternity, which

But Kierkegaard's eye does not remain fixed on the possibility of human response; it receives also the testimony of actuality. The glory of human freedom ('this is his perfection and not his merit') marks the depravity of human failure. But perhaps one should take one's starting point in the predicate and go in quest of the systematic implications of that 'depravity'. Will not the constant recurrence of failure lead to the revision of the preliminary definition of man as free? It need not do so, if the experience of failure itself contains data witnessing to an alternative to sin. That is, of course, the insistent argument of *CD*: 'Now it is unethical to say that innocence must be annulled; for even if it were annulled the moment this word is uttered, even then ethics forbids us to forget that it can only be annulled by guilt.'[6] This argument is also the concern of Climacus in his effort to measure the Christian advance beyond 'Socrates':

> In so far as the learner exists, he is after all created, and hence God must have given him the condition for understanding the truth (for otherwise he would earlier have been only an animal and that teacher who gave him the truth with the condition for understanding the truth first made him a man); but in so far as the moment is to have decisive significance (and if this is not assumed, we remain standing, after all, with the Socratic principle), he must be without the condition, and thus he must have been deprived of it. That cannot have come about by an act of God (for that is a contradiction), nor by accident (for it is a contradiction that what is lower should be able to overcome the higher). It must therefore be due to himself. If he could have lost the condition in such a way that it was not due to himself, and if he could be in the situation of loss without that being due to himself, then he would have possessed the condition only accidentally, which is a contradiction, since the condition for understanding the truth is an essential condition. Untruth is therefore not merely without the truth, but is polemic towards the truth, which is expressed by saying that the learner has himself forfeited the condition and is forfeiting it.[7]

---

speaks of the highest, calmly assumes that every man can do it, and asks therefore only whether he did it.'

[6] *S.V.* IV, p. 307 (*CD*, p. 32). This passage is not to be understood as suggesting that, while innocence can be retained, that can occur only by holding back from any actualization at all. That thought is suggested in *CD* and will be discussed below. That it is not the point of the above passage is evident by the context's emphasis on temptation to good as well as to evil (ibid., p. 311n. [ibid., p. 36n.]) and by the observation that the dread which predisposes to the actualizing leap is not an imperfection (ibid., p. 323 [ibid., p. 47]). Thus Torsten Bohlin, *Kierkegaards dogmatiska Aaskaadning i dess historiska Sammanhang* (Stockholm: Svenska Kyrkans Diakonistyrelses, 1925), p. 133, rightly insists that for the author of *CD* the possibility must remain that some individual has not sinned.

[7] *S.V.* IV, pp. 184–5 (*PF*, p. 10). For further expression of this note see ibid., p. 214 (ibid., p. 37); ibid., p. 410 (*CD*, p. 129); *S.V.* XI, pp. 130–1 (*SD*, pp. 149–50); and *Pap.* II A 310 (*Dru* 238).

That sin is rebellion, rather than inadequate endowment or accidental misfortune, reinforces the judgment of possibility. Hence it is by no means a matter of academic pedantics when Climacus writes: 'Ethics focuses on the individual, and ethically understood it is every individual's task to become a whole man; just as it is the presupposition of ethics that everyone is born in such a condition that he can become one. If no one attains that, the principle is not changed; that the demand is there is the principal point. . . .'[8]

Still the possibility of obedience imbedded in the consciousness of rebellion remains only a subjective datum which is the more easily labelled illusion as the sovereignty of sin perpetuates itself. Here is where the christological witness makes itself felt. We have said that we want to ask: Is the christological witness so fashioned as to reflect and incorporate the prospects for that more general harmonious meeting of divine intention and human response (question 3 above)? Now we have come to the point where we can see that the christological witness does more than reflect—it actually reinforces an affirmation which otherwise might be hard put indeed to maintain itself. Surely that is Kierkegaard's point in turning the Christian in his temptation to the Christ with the word, 'he, too, was tempted thus'.[9] It ought to be clear by now that the imitation of the Christ —whether one likes it or not—is a central theme in Kierkegaard.[10]

The Christ is more, of course, for Kierkegaard than a restatement of the possibility of human obedience and a specification of that possibility by illustration. Man needs more than that. We have seen that Kierkegaard does not affirm the reality of the act of freedom only to deny that act the reality of winning consequences beyond itself in the temporal process. Rather Climacus writes: 'In so far as the learner is in untruth, but is so due to himself . . . it might seem that he was free; for to be with oneself is certainly freedom. And yet he is certainly unfree and bound and exiled; for to be free from the truth is certainly to be exiled, and to be exiled by one's own self is certainly to be bound.'[11] Not that man somehow changes his whole nature by an act of that nature. To retain the language of Climacus: even our 'non-being has being in it'.[12] Thus 'Christianity assumes that subject-

---

[8] S.V. VII, p. 300 (CUP, p. 309).
[9] See particularly the long quote from S.V. XI, pp. 256-7 ('HP', CDi, pp. 366-7), quoted above on p. 181.
[10] See above, p. 184, especially notes 43-44.
[11] S.V. IV, p. 185 (PF, p. 11).
[12] S.V. IV, p. 189 (PF, p. 14): '. . . the non-being which precedes the rebirth contains more being than the non-being which preceded birth'. Cf. S.V.VII,

ivity, as the potentiality for the appropriation of this good [of an eternal happiness], is the possibility for its acceptance'.[13] But Christianity does not 'assume that subjectivity, without further ado, is all ready, or even has, without further ado, a real conception of the significance of such a good'.[14]

It is to this state of need that Kierkegaard addresses his witness to the unique meeting of God and man in the Christ: 'So it is not just a matter of course that Christ is the pattern and I merely must be willing to imitate him. In the first place, I need his help in order to imitate him; and in the second place, in so far as he is the saviour and redeemer of the race, I cannot, of course, imitate him.'[15] The witness to that unique meeting itself finds an enabling preparation in other affirmations of Kierkegaard.[16] We mention five. (1) That the world of time-space is not essentially opposed to God. (2) That God does act in the world of time-space—quite apart from Jesus of Nazareth. (3) That in his activity God loves men and boldly wills to be loved freely by man in turn. (4) That the self's relationships are constitutive of its reality (in part). (5) That the self's reality changes as and because its relationships change in this world of time-space.

All of these affirmations have already been documented with reference to Kierkegaard's works and analysed with reference to their meaning quite apart from their relationship to christology. Chapter five has shown how Kierkegaard's witness to the uniquely christological meeting of God and man incorporates these theses. Indeed one might suspect that his christology itself inspires these statements. We have hinted already and will show more clearly later that there are grounds for honouring that suspicion. But one cannot convincingly place on Kierkegaard's lips the slogan 'all theology is christology'. That becomes clear most quickly when one observes those strands in his thought which point to the impossibility of the Christ.

---

pp. 257–73 (*CUP*, pp. 267–82). In *S.V.* IV, p. 417 (*CD*, p. 135), Kierkegaard denies that one can succeed in 'killing the eternal entirely', for 'however much one may deny it, one still does not slip free from it entirely'. Thus even the demonica is not absolutely evil (ibid., p. 390 [ibid., p. 109]). And in *S.V.* IX, p. 119 (*WL*, p. 101) Kierkegaard writes: '. . . I am willing to vouch for this understanding of worldly love, that it is not entirely evil, as it is sometimes passionately represented to be, or entirely untainted; but to a certain degree good and bad. But according to the Christian understanding this "to a certain degree" is surely evil.'
[13] *S.V.* VII, p. 105 (*CUP*, p. 116).
[14] Ibid. (ibid.).
[15] *Pap.* X 1 A 132. Cf. X 1 A 134 (*Dru* 887), X 6 B 241.
[16] Here we introduce one line of response to the second and fourth questions from p. 245 above.

The diastatic rhythm tends to move towards an extreme position in which the independence of God from other beings is secured by the inclusion of all being within God. The emphasis then must rest on the whole rather than the parts. Yet Kierkegaard's works never long fit the mould of a classical monism such as Spinoza makes available. He is far too committed to the reality of individuality to accept such a pattern. With the reality of man as a given, the diastatic impulse to separate God and man finds its expression in a very dark reading of the human condition. If that impulse cannot deny the fact of the divine command without turning directly against its own intention to affirm God's lordship, it can point persuasively to the human failure to fulfil that command.

However, one may react to this settlement of the question of systematic responsibility, Kierkegaard's thought does follow this course. We are told that 'everyone, the dearest (alas, the dearest!), the most honest (alas, the most honest!), is nevertheless, when all is said and done, a coward, a traitor, a hypocrite'.[17] Such a statement pushes beyond the boundaries of descriptive generalization and invites the suggestion that the divine requirement is 'such that no man perfectly fulfil it'.[18]

The universality of sin provides sufficient grounds to support the judgment that 'our whole earthly existence is a kind of illness'.[19] But there are indications that this earth is not merely the locale of universal sin, but its cause as well. Thus it is in that principle of distinction which (it would surely seem) 'makes it possible that in the particular instance one can be guilty or not guilty',[20] that Kierkegaard finds the clue to 'total guilt'. He writes: 'He who totally or essentially is guiltless cannot be guilty in the particular instance; but he who is totally guilty can very well be guiltless in the particular instance. So then, not only by being guilty in a particular instance does a man denounce himself as essentially guilty (*totum est partibus suis prius*), but also by being guiltless in the particular instance (*totum est partibus suis prius*).'[21]

The very particularity of human action seems to be charged with

---

[17] *S.V.* XII, p. 444 (*JY*, p. 183).
[18] ibid., p. 426 (ibid., p. 164).
[19] *S.V.* VII, p. 392 (*CUP*, p. 403). Cf. ibid., pp. 157–211 (ibid., pp. 169–224). Cf. *S.V.* X, p. 289 (*CDi*, p. 287): '. . . to be a man is to be a sinful man.'
[20] *S.V.* VII, p. 461 (*CUP*, p. 471).
[21] ibid., pp. 461–2 (ibid., p. 471). [Italics his.] It is passages such as these that call forth Bohlin's charge (op. cit., p. 214) that Climacus falls into the Flacian heresy of making sin man's substance.

guilt in these formulations. *CD* offers passages which confirm this impression, despite the fact that one of the first things one must say about this book is that it is intent to reject the suggestion that man sins necessarily. But the diastatic rhythm is present beneath the surface of the argument. Thus one may make each man an Adam, whose freedom is that he need not act,[22] but whose necessity is that he can only act in sin. Haufniensis writes: 'To let freedom begin as a *liberum arbitrium* (which nowhere is to be found, as Leibnitz says) . . . which can just as easily choose the good as the evil, is to make every explanation radically impossible. To talk about good and evil as the objects of freedom is to render finite both freedom and the concepts good and evil.'[23] While aware that one does not 'explain' the origin of sin by appealing to a will free to choose between good and evil, Kierkegaard at least 'reduces' the mystery involved by arguing that 'the opposite of freedom is guilt and it is the highest thing about freedom that it unceasingly only has to do with itself, that in its possibility it projects guilt, and then posits it by itself, and if guilt is actually posited, freedom posits it by itself'.[24]

This dynamic lies behind the tendency in Kierkegaard to identify sexuality as sinfulness. If it is so that 'without sin there is no sexuality, and without sexuality there is no history',[25] then one may grant a first man the fact of alternatives and posit the necessity of sin as the consequence of sinful choice. If Adam had not sinned he would have become eternal.[26]

These turnings of thought again seem to centre in the theme of metaphysical opposition between God and man.[27] Yet the diastatic

[22] *S.V.* IV, pp. 380–1 (*CD*, p. 100): 'We have nowhere been guilty of the foolishness which supposes that man *must* sin, . . . to want to say that man sins necessarily is to want to lay the circle of the leap out in a straight line.' [Italics his.]

[23] ibid. (ibid.). [Italics his.]

[24] ibid., p. 377 (ibid., p. 97).

[25] ibid., p. 319 (ibid., p. 44). See above, pp. 165–8, for the logic leading to the ethic of racial suicide. We have shown that this tendency is countered by another. That other finds expression in *CD*, and in the connection indicated. Thus see ibid., p. 337 (ibid., p. 61): 'The sexual as such is not the sinful.'

[26] This sentence expresses the conclusion towards which the argument of ibid., pp. 350–63 (ibid., pp. 73–83) tends, though Kierkegaard resists this conclusion in suggesting that to argue so is to speak 'by way of accommodation and foolishly'. ibid., p. 363 (ibid., p. 83).

[27] Indeed they permit one to attach to Kierkegaard's thought the more common existentialist statement of incapability. Thus Walter Schulz, *Die Vollendung des deutschen Idealismus in der Spätphilosophie* (Stuttgart: Kohlhammer, 1955), pp. 274–5, shows how the judgment of impossibility follows if one defines the ideal over against aesthetic immediacy 'as the annulling of every immediacy in and through the pure (that is to say, the unconditioned) self-reconciliation': 'But this self-reconciliation

intention in Kierkegaard is essentially religious in character. Anti-Climacus puts it well in *TC*: 'Only the consciousness of sin is absolute respect, and just for this reason, because Christianity demands absolute respect, Christianity must and will appear as madness or horror to every other point of view, precisely in order that the infinite qualitative emphasis may fall upon the principle that only the consciousness of sin is the entrance . . .'[28] This passage also hints that the sovereign Lord before whom one bows is gracious. Anti-Climacus does not leave the matter in doubt: only through absolute respect can one 'see Christianity's leniency, and love, and compassion'.[29] This brings us to ask: if the prospects for a more general meeting of God and man in the sense of an affirmative human response to the divine intention are non-existent, what of that more specific christological form of meeting in personal unity?

Any hopes the reader may have had for smoother going are ill grounded and poorly rewarded at best. So long as the metaphysical statement of the general opposition of the eternal God and temporal man is in effect, no loophole is visible which would permit a particular meeting of the two—no matter how special (i.e. particular). Chapters five[30] and six[31] have shown that the christological witness at times directly incorporates such a statement of opposition and accepts (welcomes?) the accompanying judgment of impossibility. Even when the formulation does not focus on metaphysical opposition the judgment of impossibility is found to be internal to the very witness to the Christ. Thus one may deny the humanity of Jesus,[32] or define that humanity as nothingness, or assign it the task of realizing its nothingness.[33] Or one may emphasize that the work of forgiveness which the Christ brings separates God and man all the more decisively.[34] Perhaps that is how a God who is free to be related or

---

is essentially impossible, considering the structure of existence itself. The self in existence cannot reconcile itself over against *every* immediacy, because it itself always *is* immediate.' Thus existence reveals itself as the contradiction of 'immediate self-reconciliation'. [Italics his.] One can put the matter another way by saying that the requirement is that the temporal become the eternal. The definition of the terms, then, secures the impossibility of any fulfilment.

[28] *S.V.* XII, p. 65 (*TC*, p. 72). Cf. Gregor Malantschuk, *Kierkegaard's Way to the Truth*, trans. Mary Michelson (Minneapolis: Augsburg, 1963), pp. 59–60.

[29] *S.V.* XII, p. 65 (*TC*, p. 72).

[30] See above, p. 188, especially note 56.

[31] See above, pp. 218–29.

[32] On the docetic tendency in Kierkegaard's thought, see above, pp. 175–82.

[33] See above, p. 177, note 15, and pp. 186–8.

[34] See above, p. 192, note 81.

not—quite as he likes[35]—'meets' man. The unreality of such a 'meeting' appropriately restates the judgment of impossibility issuing from the context which diastatic themes in Kierkegaard's thought provide for his christology.

An impasse in thought clearly emerges as the result of this extrinsic assessment of the possibility of the Christ. It is possible and it is not possible for God and man to meet in the Christ. This impasse is explicitly recognized by Kierkegaard as far as the possibility of an affirmative human response to the divine intention is concerned. The Christian faith rejects the Socratic identification of sin with ignorance. Starting down the path opened by recognizing the difference between knowing and doing, Christiantity 'comes to show that sin lies in the will, it comes to the concept of defiance; and then in order to make the end fast, the dogma of original sin is added'.[36] Climacus tips this recognition in the direction of necessity, while still registering protest against such necessity, when he writes:

. . . by coming into being the individual becomes another, or in the moment he shall come into being he becomes another by coming into being. . . . From eternity the individual is not a sinner, so when the eternally planned being, who in birth comes into being, becomes a sinner in birth or is born as a sinner: then it is existence (*Existents*) which so surrounds the individual that every communication of immanence by withdrawal to the eternal along the path of recollection is broken off, and the predicate 'sinner', which is first applied, but is immediately applied at the moment of coming into being, gets such a paradoxically overpowering power that the act of coming into being makes him into another.[37]

Surely this is to offer us the dilemma that Reinhold Niebuhr made so famous: that sin is inevitable, but not necessary. Perhaps it lays bare the real impasse behind Niebuhr's formulation: that sin is necessary, but not necessary.[38]

[35] See above, p. 139, note 44.

[36] *S.V.* XI, p. 204 (*SD*, p. 224). Cf. ibid., p. 206 (ibid., p. 226): 'Thus, christianly understood, sin lies in the will, not in the intellect; and this corruption of the will extends beyond the consciousness of the individual. That is wholly consistent, for otherwise the question how sin began would have to come up with regard to every individual.'

[37] *S.V.* VII, pp. 508–9 (*CUP*, p. 517). In this passage Kierkegaard's choice of words conveys the impasse, as he moves from the general neutral term *Tilblivelse* ('coming into being') to the sharpened human state *Existents* ('existence'). See above p. 102, note 11. Cf. ibid., pp. 464–5 (ibid., p. 474).

[38] Reinhold Niebuhr, *The Nature and Destiny of Man* (2 vols., London: Nisbet, 1941), I, pp. 266–76. For a discussion of Kierkegaard's influence behind this formulation in contemporary theological thought, see Robert Scharlemann, 'Man: A Question to Himself', *Dialog*, Summer, 1964, pp. 172–8. The contemporaneity of the theme is not decisively beclouded by the uncertainty surrounding the question whether Niebuhr has continued to endorse this formulation. In the Scribner

In the passage from the *Postscript* which we have cited in the preceeding paragraph Kierkegaard adjoins a christological assertion to the description of how coming into existence makes man another: 'This is the consequence of the God's appearance in time, which prevents the individual from relating himself backwards to the eternal, since now he comes forwards into time to become eternal by relationship to the God in time.'[39] We may leave aside for now the question of the order of priority of the assertions made here. Their connection is the immediate concern of this discussion. And it is the case that an impasse in thought also emerges from an inquiry into the possibility of a special meeting of God and man in the Christ.

At times Kierkegaard seems to accept that judgment and even make it constitutive of his christology. Thus Anti-Climacus writes of the doctrine of the God-man: 'Never anywhere has any doctrine on earth actually brought God and man so close together as Christianity; neither could anyone else but God do it, every human discovery remains a dream, an uncertain imagination. But neither has anywhere a doctrine so painstakingly protected itself against the most shocking of all blasphemies, that God having taken this step, it then should be taken in vain as though the process ended in one thing: God and man—never anywhere has any doctrine protected itself against this as Christianity has, which protects itself by the help of the offence.'[40] Thus while Kierkegaard finds the claim of God set before man powerfully in the paradigmatic manhood of the Christ, he indicts Christendom for taking in vain the doctrine of the God-Man

---

Library edition of 1964 Niebuhr says of his use of 'the traditional religious symbols of the "Fall" and of "original sin" ': 'My only regret is that I did not realize that the legendary character of the one and the dubious connotations of the other would prove so offensive to the modern mind, that my use of them obscured my essential thesis and my "realistic" rather than "idealistic" interpretation of human nature.' (p. viii) Having said that, he lets the text stand, however. See also his response in *Reinhold Niebuhr*, ed. Charles W. Kegley and Robert W. Bretall, Library of Living Theology, Vol. II (New York: Macmillan, 1956), pp. 432–3, and his conversation with Paul Tillich at this point in *Reinhold Niebuhr: A Prophetic Voice in Our Time*, Harold R. Landon, ed. (Greenwich, Conn.: Seabury, 1962), pp. 34–38, 120. The reader will know that while we have stressed the role of metaphysical categories in the construction of the formulations, it is very clear that Niebuhr wishes to avoid all such categories. One may feel Tillich is right, after all, in his comment, 'This is not an escape from ontology', though one may want to stop short of his next word: '. . . but what is behind it is good ontology: namely, the unity of universal destiny combined with personal freedom and responsibility' (ibid., p. 37).

[39] *S.V.* VII, p. 509 (*CUP*, p. 517). On Kierkegaard's use of the phrase 'the God', see Niels Thülstrup's introduction to the *Fragments* (Princeton, 1962).

[40] *S.V.* XI, p. 227 (*SD*, p. 248).

when 'the qualitative difference between God and man is pantheistically abolished' by appeal to that doctrine.[41]

To conceive dialectics of this sort may be within the mind's capacity, but to construct such dilemmas and to confess their truth is not natural to the self. Nor can we suppose it likely that Kierkegaard, as the highly disciplined and sensitive thinker he was, found such an occupation particularly attractive. That he so often seems fully aware of the pain his contradictions cause the reason may rightly suggest that he has gone before the reader into such suffering. The material involved suggests that he writes as he does, not out of sado-masochistic glee, but because some fundamental commitment calls him to this task. In examining that commitment we may encounter not only the force which brings him to write of the Christ, despite the impasse in thought, but also the power which permits his reflection to move away from the dead centre of the dialectics sketched in this section.

2. *The Irreducible in Faith: The Primitivity of the Christological Witness*

The impelling reality of the Christ for Kierkegaard now becomes clear in three ways.

(1) The irreducible faith in the Christ redeems the judgment of possibility from the realm of theory and the mood of stubborn fantasy by witnessing to the actuality of a genuinely human affirmative response to the divine intention. Furthermore, this figure so presses in on the writer that he must speak of the presence of God at this point in a wholly extraordinary sense. In doing so, however, he can employ categories and build on affirmations which are at hand from other areas of his reflection. Thus his confession comes to be lucid as well as passionate. The christological confession itself, however, is not derivable from its wider systematic context. One may say that God and man are 'bent' towards each other without going on to speak of the God-Man. Indeed it is fully possible that much of the influence passed the other way in the development of Kierkegaard's thought.

(2) The irreducible faith in the Christ penetrates the judgment of impossibility to affirm the truth of the paradoxical claim that God and man have met in both the more general and the specifically christological senses. The Pattern is cut of real human flesh, though the design traced seems an impossibility. In him 'that which can become historical only against its own nature' *did* become historical.[42]

[41] ibid. (ibid.).
[42] S.V. VII, pp. 504–7 (CUP, pp. 512–15).

Even when Kierkegaard's christology reflects the most extreme strains of the diastatic rhythm, it never becomes fictionalist, but only pitches its paradox the higher. We have also noted how a particular emphasis on the death of the Christ characterizes the diastatic strain in the christology.[43] That emphasis is not a proof of the power of Kierkegaard's deductive reason, but is another witness to the primitivity of the Christ-event as a formative potency in his life and reflection. We shall see that this intense interest in the death of the Christ becomes a point of contact with the synthesis strand in the christological witness.

(3) The irreducible faith in the Christ impels Kierkegaard to speak of the Christ and that speech focuses and forms the rhythms of Kierkegaard's reflection. In the preceding paragraph we have seen clearly that the christological witness does not merely *focus* the diastatic rhythm, it *forms* it—or better, *re-forms* it—in clothing the judgment of impossibility with the truth claim of the paradox. Thus we see that the power of the Christ-event not only brings Kierkegaard to his witness, despite the impasse in thought concerning the possibility of the Christ. It exercises initiative over against the impasse. In the power of the Christ-event for Kierkegaard lies the explanation not only for the fact that he confesses the Christ, but also (in part) for the form and substance of that confession. In recognizing in the christology a source as well as a recipient of systematic influence, we anticipate the task of the next section. In that section we follow Kierkegaard as he moves beyond the repetition and even the reformation of the judgments of possibility and impossibility. That section does well 'follow' the present one, for such a movement would constitute an impressive testimony to the independent power of the Christ-event for Kierkegaard.

3. *The Integration of Thought and Faith: The Assimilation of Christology and its Ascendancy*

If the impossible Christ *must* be confessed, is it possible somehow to assimilate that confession within the boundaries of one's thought? The answer would seem to be 'No'. The impossibility involved is not changed by shifting the attention from the intrinsic meaning components of the assertion to the relationship of the assertion to other assertions. It is precisely the 'relatedness' of the assertion in question which is assessed in the judgment of impossibility. Yet the diastatic

[43] See above, pp. 191–2.

strain in Kierkegaard's thought does incorporate a determined effort to assimilate the impossible truth of the Christ. The reader may come to conclude that this effort is a failure—indeed Kierkegaard's own works in a way express that judgment, as we shall see. Nevertheless, the effort to assimilate the Christ is worthy of close attention, not only because it witnesses to the power of the Christ-event for Kierkegaard's reflection, but also because it points ahead to the systematic results issuing from that power and so to the systematic bearing of the event itself, as understood by Kierkegaard.

If the diastatic witness to the independence of God is to be honoured, the Christ must not be held to represent a reaction on God's part to man's sin. Climacus well shows the way:

. . . God needs no disciple in order to understand himself; and no occasion can so serve as an occasion for him that there is as much significance in the occasion as in the resolve. What then can move him to make his appearance? He must move himself and continue to be what Aristotle says of him *akinētos panta kinei*. But if he moves himself, then it is certainly not some need which moves him, as if he could not endure silence, but had to break out in speech. But if he moves himself, and is not moved by need, what other than love can it be that moves him? For love does not find the satisfaction of its need outside itself, but within itself. His resolve, which stands in no equal reciprocal relation to the occasion, must be from eternity, even though when realized in time it becomes precisely the Moment. . . .[44]

If God's resolve is eternal, it involves him no more in successiveness than in dependence. Nor need one suppose the divine purpose to involve the doubleness, the distinction, of creative *and* redemptive intentions. Rather let the Christ be seen as the consummation of the creative intention of God: 'When God had created the world he looked upon it; and behold, it was very *good*: when Christ died on the cross the word was uttered: "It is *consummated*".'[45] Another journal reference claims nothing other than the deity of the Christ as the point at which the continuity of creation and incarnation becomes clear: 'The creation was really only completed when God included himself in it. Before Christ God was certainly in the creation, but as an invisible sign, like the watermark in paper. But the creation was completed by the incarnation in that God included himself in it.'[46]

This association of creation and God's self-manifestation may seem

---

[44] *S.V.* IV, pp. 193-4 (*PF*, p. 18). [Italics his.]

[45] *Pap.* II A 93 (*Dru* 126). [Italics his.]

[46] *Pap.* X 1 A 605 (*Dru* 949). These journal references provide a background against which to view the *Postscript*'s statement (*S.V.* VII, p. 514 [*CUP*, p. 523]) that 'Christianity did not come into the world during the childhood of mankind, but in the fullness of time'.

foreign to the diastatic impulse. It is hard to claim that the true greatness of the creator's omnipresence lies in his invisibility[47] and yet argue that the creator's work is completed in his open self-manifestation in the Christ. Perhaps that is not so troubling a point, if the 'open self-manifestation' bears the character of offence. Yet the two formulations still seem to move in quite different directions. One would want to ask: 'In just what sense is God's intention to create an intention to reveal himself?'

But another problem presses more urgently. Christians who have found this world wanting have not limited their complaint to the charge that God's presence is less than self-evident. They have supposed themselves to find something else present—and one would have thought that the diastatic tradition had more than a casual investment in its judgment of human depravity. Is this really a problem? May not the assimilation effort draw upon the investment by finding in the universality and necessity of sin a parable glorifying the Christ 'who is more than an individual':[48] '. . . it is not in the interest of ethics to make all except Adam into troubled and interested spectators of guilt, but not guilty, nor is it in the interest of dogmatics to make all into interested and sympathetic spectators of reconciliation but not as reconciled.'[49]

The reality of sin marks the 'completion' of creation in the Christ a transformation of creation.[50] But the transformation does not constitute a reaction by God to some development external to himself. The eternal resolve is one: the goodness of creation is consummated in the Christ.[51] What is being suggested is that it is in the atonement that 'the determination original sin becomes clear'.[52] And what is it that one sees in that clarification? One sees that 'it belongs to the imperfection of everything human that man can only attain his desire by passing through its opposite . . . through sin one first sights blessedness'.[53] To thus incorporate sin within the divine intention is not to deface God, so long as a universal redemption is

---

[47] *S.V.* V, p. 92 ('MN', *ED*, IV, pp. 25–26). Cf. *S.V.* XIV, p. 286 ('UG', *SE*, pp. 230–1); *S.V.* VII, pp. 204–5 (*CUP*, pp. 217–18).

[48] *S.V.* IV, p. 305n. (*CD*, p. 30n.).

[49] ibid., p. 308 (ibid., p. 33).

[50] So *S.V.* VIII, p. 338 (*GS*, p. 50) says of the 'humblest man': '. . . it was he who was with the father from eternity; it was he, who came in the fullness of time; it was he, who brought to completion what the father had begun, who completed creation and transformed the shape of the world.'

[51] See above, p. 257, note 45.

[52] *S.V.* IV, p. 385 (*CD*, p. 105).

[53] *Pap.* III A 112 (*Dru* 358).

sure. Rather the fall is blessed, for 'how could all be able to be saved, if all did not need to be saved, and how could all need to be saved, if the demand were not such that no one can perfectly fulfil it'.[54] One can still 'distribute' the actualization of that redemption in time: 'As little as Christianity came into the world during the childhood of mankind, but in the fullness of time; so little does Christianity in its decisive form fit every age in a man's life.'[55]

This effort to assimilate the Christ is striking, but it is beset by serious strain. If metaphysical opposition is the dominant theme in the diastatic context, the difficulties are scarcely camouflaged. The note of movement, so alien to a timeless God, involved in the act of creation is embarrassingly underlined in an appeal to a redemptive second stage of creation (or to a third in the appropriation of redemption). If the reply is that the successiveness of God's activity is only a matter of the semblance of this time, one must ask what reality supports the semblance. An answer is hard to come by without defiling God by linking him with some world of time.

The difficulties become still more troublesome, if we recall the religious intention behind the diastatic rhythm.[56] If it is the separateness which supports authority, the distance demanded by sovereignty, which is Kierkegaard's concern, the assimilation effort which we have traced will hardly win his approval for long. For the strategy is to assimilate the Christ's irreducible reality by assimilating man, man's sin and man's redemption within God. Only then is God's independence really secure. But how then can the moral and religious intention of the diastatic rhythm be fulfilled? Man's

---

[54] *S.V.* XII, p. 371 (*JT*, p. 164). Indeed occasionally the stages of creation collapse almost totally into one. So in treating the verse 'she was forgiven much because she loved much', Kierkegaard writes: '. . . the fact of needing much forgiveness becomes an expression for the perfection of love.' (*S.V.* III, p. 293 ['LC', *ED*, 1, p. 88].) This point of view is also active in supplying the judgment 'paradox' to the insistence that 'sin is a position'. (*S.V.* XI, pp. 207–11 [*SD*, pp. 227–31].) The journal passage cited above, note 53, closes its comment on the 'imperfection of everything human' as follows: 'And consequently the imperfection lies not so much in the contradiction as in the fact that one cannot see the thing and its opposite *simultaneously*.' [Italics his.] Hayo Gerdes, *Das Christus Verstandnis des jungen Kierkegaard* (Itzehoe: 'Die Spur', 1962), p. 50, seems to address this development in Kierkegaard when he emphasizes that for Kierkegaard to believe in Christ meant 'to believe that God is at the same time love and omnipotence'. The problem, of course, lies in the *zugleich*. For a succinct comparison of the 'blessed fall' motif in Kierkegaard, Hegel, and Baader, see Arild Christensen, 'Felix Culpa-Motivet hos Sören Kierkegaard', *Meddelelser fra Sören Kierkegaard Selskabet*, August, 1954, pp. 17–20.

[55] *S.V.* VII, p. 514 (*CUP*, p. 523).

[56] See above, pp. 102–5.

responsibility to God becomes a purely local concern within the economy of the divine life—though it is not at all clear that the metaphysical development of the diastatic principle is prepared to grant entrance to the principle of distinction necessary to sustain even such a concern. Even if 'man' has some kind of modal independence, how can he muster any sense of responsibility, upon being told that God's sovereign will is universally sure?

Kierkegaard seems to see his thought tending in this direction. He proposes: 'My hearer, let us for a moment speak foolishly . . . let us then foolishly assume that God in heaven was like a weak man, who could not once find it in his heart to deny someone eternal happiness, whether he wanted it or not; so weak in fact that he, as it were, forced it on everyone, whether he wished it or not.'[57] He then steps within this 'foolish speech' in quest of some justification for moral and religious responsibility:

> Even if you believed that you had your blessedness ever so assured, you would yet still feel a deep shame every time you compared your life with those whose concern for this matter time after time filled many a moment, many an hour, whether it was the wish which occupied their attention, or the heart which was moved in gratitude, or the mind which they disciplined according to their best insight and with every power, to be well-pleasing to the giver and by which they prepared for the transition. For a sudden transition is a horrible venture; one has sometimes portrayed how horrible it must be for the intoxicated suddenly to awaken with his mind confused; one has painted the terror which must have gripped the rich man when he awakened in hell; but if it were the case with heaven's happiness that the moment a man breathed his last he awakened to this happiness, a man whose thoughts had been as far from it as the abyss is from heaven: it seems to me that this man would have to die again of shame, must wish himself away again, because heaven's happiness and his unworthiness could not stand each other. . . .[58]

It is difficult to find this argument for an aesthetic—or even baldly psychological—justification convincing. In any case it is clear in the very context of these passages that Kierkegaard was not convinced by such appeals. True, he does claim that 'it has been shown that a man would not dare become indifferent to the thought of heaven's happiness'.[59] But it is 'foolish speech'. And he moves quickly to let the fruit of that speech be an *a fortiori* argument linked with the 'serious word of seriousness, "that God is not mocked".'[60]

---

[57] *S.V.* IV, p. 142 ('EE', *ED*, III, p. 100).
[58] ibid., p. 143 (ibid., p. 101).
[59] ibid. (ibid.).
[60] ibid. (ibid., p. 102). Kierkegaard combines the several objections we have identified, when Climacus develops the component of the learner's responsibility

What one actually witnesses in Kierkegaard's thought at this point is not the assimilation of the christological witness to the diastatic rhythm, but the ascendancy of that witness within that rhythm. A journal passage from 1837 already eloquently anticipates that result: 'The birth of Christ is not only an event on earth but also in heaven. . . .'[61] Kierkegaard's interest in the kenosis motif also suggests the ascendancy of christology. One might suppose that such a formulation is introduced to free God from involvement in time. And something of that sort does perhaps lie behind the statement of the problem which the kenosis formulation addresses. But the *direction* of the formulation in Kierkegaard is clear:

> God's servant-form is . . . not a disguise, but is actual; not a parastatic body, but an actual body; and from the hour when he with the omnipotent resolve of his omnipotent love became a servant God has so to speak imprisoned himself in his resolve, and now must go on (to speak foolishly) whether he wills to or not. He cannot then betray himself; he does not have the possibility which is open to the noble king, suddenly to show that he is after all the king—which, however, is no perfection with the king (to have this possibility), but shows merely his impotence and the impotence of his resolve, that he does not actually have the power to become what he wills.[62]

Kierkegaard does mean to confess the full involvement of God in the Christ, but does not wish to have that confession beclouded by a self-contradiction. Climacus makes the point well in observing that since his sketch of the Christian advance beyond immanence 'contains no self contradiction . . . thought can thus occupy itself therewith as with the strangest proposal of all'.[63]

While the ascendance of the christological witness turns away from the metaphysical opposition often associated with the diastatic rhythm, it is quite in harmony with the religious centre of that rhythm. We have heard that centre speak: 'If the difference is infinite between God, who is in heaven, and you, who are on earth: the difference is infinitely greater between the Holy and the sinner.'[64]

---

in his 'project of thought'. We have already cited the central passage; see above, p. 247, note 7. It is clear that the heaviest weight falls on the theological objections deriving from the doctrine of creation.

[61] *Pap.* II A 594 (*Dru* 104). Indeed Kierkegaard will even permit talk of a 'change in God' to ensure that the divine love is so understood as to emphasize God's atoning activity. See *Pap.* I A 30 (*Dru* 7).

[62] *S.V.* IV, p. 221 (*PF*, p. 44). See also the passages cited above on pp. 177–8, and *S.V.* XII, p. 123 (*TC*, p. 131).

[63] *S.V.* IV, pp. 263–4 (*PF*, p. 85). Cf. *Pap.* X 2 A 354 (*Dru* 1033) and the passage from *CUP* cited above on pp. 224–5.

[64] *S.V.* XI, p. 258 ('HP', *CDi*, p. 368).

Now the same religious correction of the metaphysical emphasis may be heard in a christological context: 'God creates out of *nothing*, wonderful, you say; yes, to be sure, but he does what is still more wonderful: he makes saints (the communion of saints) out of sinners.'[65] More wonderful indeed, for sin is not nothing, not even the 'nothing' of preliminary good. Man's sin is as real as man is. Man is fully real and the reality of his sin measures the distance between him and God. But Kierkegaard spoke of more than sin. The christological witness confesses the awful measurement of man's distance from God, but confesses 'what is still more wonderful: he [God] makes saints out of sinners'.[66]

In chapter one we spoke of 'the christological centre' of Kierkegaard's thought. That speech has found its fulfilment. And the centrality of the christological witness is a unifying force, not a passive point of intersection. The confession of the Christ does not need to resort to distortion to summon to unity a body of thought flowing with the twin rhythms of diastasis and synthesis. Those rhythms tend towards the centre. We may find that suggested by the fact that clear conceptual connections exist within both rhythms between the assessments in general and specific senses of the possibility of the Christ. Even when the diastatic impulse veers off to utter a 'No!', it is the same opposition of the temporal and the eternal which marks man's mortality as sin which is the basis for the judgment that the Christ is impossible.

Perhaps, then, the integration of Kierkegaard's thought and faith is not such a momentous accomplishment. The effort to assimilate the Christ gives way to a recognition—a confession, of the Christ—still within the categories of diastasis. It seems far closer to the truth to regard that fact not as a kind of midnight conversion either to the requirement of consistency or to essentially Christian categories, but rather as an expression of the essential thrust of Kierkegaard's work throughout. What we are saying is that diastasis and synthesis do not fundamentally clash in Kierkegaard. Both rhythms serve his intent to illumine the relationship(s) between God and man. One need not resort to romanticizing to hold that his life—for all its ambiguity and anomaly—was spent to set forth the divine-human relationship (encounter is too narrow a term, dialogue too quiescent) in order that

---

[65] *Pap.* II A 758 (*Dru* 209). [Italics his.] Cf. above, pp. 102–4, note 16.

[66] The logic of the emphasis on metaphysical opposition actually deters one from the confession of this 'still more wonderful fact'. As Kierkegaard points out already in *S.V.* II, pp. 167–88 (*E-O* II, pp. 155–76), the mystic's metaphysical penitence is really superfluous, because he did not create the world.

the divine action to set that relationship right might be served. The diastatic rhythm contributes to the fulfilment of Kierkegaard's intention by its emphasis on the essential difference in nature, the abysmal distance of sin. But that rhythm never fails to speak of both God and man, for it ever sees them turned towards each other. That holds true of the man fleeing from God as well: 'Untruth is therefore not merely without the truth, but is polemic towards the truth, which is expressed by saying that the learner has himself forfeited the condition and is forfeiting it.'[67]

It may well be felt that this statement of the relationships between the rhythms sells out the diastatic tradition. It does make the claim that the metaphysical opposition of the temporal and the eternal—while striking and even frequent in Kierkegaard—is not essential to, and not finally in harmony with, the fundamental thrust of diastasis. If it should now be said that diastasis thus becomes a kind of sub-motif within synthesis, or that it is somehow dependent on the synthesis dynamic—let that word stand, so long as one realizes that the first word of faith requires the corrective of the second, if the Christian message is to maintain its internal balance and address its world with realism. In any case the two rhythms do interpenetrate. And it should not be surprising that some of the most fruitful instances of interpenetration occur in the area of christology—as in the coalescing of the concentration on the death of the Christ with the christological extension of the ethic of revelation and communication.[68] That hardly surprises, if one sees the christological witness actively confirming, even suggesting, specific formulations within both rhythms.[69] That kind of intercourse again bears witness to the fact that the Christ is a *living* centre for Kierkegaard's thought. It seems fitting that it should be so with faith's reflection concerning the Christ who does not require that nature be wounded to exalt his grace—who indeed puts in question the very simplicity of the distinction between nature and grace, as it is commonly stated. If one hears the witness of Kierkegaard's christology along these lines, the priority of the synthesis rhythm may again be confirmed—for it does seem closer to this man's intention to speak of the Christ as the meeting of God and man, than to isolate him as the 'wholly other'.[70]

[67] *S.V.* IV, p. 185 (*PF*, p. 10).
[68] See above, pp. 193–8.
[69] See above, pp. 248–55.
[70] This is not to deny that Kierkegaard does speak so of the Christ, or that the designation 'wholly other' can be so understood that it characterizes the meeting of God and man rather than cauterizes it.

In the judgments of these last pages analysis reveals the rising concern of criticism. One senses that immanental and transcendental criticism are not separated by a boundary line but merge in a zone which is anything but neutral ground. Still the distinction is useful and may well find expression in chapter divisions. So to the next chapters the task is assigned of assessing the constructive significance for contemporary theology of the Kierkegaard whom we have heard speak in these five chapters. But those chapters have surely led up to this task—and perhaps into it as well.

PART FOUR

THE LEGACY OF KIERKEGAARD AS A
SYSTEMATIC THINKER

VIII

THE DOMINANCE OF THE DIASTATIC: THE PERIL OF POLARIZATION

To SPEAK of the legacy of Kierkegaard is not as such to recount or renew a history of infidelity to a master's voice. True, Kierkegaard was contemptuous of the 'disciple' who seeks to evade personal responsibility through a fanatical submission to authority. But his was a constructive contempt—he would set this matter right—and his literary production comes to its climax in a rising concern to 'take the responsibility', to let his personal witness of faith be superimposed on the portrayal of alternative modes of life. If the intention of the subject is to be taken into account, then, it seems far better to close this book with some assessment of Kierkegaard's legacy than to try to let it stand as an effort which seeks to justify itself purely in terms of historical interest. Of course such an interest itself would draw us into this chapter, for to speak of Kierkegaard exercising influence on contemporary thought is hardly to introduce a matter of opinion. Yet much of what is said in these pages bears opinion's relationship to fact. That is true of the identification of the portion of Kierkegaard's legacy which has been appropriated and of the characterization of the process of appropriation itself. Parallels do not constitute causal relationships, after all—even in the most general sense—and autobiographical testimony is a notoriously treacherous thing. The subjective character of our assessment is, of course, still more clearly in view when we appeal for a further appropriation of the legacy. But this subjectivity will stop short of arbitrariness, if it is tutored by the substance of Kierkegaard's work and turned towards the present time and its problems.

Competent, if necessarily incomplete, reports of the history of Kierkegaard scholarship are available.[1] No need exists for a reissue of those reports and no place remains in these pages for the massive

---

[1] See Aage Henriksen, *Methods and Results of Kierkegaard Studies in Scandinavia*, trans. Annie Fausbøll (Copenhagen: Munksgaard, 1951); Aage Kabell, *Kierkegaardstudiet i Norden* (Copenhagen: H. Hagerup, 1948); and for the more recent

task of amplifying them. What is possible and may be useful is a comment on the character of that scholarship as far as it stands related to the analysis undertaken here. That comment has been suggested in the title of this section. The diastatic impulse has dominated impressively in the Kierkegaard made known by the massive literature surrounding his own works. The reader may have pieced together that comment from the conversation with the secondary literature which is found in the earlier chapters of this book. That comment can be sustained by an independent examination of the literature and at least suggested by a reading of the reviews of that literature by Henriksen, Kabell and Thulstrup.

This dominance of diastasis in the reception of the Kierkegaard heritage did not first bloom in a twentieth century disillusioned by the desperate course of external events and by depth psychology's dark version of the life within man. While much of the scholar's energy up to (and even in) the most recent time has been devoted to the considerable task of getting the authorship in readable form and, hopefully, to reading it, analysis and criticism have been offered and they have focused first and most forcefully on the diastatic. The issue of the attention may have been approval—as with such literary figures as Ibsen, Björnsen, and Strindberg. Or it may have been negative— as was true of the humanistic philosopher Höffding or the religious writer Teisen. In either case when the thought of Kierkegaard (as distinguished from the details of his life or the deviations of his psyche) came into view it was the diastatic tradition which was seen.

In the second half-century of Kierkegaard scholarship several major voices challenged the interpretative generalization we have made. Surely Hirsch, Bohlin, Lönning, and Malantschuk have written lucidly of themes which we have linked with the synthesis rhythm. It seems correct to say, however, that the work of these men —for the most part not translated into English—has not yet become a significant influence in the appropriation of Kierkegaard in English-speaking lands. Obviously, exceptional individuals appear who know the literature and have learned from it, but their presence is precisely

---

period Niels Thulstrup, 'Theological and Philosophical Kierkegaardian Studies in Scandinavia, 1945–53', trans. P. Holmer, *Theology Today*, October, 1955, pp. 297–312 and 'Studiet af Kierkegaard undenfor Skandinavien 1945–52', *Dansk Teologisk Tidskrift*, 1953, pp. 65–80; Helmut Fahrenbach, *Die gegenwärtige Kierkegaard-Auslegung in der deutschsprachigen Literatur von 1948 bis 1962* (Tübingen: J. C. B. Mohr, 1962) and Michael Theunissen, 'Das Kierkegaardbild der neuern Forschung und Deutung', *Deutsch Vierteljahrschrift für Litteraturwissenschaft und Geisteschichte*, 1958, pp. 576–612.

exceptional. While there is reason to believe that Kierkegaard has survived at least the most superficial stage of faddism ('discipleism') in the lands affected by his explosion into English, there is still a great deal of mouthing his name and in this sad business the diastatic pronunciation is preferred.

We are not trying to say that one must get through the nearly one thousand pages of Hirsch's *Kierkegaard-Studien* or past Per Lönning's highly complex Norwegian work (or the impenetrable German of his *Zusammenfassung*) or to Gregor Malantschuk's unpretentious studies in order to appropriate the synthesis strand in Kierkegaard. The works themselves had better have something to say at this point, and they do. Still the figure of Kierkegaard continues to be drawn in American classrooms in boldly, even baldly, diastatic lines. This matter is not sufficiently explained by emphasizing that the diastatic material in Kierkegaard satisfies more readily the penchant for the spectacular. We have made clear that we cannot find it to be accounted for by the relative weight the strands themselves possess in Kierkegaard. An important cause, however partial and penultimate, seems to lie in the fact that many readers come to Kierkegaard under the tutelage of guides whose service adds orientation and explanation to that of reference. If a reader first finds his way to the *Postscript* by means of *Sein und Zeit* or the *Kirchliche Dogmatik*, his selectivity will be understandable.

We have thus mentioned the two centres of intellectual energy in our time which have administered the appropriation of Kierkegaard's legacy. Since we shall not examine the vast amount of movement around or within each centre, it is hazardous even to speak of them as centres and doubly so to give them names, 'existentialism' and 'dialectical theology' (or 'neo-orthodoxy' or 'neo-————'). Is it any better to call them *fields* of energy? In any case these have been the actual executors of Kierkegaard's inheritance. There can be little doubt that we deal here with an assimilation of Kierkegaard to the writer's own concern. But that assimilation has in turn yielded many titles which would find place in a library's Kierkegaard section. And the mark of the mentor is not easily effaced.[2] Thus one finds an author

[2] It is, of course, true, as Liselotte Richter, 'Konstruktives und Destruktives in der neuesten Kierkegaard-Forschung', *Theologische Litteraturzeitung*, 1952, pp. 141–8, points out, that the history of Kierkegaard scholarship constitutes a mirror of the intellectual history of the last hundred years. Still one can question the implied relativism by noting the predominance of a single pattern and check (if not cancel) the resulting scepticism by consistent appeal to the primary literature itself. The claim for relevance does not require, or even really permit, the claim of finality.

offering a book about Kierkegaard controlled by a diastatic reading of a Barthian diastatic elaboration of a diastatic text in Kierkegaard, while Barth (of whom the author has read nothing since Vol I, Part I) shifts his position to criticize such Kierkegaardian (Barthian?) texts.

It may not be fair to claim that a great multitude reads Kierkegaard through the eyes of Heidegger and Barth—or Marcel and Niebuhr. Or it may not be objectionable to read him so. At any rate a good deal of evidence suggests that something like this has been—and is—going on. And that constitutes a second reason for saying something at this point about the appropriation of Kierkegaard's legacy by existentialism and dialectical theology.

1. *Existentialist Philosophy: The Power and Predicament of Ontological Protest*

The existentialists—despite wide and sharp differences among themselves—do seem to agree in giving what amounts to at least a formal restatement of many Kierkegaardian themes descriptive of the human condition. Kierkegaard did write of dread, freedom, decision and integrity. The enemy in mind in the marshalling of these weapons would be easily enough recognized by Kierkegaard. The critical point of human freedom links Kierkegaard's protest against the Hegelian vision with the existentialist's outrage over a mass society which even now mechanizes and manipulates human beings and confidently looks ahead to the replacement of man by more reliable machines.[3] In such a time it has seemed salutary that the mystery of individuality be called to mind. Nor is it strange that existentialists have sought to find in individuality not only a mystery upsetting simplistic diagnoses of man, but also a mandate challenging the self's passion. If the essence of a technological society is to convert means into ends,[4] if we have thus made a vaguely defined but passionately sought productivity a value beyond questioning, if we have then set about turning men and women into marketable commodities,[5] it seems quite in order for one distressed by such a time

[3] See, for example, D. S. Halacy Jr., *CYBORG: Evolution of the Superman* (New York: Harper, 1965).

[4] See Jacques Ellul, *The Technological Society*, trans. John Wilkinson (New York: Knopf, 1965). For a converging theological analysis, see Paul Tillich, 'The World Situation', *The Christian Answer*, ed. H. P. Van Dusen (New York: Scribners, 1946), pp. 1–45.

[5] Erich Fromm has presented perhaps the most damning indictment at this point. See especially his *Escape from Freedom* (New York: Farrar & Rinehart, 1941) and *Man for Himself* (New York: Rinehart, 1947; London: Routledge, 1949).

to look in hope to the primitivity of the human act of decision.[6] Kierkegaard's critique of the self who refuses in despair to be himself represents a formidable ally to one so distressed and so hoping.[7]

Yet a momentum is discernible in this appeal to individuality which carries the existentialist to positions which would draw Kierkegaard's criticism—deservedly. Sartre's atheism provides an illustration. If man's existence precedes his essence, he may well enough be said to be 'free'. If that 'freedom' is not somehow a qualification of (and so itself qualified by) some 'being' man possesses, but is his being, it would be the case that 'we are perpetually engaged in our choice and perpetually conscious of the fact that we ourselves can abruptly invert this choice and "reverse steam" . . . [and that] we are perpetually threatened by the nihilation of our actual choice and perpetually threatened with choosing ourselves—and consequently with becoming—other than we are'.[8] But the question of the end towards which this freedom should move seems as awkward a matter for this view as it is for the scientism revelling in the vision of man's accelerating control of his environment or the technocracy ardent in its romance with things. 'In anguish we do not simply apprehend the fact that the possibles which we project are perpetually eaten away by our freedom-to-come; in addition we apprehend our choice—i.e., ourselves—as *unjustifiable*.[9] To speak of 'taste' at this point is more to recognize the problem than to propose a solution.[10]

Oddly the existentialist protest threatens to come full circle to an ethic of productivity in which every authentic choice is approved—in which, indeed, the term approval is strangely out of place. This is not of course the ethic of mass culture with its homogenized man—

[6] For a summary statement at this point see Gabriel Marcel, *The Existential Background of Human Dignity* (Cambridge: Harvard, 1963).

[7] Moving out from that basis as found most pointedly in *SD*, one could find a close topical similarity between, say, *PA* and such works as Karl Jaspers' *Man in the Modern Age*, trans. Eden and Ceder Paul (London: Routledge, 1933) and Marcel's *Man Against Mass Humanity*, trans. G. S. Fraser (Chicago: Regnery, 1952).

[8] Jean-Paul Sartre, *Being and Nothingness*, trans. Hazel E. Barnes (New York: Philosophical Library, 1956), p. 465.

[9] ibid., p. 464. [Italics his.]

[10] As Sartre recognizes, ibid., pp. 614–15. Simone De Beauvoir, *The Ethics of Ambiguity*, trans. Bernard Frechtman (New York: Philosophical Library; London: Jonas & Co., 1948), p. 18, seems to resist this conclusion in writing: 'An ethics of ambiguity will be one which will refuse to deny *a priori* that separate existents can, at the same time, be bound to each other, that their individual freedoms can forge laws valid for all.' While an effort is made to develop this lead, that effort is disturbed by two problems which are at bottom one: (1) the difficulty of distinguishing between 'natural willing' and 'ethical willing', and (2) the difficulty of distinguishing between 'good' and 'bad' instances of 'ethical willing'. [Italics hers.]

but it is not a view from which effective criticism and specific reform of that culture can be launched either. That this ethic has made its mark in our time is hard to deny, however, unless one can close one's eyes to the excesses of individualism which strikingly co-exist with the vices of collectivism, as Paul Tillich has so pointedly shown.[11]

By following the clue given in Tillich's description of the onto-logical polarity of individuation and participation under the condi-tions of estrangement, the relationship of the existentialist emphasis to the structure of this study can be illumined. The title of this section shows the way. The prospect of a polarized understanding of man in which the freedom and necessity of the self are dualistically opposed to each other is a perilous one. That peril is threefold as far as the self's relationship to the other(s) is concerned: (1) That the definition of the self will be evacuated of its content through a failure to take into account the constitutive significance of the community as actuality. (2) That the energy of the self will be enervated by a failure to bring into play the resources of the community as possibility. (3) That the intention of the self will be frustrated by a failure to recognize the good of the community as *telos*.

This assessment of the peril endorses the basic convictions we have seen to underlie Kierkegaard's religious thought. It is on theological grounds that Kierkegaard asserts the significance of relationships—for both the tasks of description and prescription. One may now wish to place the blame for Sartre's excessive individualism at the door of his atheism. Knowing no God who places man in a condition of relational necessity, Sartre conceives freedom in a way which involves a second dimension of arbitrariness. Had affirmation replaced dis-belief, his appeal to freedom might have found not only the perspective of some eternal counsel determining the ideal but also that of the actual co-existence in community which defines the real.

Yet this line of argument by Sartre's theological prosecutor is at least oversimplified and possibly fundamentally distorted. It fails to take into account the fact that Sartre *does* reckon in some sense with the inevitable relatedness of human life. When writing in his most metaphysical mode, he has acknowledged the concrete facticity of the self[12] and he can close the lyrical prose of his autobiography by letting that recognition reach out to speak of 'a whole man, composed

---

[11] Paul Tillich, *The Courage to Be*, (New Haven: Yale; London: Nisbet, 1952), especially chapters four and five.
[12] So Sartre, op. cit., p. 489: 'What we have called the facticity of freedom is the given which it has to be and which it illuminates by its project. . . . It is my

of all men and as good as all of them and no better than any'.[13] Sartre's atheism is even more sharply, though surely less obviously, qualified than his individualism. Sartre after all knows what God would be like were he to be found and he is quite capable of erecting the knowledge requisite for his denial of God into a positive explanatory principle: 'Every human reality is a passion in that it projects losing itself so as to found being and by the same stroke to constitute the In-itself which escapes contingency by being its own foundation, the *Ens causa sui*, which religions call God. Thus the passion of man is the reverse of that of Christ, for man loses himself as man in order that God may be born. But the idea of God is contradictory and we lose ourselves in vain. Man is a useless passion.'[14]

This God is none other than the wholly single, independent one with whom we have found the rhythm of diastasis in Kierkegaard to be involved from time to time. One begins to wonder if Sartre does not somehow illustrate the tendency towards extreme polarization which seems to be the peril attending the diastatic tradition in religious thought. The movement of severance succeeds in banishing the reality of God only to have the idea of God return to penetrate Sartre's 'humanism'. The proceedings are conducted on the premises of metaphysics. It is the analysis of existence which exiles the *causa sui*. But the identification of the real and the ideal which is required by, and represented by, such a God returns to deify that which existence cannot justify: human choice. Since the faith proclaimed is

---

place, my body, my past, my position in so far as it is already determined by the indications of Others, finally my fundamental relation to the Other,' Cf. ibid., pp. 494ff.

[13] Jean-Paul Sartre, *The Words*, trans. Bernard Frechtman (New York: George Braziller; London: Hamish Hamilton, 1964), p. 255.

[14] Sartre, *Being and Nothingness*, p. 615. [Italics his.] De Beauvoir (op. cit., pp. 14–15) would show that the passion is not so useless after all and introduces the concern controlling our next paragraph to make the point: '. . . the genuine man will not agree to recognize any foreign absolute. When a man projects into an ideal heaven that impossible synthesis of the for-itself and the in-itself that is called God, it is because he wishes the regard of this existing Being to change his existence into being; but if he agrees not to be in order to exist genuinely, he will abandon the dream of an inhuman objectivity. He will understand that it is not a matter of being right in the eyes of a God, but of being right in his own eyes. Renouncing the thought of seeking the guarantee for his existence outside of himself, he will also refuse to believe in unconditioned values which would set themselves up athwart his freedom like things. . . . This rejection of any extrinsic justification also confirms the rejection of an original pessimism which we posited at the beginning. Since it is unjustifiable from without, to declare from without that it is unjustifiable is not to condemn it.' De Beauvoir, however, seeks to resist the conclusion that this logic repudiates ethics—see above, p. 271, note 10.

a religious appropriation of a metaphysical conception it is sterile as far as the production of specific ethical criteria is concerned. Indeed, far from permitting value to be attached to some real acts at least more readily than to others, the logic of metaphysical opposition disqualifies all acts. That same opposition keeps Sartre from recognizing facticity and commonality as more than a point (quite literally no more than that) of departure or as an antagonistic power.[15]

This discussion of Sartre may illumine the relationship of other existentialist figures to Kierkegaard as well. The diastatic tendency to identify the real and the ideal may be heard again—metaphysically in Heidegger's living towards death[16] or pragmatically in Camus' reflections on the guillotine.[17] One may again find the locating of transcendence in the human person to be linked with the absence of specific ethical determinants and the endorsement of every commitment and of none. Commitment comes to be set off decisively from the other(s)[18] and to find its ultimate point of definition in the reality of death.[19]

[15] Thus Regin Prenter is right in linking Sartre with Kierkegaard's aesthetic stage materially, ('Sartre's Concept of Freedom considered in the Light of Kierkegaard's Thought', A Kierkegaard Critique, ed. H. Johnson and N. Thulstrup, art. trans. by Margaret Grieve and H. R. Harcourt [New York: Harper, 1962], pp. 130–41.) But it would seem that Prenter has not adequately taken into account the role a doctrine of God plays formally in Sartre's analysis and evaluation of existence. Cf. Johannes Slök's chapter on the concept of existence in Heidegger, Sartre, and Kierkegaard (Forsynstanken [Hjörring: Expres, 1947], pp. 96–135), where the emphasis is placed on Kierkegaard's aesthetic concept of existence.

[16] Martin Heidegger, Being and Time, trans. from the seventh German edition by John Macquarrie and Edward Robinson (London: SCM, 1962), sections 51–53.

[17] Albert Camus, Resistance, Rebellion and Death, trans. by Justin O'Brien (New York: Knopf, 1961; London, Hamish Hamilton, 1964), pp. 173–235.

[18] Heidegger, op. cit., section 27.

[19] Cf. ibid., p. 308: 'The ownmost possibility is non-relational. Anticipation allows Dasein to understand that that potentiality-for-Being in which its ownmost Being is an issue, must be taken over by Dasein alone. Death does not just "belong" to one's own Dasein in an undifferentiated way; death lays claim to it as an individual Dasein. The non-relational character of death, as understood in anticipation, individualizes Dasein down to itself. . . . It makes manifest that all Being-alongside the things with which we concern ourselves, and all Being-with Others, will fail us when our ownmost potentiality-for-Being is the issue. Dasein can be authentically itself only if it makes this possible for itself of its own accord. . . . Dasein is authentically itself only to the extent that, as concernful Being-alongside and solicitous Being-with, it projects itself upon its ownmost potentiality-for-Being rather than upon the possibility of the they-self. The entity which anticipates its non-relational possibility, is thus forced by that very anticipation into the possibility of taking over from itself its ownmost Being, and doing so of its own accord.' [Italics his.] Michael Wyschogrod's Kierkegaard and Heidegger (New York: Humanities, 1954) stresses the difference between the concerns of the two figures at this point: 'Heidegger's attempt is to evolve an ontology that would, as it were, contain

Admittedly, the strain of synthesis can be heard more decisively in the works of other men conventionally identified as existentialists. Jaspers and Marcel come most forcefully to mind. But that fact is evidently not descriptive of their historical relationship to Kierkegaard. While Jaspers' concern to affirm the presence of transcendence, however ciphered, and his emphasis on communication make one eager to link him with the synthesis strand in Kierkegaard, it seems rather to be the case that it is the diastatic impulse—and particularly the extreme form of that impulse—which he has heard in Kierkegaard. It is difficult, of course, to assess how much of substantive importance may have passed by way of Kierkegaard's method of existential analysis to the Jaspers of *Psychologie der Weltanschauungen*.[20] But while Jaspers can find that analysis asking the right question, he clearly focuses on the diastatic in Kierkegaard in separating himself from the answers he believes Kierkegaard to have given.[21]

One is probably on surer ground in viewing Marcel as a fulfilment of the synthesis strand in Kierkegaard. But again the connection is troubled—in this case not only by the ambiguity of the historical point involved, but also by such substantive matters as Marcel's investment in a doctrine of Being which by no means represents a clear statement in the tradition in question.[22]

---

the existential challenge of Kierkegaard and yet permit ontology to remain supreme' (pp. 136–7), while 'for Kierkegaard the ethico-religious is primary and is above the ontological' (p. 43). This judgment seems materially correct, but tends to evade the question as to whether Heidegger's relationship to his ontological concepts does not include attitudes which exceed the task of description.

[20] Berlin: J. Springer, 1919.

[21] Jaspers identifies both salutary and sinister elements in Kierkegaard's challenge. Thus in *Reason and Existence*, trans. by William Earle (New York: Noonday, 1955), p. 36, he finds that Kierkegaard—and Nietzsche with whom he consistently joins Kierkegaard—'leaped toward Transcendence, but to a form of transcendence where practically no one could follow. Kierkegaard leaped to a Christianity which was conceived as an absurd paradox, as decision for utter world negation and martyrdom.' Cf. ibid., p. 48, and the whole first chapter on 'the historical meaning of Kierkegaard and Nietzsche'. Cf. Jaspers' article 'Kierkegaard, Leben und Werk', *Universitas*, 1951, pp. 1057–71.

[22] Marcel's 'An Essay in Autobiography', *The Philosophy of Existentialism*, trans. by Manya Harari (New York: Citadel, 1963) well illustrates the relationship to Kierkegaard by combining praise (p. 124) with the assertion of the historical independence of the author's development (p. 120). Cf. his *The Existentialist Background of Human Dignity*, pp. 25–26. Kenneth T. Gallagher does have support for his judgment (*The Philosophy of Gabriel Marcel* [New York: Fordham, 1962], pp. ix–x) that Marcel 'does not derive from the line of descent to which so many of the "existentialist" thinkers owe their origin, the line that is vaguely drawn from Kierkegaard and Nietzsche; the influence of these thinkers on his formation was

Existentialist writers do, then, reproduce many of the categories present in Kierkegaard's analysis of existence. Are those categories neutral in the sense that they are separable from Kierkegaard's religious affirmations? In any case they serve far more than descriptive interests in the hands of the existentialists. Judgments marking man as absurd and totally guilty do not emerge from an analysis and application of the conceptual opposition of being and existence. Still it remains the case that the substance of this faith is stated in philosophical or ontological terms. As such the faith does not generate the power or provide the principles by which the polarization of self and others might be corrected. Perhaps one must move away from the ontological orientation if one is to provide an analysis which is both closer to Kierkegaard's intention and farther from the danger we have identified. Those who ask of the significance of the later Heidegger for theology follow this trail.[23] Since Kierkegaard's intention was openly theological, while the later Heidegger's point of departure is considerably clearer than his destination,[24] it seems right to serve both the historical and the constructive interests of this chapter by inquiring now into the appropriation of Kierkegaard's legacy in another quarter—'dialectical theology'.

---

next to nil'. If one must trace formative philosophical influences, Gallagher proposes Schelling and Royce—both having been the subject for early studies by Marcel.

[23] See James M. Robinson and John B. Cobb, Jr., editors, *The Later Heidegger and Theology* (New York: Harper, 1963). One may, of course, find the salutary character of Heidegger's shift to lie (wholly or in part) in the particular metaphysics to which he bids farewell. See Schubert Ogden, 'Zur Frage der "richtigen" Philosophie', *Zeitschrift für Theologie und Kirche, 1964.*

[24] Of the *causa sui*, Heidegger says (*Essays in Metaphysics: Identity and Difference*, trans. Kurt F. Leidecker [New York: Philosophical Library, 1960], p. 65): '. . . this is the just and proper name for God in philosophy. Man may neither pray to this God, nor be sacrifice to him. Confronted by *causa sui* man may neither sink onto his knees nor could he sing and dance. Accordingly, this thinking-less-God which must abandon the God of philosophy, God as *causa sui*, is, perhaps, closer to God the divinity. In our context this means merely that thinking-less-God is less restricted in dealing with him than onto-theo-logic would acknowledge. With this remark we may have shed a little light on the path on which we find the type of thinking which is "backtracking" from metaphysics into the essence of metaphysics. . . .' [Italics his.] It must be said, too, that it is the early Heidegger who is far the more prepared to acknowledge the importance of Kierkegaard. See *Being and Time*, pp. 190, n. iv; 235, n. vi; 338, n. iii. (Though even then he criticized Kierkegaard for remaining under Hegel's domination in his ontology.) In *Holzwege* (Frankfurt: Klostermann, 1950), p. 230, he considers Kierkegaard no thinker, 'but merely a religious writer'. Cf. Heidegger's *Was Heisst Denken?* (Tubingen: Niemeyer, 1954), p. 129, for a low estimate of Kierkegaard's significance for understanding the problem of Being.

THE DOMINANCE OF THE DIASTATIC

2. Dialectical Theology: The Religious Restatement of the Peril

The principal pioneer and for long the dominant guide in this appropriation must be said to have been Karl Barth. Barth reports that while he bought Kierkegaard's *Augenblick* as early as 1909, the peak of Kierkegaard's influence came a decade later in the critical period between the first and second editions of the book on Romans. He has written of what Kierkegaard meant to him then. Above all he found in Kierkegaard an 'inexorable critique' of 'all speculation by which the infinite qualitative difference between God and man is obliterated, of all aesthetic forgetfulness in relation to the absolute claim of the gospel'. According to Barth Kierkegaard's words found their target in 'the Christianity and churchianity (which was at the same time too presumptuous and too cheap) of the theology surrounding us, from which we knew ourselves to be not really free'.[25] There is little question but that it is the diastatic rhythm in Kierkegaard which has here won acceptance. Barth has himself endorsed Hans Urs von Balthasar's identification of his early period's leading concept as diastasis.[26] What is in question—passing from this chapter's historical concern to its constructive interest—is whether the diastatic element in Kierkegaard's legacy, upon finding theological ground, avoids what we have referred to as the peril of polarization.

If the existentialist isolation of the individual from the community is to be corrected by attentiveness to the God who creates men in community and claims then for the new community in the Christ, an

[25] Karl Barth, 'Mein Verhältnis zu Sören Kierkegaard', *Orbis Litterarum*, 1963, pp. 97–100, especially p. 98. This testimony must not be disqualified by the fact that it comes in an address in Copenhagen to an audience whose objectivity might presumably be in doubt. Barth was entirely capable of sharp criticism on that occasion! The passage of time might seem a more significant impediment than the requirement of politeness. Yet a study of the second edition of the book on Romans does endorse Barth's comments. (It is essentially that second edition which stands behind the sixth German edition which is the basis for the English tranlation by Edwyn C. Hoskyns [London: Oxford, 1950]—see Barth's reference in his preface to the English edition to the book's 'second and present form' [p. vi].) There Barth does, for example, appeal to the infinite qualitative difference between God and man (p. 99), the intrinsic indirectness of the communication of the God-Man (the unveiling which veils) (p. 279) and to Kierkegaard's critique of the church (p. 395). For a compact and useful summary of the historical relationship see N. H. Söe, 'Karl Barth og Sören Kierkegaard', *Kierkegaardiana*, 1955, pp. 55–65.
[26] Karl Barth, *The Humanity of God*, trans, J. N. Thomas (Richmond: John Knox, 1960; London: Collins, 1961), p. 44, where Barth refers to 'the shrewd friend from another shore,' the author of *Karl Barth: darstellung und deutung seiner theologie* (Köln: Jacob Hegner, 1951).

absent God will hardly do. It might appear that in the very naming of God the theologian clears himself on that score. He speaks, after all, of one whom he knows. Yet Kierkegaard's thought should caution us from supposing the matter to be settled so easily. God seems to disappear, however subtly, if no perceptive activity can exist apart from him. Our discussion of what we have called the certainty motif in Kierkegaard[27] brings us all the way into the much discussed problem of the 'overcoming' of the subject-object distinction in contemporary theology.[28]

Debate surely seems possible as to Karl Barth's own position at this point. James Brown may be right in arguing that if one distinguishes between grammatical and epistemological senses of 'subject', and between *Objekt* and *Gegenstand*, one will find in Barth no repudiation of the subject-object distinction, despite his assertion that 'the subject of revelation (*sc.* God) is the Subject that remains indissolubly Subject. We cannot get behind this Subject. It cannot become an object.'[29] Brown can appeal to such statements as this: 'In His Word He comes as an object before man the subject. And by the Holy Spirit He makes the human subject accessible to Himself, capable of considering and conceiving Himself as object. The real knowledge of God is concerned with God in His relationship to man, but also in His distinction from him. We therefore separate ourselves from all those ideas of the knowledge of God which understand it as the union of man with God, and which do not regard it as an objective knowledge but leave out the distinction between the knower and the known.'[30]

[27] See above, pp. 136–40.

[28] See James Brown, *Subject and Object in Modern Theology* (London: SCM Press; New York: Macmillan, 1955) and Henning Schröer, *Die Denkform der Paradoxalität als theologisches Problem* (Göttingen: Vandenhoeck & Ruprecht, 1960).

[29] Karl Barth, *The Doctrine of the Word of God*, trans. G. T. Thomson (Edinburgh: T. & T. Clark, 1936), p. 438.

[30] Karl Barth, *Church Dogmatics* (4 vols., Edinburgh: T. & T. Clark, 1936–42) II, 1, p. 10. Cf. *The Doctrine of the Word of God*, pp. 242–3: '. . . the reality of this experience, i.e., the determination of man by the Word of God, is thought of in such a way that in it God hands something over to man, with the result that practically it passes from the hands of God to the hands of man, or viewed from man's angle, he receives something from God, in such a way that it is practically put into the hands. A "conjunction" or "synthesis" has taken place. Man's consciousness now has a "content of divine spirit", a consideration and investigation of which can be carried through. The statement *homo capax verbi Dei* suddenly comes to life. There arises in the reality of this experience as an entity capable of being met, indicated, and taken for granted a new man, new not only in being man addressed by the Word of God, new, that is, not just in Christ merely— who could or should say anything against that?—but new in himself, transformed

Yet the hymn to divine independence and sovereignty which the distinctions Brown identifies would seek to make one hear does prove threatening: 'Man is the subject of faith. It is not God but man who believes. But the very fact of a man thus being subject in faith is bracketed as the predicate of the subject, God, bracketed exactly as the Creator embraces His creature, the merciful God sinful man, i.e., so that there is no departure from man's being a subject, and this very thing, the Ego of man as such is still only derivable from the Thou of the Subject, God.'[31]

Kierkegaard's thought has made clear that the diastatic impulse may find its way to extreme positions which distort and even defeat the religious intention of the thinker. Karl Barth, writing in 1956, asks if that has occurred in his own earlier work: '. . . did it not appear to escape us by quite a distance that the *deity* of the *living* God —and we certainly wanted to deal with Him—found its meaning and its power only in the context of His history and of His dialogue with *man*, and thus in His *togetherness* with man?'[32] The judgment implied in the question becomes explicit in Barth's retrospective criticism of Kierkegaard.[33] There is little doubting that it is this early Barth who is best known to American readers. The extent to which the quantitative deficiency in the knowledge of Barth involves a qualitative distortion is, of course, a matter open to question. That Barth can put his finger on the fundamental ambivalence in his early thought does not mean that he has since found more than a verbal solution to the problem he identifies.[34]

---

in the immanent state of his humanity. This man now gains, certainly in virtue of his being claimed by the Word of God, independence and an interest of his own, as a participator in the reality of the Word. . . . And now the reality of experience of the Word of God itself no longer rests upon itself; it has become an ellipse instead of a circle, one pole of which, and that the one nearest us, opposite to God, is the man who experiences.' [Italics his.]

[31] Barth, op. ct., pp. 280–1.

[32] Barth, *The Humanity of God*, p. 45. [Italics his.]

[33] For that criticism see Barth's address, 'Mein Verhältnis zu Sören Kierkegaard', *Orbis Litterarum* 1963, pp. 97–100. Just as there is ambivalence in Barth's thought, so his relationship to Kierkegaard is dialectical. Already in *The Epistle to the Romans*, p. 495, Barth seems to move away from diastasis in endorsing Kierkegaard's stress on love as fellowship with the neighbour. We have seen, however, that it is relevant to ask how real this neighbour is. See above, p. 161, note 132; p. 162, note 135; p. 218.

[34] It should be noted that *The Humanity of God* retains the theme of the uncompromised freedom of God so important to the early Barth. God acts as a partner of man 'and the freedom in which He does *that* is His deity'. (p. 45.) [Italics his.] And it is the deity which includes the humanity, not *vice versa*. As to the christological force behind the 'new' thrust, one must reckon with the statement: 'In Jesus

It is, then, not at all clear how far dialectical theology in fact does reclaim the theological setting in the appropriation of the diastatic tradition in Kierkegaard. Perhaps the dangers discerned in the existentialist statement of that tradition may provide a clarifying test. Barth has acknowledged that under the lure of the diastatic protest 'it was a part of the exaggerations of which we were guilty in 1920 that we were able to see the theological relevance of the Church only as a negative counterpart to the Kingdom of God which we had then so happily rediscovered'.[35]

The community hardly fared much better with others sounding the diastatic warning of Kierkegaard with or without the mediation of Barth. Bultmann, for example, found that 'I cannot speak of God's action in general statements; I can only speak of what he does here and now with me, of what he speaks here and now to me'.[36] Man is 'de-secularized', in that 'God, who stands aloof from the history of nations, meets each man in his own little history, his everyday life with its daily gift and demand'.[37] It is true that for Bultmann while God 'lifts man out of his worldly ties and places him directly before his own eyes', yet that man 'is guided into his concrete encounter with his neighbour, in which he finds his true history'.[38] But the problem of continuity between the encounters, the 'moments', is not settled or even addressed as a problem. While Martin Buber might be called as a witness to the way in which 'theological existentialism' can yield a communal emphasis, it is not clear that Buber recognizes any continuity between the several Thou's the I knows. This is the background for the familiar charge levelled against Buber to the effect that his I-Thou appeal vainly tries to set back the clock in a necessarily impersonal society.[39]

Christ man's freedom is wholly enclosed in the freedom of God.' (p. 48). Still Barth does in fact move away from his early position and that movement bears positive fruit—as in the conception of divine independence as divine triune *life* (p. 50), divine freedom as the freedom for *love* (p. 48) and in Barth's rich discussion of the creation of man in community (*Church Dogmatics*, III, 2, sections 44 and 45).

[35] Barth, *The Humanity of God*, p. 62.

[36] Rudolf Bultmann, *Jesus Christ and Mythology*, (New York: Charles Scribner's, 1958; London: SCM Press, 1960), p. 66.

[37] Rudolf Bultmann, *Theology of the New Testament*, trans. Kendrick Grobel (2 vols., New York: Charles Scribner's; London: SCM Press, 1952, 1955), Vol. I, p. 25.

[38] ibid., pp. 25–26.

[39] See H. Richard Niebuhr's, *The Responsible Self* (New York: Harper, 1963), pp. 69–79, for an expansion of Buber's work through the addition of an I-You category.

Bultmann, and in his way Buber, must deal with the community in a second sense: the vertical community of the faith's history. The polarization of the self and the historical community threatens in the assertion that 'the kerygma is not interested in the "objective historicity" beyond that "that", but requires faith in the crucified and risen Christ . . . faith does not at all arise from the acceptance of historical facts.'[40] And what is faith in the crucified? 'To believe in the cross of Christ does not mean to concern ourselves with a mythical process wrought outside of us and our world, or with an objective event turned by God to our advantage, but rather to make the cross of Christ our own, to undergo crucifixion with him. . . . In other words, the cross is not just an event of the past which can be contemplated in detachment, but the eschatological event in and beyond time, for as far as its meaning—that is, its meaning for faith—is concerned, it is an ever-present reality.'[41] While Bultmann's theology has focused this peril most dramatically, one ought to be aware that the early Barth refused to give any higher place to historical scholarship and added to that refusal an appeal to Kierkegaard.[42]

[40] Rudolf Bultmann, 'The Primitive Christian Kerygma and the Historical Jesus', trans. C. E. Braaten & R. A. Harrisville, *The Historical Jesus and the Kerygmatic Christ* (New York: Abingdon, 1964), p. 25.

[41] Rudolf Bultmann, 'New Testament and Mythology', trans. R. H. Fuller, *Kerygma and Myth*, I, ed. H. W. Bartsch (New York: Harper; London: SPCK, 1961), p. 36. In this manifesto Bultmann asked whether it was necessary to go back to the historical (*historisch*) event in order to discern the historic (*geschichtlich*) fact's abiding significance ('the judgment of the world, the judgment and deliverance of man'). He replied: 'As far as the first preachers of the gospel are concerned this will certainly be the case. . . . But for us this personal connection cannot be reproduced. For us the cross cannot disclose its own meaning: it is an event of the past. We can never recover it as an event in our own lives.' (ibid., pp. 37–38.) In his reply to his critics he made the point more explicit in an autobiographical setting:'. . . I am deliberately renouncing any form of encounter with a phenomenon of past history, including an encounter with the Christ after the flesh, in order to encounter the Christ proclaimed in the kerygma, which confronts me in my historic situation.' (ibid., p. 117.) For a different reading of Bultmann at this point, see Van A. Harvey and Schubert M. Ogden, 'How New is the "New Quest of the Historical Jesus"?', *The Historical Jesus and the Kerygmatic Christ*, trans. and ed. by Carl E. Braaten and Roy A. Harrisville (New York: Abingdon, 1964), pp. 197–242. It does seem possible to quote Bultmann on both sides of the issue of the significance of the historical Jesus. See also Joseph C. Weber, 'Jesus and the Kerygma in the Light of Law and Gospel in Bultmann's Theology', *Dialog*, 1964, pp. 288–93.

[42] Karl Barth, *The Epistle to the Romans*, pp. 278–81. Thus in *Church Dogmatics*, II, 1, p. 20, Barth also turns away from an appeal to the resurrection as offering some kind of objective verification and rather places the resurrection within the revelation of God which makes the Jesus of history recognizable. This prepares for Bultmann's position: 'The real Easter faith is faith in the word of preaching which

Paul Tillich has written in a similar manner in pointing out that faith in the Christ is not vulnerable to historical scepticism:

> The problem is: Exactly what can faith guarantee? And the inevitable answer is that faith can guarantee only its own foundation, namely, the appearance of that reality which has created the faith. This reality is the New Being, who conquers existential estrangement and thereby makes faith possible. This alone faith is able to guarantee—and that because its own existence is identical with the presence of the New Being. Faith itself is the immediate (not mediated by conclusions) evidence of the New Being within and under the conditions of existence. Precisely that is guaranteed by the very nature of the Christian faith. No historical criticism can question the immediate awareness of those who find themselves transformed into the state of faith . . . one must say that participation, not historical argument, guarantees the reality of the event upon which Christianity is based. It guarantees a personal life in which the New Being has conquered the old being. But it does not guarantee his name to be Jesus of Nazareth. Historical doubt concerning the existence and the life of someone with this name cannot be overruled. He might have had another name.[43]

---

brings illumination. If the event of Easter Day is in any sense an historical event additional to the event of the cross, it is nothing else than the rise of faith in the risen Lord since it was this faith which led to the apostolic preaching. The resurrection itself is not an event of past history.' Bultmann, op. cit., p. 42. See the comparative study by Herbert C. Wolf, *Kierkegaard and Bultmann: The Quest of the Historical Jesus* (Minneapolis: Augsburg, 1965).

[43] Paul Tillich, *Systematic Theology* (3 vols; Chicago: The University of Chicago 1951–63 [London: Nisbet, 1953–65]), II, p. 114. Tillich, however, does not want to lose the 'factual element' in the 'event "Jesus as the Christ"'. (ibid., p. 107 [123].) Indeed he writes: 'Kierkegaard exaggerates when he says that it is sufficient for the Christian faith nakedly to assert that in the years 1–30 God sent his son. Without the concreteness of the New Being, its newness would be empty.' (ibid., p. 114 [131–2].) Thus he pleads for 'an *analogia imaginis*, namely, an analogy between the picture and the actual personal life from which it has arisen. It was this reality, when encountered by the disciples, which created the picture. And it was, and still is, this picture which mediates the transforming power of the New Being.' (ibid., p. 115 [132].) While 'no special trait of this picture can be verified with certainty' and 'it is impossible to push behind the analogy and to state directly what can be stated only indirectly, that is, symbolically', Tillich believes it is possible to hold to a distinction 'between an imaginary picture and a real picture' by appealing to the criterion of 'transforming power'. (ibid., pp. 114–15 [132].) For an assessment of this point at the close of Tillich's career, see D. Moody Smith, Jr., 'The Historical Jesus in Paul Tillich's Christology' and Tillich's 'Rejoinder' in *The Journal of Religion*, 1966, pp. 131–47, 184–96. Tillich rejects the suggestion (coming to him originally, he tells us, from C. H. Dodd) that the element of historical doubt is part of what he has called the 'risk of faith': 'This sounded very plausible, but it is not. For the two risks lie in different dimensions. The risk connected with a historical statement is the risk of scholarly error which may have serious consequences in the realm of finite concerns. The risk connected with the assertion of faith that Jesus is the Christ is an error about the character of my ultimate concern. It is the question of the true messiahs and the false ones. It is, in Kierkegaardian terms, a decision of infinite significance. And this decision cannot be threatened in any way by the possibility of a historical error.' Tillich then appeals to the Spirit Christology of

Introducing Tillich may well serve to illumine the difficulty which dialectical theology experiences in making an advance beyond existentialism. No one—surely not Paul Tillich!—will claim that the *Systematic Theology* gets beyond the predicament of the existentialist by routing ontology in favour of theology. Perhaps Tillich and Barth —for all their differences otherwise—stand nearer at this point than their vocabularies suggest. Barth's neo-Kantianism may not place him so far from the dark world of philosophy.[44] One may still want to analyse the paths taken very differently. It may be Tillich's involvement in metaphysics (or in the wrong metaphysics) and the early Barth's failure to check the polarizing tendency of an entirely religious diastatic impulse which yield their common difficulty with the historical dimension of faith. Or let them both retain voting privileges in the theological union—what matters for our concern is that the existential predicament of polarization is not avoided by the one or the other.[45]

Part of that predicament was seen to be the tendency to identify the real and ideal with the result that one was left quite without means of determining which alternatives would really represent authentic selfhood—or even of accepting that question meaningfully. It must now be added that the extreme diastatic position on the ground of theology—or at least in the language of theology—comes off no better. Kierkegaard's dizziness over maintaining an absolute relationship to the absolute *telos* and a relative relationship to relative

---

the third volume of his *Systematic Theology*: 'It is the bearer of the Spirit who through the Spirit has created the church and the picture of himself in the New Testament in mutual dependence. In this sense the Christian faith guarantees directly its foundation.'

[44] See Schröer, op. cit., p. 183, for the contention that the ontological paradox is still dominant for Bultmann.

[45] Emil Brunner, *Truth as Encounter*, trans. by Amandus W. Loos and David Cairns (Philadelphia: Westminster; London, SCM Press, 1964), pp. 41–50, emphasizes the contrast between Barth and Bultmann by centering their positions at the opposite poles of a *theological* diastasis. Taking Luther's word that 'God and faith belong together', he finds Bultmann sacrificing the former and Barth the latter. While Brunner's comment does illumine a difference of emphasis, we are pointing out that the practical outcome for the self's relationships to others is not great. We shall see that to be the case as far as the ethical implications of diastasis are concerned as well. A coalescence of religious and philosophical interests is represented in Miguel de Unamuno's relationship to Kierkegaard. In neither case, however, is the dominance of the diastatic significantly qualified. See Unamuno's *Tragic Sense of Life*, trans. J. E. Crawford Flitch (New York: Dover, 1954) for the endorsement of Kierkegaard's emphasis on the opposition between thought and existence (p. 115), the contra-rational character of faith (pp. 198, 257) and the goal of maryrdom (p. 327).

ends[46] finds new life in Tillich's effort to relate penultimate concerns to his ultimate concern.[47] In neither case does the struggling individual find specific light to guide him in and between situations.

This same result seems to be represented by the populous attachment to the notion of a 'religionless Christianity'. Kierkegaard identified the danger of so endlessly exalting God that one was left free 'to live just as one wants to, in a worldly view of life'.[48] Barth insists that he never did believe or intend 'a new justification of the autonomy of man and thus of secularism'.[49] We shall see that the logic of Bonhoeffer's fragments does not endorse such a result. Still, taken by itself, the diastatic statement of God's lordship may leave one quite without the principles required to expose men's servitude to false masters and summon them concretely to servanthood to God.[50] Pure diastasis simply fails to yield any material basis for distinguishing between, say, secularity and secularism. Of course that failure may claim support in dark 'religious' judgments about the capacity of man and the significance of this life. But all of this still leaves man quite to himself in the facticity of his existence.

3. Beyond Diastasis: The Call to Christian Coherence

We have said that we have both an historical and a constructive interest in speaking of the legacy of Kierkegaard. In what we have said of the dominance of the diastatic impulse the historical account has largely been completed, while the constructive appeal is hardly begun. Were our task wholly that of identifying the probable influence of this 'maker of modern theology' we should still have to speak of more than the diastatic rhythm. Perhaps that cannot persuasively be said of the existentialists, for those figures who seem most linked with the rhythm of synthesis—Jaspers and Marcel, for

---

[46] S.V. VII, pp. 335ff. (CUP, pp. 347ff.).

[47] For a critique of Tillich at this point, see Walter Kaufmann, The Faith of a Heretic (Garden City: Doubleday, 1961), pp. 136–8.

[48] Pap. X 1 A 59; cf. above, p. 103.

[49] Barth, The Humanity of God, p. 45. Were that result intended Barth would be moving consciously towards a position which would finally reproduce the fatal weakness Barth sees in existentialism—that existence and transcendence are identified. See Church Dogmatics, III, 2, p. 120, for his criticism of Jaspers at this point. In his address. 'Mein Verhältnis zu Sören Kierkegaard', Orbis Litterarum, 1963, pp. 97–100, Barth relates this danger in existentialism to Kierkegaard's 'fatal pietism'.

[50] Ethics would then be frustrated as decisively as by the Hegelian subsumption of all reality under divine necessity. See above, pp. 79–81, on the need for the synthesis rhythm, if an advance 'beyond Hegel' is to be made.

example—seem to have drawn rather scantily from Kierkegaard at this point.[51] But Tillich, the Niebuhrs, Brunner—and others— challenge the generalization which titles this chapter. But it is above all our constructive concern which requires us to say more and to speak differently than we have. Several reasons come together at this point.

(1) Something seems strangely out of joint, if the contemporary theologian is to be nourished by the past by drawing upon a diastatic tradition which—taken by itself—requires that any important help must reach the individual Christian directly from the hand of God. Let the Christian renounce false hopes or re-examine the logic of his appeal.

(2) The contemporary theologian may deem consistency a very minor virtue—if not an actual vice. The canons of a reverse rationalism equating contradiction and truth do perhaps come rather easily to the lips (not to the minds, surely!) of current theologians, who speak with a rhythm representing the extremes of the diastatic tradition. But what is at stake is not some methodological nicety which is fully detachable from the substance of faith. We have shown in this chapter the predicament towards which the diastatic impulse seems to incline, if it is not checked and balanced by some other strain. In a word, too disjunctive conceptions of divine sovereignty defeat their own intention. Concerned to confess only God as Lord the speaker may be carried by the momentum of his diastatic commitments to the point of denying man access to God through his fellows and finally (and so?) of denying the Sovereign the possibility of receiving any discipleship whatever.

This self-defeating escalation is often linked with the recruitment by the diastatic thinker of metaphysically contradictory conceptions for the task of characterizing God and man. Perhaps the key step here lies in the understanding of God's independence. Caught up in the mood of devotion, one's speech blurs recognition of God's moral absoluteness (He alone determines the good) through a moment of repentance (He alone does the good) to an ascription of metaphysical ultimacy (He alone can do the good, for He alone is). This is not a logical syllogism, and hardly a conscious progression, but it may comment accurately on the psychological environment surrounding the diastatic escalation. Whether the appropriation of some formulation of metaphysical opposition is systemic to the diastatic rhythm or not, the polarizing course of that rhythm does seem perilous.

[51] See above, p. 275, notes 21–22.

(3) At least that seems to be the judgment of impressive voices within the human community. This is a time when an author can denounce the narrow snobbishness of the literary caste as blindness compounded by the formal posture of liberation, independence, and creativity. Joined to that denunciation a plea sounds for a return to the common world and to the use of intelligence therein.[52] It is a time when artists can second the judgment against professionalism and the adulation of the artist and his personality, urging attentiveness to the whole man, including the contribution of the past to that wholeness.[53] And it is a time when scientists witness to the self-accelerating momentum of technology and speak of questing after the ultimately simple structure of things.[54]

It would be excessive to claim that this is the stuff of which the dominant temper of the age is made, but there does seem to be an increasing concern for relatedness, for relevance, within and between disciplines.[55] To be sure, such concern conducts its business on the level of description. It does not—consciously, or at least openly—propose a material solution for a time threatened with the polarization of the diastatic. But it puts the question and one wonders on what grounds the theologian declines to attempt an answer. Perhaps his business is to sing the louder his praise to a disappearing deity and surely he may dismiss the pleas of the human community as those who know not the voice of the shepherd. He may—strangely—even find solace and self-vindication, rather than discomfiture and an indictment, in the fact that organized religion seems at ebb tide in the affairs of men.[56] All this and more is possible, but one does wonder about a theological community opting for this course.

[52] See the acceptance speech made by Saul Bellow upon receiving the National Book Award for fiction for his novel *Herzog*.

[53] See, for example, Charles Biederman, *Art as the Evolution of Visual Knowledge* (Red Wing, Minnesota; 1948).

[54] Dr Ralph E. Lapp in an article 'Do Developers Regret A-Bomb?' for World Book Encyclopedia Science Service, Inc. cites Dr Cyril S. Smith's contribution to a list of reasons for the making of the atomic bomb by the group of scientists of which Smith was a member: 'Then once we got started, the desire to do the job well took over, and carried us along to the conclusion.' Lapp expands on this theme: '. . . in general, technology is remorseless. If a bomb could be made, it would be. If made, it would be used. Technology manufactures its own momentum.'

[55] This concern is manifested both in the explicit conceptual elevation of the theme of relatedness (witness the work of such men as Gordon Allport and Gardiner Murphy—and before them, George Herbert Mead) and in the increasing fluidity of the lines separating 'different' disciplines (witness the development of social psychology, biophysics, physical chemistry, etc.).

[56] To cite a single example of the many available, a 1965 Gallup pole found that of the people questioned 33% thought 'religion as a whole is increasing its in-

(4) There are sounds within contemporary theology which parallel and perhaps respond to these expressions from the world of men. This new note is heard even within those currents of thought which we have linked with the sway of the diastatic. Again Gabriel Marcel and, to a lesser extent, Karl Jaspers provide a clearer suggestion of this tendency than the much discussed but still unclarified movement within the Heidegger corpus.[57] And Karl Barth can let the development in his own theology issue in specific criticism of the diastatic Kierkegaard's failure to appreciate the fact that 'the gospel is the *glad* message of God's *YES* to man' and that that gospel is 'the message which the *community* has to give abroad to the whole world'.[58]

Barth traces the development—revision is not too strong a word— of his thought to a christological source: 'It is when we look at Jesus Christ that we know decisively that God's deity does not exclude, but includes *His humanity*. . . . In Him the fact is once for all established that God does not exist without man.'[59] It is in the probing of the meaning of the Christ that a number of other voices have arisen to challenge the reign of diastasis in contemporary theology. We shall refer to this challenge in the sections which follow. It seems to represent no more than a spirited challenge to a diastatic posture which manages to be very much still the formative mentality in contemporary theological thought, appealing to the name and using the thought of Kierkegaard in doing so.[60]

---

fluence on American life', while 45 % thought it to be losing its influence—as opposed to 69% and 14%, respectively, in 1957. (That is only the people's opinion, but they would seem to be more than accidentally related to the question at hand.) This is not merely a 'finding' of those outside the household of faith. In releasing this poll the American Institute of Public Opinion had no difficulty adding supporting testimony from prominent religious leaders.

[57] Both Marcel and Jaspers echo Kierkegaard's concern with the *presence* of transcendence and with an ethic of communication which derives from that presence. Heidegger, on the other hand, does not seem to have moved this far. Wyschogrod's judgment (op. cit., p. 138) seems correct: 'The ontology of *Sein und Zeit* is not in a position to posit a situation in which the existentialistic reception of a revelation is just that—a reception and not the production of that received. Though Heidegger's second period represents an ontological shift from the position of the first period, it is not possible to take this latter formulation as an ontology that succeeds in some new way in incorporating Kierkegaardian existence into Being because this latter understanding of Being is implicit only. It is not a philosophically reasoned argument of the concept but merely an application of it to some aesthetic problems from which it must be drawn by inference.'

[58] Karl Barth, 'Mein Verhältnis zu Sören Kierkegaard', *Orbis Litterarum*, 1963, pp. 97–100.

[59] Barth, *The Humanity of God*, pp. 49–50. [Italics his.]

[60] Perhaps a kind of bridge from the use of Kierkegaard as a representative of extreme diastasis to the new interest in the meaning of the Christ is to be found in

(5) It is therefore a matter of particular interest that other themes in Kierkegaard be heard and appropriated. Here our historical and constructive interests are joined. One could justify an effort to articulate these other themes simply in the interest of historical justice. Let us not fail to hear all sides of a Kierkegaard who set before men the various choices he saw confronting the self. But it becomes especially important to set the record right if new forces in thought, which are struggling to make themselves heard, must overcome the prestige of a figure from the past who could with at least equal right be cited on their side of the argument. Indeed a more balanced reading of Kierkegaard could very well give not only greater force but clearer unifying focus to the sounds which can be heard today.

---

the work of theologians like Tillich and Niebuhr who have not been content to settle for a diastatic description of the relationship between God and man. Reinhold Niebuhr's esteem for Kierkegaard's analysis of the self is well known. He finds that 'Kierkegaard has interpreted the true meaning of human selfhood more accurately than any modern, and possibly than any previous, Christian theologian'. (*The Nature and Destiny of Man* [2 vols., London: Nisbet, 1941–3] I, p. 182; cf. *passim*.) Tillich has argued against any total isolation of the stages, of eros and agape, from each other. (See *Love, Power, and Justice* [New York: Oxford, 1960], pp. 31–32.) Yet one wonders how much actual effect these qualifications have beyond their immediate context in the system in question. Tillich's doctrine of God tends toward a notion of static substance, as becomes clear in the second volume of the *Systematic Theology* if it was not clear already in the first. At the end of his life Tillich found 'very attractive' the suggestion that there is 'a subject and circumstance of all knowledge' which may be called God, paralleling "being" which refers to that which is 'both the object and the circumstance of all knowledge'. Thus the assertion emerges that 'being and action are two aspects of the prius of thinking, neither of them reducible to the other'. Yet he still wishes to resist putting being and doing on the same ontological level, since 'in "doing" being is presupposed (as it is in "becoming")'. See the suggestion, 'Tillich's Method of Correlation: Two Proposed Revisions' by Robert P. Scharlemann, and Tillich's 'Rejoinder', in *The Journal of Religion*, 1966, pp. 92–104, 184–96. Niebuhr has not drawn on Kierkegaard's christology significantly. Indeed scepticism concerning the degree to which diastasis is qualified in neo-orthodox theology is increased by the fact that Brunner, for all the heat of his dispute with Karl Barth on natural revelation, offers a strongly diastatic statement in the area of christology. He may want to find an alternative between Barth and Bultmann (see above, p. 283, note 45), but the alternative seems to be combining the two in a christology which leaves the solitary individual confronting the paradoxical point in time, the Christ. The diastatic moment is not only deeply rooted—it is widespread as well. Carl Braaten suggests that range in writing of the 'breakdown in the religio-cultural synthesis in the West' which 'is evident in the almost insuperable gulf between the biblical text and the contemporary sermon, in the diastasis between theology and philosophy, in the post-Kantian expulsion of nature from a theology of grace, in the retreat from ontology to phenomenology and finally to semantics, in the splitting up of the unity of history into the dualisms of *Heilsgeschichte* and *Weltgeschichte* and of *Historie* and *Geschichte* and what not.' 'The Interdependence of Theology and Preaching', *Dialog*, Winter, 1964, pp. 14–15. [Italics his.]

We have as yet offered no 'explanation' for the dominance of the diastatic in the appropriation of Kierkegaard's legacy. We believe that it has been shown that the works themselves do not require that their reception possess such a character. Perhaps a too sensationalist reading of the end of Kierkegaard's life, if not an over-punctiliar definition of the end of the passage through the stages, has contributed to the result. It was the pamphlet attack which was the first of Kierkegaard's works to find its way into German in 1861 and into Karl Barth's study in 1909. Indeed the bold lines of the diastatic tradition appear to possess an emotional appeal which the synthesis rhythm can hardly rival. In any case Kierkegaard so diagnosed his time that the sharper, more strident, tones of diastasis seem to over-shadow those other affirmations which support his message and give it substance.[61] We may deal more, then, with the tides of historical times than with the eternal relationships between types of mentality. Perhaps this 'other Kierkegaard' has belonged to a kind of 'middle distance', while the diastatic Dane seemed to offer such a clear contrast and penetrating critique of what we have thought the rest of the nineteenth century was doing and saying.

We live in a new time. If, in a certain sense, Kierkegaard did not feel that the question of the 'what' of Christianity was basic to the affliction of his time, we cannot so judge the period in which we find ourselves. The objective content of Christian claims is very much in doubt today—indeed the issue in many quarters is the more funda-mental one as to whether the faith can be said to make any claims which would have any bearing on the life of man other than as an invitation to emotional extravagance. If this was not Kierkegaard's conscious problem, he yet speaks to it. We should want to say that he does so precisely because he is a Christian theologian. Any theology speaking from an encounter with the Christ cannot long (and this generation's theologians surely cannot well longer) speak only in the diastatic mood.[62] But that is a claim which requires support and for which the support of the rest of this book will not be too great.

[61] See above, pp. 38–39 A, and *Pap.* X 2 A 475 (*Dru* 1060), X 2 A 525 (*Dru* 1072).

[62] Or if it does it runs the risk of being carried by the diastatic momentum to the point where its theological character is reduced to a matter of words. This is the basis for Gerd-Günther Grau's argument against Kierkegaard, when he claims (*Die Selbstauflösung des christlichen Glaubens* [Frankfurt: G. Schulte-Bulmke, 1963]) that Nietzsche is more honest than Kierkegaard. This chapter suggests the validity of his argument, while the entirety of the book reveals how selective one must be if one is to offer Kierkegaard as the exemplification of such dishonesty. Paradoxically the attacks on Kierkegaard by representatives of the extreme theological right at times do serve to bring into focus the selectivity of a reading like Grau's.

IX

THE CHRIST AND CHRISTIAN COHERENCE

1. *The Christ and Christian Coherence: The Substance of Faith*

IT IS only possible to suggest briefly what contributions Kierke-gaard's thought could make to contemporary theology if the diastatic caricature could be removed. It is right to make that suggestion by exploring the meaning of the christological witness which we have found to be central to his thought.

(1) In looking to the Christ there is found the central principle for Christian faith and Christian reflection: 'To believe is to believe the divine and the human together in Christ.'[1] The theologian who witnesses to the Christ offers his work as commentary on the coher-ence of God and man. The boundaries of his interest and the bent of his work are found in the relationship of God and man. He may have to speak forcefully of opposition, he will have to speak plainly of distinction,—but these speakings are adjectival, for they offer comment on the primal substantive fact he confesses: that God and man do have to do with each other and that eternal differences and existential estrangement do not efface that fact. Kierkegaard surely knew well enough that man was not God, that man was against God, and he does not turn from that knowledge when he speaks of the Christ. But even in the most severely diastatic setting the Christ still means to him the meeting of God and man. The one Christ bodies forth both the powerful presence of God and the actuality of authentic humanity. That conviction is strong enough to chasten the diastatic impulse and reform those formulations which threaten to make the meeting of God and man merely verbal and intrinsically unintel-ligible.

(2) But to say that God and man 'cohere' seems to be to say some-thing other than to say that they 'meet'. If coherence suggests 'connection or congruity arising from some common principle or relationship',[2] it implies an extensiveness and a givenness missing in

---

[1] *S.V.* XI, p. 69 ('HM', *PA*, p. 99).
[2] *Webster's Collegiate Dictionary*, fifth edition (Springfield, Mass: G. & C. Mer-riam Co., 1948), p. 195.

a 'meeting'. So are the elements of form and motion suggested. Kierkegaard would bid us sacrifice neither of these elements in our speech about the Christ. To believe is to believe the divine and the human together—in the Christ. There is an event-full character to the Christ. We shall say more of that momentarily. Now we speak of the context for that event. The event depends on the context. That is true of man's reception of the event, for if he knew nothing whatever of God, the claim of the Christ to make 'God' known would be unintelligible.[3] This subjective dependence of the event on a context leads beyond the matter of appropriation to the constitution of the event itself. Without some continuity between God and man no aspect of human reality offers itself to a meeting with God in the Christ any more readily than the centre of volition and consciousness.

Kierkegaard surely confesses the faith that something 'new' happened in the Christ. But God and man so meet in him as to make clear their fundamental coherence.[4] We have argued that the schema of the stages witness to that coherence.[5] The aesthetic quest for pleasure anticipates the Christian's experience of the true good in which the aesthetic is dethroned but not renounced.[6] Kierkegaard invites the Christian thinker to take the bold step of recognizing this relationship in addressing the man apart from the Christ. 'Between' the aesthetic and the religious stands the ethical and there lies the clue to the continuity. The existentialists *do* have something in letting the category of choice dominate their description of man. Man's being and man's fulfilment require that he choose something, so that the existentialists are right in refusing to restrict the necessity of choice to an epistemological affair. The need to choose is a matter of man's very being and is rooted in the internality of his being. One may go further and say that man quests after some kind of continuity in his choices—caprice is not his native element. How else has it come about that the existentialists' evocation of the anguish of unjustified choice has found so powerful a response in our time?

---

[3] For a recent statement of this point, see Kai Nielsen, 'God and the good: Does Morality Need Religion?', *Theology Today*, April, 1964, pp. 47–59.

[4] Erik Routley, *The Man For Others* (Derby: Peter Smith; New York: Oxford, 1964), p. 61, writes in a similar manner: 'So Jesus is "God among us": and just as we are told in the Gospel that "God loves the world", meaning that God has always loved it, so we are told in His incarnation that it is of the very nature of God to be "among us".'

[5] See above, pp. 34–39.

[6] See above, pp. 37, 113–4.

The existentialist counsel of despair accurately perceives that justification is not secured by an appeal to group convention. Kierkegaard could endorse that perception, but his conviction concerning the coherence of God and man frees him from turning back with the existentialists to the lonely courage of the self's arbitrariness. It is faith in a transcendent reality which opens the possibility of an ethical orientation.[7] Christian thinkers have not hesitated in saying that the transcendent ought is heard apart from the career of Jesus of Nazareth.[8] Kierkegaard makes such speech his own, as Valter Lindström has shown so ably in making clear how the theme of the unavoidability of the God-relationship is basic to the theology of the stages.[9] Kierkegaard would not shrink from speaking of a point of contact and would not limit that point to a formal sense of responsibility,[10] speaking rather of a sense of guilt which penetrates the totality of the self.

(3) This manner of speaking may seem to characterize Kierkegaard as some quaint figure from the distant past of the nineteenth century who is out of place in our age and hopelessly naïve in any time. Has the man who brings this figure forward, professing constructive interest, read neither Feuerbach nor Freud?[11] Or, changing the indictment somewhat, does he seriously offer this Kierkegaard, concerned as he is with the preparation for faith in the natural man, to a man 'come of age'?

The outline of an answer to these questions would run somewhat

[7] For an extended critique of the autonomy of ethics, see Paul L. Lehmann, *Ethics in a Christian Context* (New York: Harper; London: SCM Press, 1963) Part II. For a discussion of Kierkegaard's thought in terms of the relationships between personal identity, the ethical, and the religious, see Elfriede Tielsch, *Kierkegaards Glaube* (Göttingen: Vandenhoeck & Ruprecht, 1964).

[8] See, for example, John Baillie, *Our Knowledge of God* (Oxford University Press; New York: Scribners, 1939), p. 17: 'My conviction has been that the only humanity known to us is a humanity which has already . . . been confronted with the reality of God and disturbed by the challenge of His Holy Presence, and . . . it is this fact which determines the success alike of theological argument and religious appeal.'

[9] Valter Lindström, *Stadiernas Teologi* (Lund: Haakan Ohlsson, 1943).

[10] Emil Brunner's use of the concept of responsibility in connection with a distinction between a *principium essendi* and a *principium cognoscendi* is perhaps the best known example of this approach. Brunner believes himself to be in Kierkegaard's tradition, whom he praises as 'incomparably the greatest apologist or "eristic" thinker of the Christian Faith within the sphere of Protestantism'. *The Christian Doctrine of God*, trans. Olive Wyon (London: Lutterworth Press, 1949; Philadelphia: Westminster, 1950), p. 100.

[11] For a useful survey of contemporary literature carrying this critique, see Michael Argyle, 'Seven Psychological Roots of Religion', *Theology*, August, 1964, pp. 333–9.

as follows. (A) Kierkegaard never comes near claiming that faith is a self-evident medicine for despair. If a kind of momentum can be found in the stages, it is not that of a machine which pushes man irresistibly on to the affirmation of the Christian answer to the human predicament. Earlier we put this point so: 'Reality is not onto-logically weighted in the direction of the good, which is God. Sin is quite literally a possibility and the actualization of that possibility bears the mystery of any act of freedom, but none other.'[12] Kierke-gaard could accept Bonhoeffer's words: 'It is possible nowadays to find human answers to these problems too [guilt, suffering and death] which leave God right out of the picture. It just isn't true to say that Christianity alone has the answers. In fact the Christian answers are no more conclusive or compelling than any of the others.'[13]

(B) Kierkegaard does not depend for his point of contact on a particularistic conscience moralistically compiling a list of personal peccadilloes. The human predicament at the ethical stage is far more fundamental and quite other than such a procedure would suggest. The self becomes aware of its finitude. It does encounter boundary situations.[14] It knows the dread 'which is freedom's reality as possi-bility for possibility'.[15] The self thirsts for the word of acceptance, for the glad message that quite as it is, with or without its achievements, it is valued by God.[16] It is this kind of all-embracing and underlying need to which Kierkegaard's words about 'total guilt' refer, even though they are cast in an ambiguous framework.

(C) It ought to be clear that the Christian 'answer' is no release from a life of engagement and striving. It does not clearly offer an easier time of it to all who come. This, of course, does not defeat the

[12] See above, p. 202.
[13] Dietrich Bonhoeffer, *Letters and Papers from Prison*, ed. Eberhard Bethge, trans. Reginald Fuller (London: 1953 SCM Press; New York: Macmillan, 1954), pp. 142–3. Kierkegaard's openness on this point derives from his fundamental rejection of a thoroughgoing monism. Thus he could not endorse Alan Richardson's statement ('Second Thoughts: Present Issues in New Testament Theology', *The Expository Times*, January, 1964, p. 111): 'According to the classical tradition of Christian philosophy (which, of course, goes back to Greek thought), evil is essen-tially the unreal, the absolutely non-existent. Therefore it can be demythologized with plausibility. But God is defined as "He who is", the One in whom essence and existence coincide. A possible way, therefore, of characterizing God in our con-temporary thought-forms would be to say that He is the uniquely undemytholo-gizable One—. . . The historic Christian faith involves the metaphysical assertion that good and evil are not of equal ontological status.'
[14] See above, pp. 109–11, *Pap.* VII A 143 and Lindström, op. cit., p. 118.
[15] *S.V.* IV, p. 313 (*CD*, p. 38).
[16] See Gregor Malantschuk, *Kierkegaard's Way to the Truth*, trans. Mary Michel-sen (Minneapolis: Augsburg, 1963), p. 46.

psychological explanation of faith, but one might grant man the capacity to wish in ways less involved than this.[17]

We shall return below to the question of the vertification of the Christian claim. But it is in place here to note that our brief summary of how Kierkegaard sees the Christian message confronting man hardly finds a challenge in the Bonhoeffer who sent forth those tantalizing words, 'the non-religious interpretation of biblical terminology'.[18] Bonhoeffer would quite agree that—in Helmut Thielicke's words—'one cannot do away with the anxiety which threatens the nihilistic man by talking the fear-producing objects out of existence. [One may question whether we have done so thorough a job of that at that.] For the source of anxiety does not lie in the objective world but within man.'[19] Gerhard Ebeling has pointed convincingly to Bonhoeffer's testimony to the significance of boundary situations in his own experience and has gathered passages showing how Bonhoeffer let that testimony inform his thought about the age in which he lived.[20]

Thus Bonhoeffer can reliably be read as seconding Kierkegaard's insight into the fundamental dependence of man upon God. This is not true in the sense that man is nothing, but rather in the sense that the very plenitude of his being is from God and turned towards God.[21] Indeed, if the relationship miscarries, the self may not only fail to fathom its own nature,[22] but let its fundamental disquietude

[17] Feuerbach shows how the appeal to the ethical character of religion can be handled by the psychological explanation in *The Essence of Christianity*, trans. George Eliot (New York: Harper, 1957), pp. 44–49. While the Christian must concede that this explanation is possible, it seems to behove his partner in dialogue to observe that it is not necessary. Michael Argyle, 'Seven Psychological Roots of Religion', *Theology*, August, 1964, pp. 333–9, observes that the psychological approach need not be deemed a rival to religious claims, for 'it does not follow . . . that because a belief has psychological grounds it is false'. Others, of course, using the razor edge of economy, would cut away talk of some objective religious reality as having no explanatory value whatever. We comment below in discussing the Statement of Faith.

[18] Bonhoeffer, op. cit., pp. 158, 162; cf. pp. 126, 160, 164. For a thorough and reflective discussion of Bonhoeffer's use of this phrase, see Gerhard Ebeling, *Word, and Faith*, trans. James W. Leitch (London: SCM Press; Philadelphia: Fortress, 1963), pp. 98–162. See also John D. Godsey, *The Theology of Dietrich Bonhoeffer* (Philadelphia: Westminster; London: SCM Press 1960), pp. 248–60.

[19] Helmut Thielicke, 'Nihilism and Anxiety', *Theology Today*, October, 1955, p. 353. Cf. Bonhoeffer, op. cit., p. 178: 'Man is once more faced with the problem of himself. He can cope with every danger except the danger of human nature itself.'

[20] Ebeling, op. cit., pp. 151–3.

[21] See above, pp. 109–10, 133–4.

[22] Cf. Robert Scharlemann, 'Man: A Question to Himself', *Dialog*, summer, 1964, p. 172: 'That fact that man is a question and that he becomes aware of his

blossom in a world of imaginary fears. That may account for the impression of cosmic hypochondria existentialism sometimes creates.[23] What, then, is the 'religion' for which Bonhoeffer finds no place? It is the polarized extreme of diastasis, the metaphysical otherness of God and the solipsistic subjectivity of the individual that draws his fire: 'Our relation to God [is] not a religious relationship to a supreme Being, absolute in power and goodness . . . the absolute, metaphysical, infinite, etc. . . .'[24] 'Is it not true to say that individualistic concern for personal salvation has almost completely left us all? Are we not really under the impression that there are more important things than bothering about such a matter? . . . I know it sounds pretty monstrous to say that. But is it not, at bottom, even biblical?'[25] One can well understand the positive thrust of Bonhoeffer's protest to be a witness to the coherence of God and man: 'God is the "beyond" in the midst of our life.'[26]

(4) Just as Barth found 'it is when we look at Jesus Christ that we know decisively that God's deity does not exclude, but includes His humanity',[27] so did Bonhoeffer write: 'The thing that keeps coming back to me is, what *is* Christianity, and indeed what *is* Christ, for us to-day?'[28] The answer? 'Whoever sees Jesus Christ does indeed see God and the world in one. He can henceforward no longer see God without the world or the world without God.'[29] If the Christ leads us beyond the paradox of metaphysical transcendence, we surely ought not to resurrect those same intellectual puzzles in speaking of this one who is in the centre of life.[30]

---

questionability most acutely in the presence of God constitutes in brief his heritage of self-understanding. . . . Today man is just as acutely aware of his questionability, but now he stands typically not before "God" but before his "future". . . . which is that reality where the secret of human destiny is held.'

[23] See Charles Frankel, *The Love of Anxiety* (New York: Harper, 1965).

[24] Bonhoeffer, op. cit., p. 179. Cf. ibid., pp. 124, 175.

[25] ibid., pp. 125–6. Cf. ibid., p. 160: '. . . the Bible does not recognize our distinction of outer and inner. . . . The "heart" in the biblical sense is not the inward life, but the whole man is relation to God.'

[26] ibid., p. 124. Cf. ibid., p. 84: ' . . . through every event, however untoward, there is always a way through to God'.

[27] Karl Barth, *The Humanity of God*, p. 49.

[28] Bonhoeffer, op. cit., p. 122. [Italics his.]

[29] Dietrich Bonhoeffer, *Ethics*, ed. Eberhard Bethge, trans. N. H. Smith (London: SCM Press; New York: Macmillan, 1955), p. 8.

[30] W. Norman Pittenger, *The Word Incarnate: A Study of the Doctrine of the Person of Christ* (New York: Harper; London: Nisbet 1959), p. 117, states the correlation in a sentence: 'We must not look for the divinity of Jesus in the "gaps" of his humanity any more than we look for God in the "gaps" of his creation.' Cf. Bonhoeffer, *Letters and Papers from Prison*, pp. 142–3.

Here we may follow a path which Kierkegaard cuts through the heavy underbrush of theological verbiage. It is not merely that he fears that the individual will lose himself in heavenly speculation over the doctrine of the God-Man.[31] Beyond and behind that is the fundamental conviction that in the Christ the coherence of God and man becomes clear. 'He makes the divine commensurable to being a wholly ordinary man.'[32] 'First in Christ is it true that God is man's goal and measure, or measure and goal.'[33] This is not related accidentally to his person. We have seen how Kierkegaard refuses to parcel out the functions in the life of Jesus to divine and human natures.[34] One cannot isolate a human Jesus setting before us the pattern of perfect response from a divine Christ who saves us. Kierkegaard can sing of the blessedness of the royal coachman's lash [35] and speak of the pattern as the fulfilment.[36] The results of the Christ's work are no more separable by appeal to a law-gospel schema, than is the ministry itself by the employment of a two natures dichotomy. Indeed the two points are related in a way which reflects the fundamental coherence of God and man. So we are told that the Christian who struggles to resemble the pattern (and that he is to do) has God for a brother.[37]

[31] Though that is a danger, see *S.V.* XII, pp. 101–2 (*TC*, pp. 108–9).

[32] *Pap.* IX A 101; see above, p. 184.

[33] *S.V.* XI, p. 224 (*SD*, p. 245); cf. *Pap.* X 2 A 643 (*Dru* 1089). Cf. above, p. 185.

[34] See above, pp. 197–8.

[35] See above, pp. 110–1. In a similar vein, T. W. Manson writes in *On Paul and John* (London: SCM Press, 1963), p. 31: 'Salvation is primarily a radical change in man's character and disposition, not primarily a revision of his theological opinions.' See Edvin Larsson, *Christus als Vorbild* (Lund: Gleerup, 1962) on the relationship between the imitation of the Christ and the Pauline theme of being 'in Christ'.

[36] *S.V.* X, p. 46 (*CDi*, p. 45). G. W. H. Lampe, 'The Atonement: Satisfaction or Sentimentality', *Theology*, August, 1964, pp. 339–43, points the way to an elaboration of this theme by emphasizing the distinction between penal and sacrificial views of the atonement: 'In so far as I understand it, the sacrificial metaphor expresses the essential truth that Christ, in his perfect trust and obedience to the Father, by which he was able to be the channel of God's accepting and forgiving love for sinners, effected what the sacrifices portrayed but could not achieve. He removed sin out of the way, and opened up access for all men to fellowship with the Father. Thus he made it possible for us to share in his faith and obedience, to make the offering of thanksgiving and dedication which is man's duty to the Creator and our proper response to his free acceptance of us.'

[37] *S.V.* X, p. 48 (*CDi*, p. 46). See above p. 197. Cf. Canon Montefiore in *Soundings* (ed. Alec Vidler [Cambridge: University, 1962], p. 169): 'It is God's identification with mankind and his loving acceptance of the worst that man can do to him that enables a man to accept himself and God and thereby to be set on the road toward full and loving relationships with God and men. "We love because he first loved us". . . . This is atonement.' On the whole one may say that current writers do not

What is the claim made by this Christ, then? It is to be found 'not, as in other religions, in animal form—the monstrous, chaotic, remote and terrifying—nor yet in abstract form—the absolute, metaphysical, infinite, etc.—nor yet in the Greek divine-human of autonomous man, but man existing for others, and hence the Crucified'.[38] What is at stake here is not merely a matter of the disclosure of the essential coherence of God and man. It is a matter of God and man cohering in the Christ. The 'event' character of the Christ comes into focus. We are to make more of our relationship to God than the mumbling of formulas—we are to be formed into the likeness of the Christ. In Bonhoeffer's words again: 'It is not some religious act which makes a Christian what he is, but participation in the suffering of God in the world.'[39] Man is challenged not to consider a conception, but to let his very existence be changed by the Christ over against whom he stands. This is the claim of the Christ.

(5) One may, of course, diagnose this line of thought as a subtle (or even straightforward) denigration of the Christ. It is true that certain avenues for stating the significance of the Christ are closed to this approach. He is not to be exalted as a metaphysical miracle. And on the religious level, the prospects are not bright for any simple distinction by which it could be held that in the Christ for the first time man comes to know that—in Macquarrie's terms—'being is gracious'.[40] 'Grace and truth came through Jesus Christ', but he is the incarnation of the Word, 'the true light that enlightens

---

appear to be reluctant to take the corresponding step of giving weight to the human Jesus in understanding the significance of the death of the Christ. See, for example, Paul M. van Buren, *The Secular Meaning of the Gospel* (New York: Macmillan; London: SCM Press, 1963), p. 151: '"The cross" and other references to Jesus' death became summary ways of speaking of his whole history, as indeed his end seemed to his disciples, after the fact, to have been foreshadowed in all of his life. Since his life was one of solidarity with men, compassion for them, mercy toward their weakness and wrong, it is not suprising that his death, which was the consequence of his freedom to be related to men in this way, was spoken of as a death "for us". His death (which could so easily have been avoided if he had taken the way of caution, calculation, and self-interest) was regarded as the measure of the freedom for which he set other men free.' But it does not seem to be a mark of great progress to accept the traditional dichotomy, though reversing the traditional roles. It is not too soon for contemporary theologians to probe the cost for God of the loving life and death of the Christ.

[38] Bonhoeffer, op. cit., p. 179.

[39] ibid., p. 166. Cf. ibid., p. 167 and p. 179: 'Faith is participation in this Being of Jesus (incarnation, cross and resurrection).'

[40] See 'How is Theology possible?', John Macquarrie's inaugural lecture at Union Theological Seminary, in: John Macquarrie, *Studies in Christian Existentialism* (Montreal: McGill University; London: SCM Press, 1966), pp. 3–16.

every man . . . coming into the world'.[41] Furthermore, quite apart
from any concept of 'common grace',[42] the very distinction between
law and gospel can no longer be understood to present a total
separation, making it possible to reserve the gospel for Jesus.[43] In the
Christ God and man do not so meet that the best of human deeds and
the richest mortal wisdom are repudiated and the meeting itself
reduced to a verbal juxtaposition.[44]

But how, then, may the charge of forfeiting the Christ be met? A
good part of the answer must be found in what we have referred to in
this book as the 'actuality' of the Christ. The Christ of whom the
Christian speaks has the actuality of an event, not that of a concept.
Training in Christianity eloquently warns against reducing the God-
man to a truth about God and man.[45] The efficacy of the Christ is
rooted in the raw facticity of an event which in its objectivity checks
subjectivity in a way a concept never can. It ought to be noted that
even the most diastatic of Kierkegaard's utterances never relinquish
this emphasis on the event, though they surely do fail to relate that
event intelligibly to the common course of history.

(6) This emphasis on the objectivity of the Christ event must not
be turned into an escape from the claim of God in the Christ. The
givenness of this event means that this event shall be given anew to
men. Thus there arises the need for the scholarship which lays bare
the reality of that happening. Surely Kierkegaard's strictures against
the misuse of historical scholarship sound far clearer in his works
than any endorsement of a proper role for such scholarship. And

[41] John 1. 17 b and 9 (RSV).

[42] See, for example, John Baillie, *The Sense of the Presence of God* (Oxford University Press; New York: Scribners, 1962), pp. 201–2: 'I should not myself care to
speak of any saving power "apart from Christ", but should rather insist that the
Eternal Christ who was made *flesh* in Jesus of Nazareth, and the Eternal Atonement which was made *event* on Calvary, were and are the source of every "saving
process" which has at any time proved to be for the healing of the nations.' [Italics
his.]

[43] Ebeling, op. cit., p. 156, makes this point concerning proclamation, when he
writes: '. . . when given proper theological treatment law and Gospel cannot in
any way be isolated from eath other. The law interprets the Gospel and the Gospel
interprets the law. The principle of their relationship is as much a *coniunctissime*
as a *distinctissime*. The correct doctrine of law and Gospel has to show in what
respect the law precedes the Gospel, but also in what respect the Gospel precedes the
law—in such a way, of course, that the order "Gospel and law" serves to confirm the
order "law and Gospel", and on no account vice versa.' [Italics his.]

[44] For a sharply opposed interpretation of Kierkegaard's meaning, see Jan
Sperna Weiland as quoted above, p. 115, note 70, and Malcolm Diamond, p. 193,
note 83.

[45] See *S.V.* XII, pp. 101–2; cf. pp. 79, 131, 189 (*TC*, pp. 108–9; cf. pp. 83,
140–1, 200–1).

there is the danger that the quest—new or old—for the historical Jesus will derail the proclamation of the Christ by routing it through the interminable deliberations of the professors.

Yet what is at stake is not a luxury. And perhaps the very diastasis between the groves of the academe and the centre of the city can be seen to be cracking—both in the cry for the correlation of scholarship and proclamation[46] and in the signs that the world of the university is being ineluctably drawn into the commerce of human affairs. As to the essential limitations facing such scholarship, it should be noted that the understanding of the claim of the Christ event being advanced here in no way requires that the mental state of Jesus be exposed to view. Ernest Käsemann has suggested that the synoptic gospel tradition is more concerned with the historical Jesus than Bultmann supposed, in the sense that it invites investigation into the question of the continuity between the preaching of Jesus and the preaching about Jesus.[47] If this suggestion is sound, there is hope that the encounter with the Christ might go forward under the tutelage of the actuality of the Christ event.[48] That development would

[46] So, for example, Heinrich Ott, 'What is Systematic Theology?', *The Later Heidegger and Theology*, ed. James M. Robinson and John B. Cobb, Jr. (New York: Harper, 1963), p. 79. 'A single arch stretches from the Biblical texts to the contemporary preaching of the church. It is the arch of the kerygma and of the understanding of the kerygma. At each point, from the text to the sermon, it is the continuity of a single act of understanding, a single hermeneutical process. It is a matter of the same kerygma becoming audible today as then, that is, of the witness being trans-lated to our side of the shore.' Cf. ibid., p. 81, note: '. . . exegetical, systematic, and practical theology should not be artificially separated and isolated one from the other. They are in continuity one with the other. Only on technical grounds of a division of labour did the various theological "disciplines" arise. Originally they were one.' Carl Braaten's 'The Interdependence of Theology and Preaching', *Dialog*, Winter, 1964, pp. 12–21, provides a useful statement of Ott's and Ebeling's concern at this point, though Braaten himself regards the concern to demonstrate a basis for christological statements in the pre-resurrection Jesus 'as a reactionary tendency that can only introduce once again a great uncertainty into the preaching of the Christ and place faith in reliance upon the shakiest foundation'. ibid., p. 20.

[47] Ernst Käsemann, 'The Problem of the Historical Jesus', *Essays on New Testament Themes*, Studies in Biblical Theology, No. 41 (London: SCM Press; Naperville: Allenson,1964). See also Ernst Fuchs, *Studies of the Historical Jesus*, Studies in Biblical Theology, No. 42 (London: SCM Press; Naperville: Allenson, 1964). In relation to Bultmann's scepticism about the historical element in the Gospels, it is interesting that his colleague in the methods of form criticism, Martin Dibelius, has considerable confidence in the essential reliability of the tradition. For a concise statement at this point see his *Jesus*, trans. C. B. Hendrick and F. C. Grant (London: SCM Press, 1963). With respect to the dispute concerning the degree of Bultmann's scepticism, see page 281, note 41 above.

[48] See the summary article by Norman Perrin, 'The Challenge of New Testament Theology Today', *Criterion*, Spring, 1965, pp. 25–34, for a discussion of

be welcomed by Kierkegaard's fundamental call to Christian coherence and more specifically by his recognition of man's rootage in the communities of space and time.

(7) We have shown how important the concept of community is for Kierkegaard. His works may permit appeal to his name by those who isolate the individual, but they more basically challenge such appeal and may serve to correct the tendency towards the polarized subject in contemporary theology. Man *is* self and race. He will flee from 'shut-in-ness' to disclosure—a disclosure bearing substantive, constitutive significance for the selves in question. From Kierkegaard's thought the contemporary theologian could learn of both the human community and the Christian community and come to recognize the distinction at this point without permitting that distinction to drive a hard line between the two communities of man.[49]

Indeed those efforts on the contemporary scene to explore the communal dimension of the Christ event do not violate the main thrust of Kierkegaard's christology. An important part of that effort is to warn against a purely individualistic reading of the divine intention in the Christ event.[50] A still more pressing part is to correct the tendency to characterize the result of the Christ event in terms of a purely individualistic salvation. Here again the actuality of the event

---

efforts following Käsemann's suggestion. Käsemann, like most of the 'New Questers', still understands himself to be fighting a two-front war with the 'kenosis view of the historizers' a very real threat. The work of Wolfhart Pannenberg provides a more exhilarating contrast to the 'docetism of the enthusiasts', though it may be doubted whether it is possible to limit faith to a confidence with respect to the future. See *Offenbarung als Geschichte*, ed. Pannenberg (Göttingen: Vandenhoek & Ruprecht, 1961). A useful summary of Pannenberg's concern and the literature growing up around it is available in an article by Carl E. Braaten, 'The Current Controversy on Revelation: Pannenberg and his Critics', *The Journal of Religion*, 1965, pp. 225–37.

[49] Such a refusal to draw the line so firmly may be found in Bonhoeffer's *Sanctorum Communio* (Munich: Chr. Kaiser, 1954; Eng. tr. Collins, 1963). Bonhoeffer was twenty-one years old when he submitted this work to the theological faculty of the University of Berlin, but it already points the way to the letters from prison by rejecting any specific ritualistic or religious distinction which would separate the church from other communities.

[50] So T. W. Manson, *The Teaching of Jesus: Studies in its Form and Content* (Cambridge: University, 1931), pp. 227ff: 'His [Jesus'] mission is to create the Son of Man, the Kingdom of the saints of the Most High, to realize in Israel the ideal contained in the term. This task is attempted in two ways: first by public appeal to the people through the medium of parable and sermon and by the mission of the disciples: then, when this appeal produced no adequate response, by the consolidation of His own band of followers. Finally, when it becomes apparent that not even the disciples are ready to rise to the demands of the ideal, He stands alone, embodying in His own person the perfect human response to the regal claims of God.'

comes into focus. Surely Kierkegaard witnesses to the facticity of the event when he writes that first in the Christ does God become man's measure and goal. He is not speaking of a change in God,[51] but of a change in a man fashioned through his relationships and now confronted by the Christ.

One cannot doubt that Kierkegaard would want us to understand that 'God becoming our measure and goal' altogether concretely in the testimony of deeds. The Christ event both challenges and enables man to make the fitting response.[52] The fundamental coherence of God and man is celebrated and consummated in the meeting of God and man in the Christ and through the kerygmatic witness finds new Christomorphic fulfilment.[53] That fulfilment recognizes the community as *telos*. Perhaps Teilhard de Chardin combines these elements when he writes:

Christ, principle of universal vitality because sprung up as man among men, put himself in the position (maintained ever since) to subdue under himself, to purify, to direct and superanimate the general ascent of consciousness into which he inserted himself. By a perennial act of communion and sublimation, he aggregates to himself the total psychism of the earth. . . . The universe fulfilling itself in a synthesis of centres in perfect conformity with the laws of union. God, the Centre of centres. In that final vision the Christian dogma culminates.[54]

John Knox has also stressed the theme of community, rather less pessimistically than Manson. See Knox's *The Man Christ Jesus* (Chicago: Willett Clark, 1942), *Christ the Lord* (Chicago: Willett Clark, 1945) and *The Meaning of Christ* (New York: Scribner's, 1947).

[51] See above, pp. 194–6.

[52] See above, p. 182, note 36 on the pattern as the fulfilment, and above, p. 194, note 85, on the miracle of suffering love which 'moves everyone who has a heart'. Cf. P. T. Forsyth, *The Work of Christ* (New York: Hodder & Stoughton, 1931; London: Independent Press, 1946), p. 194: 'He [Christ] is thus not only the pledge to us of God's love, but the pledge to God of our sure response to it in a total change of will and life.' See, too, the quotation from Canon Montefiore, above, p. 296, note 37.

[53] This seems to be the direction in which Ernst Fuchs (see his *Studies of the Historical Jesus*, Studies in Biblical Theology, No. 42 [London: SCM Press; Naperville: Allenson, 1964]) and Ebeling (see 'Word of God and Hermeneutics', op. cit., pp. 305–33) go in proposing as the purpose of exegesis the bringing into being of a new linguistic occurrence of the Word of God. It is possible, however, to wonder whether the recognition of the community is realistically retained in the face of the individualistic and intellectualistic tendencies present in the formulations of this proposal. See below, p. 312, note 91.

[54] Teilhard de Chardin, *The Phenomenon of Man*, trans. Bernard Wall (London: Collins; New York: Harper, 1961), p. 294. Cf. this statement: 'The essence of Christianity is neither more nor less than the belief in the Unification of the world in God by the Incarnation.' Quoted from *La Religion du personell* by C. E. Raven, *Teilhard de Chardin: Scientist and Seer* (London: Collins; New York: Harper, 1963), p. 193.

The meaning of the vision is far from fully clear, but it seems to make contact at points with Kierkegaard's thought which implies the goal of a deeper and more inclusive community.[55] One may find a more sober and perhaps a more acceptable manner of seeing the Christ as both the means and the momentum of a movement towards community, if one combines the current interest in word as encounter[56] with attempts to follow the implications for faith of a philosophy of symbolic forms.[57] H. R. Niebuhr's posthumous volume *The Responsible Self* offers intriguing clues at this point.[58] We shall return to this topic below, when we relate Kierkegaard's views and use of different kinds of communication to the Statement of Faith.

(8) Despite the general dominance of diastasis in contemporary theology, we have been able to identify tendencies which reflect

[55] For another effort to connect the Christ with the vision of a universal community, see Karl Rahner, *The Church and the Sacraments*, trans. W. J. O'Hara (London: Burns & Oates; New York: Herder, 1963), p. 13: 'Even though in biblical as well as in present-day official ecclesiastical terminology "Church" and "Body of Christ", too, always signify the society comprising the whole of mankind called to supernatural salvation in Christ, with its juridical build and the hierarchical, social, organized structure given to it by Christ, that does not alter the fact that this organized association of those who are called to redemption, and the personal acceptance of the call by the individual, are in fact preceded, even chronologically, by a consecration of the whole of mankind which took place in the incarnation and death on the cross of the eternal Word of the Father.'

[56] While Fuchs and Ebeling are perhaps best known for this concern, Karl Heim placed great emphasis on this theme. See, for example, his *Jesus the Lord*, trans. D. H. van Daalen (Edinburgh: Oliver & Boyd, 1959; Philadelphia: Muhlenberg, 1961), p. 149: 'The peculiar thing about the sound of a word, which distinguishes it from all other sounds, is that in the hearing of this sound an encounter is effected between you and me. I hear the word that you speak. I speak the word that you hear. We meet one another because I know that speaking on your part and hearing on my part are the same act. In speaking and hearing therefore there is something common to you and to me, to the world of your consciousness and to the world of my consciousness, though these worlds are altogether inaccessible to each other.'

[57] A massive literature, of course, has followed Ernst Cassirer's development of a *Philosophy of Symbolic Forms* (3 vols., New Haven: Yale, 1953–7). Of special interest are Stephen Pepper's employment of this approach in studying metaphysics (see *World Hypotheses* [Berkeley: University, 1961]) and Stephen Toulmin's in studying the philosophy of science (see 'Contemporary Scientific Mythology', *Metaphysical Beliefs* [London: SCM Press, 1957]).

[58] See the passages from the Earl Lectures included in *The Responsible Self*, pp. 147–78. These pages seem to take up a theme already found in Niebuhr's *The Meaning of Revelation* (New York: Macmillan, 1946), pp. 124–5: 'Not with complete clarity, to be sure, yet as in a glass darkly, we can discern in the contemporary confusion of our lives the evidence of a pattern in which, by great travail of men and God, a work of redemption goes on which is like the work of Christ. . . . The story of Jesus, and particularly of his passion, is the great illustration that enables us to say, "What we are now doing and suffering is like this." '

(without necessarily deriving directly from) the substantive thrust of Kierkegaard's thought towards the coherence of God and man. Such tendencies—or less ambitiously, soundings—as the concern with christological community are essentially crippled, however, if the intention involved is deprived of the principles by which it can find concrete fulfilment. It is not clear how the situationalism still regnant in theological ethics represents an advance over the situationalism of the existentialist who is unable to assess authenticity by reference to any standard external to the sheer act itself. We badly need a closer study of Kierkegaard's ethics, including a scrutiny of such themes as communication, the universal human, and honesty. Beyond and beneath that, the thrust of his thought towards the coherence of God and man invites inquiry into the possibility of reopening the rubric of natural law. We hear today eloquent testimony to man's communion with nature.[59] Is the import of that communion to be restricted to matters of description?[60]

The predicament in ethics affects, of course, the call of the new christology which we have linked with the central motif of Kierkegaard's religious thought. It may be fine to insist that the claim of the

[59] No one has pleaded more persuasively than Joseph Sittler for a consideration of this theme. See his 'Nature and Grace: Reflections on an Old Rubric', *Dialog*, Autumn, 1964, pp. 252–7, where he takes up the theme of his controversial address to the Assembly of the World Council of Churches in New Delhi. This number of *Dialog* has its theme 'Creation and Redemption', and a number of the articles are relevant to our concern. Harold H. Ditmanson's 'The Call for a Theology of Creation', pp. 264–74, provides a useful summary of recent theological literature on the subject, as well as several substantive comments by the author. A number of the pieces in the Sittler Festschrift also, quite appropriately, involve this theme. See Philip J. Hefner, ed., *The Scope of Grace, essays on Nature and Grace in honor of Joseph Sittler* (Philadelphia: Fortress, 1964).

[60] Reinhold Niebuhr, who is hardly the type of theologian who can most easily be classified as isolated from life in the world of men, has shown interest at this point. Thus in *The Nature and Destiny of Man* (2 vols., London: Nisbet, 1941–3), II, p. 263, he writes: '. . . it is important to recognize the validity of principles of justice, rationally conceived, as sources of criticism for the historical achievements of justice in living communities. If the mediaeval and modern secular theories of natural law claim too much for these rational principles of justice, both secular and Reformation relativists frequently dismiss them as irrelevant or dangerous. Karl Barth's belief that the moral life of man would possess no valid principles of guidance if the Ten Commandments had not introduced such principles by revelation, is as absurd as it is unscriptural.' Yet Niebuhr's own work in the area of 'ethical principles' by no means leaves the Christian with very specific guidance. The principles of 'order' and 'freedom' seem at the point of cancelling each other out, and no unambiguous statement of 'equality' is available. For a sharper contrast to the dominant mood at this point, see, for example, Bernard Häring, *The Law of Christ* (2 vols., Westminster, Maryland: The Newman Press; Cork: Mercier, 1964–5) and *Toward a Christian Moral Theology* (South Bend: University of Notre Dame Press, 1966).

Christ is not that of a metaphysical puzzle upon man's opinions. But what is it like—quite concretely now—to be the 'man for others'? If this is not to be a return to the 'what would Jesus do' ethic, if being a Christian is not a special form of existence,[61] how are we claimed by the Christ today? What does it mean to 'participate in the suffering of God in the world'?[62]

(9) Perhaps this dilemma ought to turn us back to more conventional theological tasks. The failure to depart from the polarized picture of the solitary Christian awaiting an ethical revelation from his Lord may reflect both the incapacity and the disinclination of the diastatic thinker. Kierkegaard's thought should have made clear to us how linkage to particular ethical norms is shunted aside by a belief in a Lord whose independence permits him to recognize nothing outside himself. Perhaps it would be useful to address quite directly the task of stating the doctrine of God in contemporary idiom. A weakness at this point seems to be indicated in several of the more recent calls to a new christology. Perhaps Bishop Robinson's call to follow the 'Man for others' would have been more convincing, had he not linked it with a Tillichian concept of being which seemed —and seems—ill paired with such a call to commitment.[63]

What does the Christ's claim upon life at its centre mean for Christian reflection about the God and father of our Lord Jesus Christ? A certain kind of speaking about God may divert those within the household of faith from their true calling to christomorphic life and drive others away from the church's door through its irrelevant, or even its nonsensical character. But discourse about God can be wholly expulsed only on pain of reducing the claim of the Christ to arbitrariness.[64] It is perhaps too early to expect from the

---

[61] See Bonhoeffer, *Letters and Papers from Prison*, p. 166.

[62] ibid.

[63] It is notable that Alasdair MacIntyre, who might seem a fair target for *Honest To God*, finds that Tillich's theology vacillates between making the matter of first importance being itself and making it our own subjective concern. He observes that Tillich manages to escape from this dilemma, when he 'slips into ascribing to God predicates which we would normally take to imply that God was a being. God creates and reveals himself, for example.' But the best that Tillich can manage is 'a verbal triumph over the atheist, the substance of atheism has been conceded'. ('God and the Theologians', *The Honest to God Debate*, ed., David L. Edwards, pp. 219–20.) [Italics his.] Cf. Walter Kaufmann's critique of Tillich in his *Critique of Religion and Philosophy* (New York: Harper, 1958; London: Faber: 1959), pp. 124–30.

[64] See the article by Kai Nielsen cited above, p. 291, note 3. This seems to be Paul M. Van Buren's problem (op. cit.), for he surely fears the prospect of irrelevant talk about God more than that of arbitrary talk about the Christ. (Though he can speak of Jesus meaning 'whatever "God" means'—see ibid., pp. 139, 147.)

new christological thinkers much of substance on the doctrine of God and it is in any case too late in this book to speak extensively on *any* subject. But it is clear that what such discourse *must not* do is to deny the claim of the Christ a meaningful theological context. Rather it should derive its clues for the constructive task from the reality of the Christ claim.[65]

Kierkegaard declares that the Christian proves the existence of God by his obedience[66]—in doing that he must to some extent illumine the nature of God. The Christian understanding of God must hold that time is meaningful and obedience important to God.[67] That much follows from the reality of the coherence between God and man. The contemporary theologian finds here an opportunity to enter an heritage rooted in the biblical understanding of the Living God, who is not defiled by his involvement in the world of time.[68] Perhaps most prominent among the instruments which offer themselves for the task of contemporary restatement of this heritage is process philosophy. In this instance one has no difficulty speaking of God as being involved in temporality—indeed He is temporal.[69] The problem lies on the other side of the matter. We still lack a full

---

If the metaphysically remote God of extreme diastasis is 'no more' (to paraphrase the title of Werner and Lotte Pelz' *God is No More* (London: Gollancz, 1963; Philadelphia: Lippincott, 1964]), that may be counted to the good, but we surely must not suppose that we are then done with the doctrine of God. Chapter eight should have made clear the peril of that course. The argument of the present chapter seeks to show that the reality of God is not only a matter of importance to the professional theologian.

[65] In a way this is to suggest a path towards reconstruction paralleling one found in Kierkegaard and discussed under 'The Assimilation of Christology and Ascendancy', pp. 256–64, above.

[66] *S.V.* VII, p. 476 (*CUP*, p. 485).

[67] See above, pp. 120–4 on the way in which Kierkegaard understands the life of man to 'matter' to God.

[68] Robinson himself affirms this heritage in his contribution to *The Honest to God Debate*, p. 262, where he backs off from the notion of static substance so easily linked with the image of being-itself. To enter the heritage which emphasizes the Living God the theologian need not overleap the years separating the biblical witness from his own time. See Frederick Sontag's discussion of such figures as Ockham, Eckhart and Cusanus on 'possibility' as a divine attribute in his *Divine Perfection: Possible Ideas of God* (New York: Harper; London: SCM Press, 1962).

[69] The classical documents in this case continue to be Alfred North Whitehead, *Process and Reality* (New York: Harper Torchbook, 1960) and Charles Hartshorne, *The Divine Relativity* (New Haven: Yale, 1948). Hartshorne has also provided a very useful summary of his argument in the first chapter of his (with William L. Reese) *Philosophers Speak of God* (Chicago: University, 1953) and Whitehead stated some of the religious implications of his thought apart from the intricacies of *Process and Reality* in his Lowell Lectures of 1962 (*Religion in the Making* [New York: Macmillan, 1960].

scale theological exploration of the import to Christian thinking of, for example, Whitehead's reflections concerning the 'primordial nature of God'.[70] One might await the outcome of such an exploration the more hopefully, if it were tutored by the resources available in the past—for example—in Augustine's wisdom concerning the divine Trinity.

Many will feel that the most severe problem facing this line of theological reflection still remains that of giving adequate place to, while making significant sense of, the assertion that in the Christ the word did become flesh and dwelt among us. The doctrine of the person of the Christ is not an antique, real only in the quaint dust of the textbook world. Its reality bears upon the Christian community with the force of a requirement. 'But who do you say that I am?'[71] The basis and the boundaries for a Christian reply are given in the thrust of Kierkegaard's thought towards the coherence of God and man in the Christ. This leaves much room for reflection—as Alan Richardson has said: 'We are free to suggest any theory about the mode of the Incarnation which commends itself to us, provided that we do not lose sight of the fundamental truth that God and man are brought together in the Person of Jesus Christ.'[72] The response of Christian theologians to this requirement and this freedom has not been encouraging. Perhaps developments in Logos christology, such as the work of Lionel Thornton and Norman Pittenger, represent the most promising replies.[73] But it does not seem too much to hope that

[70] Perhaps Daniel D. Williams' *God's Grace and Man's Hope* (New York: Harper, 1949) and Bernard Meland's *The Realities of Faith* (New York: Oxford, 1962) come closest to such an exploration, but neither work chooses precisely this focus. See also John Cobb, Jr., *A Christian Natural Theology* (Philadelphia: Westminster, 1965; London: Lutterworth, 1967).

[71] Matt. 16. 15 (RSV).

[72] Alan Richardson, *Creeds in the Making* (London: SCM Press, 1951), pp. 84–85. Richardson prepares for this comment by remarking that Chalcedon stated a 'principle, not a theory'. Thus it 'permits the formulation of theories provided that the principle is safeguarded in them'. ibid.

[73] See Lionel Thornton, *The Incarnate Lord* (London: Longmans, Green, 1928) and Pittenger, op. cit. (It should be noted that Pittenger is critical of Thornton, arguing that Thornton has failed to protect the reality of the humanity of Jesus— ibid., pp. 107–9.) Pittenger's own effort to state the Incarnation in meaningful terms is significantly supported by a 'process' view of human identity. This effort seems to be following the warning of I. A. Dorner (see the translation of Dorner's *System of Christian Doctrine. The Doctrine of Christ* in *God and Incarnation in Mid-Nineteenth Century German Theology*, ed. and trans. by Claude Welch [New York: Oxford, 1965], pp. 233–4) that 'it is . . . necessary to give up the path of attempting to attain the personal living unity of the God-man by means of the *persona* (divine or human) as the bond of unity, because on grounds of logic and fact the ego cannot thus be put at the apex as the bond of unity; rather the personality of

the new christological interest, gaining its second wind, but still following its sound sense for the central Christian reality of God's claim in the Christ, may yield new efforts to explicate the personal meeting of God and man in the context of fundamental Christian coherence.

2. *The Christ and Christian Coherence: The Structure of Faith*

This book studies Kierkegaard as a *systematic* thinker. This formal focus is not forced upon the subject. Kierkegaard not only defends the validity of the principle of contradiction in theology,[74] he lets himself be guided by that principle. His thought manifests a truly remarkable (we shall not say 'for theologians') sensitivity to the requirements of internal consistency. There is a centre and there are rhythms in this man's reflection. This book has shown nothing more clearly than that. It has, of course, more than once shown Kierkegaard approaching the precipices of contradiction. But it has shown the thinker reconsidering, re-examining his 'data', if you please, and working his way through to a more harmonious view, though to one reflecting the strain of the passage. Indeed it seems to be Kierkegaard's fundamental consistency which first puts him in trouble by causing him to follow out the full implications of an affirmation (one might better say his consistency puts him on to the trouble inherent in certain commitments), and then provides one of the instruments by which his thought moves to more secure ground.

This internal coherence is not an 'accidental' matter. It is not to be explained as a hangover from Hegel or as a matter of personal idiosyncrasy. Rather we encounter here a methodological expression of the fundamental coherence of God and man. If God has commerce

---

Christ can only be the result of the process of the *unio*. . . . The ego is continually present only as an act.' [Italics his.] The more difficult question for Pittenger, of course, is whether his appeal to the 'epigenetic' or 'emergent' character of evolution will bear the weight required by the Christian witness to the uniqueness of Jesus. Is it sufficient to suggest Shakespeare as the instance of the 'classical'(definitive) dramatist to picture what is meant by the 'finality' of the Christ? Still Pittenger is not rendered mute by these difficulties. See op. cit., chapters seven, ten and eleven. The widespread use of the kenosis motif in contemporary christology also seems on the whole to move in the direction of protecting the humanity of Jesus. That is most clear in its negative function of releasing the thinker from commitment to a metaphysical contradiction as the core of his christology. But it does not provide an adequate positive statement. The metaphysical problems, evicted (or at least dethroned) from their relevance to the actuality of the Christ, return to afflict the discussion of his possibility.

[74] See above, pp. 18–21.

in the world of men, if God and man actually meet in the Christ, the deep human drive for order, for making sense, will not be frustrated by the reality of this relatedness or by Christian discourse about it. Man today may not seek the rule of reason in the grand manner of Hegel—but then Kierkegaard is his fellow at this point, too. But spurred on by the great accomplishments and greater prestige of science, he remains unshaken in his practical faith that nature and its perils will finally be wholly subdued by reason. And while Kierkegaard's message of coherence may chastise the modern for the naïveté of his confidence and quarrel with him concerning the scope of reason's relevance (coherence does not mean the collapse of difference), it basically endorses the quest for meaningfulness.

We have tried in this book to expose and oppose the caricature of Kierkegaard as an apostle of irrationalism. The Kierkegaard to whom we have tried to give voice may cause more than mild surprise in some quarters. There is a special Kierkegaard problem at this point. But one must say that considerable shock would be registered throughout the human community upon the introduction of evidence suggesting that any Christian theologian was concerned with the requirement of consistency and faithful in his response to that requirement. The man outside the household of faith has learned (been taught) to assume that theologians dwell in that heavenly land where one can 'have it both ways'. Whether it is a matter of saying that sin is inevitable, but not necessary;[75] or of acknowledging human reality in its own sphere, but denying it—and presumably its sphere of reality—meaning for God;[76] the double truth theory seems to lurk behind every utterance of the reverend professors. Perhaps the worst example of this type of blatant contradiction comes to view in theologians who take to hand the task of justifying human suffering.

Now it is perfectly true that theological discourse about the relationship between God and man which has a fine place for everything

---

[75] See above, pp. 253–4, for this formulation in Kierkegaard and Reinhold Niebuhr. It is this formulation of freedom and necessity, taken out of the context of sin, which mars D. M. Baillie's fine book *God Was In Christ* (London: Faber; New York: Scribner's, 1948) by an effort to illumine the 'paradox of the Incarnation' by the 'paradox of grace'. (pp. 106–33.) Though Baillie's effort to relate the Christ to broader Christian categories represents a sound formal principle, the content of his formulation remains a contradiction.

[76] One finds an illustration in James Collins' appeal to the formula *tanta similitudo, major dissimilitudo*. (*The Mind of Kierkegaard* [Chicago: Henry Regnery, 1953], pp. 150–1.) Collins is right in finding that principle opposed to Kierkegaard's procedure. For we have seen (above, pp. 124–8) that while Kierkegaard moves towards such a formulation, he moves the more decisively away from it.

and firmly puts everything in its place does not well cohere with life as we know it on this planet. We encounter gaps, incongruities—and more fundamentally, mysteries.[77] The complexity and incompleteness of his data may suggest that the best course for the theologian is to strive for an organic rather than a geometric consistency. But this is a second word that should hardly be uttered since the first word is so little heard today. And that is so despite the fact that the mandate of consistency is not an arbitrary external burden, but one deriving from the substance of the faith—indeed from the meaning of the Christ who stands at the centre.

'You are Christ's and Christ is God's.'[78] The call to consistency does not involve a naked dependence on the ever narrower reality of the Christ event receding in time. Obviously men did not first incline to the use of intelligence when Jesus of Nazareth made his appearance in history. But Kierkegaard's thought requires us to relate the event to a 'given' in quite another sense. God does not accept the principle of consistency as some great compromise forced upon him by his will to be incarnate in the Christ. God and man cohere before the Christ —and therefore in the Christ. God is in some significant way(s) like man. That surely puts the matter wrong way first. And we do not mean that God is the supreme rationalist, the epitome of order—as death is undisturbed by any movement whatever. But the life of God is not chaos—his consistency is conveyed by his activity. Perhaps 'consistency' still bears too much the tones of death: this, the living God, is the supremely faithful one. He makes and keeps covenant with man.

We shall mention only one further implication of this line of thought. Intrinsic to the affirmation of the faithfulness of God is the assumption that what God wills is characterized by an essential consistency. A Christian ethicist would presumably be interested in the character and content of God's will. We have already noted the dominance of situationalism in contemporary theological ethics. We may now add that those who reject the quest for final or even for some degree of 'middle' principles cannot appeal to the doctrine of God for support[79]—that is, if Kierkegaard has seen matters rightly at this point. If the good or the right changes, it does so only because

---

[77] Cf. Gabriel Marcel's distinction between 'problems' and 'mysteries' in his essay 'On the Ontological Mystery', *The Philosophy of Existentialism*, trans. Manya Harari (New York: Citadel, 1963), pp. 9–46.

[78] I Cor. 3.23 (RSV).

[79] Paul Tillich outlines such an appeal in his *Theology of Culture* (New York: Oxford, 1959), pp. 10–29.

the situations upon which God places his self-identical claim change. And yet one may wonder whether the prospect of continuity between the situations has not been dismissed too casually—particularly so, if the creatures who make up the reality of these changes come from the hand of the one God and do so in such a way that their relationships to each other are essential to their very selfhood.

In this section we have explored the connection between the thrust of Kierkegaard's thought towards the substantive coherence of God and man and the requirements of consistency for discourse about that reality. But in that thrust more is implied for Christian discourse than the requirement and reality of structure for faith. After all the coherence in question might be precisely internal and nothing more than that. Christians cannot settle for the coherence of a symbol system which itself is isolated from the world of men. That could occur in two ways: (1) if this coherent symbol system failed to be communicated to modern man, (2) if, upon being communicated, it fundamentally frustrated the wisdom and experience of the human community. Both possibilities lead us into a final section.

3. *The Christ and Christian Coherence: The Statement of Faith*

A concern with communication does not need to be grafted unto Kierkegaard's faith in a mechanical fashion. Such concern grows out of the living centre of the faith: the Christ who is God's authoritative word to man. As such, this Christian faith is intrinsically bent towards disclosure, openness, dialogue and is the enemy of that religious brand of concealment which hides its fragile treasures from the light of day.[80]

The thrust towards communication is found in the christological centre of this faith, but the forms for communication are not. The appeal to the Christ does not 'freeze' the matter of forms. Kierkegaard would be as ready as any man to put forward the argument that the only way the unchanging truth of the gospel can be conveyed in this world of time is by means of changing the forms of expression. One can reach that conclusion by moving straight ahead from the fundamental thrust of Kierkegaard's thought towards the coherence of God and man. There is a connectedness between God and man and

---

[80] Viewed in this light, it does not seem surprising to find Kierkegaard saying that the 'reality of his significance' lay in a distinctive concept 'of what communication is'. (*Pap.* VIII 1 A 466 [*Dru* 722].) Near at hand at this point, though not itself the focus of the discussion, lies Kierkegaard's ethic of communication.

the Christ represents the celebration and consummation of that coherence, not its repudiation. Thus it is wholly appropriate that discourse about the Christ open itself to the forms of understanding and expression current in any particular period of time.

A more specific foundation for attributing to Kierkegaard an openness to new ways of stating the faith is to be found in his comments about, and even more strikingly perhaps in his use of, 'indirect communication'.[81] Surely one of the significant functions the structure of the stages serves is to engage the reader—not simply by virtue of the colour and drama of its fictional characters—but by finding a point of entry to Christian categories within the convictions and through the conceptions of the other stages of existence.[82] Kierkegaard believed that entry could only be made by personal decision and he surely did not give too few words to the explicit denunciation of attempts to state the faith in such a way as to disguise the reality of the leap involved. Perhaps this is part of Kierkegaard's meaning in speaking of the Christian category (a category, not a· concession!) of paradox as the way of relating eternal truth and an existing individual.[83] At least Kierkegaard so understood the eternal truth to which he would bear witness, the faith he would state, that though it be born in the eternal resolve of God himself, it waits upon the free affirmation of men who may very conceivably direct their passion to other ends. Any 'communication' of this truth cannot be 'direct', for it requires more of the hearer than the non-committal reception and filing of some item of information.[84]

All of Kierkegaard's work was indirect in this sense that it served to confront the reader with his need to choose. But his work encourages an emphasis on an indirectness of the means of communication as well. While his decision may very well go against faith, it is desirable that the addressee of the Christian message should be exposed to all the relevant 'data' available. Kierkegaard did not believe that every scrap of the data could be stated in a verbal form.[85] There is greater

[81] See above, pp. 28–43.
[82] Thus in *Pap.* IX A 448 (*Dru* 849) Kierkegaard says that his effort to depict what it means to be a Christian and a Christian's relationships to the world receive little help from the old doctors of the Church, for 'they did not know the world'.
[83] *Pap.* VIII 1 A 11 (*Dru* 633).
[84] It should be noted that this emphasis on decisive appropriation is retained, even when the discussion of indirect communication is placed in a strongly diastatic context—as when Kierkegaard speaks in *TC* of the impossibility of direct communication in the case of the God-Man.
[85] See the passages quoted above, pp. 26–27, and *Pap.* IV B 1, p. 145.

hope that the elusive aspects of reality can be suggested by such instrumentalities as music which expresses immediacy,[86] drama which portrays the inner history of the self,[87] and fantasy which creates the reality of the other as genuine possibility and not as dead facticity.[88] The artist serves the man of faith well, not because he plays with an imaginary world, but because his 'imagination' corresponds to the character of life in all its complexity.[89]

The appeal to these 'indirect' media of communication suggests that the picture of an isolated cognitive subject distorts the true nature of things. As a knower the self may stand in a certain such isolation, but beneath and before such separateness lies the base of the fundamental relatedness of self and other. The indirect mode of communication resonates to the immediacy of man's relatedness in ways not possible for speech which requires that the living current of relatedness be fixed with definiteness.[90] While Kierkegaard may speak less often, and surely less dramatically, of this primal communal dimension than of the uniquely individual element, his understanding of the individual as 'self and race' formulates this reality as a principle to which his analyses of dread and despair give powerful amplification.[91]

Thus while Kierkegaard must be counted with those who are open to new forms for stating the faith, he offers no support to anyone who would propose the particular newness of removing all language which suggests and evokes in favour of formulations which are

[86] *S.V.* I, pp. 51–52 (*E-O* I, pp. 55–56). This passage also points out the way in which language is superior to music as a means of expression.

[87] *S.V.* II, pp. 122ff. (*E-O*, II, pp. 112ff.).

[88] See *Pap.* XII A 288, 328, IX A 95; and *S.V.* XI, p. 144 (*SD*, pp. 163–4). See also Arild Christensen, 'Der junge Kierkegaard als Schrifstellerpersönlichkeit', *Orbis Litterarum*, 1963, pp. 26–47, for a discussion of the early Kierkegaard's interest (especially in the dissertation) in the doubleness of myth.

[89] Cf. Denis de Rougemont, 'Religion and the Mission of the Artist', *Spiritual Problems in Contemporary Literature*, ed. Stanley R. Hopper (New York: Harper, 1957), p. 186: 'Art is an exercise of the whole being of man, not to compete with God, but to coincide better with the order of Creation, to love it better, and to re-establish ourselves in it.'

[90] *Pap.* IV B 1, p. 145: 'Immediacy has no relationship, for as soon as a relationship is present, the immediacy is cancelled.' Here Kierkegaard suggests the mood of Henri Bergson's *An Introduction to Metaphysics*, trans. T. E. Hulme (New York: G. P. Putnam, 1912).

[91] See above, p. 106, note 23, for John Wild's comments which relate Kierkegaard to a 'field conception of man'. It may be questioned whether Gerhard Ebeling's theology of the Word, with which this chapter's concern has identified at points, does adequately recognize this dimension. For a forceful putting of the question see an earlier work in this series, Philip Hefner's *Faith and the Vitalities of History*, ed. Jaroslav Pelikan (New York: Harper and Row, 1966), pp. 156–67.

altogether definable. As for the prospect of 're-mythologizing' the faith, Kierkegaard's voice again seems to speak caution. From his viewpoint scepticism would be present over the accessibility of the reality in question to the deliberations of the august council in charge of revisions. That scruple might not deter one, were it not for the fact that the Christian reality involves an historical tradition in which a rich mythos has borne witness to the complex of events which forms at once the source, centre and telos of that tradition.[92]

There is, of course, the danger that this line of thought will be commandered to support a tendency towards obscurantism and rigidification. Oddly those tendencies often come together in the worst breed of theology available. The counsel of the last several paragraphs is not a way back to that golden garden where the theologian can 'have it both ways'. Christian faith and Christian discourse are structured. Kierkegaard was concerned to be consistent and precise in his use of words and his life climaxes in the increasing affirmation and exemplification of the principle that the Christian must take a stand, exposing himself to all the consequences of that stand. The directness of such commitment honours and even serves the principle of indirect communication as a goal: that the need for choice be impressed on the hearer.[93] Whether this highly direct commitment can accommodate an indirectness of means of statement depends on the character of the reality to be expressed and on the prospect of inter-subjective participation in that reality. And those questions bring us to the second of the concerns which control this final section: Does the faith finally fail to cohere in that, while it may be internally consistent and may even be communicated

---

[92] Cf. Kierkegaard's emphasis on the presence of the Christ in the word spoken at the altar on the occasion of holy communion, where 'every word is said exactly as it was handed down by the fathers' and 'he is himself personally present, . . . it is he who speaks'. (*S.V.* X, p. 278 [*CDi*, p. 278]; cf. *ibid.*, p. 313 [ibid., p. 305].) This emphasis surely does not reflect a verbalism, for Kierkegaard is well aware of the 'dialectical' character of any revelation—see *S.V.* VII, p. 24n. (*CUP*, p. 35n.); cf. the passages quoted above, pp. 235–8. But Kierkegaard would have the dialectics and ambiguity involved be that of the authentic Christian claim centred in the facticity of the Christ event.

[93] *Pap.* X 1 A 235: '"Witness" is . . . the form of communication which most truly strikes the midpoint between direct and indirect communication. Witness is direct communication, but it still does not bring the contemporary to the Moment.' Cf. *S.V.* XII, p. 125 (*TC*, pp. 133–4). This point does not seem to be given sufficient weight by Harmut Metzger (*Kriterion christlicher Predigt nach Sören Kierkegaard* [Göttingen: Vandenhoeck & Ruprecht, 1964]) who stresses the distinction between proclamation and contemplation in such a way as to diminish the value of the pseudonymous works. This weakness also mars the discussion of James Collins, op. cit., pp. 34–42.

meaningfully, it does materially frustrate the wisdom and experience of the human community.

It is a mistake to picture Kierkegaard as one who revels in the fact that all of his experience counts against his faith. Yet it is understandable that such a mistake should be made. Kierkegaard does, after all, say that 'belief in the Son of God is the evidence'.[94] But such single references occur within a body of thought which fundamentally thrusts towards the coherence of God and man. It is to and in the world of men that God speaks. Here Kierkegaard's thought can serve to point up the contradiction internal to the notion of self-authentication. It is surely impossible for man to renounce all his experience and reflection—they abide ineradicably to form the context which gives meaning to any reference to authentication. If the word of God is accredited as true, it is so in relationship to the world of time in which men must live. The word may bring a new factor into play and may thus force a revised interpretation of other factors in experience,[95] but that word cannot in a literal sense authenticate itself. Wholly by itself the word can be said to be neither true nor false, for these terms assess relatedness. Of course a wholly unrelated word would in perfect consistency never be entrusted to a hearer who has no choice about his being a spatial-temporal, related being.[96]

The same kind of comment must be made about the possibility of identifying Kierkegaard with the view that the verification of the Christian claim(s) is eschatological.[97] While Kierkegaard may say

[94] *Pap.* X 1 A 481 (*Diary* 201).

[95] Gerhard Ebeling speaks of such a process of revision and clarification, when he writes ('The New Hermeneutics and the Early Luther', *Theology Today*, April, 1964, p. 46): 'This understanding of language is not defined from the point of view of signification, but from the viewpoint of the word event which must be accounted for and which, in turn, enables such accountability. The hermeneutical result is, therefore, that the very word as such is of hermeneutical importance and is able to illumine, to bring about clarity and to give life.'

[96] Cf. Ronald W. Hepburn's critique of the notion of self-authentication in *Christianity and Paradox* (London: Watts, 1958), pp. 24–59. See also James Barr, *The Semantics of Biblical Language* (London: Oxford, 1962), for a critique of a comparable approach to be found in the 'mystique of word studies'.

[97] For a statement of this view, see John Hick, *Faith and Knowledge* (Ithaca: Cornell, 1957), p. 152: 'The theist and the naturalist do not, *qua* theist and naturalist, necessarily expect different events to occur in the temporal process. They do not make characteristically differing historical predictions. But the theist does and the non-theist does not expect that when history is completed it will be seen to have led to a particular end-state and to have fulfilled a specific purpose, namely, that of creating "children of God". And this expectation assures for Christian theism the indubitable status of an assertion.' And further: 'The logical peculiarity of the claim is that it is open to confirmation but not to refutation. There can be conclusive

that 'eternity is the true repetition',[98] he must fundamentally be understood to be saying that the Christian message witnesses to and itself bodies forth the powerful presence of God in this life—a presence paradigmatically real in the Christ who is the temporal expression of God's eternal resolve.[99] We have traced the movement of Kierkegaard's thought regarding the efficacy of the Christ to that point where an actual issue of faith is granted despite strong counter pressures.

In Kierkegaard's view Christian faith is related to reality as we know it in two ways: (1) that faith prescribes for reality by enunciating the claim of God upon the existence of man, and (2) that faith describes reality by offering a perspective which makes the most comprehensive and coherent sense out of man's existence. The two points are intimately connected, for the prescriptive function of faith would be reduced to arbitrariness, were it not rooted in an accurate analysis of existence[100] and the descriptive perspective finds its superiority centred in its clarification of man's need for a prescriptive word and of the way in which that need is met.

If Kierkegaard so conceived of the bearing of Christian faith on the reality of life in this world of men, he hardly could dismiss any agency concerned with the process of clarifying and establishing meaning in that world. In fact the man of faith holding to the coherence of God and man must feel an instinctive affinity to the representatives of such an agency. An absolutely essential presupposition for relevance is meaningfulness; the gospel cannot save, if it makes no sense.

Faith offers itself as a pattern of meaning, a way of seeing life,

---

evidence for it if it be true, but there cannot be conclusive evidence against it if it be untrue. For if we survive bodily death we shall (presumably) know that we have survived it, but if we do not survive death we shall not know that we have not survived it. The verification situation is thus asymmetrical. However, the religious doctrine at least is open to verification and is accordingly meaningful.' (ibid., p. 150.) Cf. I. M. Crombie's contribution to *New Essays in Philosophical Theology*, ed. A. Flew and A. MacIntyre (London: SCM Press, 1955).

[98] See above, pp. 220–1, note 87, for the expression of this theme in Kierkegaard. We make clear there that Kierkegaard does not try to realize anything of evidential value from this appeal (as indeed one must not).

[99] See above, pp. 120–2.

[100] Kierkegaard is often pictured as asserting precisely such an unrooted and unrelated ethic. See, for example, Raymond E. Anderson, *Kierkegaard's Theory of Communication*, an unpublished doctoral dissertation submitted to the University of Minnesota at Minneapolis, 1960, pp. 427–8: 'Existence-Communication, as he [Kierkegaard] understands it, must respect the principle that "ought" discourse is grounded not in cognition, but in passion.'

which orders experience through the relationships of God, self, and other(s). It does, then, address the real world and the man who comes to faith does so in a process of relating an interpretive pattern to the world he finds about him. It seems, therefore, rather exaggerated to say, as Alasdair MacIntyre does, that 'the transition is not in objective considerations at all, but in the person who comes to believe . . . the man who has come to believe can only give us his reasons for believing by relating a segment of his autobiography'.[101]

In any case coming to faith is not that kind of autobiographical segment which cannot be undone.[102] And if one attends to the central thrust of Kierkegaard's thought towards coherence, one can imagine him affirming the concept (if not using the term) of falsifiability in relation to faith. Such specific items as Kierkegaard's fondness for the Johannine 'do and you shall know' lead on to this conclusion. But more importantly the basic thrust of his thought suggests that the Christian faith does not force life into its form, but quite literally 'cohers' with man's situation in existence. If sizable segments of experience simply fail to yield themselves to the illumination of faith, if life thus resists being—in Kierkegaard's characteristic phrase— 'Christianly understood', if the Christian viewpoint identifies an ideal which cannot be real in this real world, then faith has been falsified.

Can one go the next step and speak of some kind of positive verification of the Christian faith claim? Or is one left in the position of simply recognizing the Christian perspective as not yet having lost its voice, though it never can hope to make its claims good? Kierkegaard's works make possible a kind of penultimate role for evidence. Indeed those works themselves involve such an appeal to man's self-awareness. That plea will be easily dismissed if one defines admissible data so narrowly as to exclude the distinctively human realities which are the very stuff of Kierkegaard's concern. On this score one must count as gain the increasing openness to the complexity of data manifested by philosophers and scientists. Items illustrative of this tendency are not far to find :(1) Witness the scien-

[101] Alasdair MacIntyre, 'The Logical Status of Religious Belief', *Metaphysical Beliefs*, ed. by Alasdair MacIntyre and R. G. Smith, p. 209. In a similar way R. M. Hare, *The Language of Morals* (Oxford: Clarendon, 1960), p. 69, suggests that 'if pressed to justify a decision completely, we have to give a complete specification of the way of life of which it is a part. . . . If the inquirer still goes on asking "But why *should* I live like that?" then there is no further answer to give him. . . . We can only ask him to make up his own mind which way he ought to live; for in the end everything rests upon such a decision of principle'. [Italics his.]

[102] See above, pp. 207–8, on the possibility of a 'fall' from faith.

tists who decline to identify their formulations with things-in-themselves, stressing instead that they deal with highly selective models in whose production a kind of faith running ahead of evidence is involved.[103] (2) Witness the tendency of contemporary scientists to incorporate a recognition of uncertainty and contingency into the models themselves.[104] (3) Witness the tendency of linguistic philosophers to recognize increasingly the plurality of languages with each language possessing its distinctive logic.[105] Witness the consideration being given to the possibility that 'person language' possesses a 'logically primitive' character.[106]

It behoves the theologian to act responsibly over against these overtures from the fields of philosophy and science. It is not seemly for him to bank these offerings in a *tu quoque* argument[107] and go his

---

[103] On this point, see Ian Ramsey, *Models and Mystery* (Cambridge: Oxford, 1964). Ramsey draws heavily on Max Planck's distinction between 'analog' models and 'literal' models with the stress in the sciences falling on the former. Michael Polanyi has argued in several works that heuristic vision has a role in every act of knowing. With respect to scientific knowing, see particularly Polanyi's *Personal Knowledge* (Chicago: University, 1958; London: Routledge, 1962) pp. viii, 27, 29, and chapter vi.)

[104] The mood of these scientists hardly supports the principle 'if what we know cannot be proved then it is not knowledge at all', which J. Heywood Thomas, *Subjectivity and Paradox*, (Oxford: Blackwell, 1957), p. 90, depends on in linking Kierkegaard with the identification of religious faith as subjective passion.

[105] Thus from the fathers themselves: 'It is interesting to compare the multiplicity of kinds of words and sentences with what logicians have said about the structure of language (including the author of *Tractatus Logico-Philosophicus*).' (L. Wittgenstein, *Philosophical Investigations*, trans. G. E. M. Anscombe [New York: Macmillan, 1953; Oxford: Blackwell, 1958], p. 12e.) And: '. . . I do not wish to deny that . . . a statement may properly be said to be meaningful even though it is neither analytic nor empirically verifiable. I should, however, claim that there was at least one proper use of the word "meaning" in which it would be incorrect to say that a statement was meaningful unless it satisfied the principle of verification; and I have, perhaps tendentiously, used the expression 'literal meaning' to distinguish this use from the others . . .' (A. J. Ayer from the introduction to the *second* edition of *Language, Truth and Logic* [London: Gallancz; New York: Dover, 1946], p. 15.) Cf. Martin Jarrett-Kerr, 'Christianity and the Four Cultures', *Theology*, June, 1964, pp. 237–43.

[106] See, for example, P. F. Strawson, *Individuals* (London: Methuen, 1959). The basic concern of this chapter seems in accord with Strawson's effort to emphasize the aspect of objective embodiment, while not arguing that all personal acts are strictly observable. Robert H. King has drawn some theological hints from Strawson in an article, 'The Concept of Person', in *The Journal of Religion*, 1966, pp. 36–44. In that article King also comments on G. E. M. Anscombe's proposal (*Intention* [Oxford: Basil Blackwell, & Mott, 1957]) that intentional action description has a distinct logical form.

[107] This is not to deny that a formidable argument can be constructed along those lines. See, for example, Wm. W. Bartley III, *The Retreat to Commitment* (New York: Knopf, 1962; London: Chatto & Windus, 1964).

way undisturbed. Such banditry will easily be recognized and exposed for what it is. The biologist, for example, will protest: 'Contrary to a common impression, the Uncertainty Principle does not provide a convenient slot into which to insert a god-of-the-gaps. It, together with the Principle of Relativity, simply means that science makes relativistic and probabilistic statements, not absolute statements. This does not alter science's ability to make extremely precise statistical predictions.'[108]

The theologian who follows Kierkegaard's lead would rather welcome the overtures from other fields and find in them the invitation to genuine dialogue. In his time Kierkegaard acknowledged the validity of scientific method within its sphere. In our time, even while we are recognizing the plurality of spheres more clearly than some decades ago, we are becoming aware of how difficult it is to wall those spheres off from one another. This situation may cause one to predict the cessation of the 'truce' between religion and science. It may also, however, be welcomed as the context for a new effort to explore the coherence of faith and life in ways quite unanticipated in Kierkegaard's time. But the spirit of such exploration would be wholly Kierkegaardian, if it were to go on not merely in the dry air of classrooms, but in impassioned efforts to understand man's predicament and heal his wounds in this perilous time. The ominous power of technology itself may serve finally, then, not as enemy but as ally, by forcing men to a new dialogue in quest of the proper ends of human life.

In a way such a development would be a 'reduplication' of the course Kierkegaard's authorship traces in the stages. Now, as then, it would be proposed that the Christian perspective meet and pass its test in the hard reality of existence. We need not seek to show again how Christian faith does—in Kierkegaard's view—represent the answers to the problems developing within the dynamic of the stages. The God one finds is the God one needs and one shall not make bold

---

[108] William T. Keeton (Biologist from Cornell University), 'Is Theology Based on Evidence?', *Dialog*, Spring, 1965, p. 101. And the philosopher will surely add his 'Amen'. Thus H. D. Lewis writes in his review of J. Baillie's *Sense of the Presence of God* in *The Journal of Theological Studies*, 1964, p. 233: 'Professor Baillie leans heavily on G. E. Moore's distinction between the meaning of an affirmation and the analysis of it and on Russell's idea of "knowledge by acquaintance", but he pays no heed to well-known discussions of the former principle or to the severe limitations which Russell himself would have placed on knowledge by acquaintance. We can certainly not pass without further argument from notions like these to insistence on acquaintance with religious realities of which Moore and Russell themselves would have denied all awareness.'

to offer God some greater praise.[109] One does not have to invent needs today. The scope of need may have been considerably broadened, though Kierkegaard's discussion of the problems of the self hardly seems to have fallen on stony ground. In any case the key point facing this new summons to Christian faith would still be the mandate to furnish moral insight in the world of men. The ethical stage is the key element of continuity in the development of the stages and can become the field in which faith in God and the life of the world come to cohere today in unprecedented ways. Should that occur it would not involve a renunciation of the christological centre of the faith Kierkegaard confessed. Rather it would amount to a new expression of the salutary and wholly Kierkegaardian movement away from the derailment of faith in metaphysical belief and towards the living response to the claim of God in the Christ.[110]

One would then no longer be debating how the hypothesis that God works faithfully for man's good at every point in time can be meaningful tested.[111] One would have taken up the task of response in which faith is tested by its results.

Now it certainly is not clear that Christian faith will emerge from all of this victorious—or, since we should not propose that the process outlined take the form of warfare, that it will find itself verified. Did we know that, our life now would not be one of faith. Furthermore, in the very nature of the case Christian faith cannot show itself to be the only or even the best possible counsel for the human condition.[112] Thus the Christian cannot require that his time cast no glance at other candidates bidding to fill the moral vacuum. Indeed, perhaps in the relation to such other candidates lies the ultimate test of the

[109] See above, p. 201, for the powerful passage from *CDi* appealing to man to love God purely and simply because one needs him'.

[110] Thus one would be following out the lead Kierkegaard provided when he wrote of 'understanding for one's self in the inwardness of appropriation. . . . Meaning lies namely in the one meditating and in the understanding of the one meditating on the discourse'. (See above, p. 27, note 70.)

[111] See R. B. Braithwaite, *An Empiricist's View of Religious Belief* (Cambridge: University, 1955), pp. 6–7.

[112] At this point MacIntyre, loc. cit., is right in holding that 'there is no logical transition which will take one from unbelief to belief. . . . There are no logical principles which will make the transition for one. There are no reasons to which one can appeal to evade the burden of decision.' Cf. Anderson, op. cit., p. 426. Wolfhart Pannenberg does seem to disagree in seeking, for example, to achieve 'with the methods and criteria applied everywhere else today . . . a proven knowledge of the resurrection of Jesus as an event which happened at a certain time, a knowledge which could be the basis of our faith'. (Wolfhart Pannenberg, 'Did Jesus Really Rise from the Dead?', *Dialog*, 1965, p. 129.) The suggestions which this chapter contains share at many points both Pannenberg's targets and

openness of Christian faith to this world. Being Christian is not simply an exercise in inwardness. There are 'inter-subjective' dimensions to this reality, for the believer knows the support and correction of the Christian community[113] and seeks discourse about a common world with the human community. Indeed if the Christian is in fact genuinely bent on coherence and not coercion, he will welcome dialogue with other faiths, as freely as the discourse with other disciplines.[114] For it is through such open and honest conversation that the polarization of our time may be checked and co-operative efforts be born which prevail against those forces which imperil our existence and erode our well-being.

---

his amunition. But his claims do seem excessive, particularly in view of his acknowledgement of the 'metaphorical' character of language concerning the resurrection and his use of a 'psychological' argument along the following lines: 'The enthusiasm of an ultimate devotion in the face of all obstacles which leads to sacrificing one's own life could not arise out of deceit.' (ibid., p. 134.)

[113] See above, pp. 209–14.

[114] John Taylor, *The Primal Vision* (London: SCM Press; Philadelphia: Fortress Press, 1963), pp. 113–14 writes of such genuine openness: 'Either we must think of the Christian Mission in terms of bringing the Muslim, the Hindu, the Animist into Christendom, or we must go with Christ as he stands in the midst of Islam, of Hinduism, of the primal world-view, and watch with him, fearfully and wonderingly, as he becomes—dare we say it?—Muslim or Hindu or Animist, as once he became Man, and a Jew. Once, led by the Spirit, the Church made its choice in this matter at the Council of Jerusalem and dared to win the Gentiles by becoming Gentile. Paul and those who followed him did not wait for history to reduce the Graeco-Roman world to chaos and drive its derelicts into the arms of the Church. They claimed that world in its strength and reformulated the Gospel in the terms of its wisdom. So Christ in his Church answered the call of the Greeks; he came where they were and became what they were. From within their own culture he challenged their strength and judged their wisdom. He turned their world upside down, just as he had turned Judaism upside down—just as, indeed, if he enters our Churches today, he turns our Christianity upside down. So he would challenge and judge and revolutionize the African world-view; but he must do it from the inside.'

BIBLIOGRAPHY

I KIERKEGAARD'S WRITINGS

A list is available in the Bibliographical Note and Table of Abbreviations, pages ix–xi.

II SELECTED SECONDARY BIBLIOGRAPHY

A much wider range of secondary literature may be identified by reference to A. The selection in B offers a sampling of diverse styles of Kierkegaard scholarship and stresses recent publications and studies which bear (whether in affirmation, analogy or dissent) upon the systematic bent of this book. Limitation of space has dictated the exclusion of nearly all studies specializing in figures of systematic and historical importance to Kierkegaard.

A General Bibliographical Essays and Materials

FAHRENBACH, HELMUT, *Die gegenwärtige Kierkegaard Auslegung in der deutschsprachigen Literatur von 1948 bis 1962.* Tübingen: J. C. B. Mohr, 1962.

HENRIKSEN, AAGE, *Methods and Results of Kierkegaard Studies in Scandinavia; a historical and critical study.* Köbenhavn: Munksgaard, 1951.

HIMMELSTRUP, JENS, ed. *Sören Kierkegaard, international bibliografi.* Köbenhavn: Nyt Nordisk, 1962.

KABELL, AAGE, *Kierkegaardstudiet i Norden.* Köbenhavn: H. Hagerup, 1948.

THEUNISSEN, MICHAEL, 'Das Kierkegaardbild der neuern Forschung und Deutung,' *Deutsche Vierteljahrschrift für Litteraturwissenschaft und Geistesgeschichte,* XXXII (1958), 576–612.

THULSTRUP, NIELS, ed. *Kierkegaardiana,* I (1955–). (Published by the Sören Kierkegaard Society, Köbenhavn, and including reviews and review essays; for such materials prior to 1955, see *Meddelelser fra Sören Kierkegaard Selskabet* [1949–55].)

THULSTRUP, NIELS, 'Studiet af Kierkegaard undenfor Skandinavien 1945–52,' *Dansk Teologisk Tidskrift* XVI:2 (1953), 65–80.

THULSTRUP, NIELS, 'Theological and philosophical Kierkegaardian studies in Scandinavia, 1945–53,' *Theology Today* XII:3 (October, 1955), 297–312.

THULSTRUP, NIELS, 'Ziele und Methoden der neusten Kierkegaard-Forschung mit besonderer Berucksichtigung der skandinavischen,' *Orbis Litterarum* X:1–2 (1955) 303–18.

B Selected Secondary Studies

ADORNO, THEODOR, 'Kierkegaards Lehre von der Liebe,' *Zeitschrift für Religions und Geistesgeschichte* III: (1951), 23–38.

AMUNDSEN, V., *Sören Kierkegaards Ungdom, hans Slaegt og religiöse Udvikling.* Köbenhavn: G.E.C. Gad, 1912.

ANDERSON, ALBERT, 'Ignorance and Enlightenment: A Study in the Religious Philosophy of J. G. Hamann (1730–1788).' Unpublished doctoral dissertation, Harvard University, 1964.

ANDERSON, RAYMOND E., 'Kierkegaard's Theory of Communication.' Un-published doctoral dissertation, The University of Minnesota, 1960. *Dissertation Abstracts*, XX:10 (1960), 4213.

ANZ, WILHELM, *Kierkegaard und der deutsche Idealismus*. Tübingen: J. C. B. Mohr, 1956.

ANZ, WILHELM, 'Philosopnie und Glaube bei Sören Kierkegaard,' *Zeitschrift für Theologie und Kirche* LI:1 (April 1954), 50–105.

ANZ, WILHELM, 'Zum Sokratesverständnis Kierkegaards,' *Orbis Litterarum*, XVIII:1–2 (1963), 1–9.

BEJERHOLM, LARS, '*Meddelelsens Dialektik*'. Lund: Haakan Ohlsson, 1962.

BJÖRKHEM, JOHN, *Sören Kierkegaard i psykologisk belysning*. Uppsala: Nyblom, 1942.

BOHLIN, TORSTEN, *Kierkegaards dogmatiska aaskaadning i dess historiska samman-hang*. Stockholm: Svenska Kyrkans Diakonistyrelses, 1925.

BOHLIN, TORSTEN, *Kierkegaards tro och andra Kierkegaardstudier*. Uppsala: Svenska Kyrkans Diakonistyrelses, 1944.

BOHLIN, TORSTEN, *Sören Kierkegaards etiska aaskaadning med särskild hänsyn till begreppet den enskilde*. Stockholm: Svenska Kyrkans Diakonistyrelses, 1918.

BRANDT, F., *Sören Kierkegaard*. Stockholm: Natur och Kultur, 1955.

BRANDT, F., *Sören Kierkegaard: His Life and His Works*. København: Det danske Selskab, 1963.

BRANDT, F., *Sören Kierkegaard og Pengene*. København: Levin and Munksgaard, 1935.

BRANDT, F., *Syv Kierkegaard Studier*. København: Munksgaard, 1962.

BRUNNER, EMIL, 'Das Grundproblem der Philosophie bei Kant und Kierke-gaard,' *Zwischen den Zeiten*, II:6 (1924), 31–47.

BRUNNER, EMIL, 'Sören Kierkegaards Budskap,' *Janus*, VII:1, 3 (1939), 225–44.

BUKDAHL, JÖRGEN, 'Indrömmelse, dens plads i Sören Kierkegaards kristendoms-forstaaelse og vaekkelseaktion,' *Dansk Teologisk Tidskrift*, XXVI:2 (1963), 96–124.

BUKDAHL, JÖRGEN, *Sören Kierkegaard og den menige mand*. København: Munks-gaard, 1961.

CARNELL, E.J., *The Burden of Sören Kierkegaard*. Grand Rapids: Eerdmans, 1965.

CHRISTENSEN, ARILD, 'Felix Culpa-Motivet hos Sören Kierkegaard,' *Meddelelser fra Sören Kierkegaard Selskabet* V:1 (August, 1954), 17–20.

CHRISTENSEN, ARILD, 'Der junge Kierkegaard als Schrifstellerpersönlichkeit,' *Orbis Litterarum*, XVIII:1–2 (1963), 26–47.

CHRISTENSEN, ARILD, 'Sören Kierkegaard Individuationprincip,' *Dansk Teologisk Tidskrift*, XVI:4 (1953), 216–36.

CHRISTENSEN, V., *Sören Kierkegaards Vej til Kristendommen*. København: Munks-gaard, 1955.

COLLINS, JAMES, *The Mind of Kierkegaard*. Chicago: Henry Regnery, 1953.

COPP, JOHN DIXON, 'The Concept of the Soul in Kierkegaard and Freud.' Doctoral dissertation, Boston University, 1956. Madison, Wisconsin: The Microcard Foundation for the American Theological Association, 1956.

DIAMOND, MALCOLM, 'Kierkegaard and Apologetics,' *The Journal of Religion*, XLIV (April, 1964), 122–32.

DIEM, HERMANN, *Kierkegaard's Dialectic of Existence*. Translated by H. Knight. Edinburgh: Oliver and Boyd, 1959.

DIEM, HERMANN, *Philosophie und christentum bei Sören Kierkegaard*. München: C. Kaiser, 1929.

DIEM, HERMANN, *Sören Kierkegaard Spion im Dienste Gottes*. Frankfurt: S. Fischer, 1957.

DUPRE, LOUIS, *Kierkegaard as Theologian*. New York: Sheed and Ward, 1963.

ELHARD, LELAND, 'Faith and Identity.' Unpublished doctoral dissertation, The University of Chicago, 1965.

FILSKOV, V., 'Lögstrup-Olesen Larsen og "Den etiske fordring",' *Tidehverv*, XXXII:1 (1958), 7–12.

FISCHER, HERMANN, *Subjectivität und Sünde; Kierkegaards Begriff der Sünde mit ständiger Rücksicht auf Schleiermachers Lehre von der Sünde*. Itzehoe: H. Dorbandt, 1963.

FRIEMOND, HANS, *Existenz in Liebe nach Sören Kierkegaard*. Salzburg und München: Pustet, 1965.

FRITZSCHE, HELMUT. *Kierkegaard Kritik an der Christenheit*. Stuttgart: Calwer, 1966.

GARELICK, HERBERT M., *The Anti-Christianity of Kierkegaard. A Study of Concluding Unscientific Postscript*. The Hague: Martinus Nijhoff, 1965.

GATES, JOHN A., *Christendom Revisited: A Kierkegaardian View of the Church Today*. Philadelphia: Westminster, 1963.

GEISMAR, E., *Lectures on the Religious Thought of Sören Kierkegaard*. Minneapolis: Augsburg, 1937.

GEISMAR, E., *Sören Kierkegaard*. 6 vols. Köbenhavn: G. E. C. Gad, 1926–8.

GEORGE, ARAPURA GHEVARGHESE, *The First Sphere; A Study in Kierkegaardian Aesthetics*. New York: Asia Publishing House, 1965.

GERDES, HAYO, *Das Christus Verstandnis des jungen Kierkegaard*. Itzehoe: 'Die Spur,' 1962.

GERDES, HAYO, *Das Christusbild Sören Kierkegaards, vergleichen mit der christologie Hegels und Schleiermachers*. Düsseldorf: Eugen Dietrichs, 1960.

GIESS, LUDWIG, *Liebe als Freiheit; eine Kierkegaard-aneignung*. Temeschburg: H. Anwender and Sohn, 1939.

GRAU, GERD-GUNTHER, *Die Selbstauflösung des christlichen Glaubens*. Frankfurt: G. Schulte-Bulmke, 1963.

GRIMAULT, MARGUERITE, *La Mélancholie de Kierkegaard*. Paris: Aubier-Montagne, 1965.

HAMILTON, KENNETH, *The System and the Gospel*. New York: Macmillan, 1963.

HANSEN, KNUD, *Sören Kierkegaard*. Köbenhavn: Gyldendal, 1954.

HANSEN, SIEGFRIED, 'Die Bedeutung des Leidens für das Christusbild Sören Kierkegaards,' *Kerygma und Dogma*, II:1 (1956), 1–28.

HEIBERG, P. A., *En Episode i Sören Kierkegaards Ungdomsliv*. Köbenhavn: Gyldendal, 1912.

HEIBERG, P. A., *Et Segment af Sören Kierkegaards religiöse Udvikling*. Köbenhavn: Gyldendal, 1918.

HEIBERG, P. A., *Sören Kierkegaards religiöse Udvikling. Psykologisk Mikroskopi*. Köbenhavn: Gyldendal, 1925.

HEINECKEN, MARTIN J., *The Moment Before God*. Philadelphia: Muhlenberg, 1956.

HEISS, ROBERT, *Die grossen Dialektiker des 19 Jahrhunderts: Hegel, Kierkegaard, Marx*. Köln: Kiepenheuer and Witsch, 1963.

HELD, MATTHEW, 'The Historical Kierkegaard: Faith or Gnosis,' *The Journal of Religion*, XXXVII:4 (October, 1957), 260–6.

HELWEG, H., *Sören Kierkegaard; en psykiatrisk-psykologisk Studie*. Köbenhavn: Hagerup, 1933.

HIMMELSTRUP, JENS, *Sören Kierkegaards Opfattelse af Sokrates*. Köbenhavn: Busck, 1924.

HIRSCH, EMANUEL, *Kierkegaard-Studien*. 2 vols. *Gütersloh:* C. Bertelsmann, 1930–3.

HÖFFDING, H., *Sören Kierkegaard som Filosof*. Köbenhavn: Philipsen, 1892.

HOLM, SÖREN, *Grundtvig und Kierkegaard*. Köbenhavn: Nyt Nordisk, 1956.

HOLM, SÖREN, *Sören Kierkegaards Historiefilosofi*. Köbenhavn: Bianco Lund, 1952.

HOLMER, PAUL L., 'Kierkegaard and Ethical Theory,' *Ethics*, LXIII (April, 1953), 157–70.

HOLMER, PAUL L., 'Kierkegaard and Logical Theory,' *Kierkegaardiana*, II (1957), 23–44.

HOLMER, PAUL L., 'Kierkegaard and Religious Propositions,' *The Journal of Religion*, XXXV:3 (July, 1955), 134–57.

HOLMER, PAUL L., 'On Understanding Kierkegaard,' *A Kierkegaard Critique*. ed. H. Johnson and N. Thulstrup. New York: Harper, 1962. Pp. 40–53.

HOLMER, PAUL L., 'Sören A. Kierkegaard,' *Christian Ethics, Sources of the Living Tradition*. ed. Waldo Beach and H. Richard Niebuhr. New York: Ronald Press, 1955. Pp. 414–44.

HYGEN, JOHAN B., 'Opposisjonsennlegg ved cand. teol. Per Lönnings disputas for den teologiske doktorgrad 5 maj, 1955,' *Norsk Teologisk Tidskrift*, LVII:1 (1956), 23–56.

JASPERS, KARL, 'Kierkegaard. Leben und Werk,' *Universitas*, VI:2 10 (1951), 1057–71.

JOHNSON, HOWARD and THULSTRUP, N., ed. *A Kierkegaard Critique*. New York: Harper, 1962.

JOR, FIN, *Sören Kierkegaard, den existerende tenker*. Oslo: Land og Kirke, 1954.

JORGENSEN, CARL, *Sören Kierkegaard; en biografi med saerligt henblik paa hans personlige etik*. 5 vols. Köbenhavn: Nyt Nordisk, 1964.

KÜHLE, SEJER, *Sören Kierkegaards barndom og ungdom*. Köbenhavn: Aschehoug, 1950.

KUHR, VICTOR, *Modsigelsens Grundsaetning*. Köbenhavn: Gyldendal, 1915.

LARSEN, OLESEN K., 'Gensvar til K. E. Lögstrup,' *Tidehverv*, XXXI:5–6 (1957), 51–65.

LARSEN, OLSEN K., 'Nogle bemaerkninger om forholdet mellem humanisme og kristendom,' *Tidehverv*, XXXI: 7–8 (1957), 77–84.

LARSEN, OLESEN K., 'Den uendelige Fordring og Kaerligheden til Naesten,' *Tidehverv*, XXVI:3–4 (1952).

LARSEN, OLESON K., 'Zur Frage des Paradoxbegriffes in "Philosophische Brocken" und "Abschliessende unwissenschaftliche Nachschrift",' *Orbis Litterarum*, X:1–2 (1955), 130–48.

LINDSTROM, VALTER, *Efterföljelsens Teologi hos Sören Kierkegaard*. Stockholm: Svenska Diakonistyrelses, 1956.

LINDSTROM, VALTER, 'Eros och agape i Kierkegaards aaskaadning,' *Kierkegaardina*, I (1955), 102–13.

LINDSTROM, VALTER, 'Kierkegaards bewaffnete Neutralitat,' *Orbis Litterarum*, X:1–2 (1955), 148–56.

LINDSTROM, VALTER, *Stadiernas Teologi, en Kierkegaard Studie.* Lund: Haakan Ohlssons, 1943.

LÖGSTRUP, K. E., 'Christentum ohne den historischen Jesus,' *Orbis Litterarum*, XVIII:3–4 (1963), 101–12.

LÖGSTRUP, K. E., 'Forholdet mellem den naturlige kaerlighed og kaerlighed til naesten,' *Tidehverv*, XXIX:4 (1955), 33–43.

LÖGSTRUP, K. E., *Kierkegaards und Heideggers Existenzanalyse und ihr Verhältnis zur Verkündigung.* Berlin: Erich Blaschker, 1950.

LÖGSTRUP, K. E., 'Opgör med Kierkegaard's "Kaerlighedens Gerninger",' *Tidehverv*, XXIX:6 (1955), 52–61.

LÖGSTRUP, K. E., 'Svar til Olesen Larsen,' *Tidehverv*, XXIX:10 (1955), 97–109.

LÖGSTRUP, K. E., 'Svar til Olesen Larsen,' *Tidehverv*, XXX:1 (1956), 6–12.

LÖNNING, PER, 'Kierkegaard's "Paradox",' *Orbis Litterarum*, X:1–2 (1955), 155–66.

LÖNNING, PER, *'Samtidighedens Situation'; en studie i Sören Kierkegaard's kristendomsforstaelse.* Oslo: Land og Kirke, 1954.

LÖNNING, PER, 'Sören Kierkegaards Kristusbillede,' *Kierkegaardiana*, VIII (1962), 75–88.

LOWRIE, WALTER, *Kierkegaard.* London: Oxford, 1938.

MAGEL, CHARLES R., 'An Analysis of Kierkegaard's Philosophic Categories.' Unpublished doctoral dissertation, The University of Minnesota, 1960.

MAGNUSSEN, RIKARD, *Sören Kierkegaard, set udefra.* Köbenhavn: Munksgaard, 1942.

MALANTSCHUK, GREGOR, 'Kierkegaard and Nietzsche,' *A Kierkegaard Critique.* ed. H. Johnson and N. Thülstrup. New York: Harper, 1962.

MALANTSCHUK, GREGOR, *Kierkegaard's Way to the Truth.* Translated by Mary Michelsen. Minneapolis: Augsburg, 1963.

MALANTSCHUK, GREGOR and SÖE, N., 'Sören Kierkegaards Angreb paa Kirken,' *Kamp Mod Kirken.* Köbenhavn: Munksgaard, 1956.

MALANTSCHUK, GREGOR, 'Sören Kierkegaard's Teori om Springet og hans Virkelighedsbegreb,' *Kierkegaardiana*, I (1955), 7–15.

MALANTSCHUK, GREGOR, 'Das Verhältnis zwischen Wahrheit und Wirklichkeit in Sören Kierkegaards existentiellem Denken,' *Orbis Litterarum*, X:1–2 (1955), 166–78.

METZGER, HARMUT, *Kriterion christlicher Predigt nach Sören Kierkegaard.* Göttingen: Vandenhoeck & Ruprecht, 1964.

MILLER, LIBUSE LUKAS, *In Search of the Self: the individual in the thought of Kierkegaard.* Philadelphia: Muhlenberg, 1962.

NICHOLS, WILLIAM JACK, 'Education and the Philosophy of Sören Kierkegaard.' Doctoral dissertation, Ohio State University, 1958. Ann Arbor, Michigan: U. Microfilm, 1959. *Dissertation Abstracts* XIX (1959): 12, 3252–3.

NIEDERMEYER, GERHARD, *Sören Kierkegaard und die Romantik.* Leipzig: Quelle & Meyer, 1910.

NIELSON, WILLIAM M., 'Kierkegaard on Change, History, and Faith.' Unpublished doctoral dissertation, Harvard University, 1949.

PAULSEN, ANNA, *Sören Kierkegaard, Deuter unserer Existenz.* Hamburg: Friedrich Wittig, 1955.

PELIKAN, JAROSLAV, *Fools for Christ*. Philadelphia: Muhlenberg, 1955.

PIVCEVIG, EDO, *Ironie als Daseinsform bei Sören Kierkegaard*. Gütersloh: Gütersloher, 1960.

PRENTER, REGIN, 'Mennesket his Sören Kierkegaard,' *Studia Theologica*, II:1 (1949).

PRICE, GEORGE, *The Narrow Pass*. London: Hutchinson, 1963.

REHM, WALTER, *Kierkegaard und der Verführer*. Munich: Hermann Rinn, 1949.

RITSCHL, D., 'Kierkegaards Kritik an Hegels Logik,' *Theologische Zeitschrift*, XI:6 (November/December 1955), 437–66.

ROHRMOSER, GÜNTHER, 'Ernst oder Ironie?—Eine Zwischenbemerkung zu Interpretation Kierkegaards,' *Archiv für Geschichte der Philosophie*, XLIV:1 (1962), 75–87.

ROOS, H., *Sören Kierkegaard and Catholicism*. Translated by R. M. Brackett. Westminster: Newman, 1954.

ROOS, H., 'Sören Kierkegaard und die Kenosis-Lehre,' *Kierkegaardiana*, III (1957), 54–60.

SCHÜEPP, GUIDO, *Das Paradox des Glaubens; Kierkegaard's Anstosse für die christliche, Verkündigung*. München: Kösel, 1964.

SCHRÖER, HENNING, *Die Denkform der Paradoxalität als Theologisches Problem*. Göttingen: Vandenhoeck & Ruprecht, 1960.

SCHULZ, WALTER, 'Existenz ynd System bei S. Kierkegaard,' *Wesen und Wirklichkeit des Menschen*. Göttingen: Vandenhoeck & Ruprecht, 1957.

SCHULZ, WALTER, *Die Vollendung des deutschen Idealismus in der Spätphilosophie*. Stuttgart: Kohlhammer, 1955.

SLÖK, JOHANNES, *Die Anthropologie Kierkegaards*. Köbenhavn: Rosenkilde und Bagger, 1954.

SLÖK, JOHANNES, *Forsynstanken*. Hjörring: Expres, 1947.

SLÖK, JOHANNES, 'Kierkegaards Bestimmung des Begriffes "Gottes Wort",' *Orbis Litterarum*, X:1–2 (1955), 236–45.

SLÖK, JOHANNES, 'En Studie i Kierkegaards Erkendelsesteori,' *Dansk Teologisk Tidskrift*, IV (1941), 45–56.

SLÖK, JOHANNES, 'Tre Kierkegaard-tolkninger,' *Kierkegaardiana* I (1955), 89–101.

SLÖK, JOHANNES, 'Das Verhaltnis der Menschen zu seiner Zukomst,' *Orbis Litterarum*, XVIII:1–2 (1963), 60–79.

SÖE, N. H., 'Sören Kierkegaards laere om paradokset,' *Nordisk Teologi, Ideer och Männ, festskrift till Ragnar Bring*. Lund: Gleerup, 1955. Pp. 102–22.

SPONHEIM, PAUL R., 'Kierkegaard and the Suffering of the Christian Man,' *Dialog* III:3 (Summer, 1964), 199–207.

SVENDSEN, PAULUS, 'Opposisjonsennlegg ved cand. teol. Per Lönning's disputas for den teologiske doktorgrad, 5 maj, 1955,' *Norsk Teologisk Tidskrift*, LVII:1 (1956), 1–23.

SWENSON, DAVID F., *Something About Kierkegaard*. ed. Lillian M. Swenson. 2nd rev. ed. Minneapolis: Augsburg, 1945.

THEUNISSEN, MICHAEL, *Der Begriff Ernst bei Sören Kierkegaard*. Freiburg/München: Karl Alber, 1958.

THOMAS, J. HEYWOOD, *Subjectivity and Paradox*. Oxford: Basil Blackwell, 1957.

THOMTE, REIDAR, *Kierkegaard's Philosophy of Religion*. Princeton: Princeton University, 1948.

THOMTE, REIDAR, 'New Reflections on the Great Dane,' *Discourse* VI:2 (Spring, 1963), 144–55.

THULSTRUP, MARIE, 'Kierkegaards "onde verden",' *Kierkegaardiana*, I (1955), 42–55.

THULSTRUP, MARIE, 'Sören Kierkegaards martyrbegreb,' *Dansk Teologisk Tidskrift*, XXVII:2 (1964) 100–14.

THULSTRUP, NIELS, 'The Complex of Problems called "Kierkegaard",' *A Kierkegaard Critique*. ed. H. Johnson and N. Thulstrup. New York: Harper, 1962. Pp. 286–96.

THULSTRUP, NIELS, 'Kierkegaard og den filosofiske Idealisme,' *Kierkegaardiana*, VIII (1962), 88–105.

THULSTRUP, NIELS, 'Kierkegaards Verhältnis zu Hegel,' *Theologische Zeitschrift*, XIII:3 (May–June 1957), 200–26.

TIELSCH, ELFRIEDE, *Kierkegaards Glaube*. Göttingen: Vanderhoeck & Ruprecht, 1964.

VETTER, AUGUST, *Frömmigkeit als Leidenschaft: eine Deutung Kierkegaards*. 2nd aufl. Feriburg: K. Alber, 1963.

WAGNDAHL, PER, *Gemenskapsproblemet hos Sören Kierkegaard*. Lund: CWK Gleerup, 1954.

WEILAND, JAN SPERNA, *Humanitas Christianitas*. Te Assen Bij: Van Gorcum, 1951.

WHITE, WILLIE, 'Faith and Existence; a study in Aquinas and Kierkegaard.' Unpublished doctoral dissertation, The University of Chicago, 1965.

ZUIDEMA, SYTSE ULBE. *Kierkegaard*. Translated by David H. Freeman. Grand Rapids: Baker Book House, 1960.

INDEX OF NAMES